Britain, France and the Empire 1350–1500

Margaret L. Kekewich and Susan Rose

palgrave
macmillan

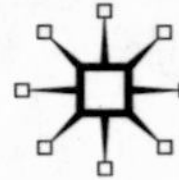

Published 2005 by
PALGRAVE MACMILLAN
Houndmills, Basingstoke, Hampshire RG21 6XS and
175 Fifth Avenue, New York, N.Y. 10010
Companies and representatives throughout the world

PALGRAVE MACMILLAN is the global academic imprint of the Palgrave Macmillan division of St. Martin's Press LLC and of Palgrave Macmillan Ltd. Macmillan® is a registered trademark in the United States, United Kingdom and other countries. Palgrave is a registered trademark in the European Union and other countries.

ISBN 0–333–68973–9 hardback
ISBN 0–333–69075–3 paperback

This book is printed on paper suitable for recycling and made from fully managed and sustained forest sources.

A catalogue record for this book is available from the British Library.

Library of Congress Cataloging-in-Publication Data

Kekewich, Margaret Lucille, 1939–
Britain, France, and the empire, 1350–1500 / Margaret L. Kekewich and Susan Rose.
p. cm.
Includes bibliographical references and index.
ISBN 0–333–68973–9 (cloth)—ISBN 0–333–69075–3 (pbk.)
1. Great Britain – Foreign relations – France. 2. Great Britain – Foreign relations – 1066–1485. 3. Great Britain – Colonies – History – To 1500. 4. France – Foreign relations – Great Britain. 5. Imperialism – History – To 1500. I. Rose, Susan, 1938– II.

DA47.1.K44 2004
327.41011′09′024—dc22

2004052831

10 9 8 7 6 5 4 3 2 1
14 13 12 11 10 09 08 07 06 05

Printed in China

For Peter and Michael
two patient husbands

Contents

List of Illustrations

List of Maps and Figures

Maps

Figures

Acknowledgements

The authors and publishers wish to thank the following for permission to use copyright material:

Agence photographique de la réunion des musées nationaux, for the illustrations *Les Très Riches Heures du Duc de Berry: Le calendrier. Le mois d'Octobre.* Chantilly, musée Condé © photo RMN – R. G. Ojeda; *Les Très Riches Heures du Duc de Berry: Le calendrier. Le mois de Février.* Chantilly, musée Condé © photo RMN – R. G. Ojeda, reproduced courtesy of Agence photographique de la réunion des musée nationaux;

Bibliothèque Nationale de France, for the illustration of *The Martyrdom of St Erasmus*, reproduced courtesy of Bibliothèque Nationale de France;

British Library, for the illustrations of *The Coronation of Charles VI of France* (Royal 14 D IV f. 133); *The Bedford Book of Hours, Duchess Anne at Prayer* (Add. 18850 f. 257b); *Hans Behem Preaching to the Common People, Niklashausen, Germany* (IC. 7452); *War at Sea*, from the Warwick Pageant (Cotton Julius E. IV art. 6); all reproduced by permission of the British Library;

Centre des monuments nationaux, for the photograph of Bourges, Palais Jacques Coeur (the house of Jacques Coeur at Bourges), © Centre des monuments nationaux, Paris;

Peter Fawcett, for the photographs of the castle at Angers, France, King René's gatehouse, and the castle at Angers, the curtain wall; both reproduced by permission of Peter Fawcett;

Hodder Arnold, for the map of the Burgundian State from David Nicholas, *The Transformation of Europe, 1300–1600* (1999) © David Nicholas, 1999, reproduced by permission of Hodder, Arnold;

Routledge Publishers, for figure 1: 'Building workers' wages, 1264–1532, expressed in terms of a shopping basket of consumables', from E. H. Phelps Brown and S. V. Hopkins, *A Perspective of Wages and Prices* (1981), reproduced by permission of Routledge;

Royal Commission on the Ancient and Historical Monuments of Scotland, for the illustration of Linlithgow Palace, Scotland, copyright © Royal Commission on the Ancient and Historical Monuments of Scotland;

Stad Brugge, for the illustration of *The Ursula Shrine* (detail) from Hans Memling, Stedelijke Musea Brugge, Memlingmuseum-Sint-Janshospitaal, reproduced courtesy of Stad Brugge;

The Warburg Institute, for the illustrations of *A religious procession at Strasburg*; *A Mass for the dead at a tomb, Switzerland*; *A ball at the court of Albert Bavaria*; *A peasant's life*: a woodcut from Germany, and the *Martyrdom of St Apollonia*, reproduced by permission of the Warburg Institute;

Wolfgang Kaehler Photography, for the photograph of the Holstentor, the landward gate to Lübeck, © Wolfgang Kaehler.

Every effort has been made to trace the copyright holders but if any have been inadvertently overlooked the publishers will be pleased to make the necessary arrangement at the first opportunity.

Preface

Did the changes in the kind of authority wielded by princes in north-western Europe between 1350 and 1500 and the cultural assumptions that underpinned it mean that the attitudes and practices associated with the Renaissance had begun to develop? Did the close engagement of members of the laity with the Christian religion and the criticisms that many of them, together with their priests, directed at the Church hierarchy mean that a climate congenial to reformation already existed? Living as we do in an era that was largely shaped by the social, ideological, political, cultural and economic developments of the following five hundred years in Europe these are arguably the most interesting questions to ask about the late Middle Ages. Yet there were also features of the period that make it distinctive for other reasons. The impact of the population collapse following the catastrophic plague known as the Black Death, changes in land tenure, the expansion of trade, dynastic upheavals and the improved administration of justice are some examples of important changes that were not closely associated with the emergence of a new cultural and ideological order.

No account of a period as rich in action, ideas and artefacts as 1350 to 1500 will be comprehensive and some hard decisions have been made to enable us to provide even the present amount of narrative, evidence and interpretation within a moderate compass. This book concentrates on north-western Europe, namely the area occupied by the modern states of Germany, France, the Netherlands, Belgium, Switzerland, Great Britain and Ireland (see Map 1). Much of France belonged to the southern, Mediterranean region and eastern Germany and Bohemia were part of central Europe, but since one of our themes is the gradual emergence of nation states it would be difficult to answer questions about why France was a realm successfully united under an authoritative prince by 1500 whilst the Empire was not, without looking to the south. Similarly any study of the strong challenge posed to orthodox Catholicism in the late fourteenth and early fifteenth centuries would be seriously impaired without a discussion of Bohemia. Countries on the fringe of the region, such as the Baltic lands and the various states of Spain and Italy, are mentioned when it is necessary to an understanding of developments in the main area of study. The Papacy as head of the Catholic Church, although located in Italy rather than Avignon for about half the period, is discussed, although its political importance as prince of an Italian state is only touched on.

The term 'Europe' entered common usage, according to John Hale, during the 150 years after 1450: perhaps a sign of the growing secularisation of society,[1] since before then the term 'Christendom' was normally used to refer to the same geographical area. During the later Middle Ages Europe was largely unaffected by or even aware of a 'wider world' until the last years of the fifteenth century. There was some sketchy knowledge of the East and of China but apart from that

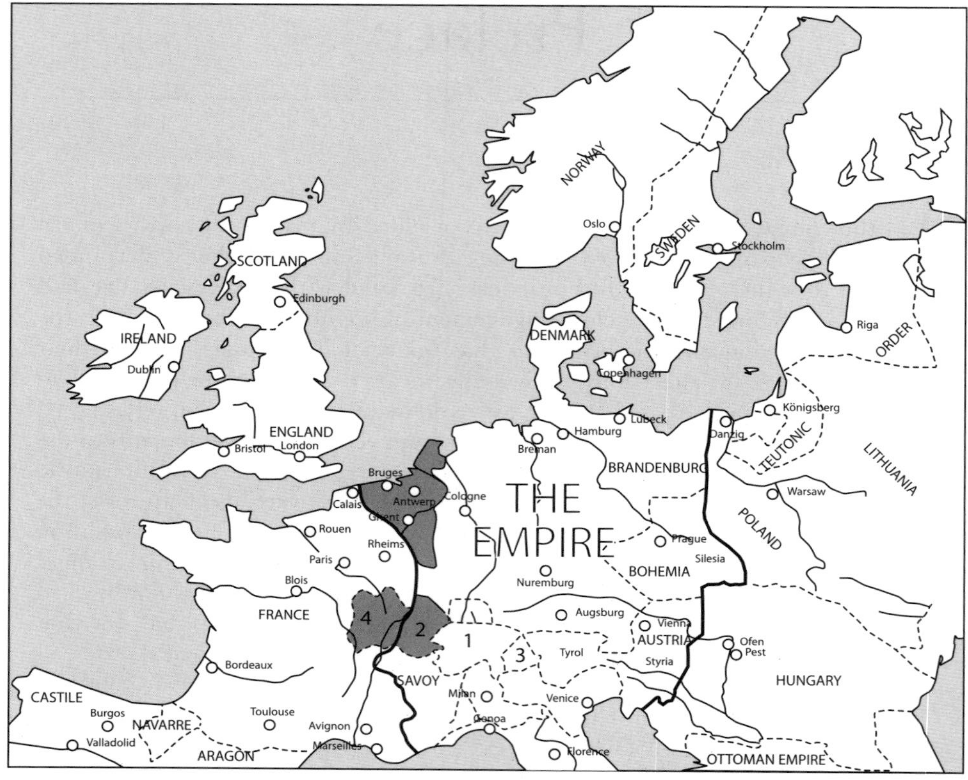

— Boundary of the Empire
■ Possessions of the Dukes of Burgundy

1 Swiss Confederation
2 Franche Comté
3 Grissons
4 Duchy of Burgundy

Map 1 Northern Europe in 1460

the known world was bounded by Iceland to the north and the coastlands of North Africa to the south. North-western Europe did have a distinctive economic and cultural character during the late Middle Ages. There were strong trading links between the different parts of the British Isles and between them and the merchants of northern and western France, the Low Countries, the Baltic coast of Germany and city states such as Cologne. Latin and, to a lesser extent, French and Italian were languages spoken or understood by many members of the ruling classes, the clergy and the merchants. The more educated and mobile peoples of all these countries shared the same mental world, which was defined by their commitment to Christianity with its ethical code, and the culture that was associated with it. The state that best typified this culture was Burgundy, which rose, flourished and finally disappeared in the course of the late fourteenth and fifteenth centuries. An example of the way in which cultural assumptions were shared is the fate of a painting of the Last Judgement commissioned from the

Flemish artist Hans Memling. It was on its way by sea to Italy when a Baltic pirate seized the ship and its cargo. Perhaps wishing to show some kind of remorse he presented the painting to his parish church when he returned to port in Danzig, where it can still be seen.

The starting date involves looking at society after it had suffered the catastrophe of the Black Death and a sudden collapse in population. By finishing at the threshold of the sixteenth century we have a period that can be analysed for signs of continuity and change both to establish any defining characteristics it may have possessed and to anticipate features of the early modern period. These issues have been keenly debated: J. Huizinga, for example, in *The Waning of the Middle Ages*, which deals with the culture of France and Burgundy, has seen the period as one of pessimism and even decadence. Denys Hay in his work *Europe in the Fourteenth and Fifteenth Centuries* generally avoids any overall judgement. B. Guenée in *States and Rulers in Later Medieval Europe* suggests that it was a time of transition when it could be said that 'the medieval State gradually gave way to the modern'.[2] In the *Handbook of European History, 1400–1600*, the fifteenth century is seen as a mere prelude to the Renaissance and the Catholic and Protestant Reformations. The editors speak of a 'gradual, fluctuating . . . blending of "late medieval" with "early modern"'. They reject Burckhardt's idea that in the Middle Ages human consciousness 'lay as though dreaming or half-awake beneath a common veil', but emphasise the great depression of the fourteenth century as a catalyst for change.[3]

All periods of history have an element of transition and in an area as large and diverse as north-western Europe change took place at different rates. Life for a peasant farmer in the far south-west of Ireland or Bavaria would have differed little between 1350 and 1500. There were also groups of people in both urban and rural society who would not have shared the experience of the majority of men. Joan Kelly-Gadol has asked 'Did Women have a Renaissance?'[4] and we can just as legitimately enquire into the opportunities that most women enjoyed to buy and sell, worship and participate in any kind of public life independently of their menfolk in the late Middle Ages. Marginal people, the very poor, vagrants and lepers could not participate fully in religious or political life and non-Christians and heretics were deliberately excluded from it. Yet some of these people could act as catalysts for change, often by very reason of their total or partial alienation from conventional life.

Even before the advent of printing in the second half of the fifteenth century the history of the late Middle Ages in Europe can draw on more plentiful sources of records than in any previous period. Some institutions, notably the government and legal system of England, the Catholic Church (especially the Papal Chancellery) and some town councils, have never been seriously disrupted. Despite wars, revolutions and religious upheavals other archives survive in part. The growth in lay literacy and numeracy led to a proliferation of letters, journals and accounts; there were so many of them that a decent quantity have survived despite the fact that they were not valued highly at the time. The fourteenth century was the first great age of collectors: the Emperor Charles IV was avid for holy relics and housed them royally, Charles V of France and his brothers showed a fine discrimination in commissioning illuminated manuscripts, and devotional and historical works for their chapels and libraries. Archaeology used to be regarded as mainly a science for antiquity but excavations on royal palaces such as the Louvre and village sites such as Wharram Percy in Yorkshire have thrown new light on medieval life styles. Recent decades have generally seen a greater willingness to consider any evidence from the past, including quite humble records such as popular songs and ballads, and artefacts such as the contents of refuse tips. The survival of documents and artefacts, however, and the motivation of historians to present them through publication varies greatly although the situation has improved in recent decades. More material from east European archives is gradually becoming available and the heightened national consciousness of areas such as Brittany and Wales has led to the same result.

This book is divided into three sections, addressing first the social and economic aspects of the period. The second section looks at the exercise of sovereignty (supreme political authority) and its essential connection with warfare. The third section discusses the way in which the culture of north-western Europe was changing; it includes developments in religion and gathers evidence from throughout the book to assess how far the Reformations and the Renaissance were anticipated during the period.

Chapter 1 is concerned with the impact of changing conditions of land tenure, changes which were expedited by the arrival of the Black Death in Europe and the consequent decline in population. Marxist historians such as Robert Brenner have debated the long-term consequences of these changes and seen in them an example of class struggle.[5] Other historians have resisted this interpretation, insisting that medieval society was divided into orders, not classes, and that conflicts were often generated by local conditions and particular loyalties that cannot be accounted for by one big theory. In Chapter 2, a contrast is drawn between areas of Europe that were highly urbanised, such as Flanders, the cities of France, Germany, southern England and Lowland Scotland. While in Italy cities managed to retain at least the outward forms of political independence, in the north they were invariably dominated by their princes. The commercial elites enjoyed great wealth and developed their own cultural forms of expression but when they attempted to gain political power they were suppressed. Part I closes with a discussion of popular unrest and revolt, drawing on social and economic evidence to account for the part played by the peasantry, townsfolk, minor clerics and nobles.

Part II opens with Chapter 3, which considers the theories underpinning ideas about what constituted good government. The work of Quentin Skinner[6] and historians who have emulated him will inform a discussion of continuity and change in the ethical values of late medieval commentators. An account of political developments in the countries of north-western Europe concentrates on the development of the institutions of government and how they interacted with dynastic crises. The question will be raised of how far each realm was a nation state by the end of the period and of what factors contributed to their success or failure. Chapter 4 opens with a discussion of the idea of a just war and of how far military theorists were diverging from the authorities of antiquity. The whole concept of a late medieval military revolution as propounded by Andrew Ayton and J. L. Price is interrogated through an examination of the kinds of war that were fought during the period, and changes in logistics.[7] Part II ends with some answers offered to the question of how far the enhancement of princely authority and changes in military practice and funding promoted the emergence of nation states.

In Part III, Chapter 5 considers both orthodox religious belief and practice and the changes brought about by the increasing involvement of the laity, ordinary priests, monks and friars, and quasi-monastic orders such as the *Béguines* and the Brethren of the Common Life. The argument of Eamon Duffy in his *The Stripping of the Altars*, that all this led to a flourishing and healthy church life, is opposed to the traditional approach of Protestant historians that it was ripe for reform, and of Huizinga that it showed an unhealthy preoccupation with death and decay.[8] Steven Ozment contends, against the optimism of historians like Duffy, that by the late Middle Ages the gap between the sacred and the profane had become unbridgeable.[9] Chapter 6 looks at the continuities and changes in court culture, learning in the universities and the growing influence of humanism, and the culture of the towns. Part III and the book conclude with an assessment of the extent to which culture was changing and of how far this was attributable to intimations of a renaissance in learning and art and an increasingly secular society.

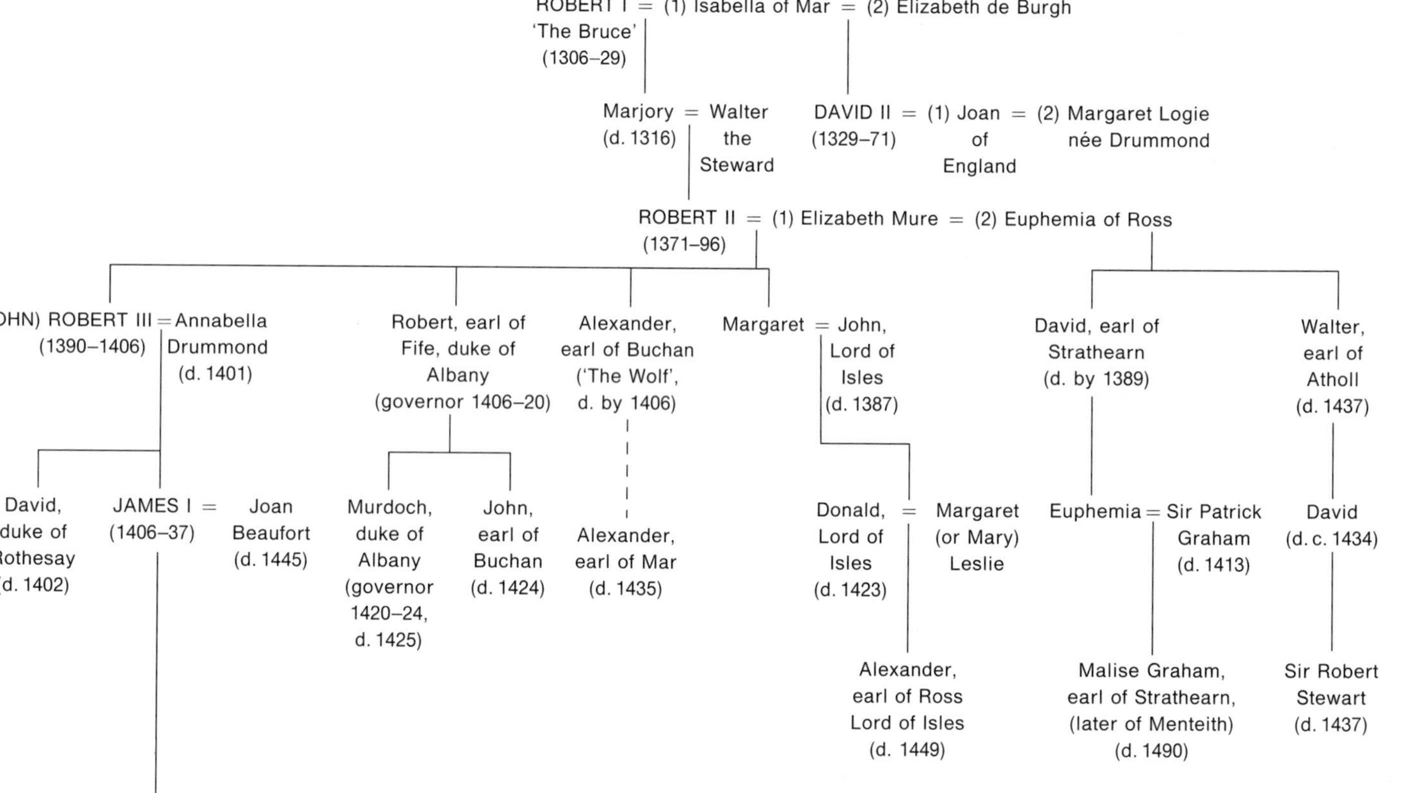
ROBERT I = (1) Isabella of Mar = (2) Elizabeth de Burgh
'The Bruce'
(1306–29)
Marjory = Walter
(d. 1316) the
Steward
DAVID II = (1) Joan = (2) Margaret Logie
(1329–71) of
England
née Drummond
ROBERT II = (1) Elizabeth Mure = (2) Euphemia of Ross
(1371–96)
(JOHN) ROBERT III = Annabella
(1390–1406) Drummond
(d. 1401)
Robert, earl of
Fife, duke of
Albany
(governor 1406–20)
Alexander,
earl of Buchan
('The Wolf',
d. by 1406)
Margaret = John,
Lord of
Isles
(d. 1387)
David, earl of
Strathearn
(d. by 1389)
Walter,
earl of
Atholl
(d. 1437)
David,
duke of
Rothesay
(d. 1402)
JAMES I = Joan
(1406–37) Beaufort
(d. 1445)
Murdoch,
duke of
Albany
(governor
1420–24,
d. 1425)
John,
earl of
Buchan
(d. 1424)
Alexander,
earl of Mar
(d. 1435)
Donald, = Margaret
Lord of (or Mary)
Isles Leslie
(d. 1423)
Euphemia = Sir Patrick
Graham
(d. 1413)
David
(d. c. 1434)
Alexander,
earl of Ross
Lord of Isles
(d. 1449)
Malise Graham,
earl of Strathearn,
(later of Menteith)
(d. 1490)
Sir Robert
Stewart
(d. 1437)

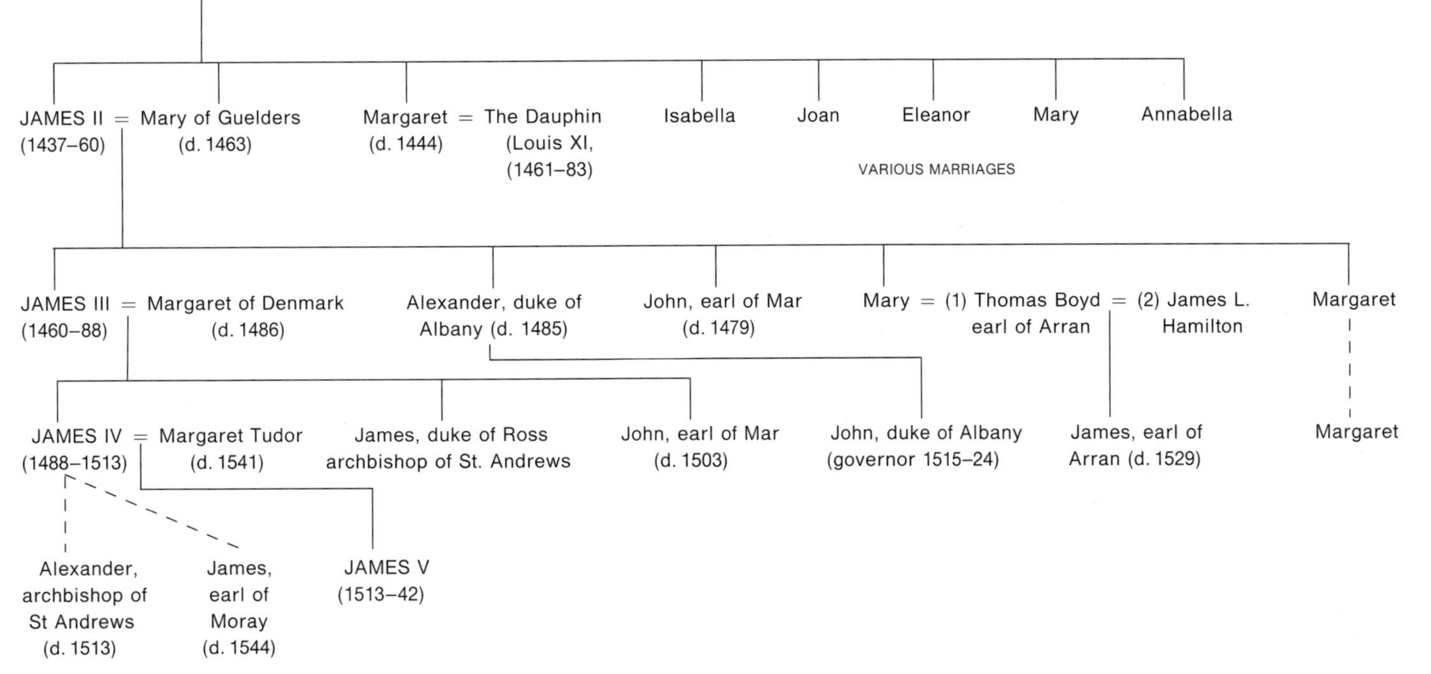
JAMES II = Mary of Guelders
(1437–60) (d. 1463)
Margaret = The Dauphin
(d. 1444) (Louis XI,
(1461–83)
Isabella
Joan
Eleanor
Mary
Annabella
VARIOUS MARRIAGES
JAMES III = Margaret of Denmark
(1460–88) (d. 1486)
Alexander, duke of
Albany (d. 1485)
John, earl of Mar
(d. 1479)
Mary = (1) Thomas Boyd = (2) James L.
earl of Arran
Hamilton
Margaret
JAMES IV = Margaret Tudor
(1488–1513) (d. 1541)
James, duke of Ross
archbishop of St. Andrews
John, earl of Mar
(d. 1503)
John, duke of Albany
(governor 1515–24)
James, earl of
Arran (d. 1529)
Margaret
Alexander,
archbishop of
St Andrews
(d. 1513)
James,
earl of
Moray
(d. 1544)
JAMES V
(1513–42)

The rulers of Scotland

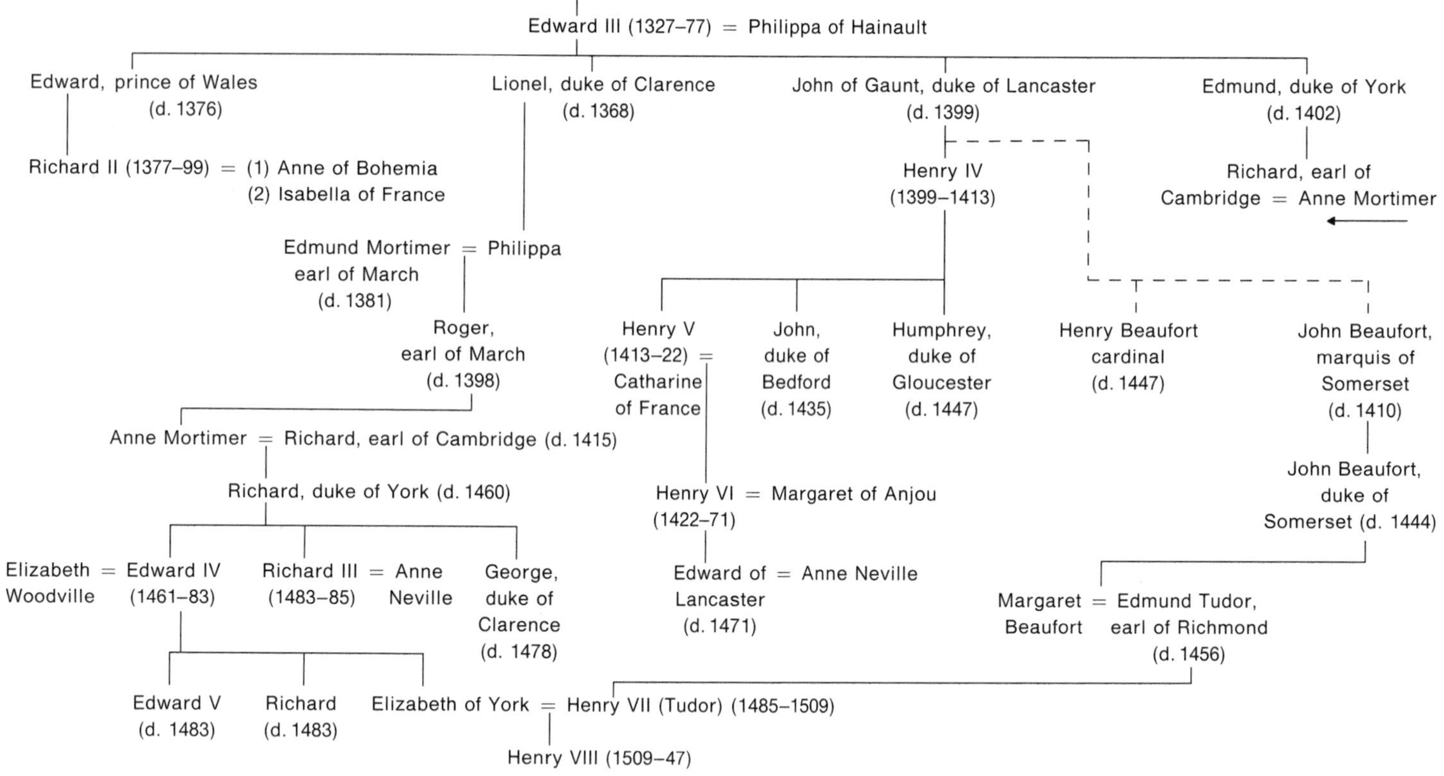

The rulers of England

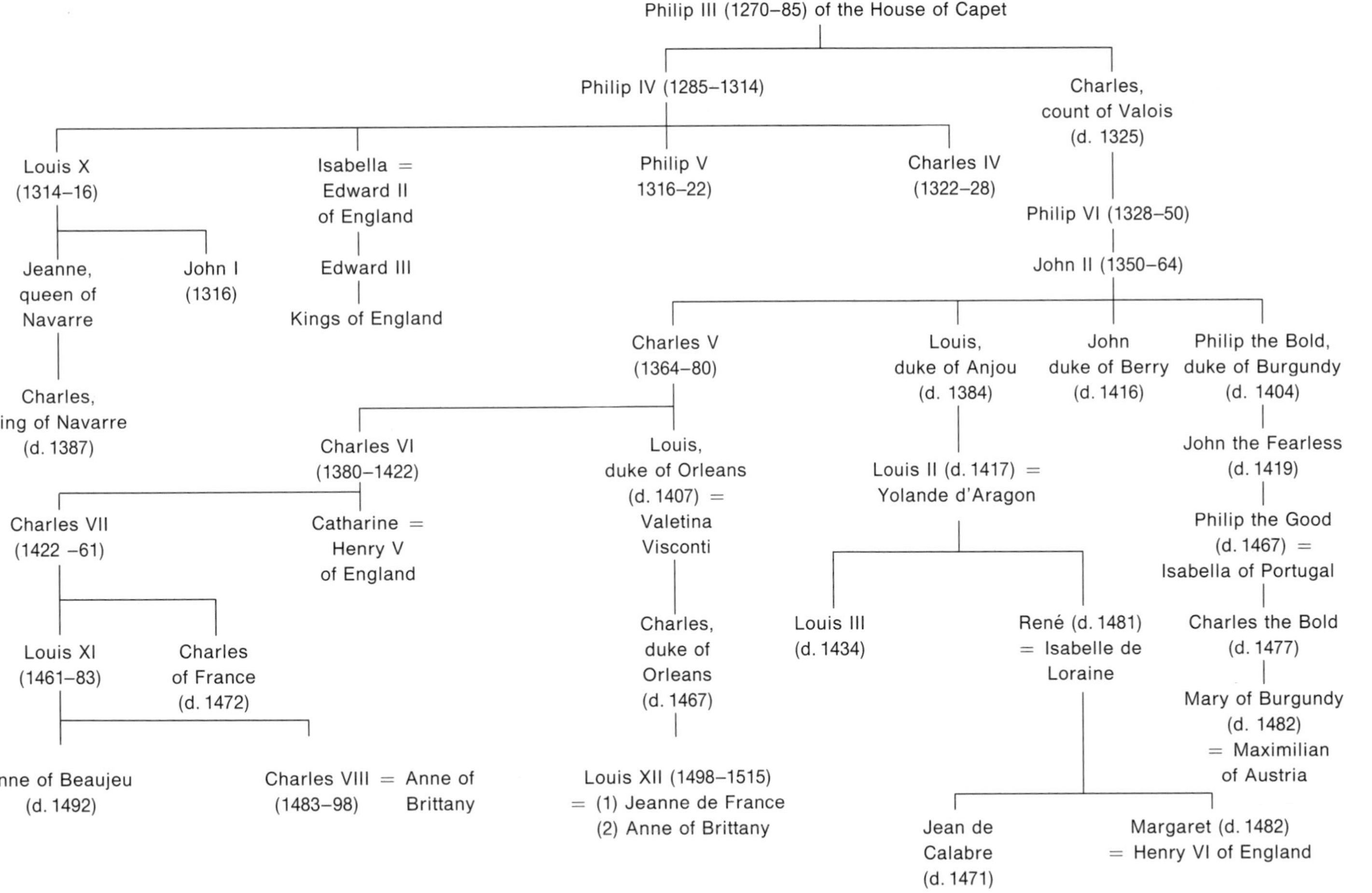

The rulers of France and Burgundy

Part I

The Social and Economic Context

1

The Countryside and its People

INTRODUCTION: THEMES AND SOURCES

This chapter is concerned with some of the basic questions that arise in any consideration of the later medieval period in our chosen area. The first section will look at what is known or can be estimated about population levels at this time. The impact of the infectious disease known by later generations as the Black Death will be considered along with the problem of what happened in the years after this demographic catastrophe. Given that the majority of the population lived in rural villages we will move on to consider the living conditions of the peasantry. These have both legal and economic implications. Legally the issues centre on the personal status of a peasant and his family. Was unfree status, or villeinage, widespread at the start of our period? Did it decline over the fifteenth century, and if so, why? Were regional variations noticeable and important? In the economic sphere we need to consider the factors which influenced the prospects and fortunes of villagers. Was the decline in population, which is universally accepted, a blessing in disguise for the survivors? Did the destruction wrought by war have some influence? Can we answer the question of whether the standard of living of countryfolk rose or fell during our period? Section 1 (iii) will look more closely at the households and families of those who lived in the countryside, both men and women, lords and peasants. The issues of change over the period, and of differences between regions, will again come to the fore, as will the importance of differing roles within the family and within society. The wider questions with which we are concerned in this book, the changes associated with concepts like the Renaissance and Reformation and the possible emergence of nation states, will be somewhat in the background but will be addressed where appropriate.

These questions have received a great deal of attention from scholars, particularly since the 1930s. The work of Robert Brenner, from a Marxist point of view, remains extremely influential though first put forward in 1976. His views and those of his opponents are contained in *The Brenner Debates: Agrarian Class Structure and Economic Development in Pre-industrial Europe.*[1] Brenner's main concern was to interpret the economic and social history of the countryside in our period in terms of the exploitation of the peasantry by their overlords, with 'class conflict' and even revolt as the inevitable result. His work and that of his followers, most notably Rodney Hilton, places a great deal of emphasis on the legal status of tenants, whether they were unfree or free, whether relationships between lords and villagers were harmonious or full of conflict.[2] Guy Bois's book on eastern Normandy from 1300 to 1500, translated into English as *The Crisis of Feudalism*,[3] puts forward a rather different interpretation. In his view the problems caused by the population fall beginning in the mid-fourteenth century, and the devastation caused by the Hundred Years War in Normandy, led to economic problems which were particularly severe for the landowners, leading them to seek out other means of maintaining their lifestyle. Some scholars have turned principally to a model based on the ideas of Thomas Malthus to explain developments in late medieval Europe; others prefer explanations which look more closely at market forces or the increasing 'commercialisation' of society; while yet others look primarily to the importance of issues affecting relationships between lords and peasants, the terms on which land was held, the power of the lords and the oppression of the peasants, for explanations. Hatcher and Bailey's *Modelling the Middle Ages: The History and Theory of England's Economic Development* very usefully sets out the various theories before suggesting its own approach.

The Malthusian model, linked with the names of Postan for England and Le Roy Ladurie for France, sees the decline in population as the major factor in developments in the agrarian economy in the fourteenth and fifteenth centuries. It is suggested that the population decline began before the storm of the Black Death broke over western Europe. Some influence can be attributed to the famine years of 1315–18 but the underlying cause was that the population increase in the thirteenth century had outrun the capacity of the land, and the way in which it was farmed, to support that number of people. The problem with this view is that after the balance between resources and population had been restored, population would be expected to rise once more. For both England and France the evidence clearly suggests that this did not happen but that, after the abrupt falls caused by the plague of 1348–9, the decline continued albeit at a much slower rate. As Hatcher and Bailey have pointed out, 'the inability of the population to rise during a prolonged era of very high wages and abundant cheap land' (which did exist after 1350) 'poses a major problem'[4] for theories of this type. The 'commercialisation' theory looks closely at improvements in agriculture, in commerce and trade and in communications, and tends to take a much more positive view of the economy and society of our period. Its major problem is difficulties with the evidence available for this kind of discussion and the degree of regional variation.[5] Arguments based solely on the 'class power of landlords and tenants' can sometimes seem to 'fly in the face of both evidence and common sense'.[6]

What are the sources available for this kind of study? In England much basic information comes from estate records, which survive in large numbers. These are overwhelmingly either financial or legal, either accounts and rent rolls and the like, or the records of the seigneurial or manor courts. The longest series tend to be concerned with estates belonging to the Church, whether to a bishop or other ecclesiastic or to a religious house. All were collected for the purposes of the lord of the land and reflect his priorities and concerns, not those of the villagers. The surviving manorial accounts also perhaps give too much prominence to estates belonging to the Church. The rate of survival has been much higher for documents coming from cathedrals or religious houses than for those from lay estates. They are also not spread evenly geographically across the whole country. They naturally relate to the domain lands directly farmed by the lords, which probably produced considerably less for the market than the lands in the hands of the peasants, whether leased or held on some feudal tenure. Nevertheless the comparative richness of the English sources does allow some conclusions to be drawn even if not all are free from controversy. Some personal papers from members of gentry or noble families in the fifteenth century remain, for example, in such well-known series as the Paston Letters and Papers, but their survival is largely a matter of accident, making it hard to draw general conclusions. The records of central government are also useful in some respects; for example, the intimate details of peasant life to be found in Hanawalt[7] are derived largely from the Coroner's Rolls recording investigations into sudden deaths.

This situation contrasts forcefully with that in Scotland and Ireland. A recent writer on the Scottish economy and society has lamented that the 'central difficulty is the scarcity of evidence.'[8] A somewhat similar problem exists for Ireland, compounded by the fact that not only are most of the records legal and political in nature, relating to the establishment of Anglo-Norman control of the island, but also many are only known from the summaries in nineteenth-century calendars as the originals were destroyed in the Irish Civil War in the 1920s.[9]

In France and the states of the Empire official records from various sources are the most plentiful. In France, seigneurial and ecclesiastical records were often destroyed during the Revolution. Bois found only the abbey of Montvilliers could supply a fairly complete series. Duby, in the area between Grenoble and the sea, relied extensively on the fortunate survival of an inventory of the possessions of the Order of St John of Jerusalem drawn up in 1338.[10] Much more generally useful are the tax records relating to the royal, or local or municipal administration. In the south of the country another source is the many notaries' books that survive from even quite small communities. In this area, it is clear that the lack of seigneurial records and the relative frequency of tax records make it easier to look at, for example, the different levels of wealth in a community than the relations between lords and peasants. The fragmented nature of the Empire, without one recognised centre of government, means that the survival of useful sources is extremely patchy, depending largely on local conditions. Examples of fortunate survivals are the accounts of the *Burggrafen* of Drachenfels near Bonn for the years 1458–63 or the *Standebuch* from Nuremberg. This was put together in 1568, portraying 'a true description of all the ranks on earth, high and low, religious and secular, and of all arts, crafts and trades from the greatest to the humblest', a total of 114 catergories. It is valid for our period because, in the opinion of Christopher Friedrichs, it 'could have been published 200 years earlier', given the stability of German society over that period.[11] In all areas archaeological evidence and visual and literary sources can also be very helpful if used with care.

(i) POPULATION

In 1350, two years after the first fearful outbreak of the plague in western Europe, it would not have been surprising if most rural societies were in a state of shock.

The precise nature of the disease, which ravaged Europe, has been disputed. Some have pointed out that the bubonic form of classic plague (characterised by buboes or swellings in the glands under the arm, in the neck and in the groin and spread by the bites of rat fleas) is not especially infectious. They have favoured the pneumonic form of the disease (spread by coughing or sneezing) as responsible for the high death rate. Others have claimed that the symptoms described by chroniclers are not always typical of this disease but could be some other infection.[12] No chronicles mention the enormous numbers of dead rats that would have been noticeable before the disease spread to humans. The fact remains that within little more than a year the death rate had soared. In some few villages all the inhabitants lay dead; in others the toll was much smaller, but even so, the basis of what passed for normal life had been disrupted. It is surprising that we do not read of more cases of disturbed behaviour, of more sects like the Flagellants (who wandered Europe beating each other's backs till the blood ran, to expiate the sins which, in their eyes, had caused the appalling visitation of the plague), of more attacks on 'outsiders' especially, of course, the Jews. Henry Knighton's description of the countryside of England in his chronicle makes clear the air of desolation that pervaded many places.

> Sheep and cattle went wandering over fields and through crops and there was no one to go and drive then off or herd them so that the number cannot be reckoned which perished in the ditches in every district for lack of herdsmen: for there was such a lack of servants that no one knew what he ought to do.[13]

Yet when we attempt to turn from emotive and chilling accounts of the progress of the plague itself to a more sober assessment of the effects of these events in terms of population, economic activity and the lives especially of those who lived in the countryside we find that it is very hard to locate either reliable and soundly based quantitative evidence, or interpretations and explanations of the consequences of this disruption which are accorded universal respect. The disastrous epidemic, whatever the nature of the disease, was not a 'one-off' event; there were severe recurrences in 1361–2, 1369 and 1375 and at intervals, with decreasing severity, throughout the fifteenth century.With regard to numbers, it is not easy to find the answers to questions like, How many died? What proportion was this of the population? Was the death rate worse in towns or in rural areas? Were all areas equally affected? The problem very often is that either reliable evidence of any kind is lacking or the evidence that does survive was collected for quite other purposes and must be subjected to considerable interpretation. An estimate of medieval European populations is shown in Table 1.

If we begin with England we find that, while there is a measure of agreement among scholars that the medieval population reached its peak *circa* 1300, estimates of the size of that peak vary considerably from about 6 million on the one hand to about 3.75 million on the other. Two sources, Domesday Book from 1086 and the first poll tax records from 1377, provide 'anchor points' for calculations but both have limitations. Neither was intended as a population record; Domesday only records landholdings, with some mention of the number of individuals in different groups. Some places of great importance, including London and Bristol, are entirely omitted. We cannot even be sure if each holding mentioned in

Table 1 Medieval European population estimates

	In millions		
	AD 1000	AD 1340	AD 1450
South			
The Balkans	5	6	4.5
Italy	5	10	7.5
Iberia	7	9	7
West and Central			
France and Low Countries	6	19	12
British Isles	2	5	3
Germany and Scandinavia	4	11.5	7.5
East			
Russia	6	8	6
Poland and Lithuania	2	3	2
Hungary	1.5	2	1.5
Total	38.5	73.5	51

Source: Based on figures from the *Fontana Economic History of Europe*, vol. 1, ed. Carlo M. Cipolla.

Domesday was that of one family or of more. The first poll tax applied only to those over 14 and it is very hard to estimate the degree to which the tax was evaded. Other documents, which exist for certain manors at certain dates, known as *manorial extents* (detailed descriptions of a manor, its inhabitants and economic resources, drawn up for the benefit of the lord) have also been used. Here the problem is that there is no way of knowing how typical a village was or how well its fortunes relate to those of the country as a whole. Calculations from records like those already mentioned also necessitate the use of a 'multiplier' to convert figures for families or households into population totals. The choice of this multiplier as well as the calculation of total households can greatly alter the final result. For example, for the village of Hanborough in Oxfordshire, estimates of the total population at the time of Domesday vary from 109 to 140–55 depending on the multiplier chosen. There were 20 villeins, 6 *bordars* (cottagers), and 5 slaves in this village in 1086 but should we multiply the total of 31 'families' by 3.5, or 4.5, or 5?[14]

The rate of population growth in England in the twelfth and thirteenth centuries is usually seen as being quite high. There is evidence of more and more land being brought into cultivation (which presupposes that there was a growing demand for foodstuffs and more mouths to feed). This included land not really suitable for growing grain, like the poor soils of the Chilterns and Breckland. Extents, where they exist, reveal higher total figures than those in Domesday. For Hanborough again, in the Hundred Rolls, 90 tenants are listed in the 1270s. A very good set of figures for Taunton in Somerset suggests that the number of adult males rose 228% between 1212 and 1312.[15] A final conclusion, however, on the population of England before the arrival of the plague, remains elusive, particularly if possible population losses in the bad harvest years at the beginning of the century are also taken into account. This uncertainty clearly feeds into similar attempts to calculate the population after the plague struck. Here the focus has been on the 1377 poll tax figures as we have said, but to what extent are they undermined by evasion? And what proportion of the population was under 14? Rates of evasion have been calculated at anything from 5% to 25%; the under 14s may have been as high a proportion of the total population as 40–50%; figures of this magnitude have been found in pre-industrial societies like modern Iran or some African states. As James Bolton points out, a high figure for under 14s and a high evasion rate raises the post-plague population total to about 3 million. This then presupposes a pre-plague population peak of some 6 million in the 1340s, with the possibility of up to 7 million at the beginning of the century, if the idea that the famines of 1315–17 had already caused some decline in the population is accepted.[16] Campbell has suggested a mid-fifteenth-century minimum of under 2 million; this is less than the total at the time of Domesday.[17]

In Scotland there are no records that relate to the period of the first arrival of the plague in the British Isles. The conclusion that the impact of this and later visitations was as severe here as further south has been drawn from the amount of waste (i.e. land not producing any income for the Crown) in the Exchequer Rolls for 1358–9. Some later evidence directly mentioning plague comes from the accounts of Coldingham Priory for 1362–3, which make plain the falling revenue from the estates and the decline in farmed acreage.[18] Mary Lyons's work on famine and plague in Ireland in the fourteenth century has led her to conclude that the combination of the wars with Scotland in 1315–18 and a period of exceptionally wet weather had led to a population collapse before the advent of the plague. There are, however, no firm figures for the total population at any point in our period.[19]

For France, rather similar problems concerning total population figures at key dates, urban and rural differences and the reliability of the figures that are available, present themselves. Miskimin points to the severe effect of the famine years 1315–17 in France. He mentions the fivefold rise of the price of wheat in Paris between July 1314 and April 1316 but has no figures for the total population either at this time or later after the advent of the Black Death.[20] Some figures are supplied by Froissier, who suggests that France had a total population of *c.*6,200,000 in 1100; 9,000,000 in 1200; and 22,000,000 in 1328. His final figure, high though it seems, is comparable with the 21,000,000 in 1300 put forward by Rösener.[21] The estimates made by Le Roy Ladurie have won wide acceptance; he suggests that the total population of France (within her seventeenth-century frontiers) in 1328 can be estimated at between 15 and 18.3 million.[22] Bois's work on eastern Normandy takes a close look at the sources, whether, for example, ecclesiastical (the Eudes Rigaud survey, a list of parishes and their resources dating from *c.*1240) or fiscal (the records of the *monnéage* or *fouage*, a form of hearth or household tax). This tax was supposedly raised at three-yearly intervals for the benefit of the Duke of Normandy. The records are dispersed and not easy of access; there are also problems caused by exemptions and the definitions of a 'hearth'. Nevertheless, the tax records, used judiciously with other sources, do allow some conclusions to be drawn. In the county of Longueville, between

Dieppe and Rouen, the population seems to have stagnated or declined very gradually between 1314 and 1347. Using the records of the *monnéage* collected in 1380 compared with those for 1347 in the same area, population levels seem to have collapsed by more than 50%, with the sharpest falls in small market towns. The decline in the immediate aftermath of the first advent of the plague seems to have been nearer 30% but further falls took place, particularly in the later years of the century as the epidemic returned.[23]

In the South of France in Languedoc, Le Roy Ladurie found a somewhat similar pattern. Despite the violent suppression of the heresy, the *Albigensian* crusade did not seriously interrupt the steady rise in population, which had begun *c.*1000. Between 1222 and 1340, from 400 to 500 new *bastides* or planned fortified towns were established in the region. The first plague (which, by a long-standing story, is held to have entered Europe in a ship that docked in Marseilles) caused very heavy loss of life particularly in closed communities. Only seven out of 140 preaching friars were left alive in Montpellier; perhaps overall the death rate reached 50%.[24] The evidence of deserted villages has also been used to try and assess the decline in population. However, this needs very careful handling since it may be due to factors like the poverty of the land, or insecurity caused by war, as much as to depopulation. These all influenced the story of the village of La Cicogne, belonging to the canons of St Martin of Tours. This settlement was completely abandoned by 1440; in 1450 a peasant, Perrin Bordebure, took over the land and built a simple thatched hut. Ten years later he had a new tiled house and a prosperous holding and had founded a family.[25]

The situation both as regards population levels and as regards the effects of plague was rather different in the Netherlands, particularly Flanders. At the beginning of the fourteenth century, this was one of the most densely populated areas of Europe and also one of the most urbanised. Ypres, a town of some 22,000 persons in 1315, is thought to have lost 10% of her population to starvation or the after-effects of dearth in the famine years of 1315–17. Figures of 14,000 in 1360 and 9,390 in 1437 have been calculated using the somewhat arcane method of relating the number of fullers needed to make a piece of cloth to the total cloth production in the town and the percentage of fullers present in Ghent and Bruges, using militia records![26] An estimate for Bruges suggests that the town had between 35,000 and 40,000 inhabitants in the late 1330s, a total which did not alter greatly during the remainder of the century. Ghent was, by contemporary standards, a very large town with 60,000 people *c.*1358–9 and 45,000 by the end of the fifteenth century. Calculation of the rural population is extremely difficult. The first survey with anything like comprehensive coverage, though there are still many omissions, dates from 1469. This seems to indicate a total of some 450,000 in rural areas outside the big cities. Nicholas relates this to a density of 172 per square mile (66.5 per square kilometre) in *c.*1320 and 151 per square mile (58 per square kilometre) in *c.*1450. This would equate to a population loss of some 20% but not all may be due to plague and its associated consequences. The Netherlands was also exposed to the dangers of flooding by the North Sea if the dikes were not properly maintained or if tidal surges occurred during storms. The experience of the district of Weert shows how disastrous this could be. This island was on the Scheldt, south of Antwerp. It was bought by St Bavo's

Abbey in 1240 and diked, with the river being diverted westward. Damage to the dikes occurred in 1334 but was soon repaired and between 1353 and 1365 the population grew by 43%. In 1375 there were catastrophic floods and by 1395 the number of holdings had fallen by one-third. The great flood of St Elizabeth's day, 19 November 1404, was a disaster for the entire region.[27] Some peasants may have moved to the towns to escape the floods but this movement of population leaves little trace in the records.

An attempt has been made to deny that the Black Death had much effect in Flanders, using the lack of comment in the town chronicles as a major piece of evidence. The plague of 1348–9 certainly reached Bruges, causing the Count to authorise the opening of two new cemeteries. The death toll on this eruption may have been relatively low at about one-quarter to one-sixth of the population. The disease struck with a vengeance, however, in later years, particularly 1368–9 when the death rate in Ghent, for example, rose alarmingly. Nicholas's final conclusion is, however, that Flanders was so densely populated that the losses were never severe enough to cause village desertions there, in striking contrast to what happened in England, Germany and France.[28]

In the northern Netherlands in a study of the area between the rivers Lek and Waal, south of Utrecht, at this period, the author feels able only to point to a population peak in the fourteenth century followed by a long decline. Any crisis caused by the Black Death seems to have been much less severe than in other European states but population levels were not restored to peak levels until the eighteenth century.[29] In the German lands further to the east, and to the south along the Rhine and in Bavaria, there are similar difficulties in putting forward detailed figures for the population. The most common way to try and assess the trend, which it is agreed is that of a declining population, is to look at figures for abandoned villages. These, of course, differ from region to region, being highest in wooded or mountainous areas like the Harz or Thuringia and lowest in the north-west and the lower Rhine valley. A figure of 170,000 settlements in around the year 1300 has been generally accepted for Germany, within its 1937 borders, decreasing to about 130,000 in 1500. There is, however, the problem, already mentioned, that not all settlements were necessarily abandoned because of a sudden catastrophe like plague or even a gentler drop in population. Villagers may have moved to a more favourable location for agriculture, or for communications, or to join a larger settlement for protection in unsettled times, or because of an unexpected disaster like a flood.[30] A Brandenburg land census of 1375 confirms that in this region the effects of the Black Death were evident to some extent, since it records that peasants had abandoned their holdings because of death or flight to more fertile lands.[31] Some more information comes from the towns of the Hanseatic League. In 1348–9, in Luneberg, 36% of the town councillors died; in Wismar 42% and in Revel 27%.[32] Further east, in central Poland, outside the boundaries of the Empire, in contrast, the people seem to have escaped the plague almost entirely and there is some evidence of very robust population growth averaging as much as 3.8% per annum. An attempt at the overall calculation of the population of Germany within its 1914 borders has suggested a total of 14 million for 1300, 9 million for 1400, 8–9 million in 1450 and 9–10 million in 1500.[33]

To many historians, the truly extraordinary feature of this demographic collapse is not that an infectious disease could have caused such havoc but that, once the epidemic had burned itself out, it was followed not by a sustained recovery but by a long period of either continued decline or stagnation. The English population may have numbered only 2–3 million in the 1520s.[34] Le Roy Ladurie bewails the 'tragic demographic situation of the fifteenth century' in France, and suggests that 'the scarcity of people' coloured most aspects of economic and social life in the period. This feature of life in late medieval Europe is of great importance because so much emphasis has been placed on the decline in population as an explanatory factor of the way in which life seems to have changed for many of those living in country villages.

(ii) LAND, LORDS AND PEASANTS

In looking at the conditions of life for the rural population of our study area, we should note what John Langton has written:

> It is not simply that the peasantry in different parts of Europe had a different story, nor even that within any one part of Europe there are different stories for different groups of peasants, but that for each particular peasantry a number of different, equally valid, stories can be written.[35]

There are features of medieval rural life which were almost universally constant – the dependence on the weather, the rhythm of the farming year – but in other ways each village community, even each peasant family, was faced with different circumstances and reacted to them in different ways. A German artist pictured this daily round in a woodcut made in 1477 (see Illustration 1). This is the reality that lies beneath attempts to 'model' or explain the peasant economy and other aspects of peasant life, already mentioned.

Contemporary historians' attention has shifted away from the death rate, whether from plague or other causes in our period, as the key explanatory factor in population levels, to the question of fertility and the birth rate. This is, of course, very hard to calculate in the absence of sources which allow any reliable estimates to be made of the age of women on marriage or of the number of women who never married. Both of these factors are of crucial importance in determining the fertility of a society; the lower the average ages of women at marriage the greater the number of fertile years and the possible number of births. It can certainly also be argued that the frequent return of the plague led to a continued high death rate, often of the youngest and potentially most fertile members of society, which could have had the effect of negating the usual surge in births which often follows a demographic catastrophe. If women in fifteenth-century England tended to marry in their late twenties (as was certainly the case in the seventeenth century), the birth rate would not have been high enough to counter the losses from plague and other infectious diseases. An argument that this was the case has been put together, based on the belief that women were much more involved in work outside their families in the aftermath of the Black

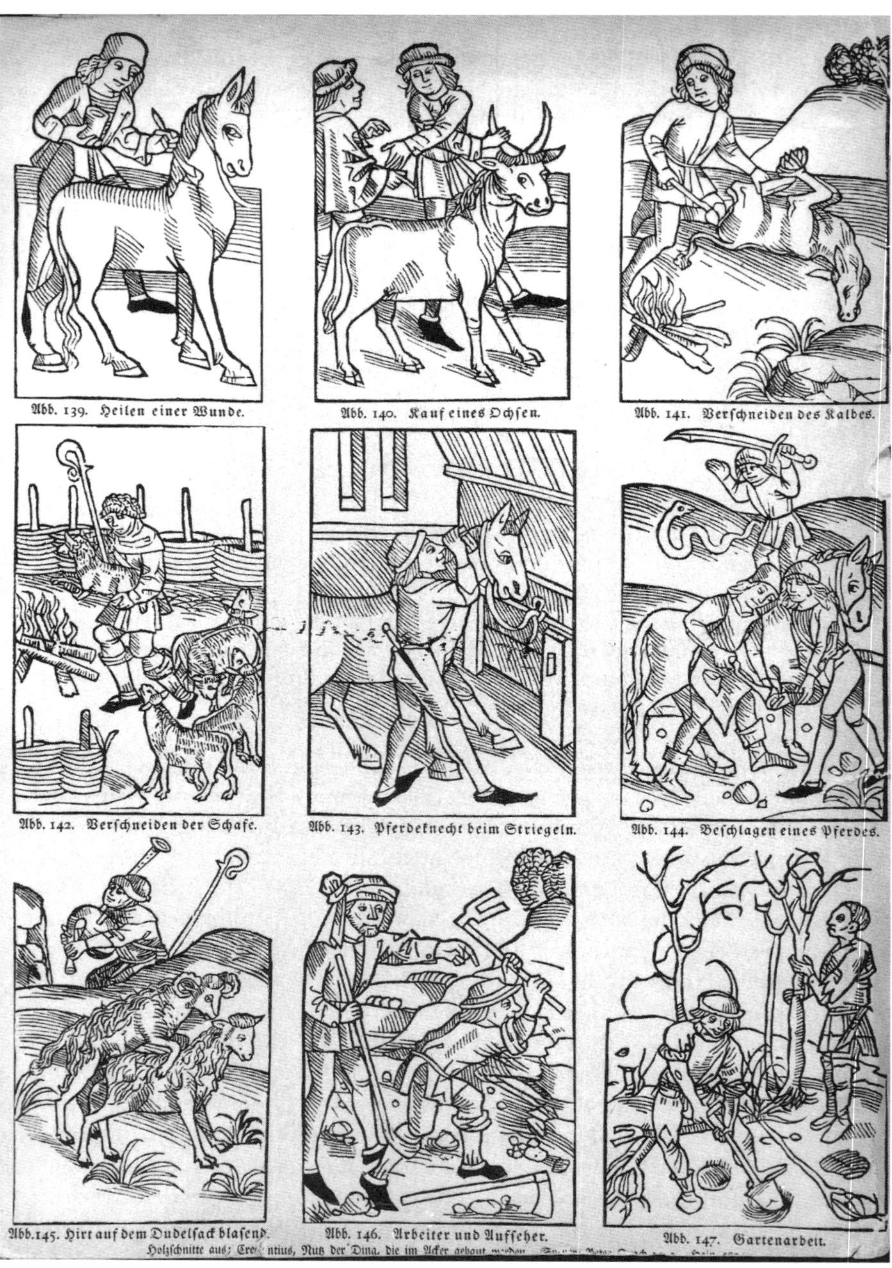

Abb. 139. Heilen einer Wunde.
Abb. 140. Kauf eines Ochsen.
Abb. 141. Verschneiden des Kalbes.
Abb. 142. Verschneiden der Schafe.
Abb. 143. Pferdeknecht beim Striegeln.
Abb. 144. Beschlagen eines Pferdes.
Abb. 145. Hirt auf dem Dudelsack blasend.
Abb. 146. Arbeiter und Aufseher.
Abb. 147. Gartenarbeit.

1 A peasant's life: a woodcut from Germany

This woodcut, made by Peter Drach from Speyer in Germany in 1477 for the book *Commodorum Ruralium Libri*, shows some of the daily activities of a peasant. It does not demonise the peasant figure unlike some other contemporary material. It shows the peasant treating a wound on a horse, buying an ox, butchering a calf and a sheep, grooming and shoeing his horse, playing the bagpipes, working under supervision and in the garden.

Death. Since many of the survivors of the plague were able to earn higher wages, the demand rose for items like better-quality textiles, pottery and leather and metalwork. This increased the opportunities for women to find employment in towns and made them much less inclined to marry early. Goldberg has claimed, using evidence from the York records, that about 'the second to the fifth decade of the fifteenth century' represents 'the high point of female economic activity', with some women beginning to fill 'male economic niches'.[36] There is some similar evidence from Essex, but even so, doubts remain as to whether any single-issue explanation is adequate for something as complex as the demographic development of a society over more than a century.[37]

It is also the case that particularly as far as England and France are concerned, political factors may have had considerable influence on population levels and the ability of society to recover from a severe demographic downturn. Bois has suggested, for his research area in Normandy, that there was a crisis in 1410–22 followed by a 'difficult recovery' in 1422–35, and that an 'economic and demographic renaissance' began c. 1450.[38] Most dramatically, however, he speaks of the period 1435–*c.*1450 as 'Hiroshima' in Normandy.[39] These dates can be closely linked to English campaigns in northern France and the internal conflicts in France which occurred simultaneously. The crisis years correspond to the gradual worsening of Anglo-French relations under Henry IV, and the successful campaigns of Henry V. The 'recovery' coincides with the relatively stable period of English rule in Normandy, while the renaissance begins with the victory of Charles VII over the English and their expulsion from Normandy. The years of real deprivation, 1435–50, saw, in Bois's view, society undermined, initially by a peasant uprising in the Caux region and famine in 1435–8. These events were followed, from 1438 to 1450, by a rising tide of general insecurity and violence reflecting the weakening of English control. This plausibly caused depopulation and misery. The evidence of vacant fiefs immediately after the French reconquest indicates that between 80 and 90 per cent of the countryside was devastated.

In England the gradual rise in population, which gathered pace on the Continent from the middle of the fifteenth century, was postponed until the first decades of the sixteenth century. The prolonged period of insecurity and civil strife known as the Wars of the Roses was combined, in the second half of the fifteenth century, with a severe economic depression. This was less dramatic than events in Normandy but may have contributed to low levels of fertility.

The lands of the Empire as ever show great regional differences in matters such as nuptuality or fertility. It is noticeable that, in some rural areas, baptisms (which always immediately followed birth because of the fear that unbaptised babies could not achieve salvation) are clustered in the winter months. It is hard to tell whether this was accidental or deliberate 'family planning' to ensure that a baby arrived in the quietest months of the farming year. It has also been widely claimed that marriage occurred relatively late (in the mid-twenties for women, at 30 for men) and only when the couple concerned could set up a separate household. The idea that women took over some economic activities from men in the years following the population losses of the plague period, mentioned above, is to some extent supported by evidence, from towns like Frankfurt, Trier, Basel and Friedberg, that over a quarter of heads of households were women.[40]

We can also attempt to understand peasant society in late medieval Europe by focusing closely on the ways in which land was held and cultivated, the obligations of peasants, and the powers of lords. The general decline in population is not denied; the precise figures may be lacking but the trend is unmistakable. Few peasants, especially in those areas of northern Europe that are our concern, owned their land in the full sense of the term. Almost all owed some sort of allegiance to an overlord. The extent of their obligations, however, varied widely. A proportion was unfree, villeins or serfs. These villagers owed service to their lord in return for their landholdings, normally expressed in terms of so many days' work, usually both per week and at ploughtime or harvest. It was by means of this service that the land cultivated by the lord himself, his *demesne*, was worked. As well as this service, unfree peasants would be burdened by other obligations; these might involve a proportion of their own produce being due to the lord. Payments could be made to the lord – usually in kind (that is, in goods or beasts) – on the death of a villager and the passing of his holding to his heir (*heriot*), or on the marriage of a daughter (*merchet*). They were also bound to attend the lord's court, the manorial court; it was in fact a mark of their servitude in England that recourse to royal courts was forbidden them. It was, however, the case that in some places, though the peasants were personally free, they still owed dues of one kind or another to the local *seigneur* or lord. This system, with its mixture of obligations relating to land holding and personal obligations (which had almost as many variations as there were manors or villages), had never been universal or unchanging. At the beginning of our period the proportion of country people who were unfree and the precise meaning of that status both legally and personally varied widely both between and within the lands of the kings and princes in our study area.

France

By 1300 the demesne lands in many areas of France were largely cultivated by paid labourers. Contamine considers that personal serfdom only existed in a few places, in the Beauvaisis, Beauce, Bordelais, Lyonnais and Mâconnais regions of France. By 1400 it was found in even fewer places.[41] Lords found that, taking into account the obligation to provide food for those providing labour service, it was in fact cheaper to employ servants who did not enjoy this privilege. A man harrowing Church lands at Bayeux could claim, per day worked, 'a white loaf, a brown loaf, a measure of beer and three herrings or five eggs'. In 1315, Thierry D'Hireçon (who owned land in Artois) found that the cost of food for those who owed him forced labour, ploughing with eleven four-horse ploughs for half a day, was the same (30 *sous*) as one-third the annual wages for a paid servant.[42]

The situation in France was also made more complex by the climatic and agricultural difference between the South, where vines and olives dominated the landscape, and the North, where arable crops and stock-rearing were most important. There were also differences between the mountainous areas and those on the plains; those ruled directly by the king and those forming part of the *apanages* or semi-independent provinces of the highest nobility. We will concentrate here on two case studies of contrasting areas, Normandy and Languedoc.

Bois, in his study of eastern Normandy, feels able to state categorically,

> the problem of serfdom will not be raised here since it is an established fact that one of the most typical characteristics of Norman society is the almost total absence of serfdom.[43]

By the fourteenth and fifteenth centuries the peasants of Normandy can be divided into two groups, *laboureurs* (husbandmen) and *manouvriers* (smallholders). Normally a husbandman owned at least one plough and a plough team; the smallholder was dependent on his own physical strength alone. Their lives were almost symbiotic; the *laboureur* could not cultivate his holding without the aid of the paid work of the *manouvrier*; similarly the *manouvrier* could not subsist on his tiny holding without the money he earned from paid labour.[44] Their fortunes varied throughout the fourteenth and fifteenth centuries with there being a tendency for holdings to grow in size in the difficult years after 1350. When the ending of the war with England greatly improved the economic fortunes of Normandy, the smallholders, who lived precarious lives on the edge of destitution, seem to have increased in number perhaps because more work was available. The apparent stability of peasant society at this time with its continuing division into two parts is, perhaps, largely due to the fact that 'the most efficient unit of production was an average family-sized holding' worked by the holder with occasional paid help. On holdings like this were produced cereals, mainly winter wheat but also rye, some flax and hemp and also *rabette*, an ancestor of oil-seed rape. Apple orchards for cider were common round Rouen, while virtually all peasants had livestock of some kind.

Although these peasants were not serfs, we must not imagine that they were, therefore, free of obligations to their *seigneur*. The most prominent was, of course, rent for their holding. This was usually paid in money by our period and there seems to have been a dramatic fall in rents from the end of the fourteenth century to *c*.1450. This is attributed almost entirely to the fall in population levels; as one author puts it, 'too few men for too much ground'.[45] The count of Tancarville's rents, for example, diminished by 700 *livres tournois* between 1400 and 1459–60. Other *seigneurs* seem to have experienced a fall averaging 50 per cent. As well as rent, peasants were also burdened with other obligations: one of the heaviest was the requirement to grind all corn at the lord's mill. This could lead to the payment to the lord of a proportion of the harvest varying from every twelfth to every twenty-fourth sheaf. Markets too provided a resource that could be exploited by the *seigneur*, with dues payable on every transaction or on the right to display goods. The overall economic picture, however, of the late medieval period in the Norman countryside is of a severe decline in the income from land on the part of the lords (the essence of the 'crisis of feudalism') and a degree of stabilisation for the peasants. Much of the blame for this situation can be laid, as we have seen, on the war with England. There were also much increased demands for taxes by the Crown. The notorious *gabelle*, or salt tax, was first introduced in March 1341. Subsidies and later hearth or household taxes were also frequently demanded, eventually becoming a permanent feature of French life.

After 1450, very gradually things began to improve for the peasants on their smallholdings. The population began to rise but wage rates remained high. Villages that had been deserted were once more populated. Rents remained low, allowing peasants with larger holdings to build up enough savings to buy plough teams. A surviving cartulary from the village of Berneval shows clearly how the tithes due on grain, and flax, hemp and *rabette*, began to rise steadily from about 1480; in this seigneury agricultural production recovered well. By the end of our period, in this area of France, an average peasant was, according to Bois, 'a strong well-fed man who worked, produced and procreated without let-up'.[46]

Superficially the situation for the local *seigneurs* was less favourable. Their income from land had been in decline since before the disasters of plague, war and occupation had struck and they lacked the resources needed to restore the profitability of their estates even after the return of peace. Most of their land was leased, usually to a farmer who could drive a hard bargain when it came to setting the rent. Only in one aspect of agriculture did the future look brighter. Some lords, for example the count of Tancarville, were fortunate in possessing more grassland than arable, especially meadows along the Seine. Here the general rise in the prices for livestock ensured that rent for Tancarville's marshlands of Radicatel soared from 340 *livres tournois* in 1459 to 850 *livres tournois* in 1502. The balance between the fortunes of lords and peasants, which, despite the very difficult times through which Normandy passed in this period, had been generally in favour of the peasants, would not long remain so in the sixteenth century. This interpretation of the economic fortunes of the countryside and the people who lived there lays much more emphasis on the relationship between lords and peasants and on factors like war than on population levels. In the opinion of Bois, the so-called 'crisis of feudalism' drove the *seigneurs* to seek their fortunes away from their estates, in service to the Crown and attendance at court, leaving the peasantry to follow a different fate.

Le Roy Ladurie, in his study of the peasantry of Languedoc, concentrates largely on a later period. He does, however, make some very similar points to Bois with regard to the economic fortunes of the countryside in the south-west of France in the period *c.*1349–1500. The demographic collapse, so evident after the advent of the plague, in many ways worked to the advantage of the villagers. The cultivated area, particularly among the swampy coastlands of the Golfe de Lion (to the west of Marseilles), retreated, with blocked drainage channels and rampant malaria increasing the feeling of desolation. In the mountains, the foothills of the Pyrenees, forests reclaimed once farmed land and wild animals, boar, deer, and even bears roamed freely. Holdings consisted of freehold land or tenancies in perpetuity; servile tenancies were unknown. The peasant families who had survived now had larger holdings. Le Roy Ladurie remarks on how the peasantry of Languedoc 'had derived its prosperity from the genocide that had been perpetrated on its predecessors by bacilli, economic crisis, brigandage and the English'.[47]

At Saint-Thibéry, in the Hérault, in 1460, 189 landholders shared the same area which had supported 357 in 1390. Moreover, many now held estates of a reasonable size; there was no polarisation between the very few wealthy and a great mass of wretchedly poor cultivators. Le Roy Ladurie speaks of the way in which the tax surveys of the region make clear that there was a considerable group of peasant proprietors with around ten hectares of land who could feed themselves and produce a small surplus for the market, a 'yeomanry' (he uses this English term).[48] Wages, whether in money or in kind, were high; around 1480, the daily wage of a labourer tending vines was twice that paid at the end of the sixteenth century. The most prosperous peasant families were those who held a plot of a reasonable size and were able to cultivate it largely by the work of family members. The South benefited from the fact that it could produce certain specialist crops; these included olives and wine but also, particularly during the fifteenth century, the blue dyestuff, woad. This was grown near Toulouse and was exported to both the Spanish and the English cloth industries. Large landowners suffered from a sharp decline in rents similar to that noted by Bois. They could do much better if they turned away from leasing land and instead exploited it directly, a course followed successfully by the canons of Narbonne. They ran their lands at Bastide-Redonde and Vedilhan with the aid of an employee known as the *bayle*, who was in charge of the day-to-day running of the estate.[49] Between 1480 and 1500 in Languedoc, a 'sturdy, vigorous, well-nourished populace', reaped the benefits of land easily available at low rents,[50] benefits largely due to the decline in population and which would evaporate when the rapid population growth evident from 1450 really took off.

England

Perhaps because of the number of sources that survive, more work has been done in England on village life and agriculture than elsewhere. Bruce Campbell has based his *English Seigniorial Agriculture, 1250–1450* on several large databases including one with details from over 2,000 sets of manorial accounts, dating from this period, from Norfolk alone. Others add further details from *Inquisitions post Mortem*, documents which were drawn up after the death of a landowner and which included details of his estates. Certain differences with France are immediately clear; the matter of unfree personal status was a live issue for English peasants in 1350 and for some time thereafter. It may be the case that as few as one-third of villeins actually performed week work at the end of the thirteenth century but the theoretical obligation to do so remained, and 'boon work' during the harvest period might be demanded by many landlords from their villagers. The defects in the system of customary labour services from a lord's point of view, which we have already noted above for a lord in Artois, are, however, also manifest for England by entries in manorial custumals (lists of the obligations of the peasants on an estate drawn up for the use of the bailiff or reeve) like that for Battle Abbey from 1307.

> And he (John of Cayworth) ought to harrow for two days at Lenten sowing with one man and his own horse and his own harrow, the value of the work being 4d, and he is to receive from the lord on each day 3 meals of the value of 5d, and then the lord will be at a loss of 1d. Thus his harrowing is of no value to the service of the lord.[51]

In such circumstances the pressure on a lord to commute labour services for money rents is clear. Nevertheless, the stain of villein status remained and in some cases was bitterly resented by those villagers concerned. In one well-known case in 1293 a tenant of the earl of Gloucester in Worcestershire threw himself into the River Severn and drowned when the lord's bailiff tried to insist that he held his land on a servile tenure.[52] In 1336 the tenants of Vale Royal Abbey in the villages of Darnall and Over got together and claimed that the abbot had attempted to 'put them in close confinement in shackles as though they were villeins and forced them to serve him in all villein services'. It was their position that they were in fact 'free and held their lands and tenements from aforetime by charter of the Lord the King'. The group refused to give up the fight despite pressure from the abbot and in fact eventually presented a petition to the king in Parliament. The result of this is not known but the group or some of their supporters were then accused of attacking the abbot and his servants and bringing them by force to the king, who was at Stamford. In the fracas an abbey servant was killed, but even after this the bondmen continued their case in the royal courts. It was all to no avail, however; the abbey chronicle finally records triumphantly;

> The bondmen . . . returned to the abbot their lord . . . and the abbot put them all in fetters as his bondmen. And so it came to pass that, touching the Holy Gospels, they all swore they were truly the bondmen of the abbot and convent and that they would never claim their freedom against them and their successors. And for many Sundays, they stood in the choir in the face of the convent, with bare heads and feet, and they offered wax candles in token of subjection.[53]

More notably, in 1381, at the meeting between the young Richard II and Wat Tyler at Smithfield, at the climax of the Peasants' Revolt, one of the most important of the demands made by the rebels' leader was, 'that there should be no more villeins in England and no serfdom nor villeinage but that all men should be free and of one condition'.[54]

The pressure from tenants against unfree status continued during the fifteenth century. The tenants of the bishop of Worcester, one of the best documented of all medieval estates, seem to have refused to pay their normal rents in 1433 and also the special due (*recognition*) payable on the ending of a vacancy in the diocese. In 1450 a survey of the estates of the bishopric included comments regarding several manors on the lines of 'they refuse the customs'. A sixteenth-century writer expostulated angrily regarding his tenants, 'the peasant knaves be too wealthy . . . they know no obedience, they regard no laws, they would have no gentleman, they will appoint us what rent we should take for our grounds'.[55]

It is largely true that villein status had fallen into desuetude by the first years of the sixteenth century. The decline in population favoured tenants who could play one landlord off against another to get the best terms. Landlords found it counterproductive to attempt to enforce customary service grudgingly performed rather than to pay for hired labour, or to lease land to free tenants. By the middle of the sixteenth century personal status was no longer linked to the tenure of land: neither of the two main categories of tenant holdings which existed, leases on varying terms and the so-called customary tenures, implied unfreedom. Customary tenures did include an obligation to observe the ancient customs of the manor but were equated with *copyhold* (title based on a copy of the relevant entry in the manor court roll) tenures. Sir Thomas Littleton, for example, described these thus:

> it is to be understood that in divers lordships and divers manors there be many and divers customs ... and whatsoever is not against reason may well be admitted and allowed.[56]

How can this change be accounted for? The demographic collapse following the Black Death (Postan), a stage in the development of the 'class struggle' (Hilton), and the result of what can be conveniently called 'market forces' (Britnell, and Dyer) have all been given a role in developments. The richness of the surviving sources already mentioned makes it hard to come to any one conclusion. The individual circumstances of families, communities and manors, the nature of their land, the character of their lord, even the political situation with the prevalence of war and civil strife in the fifteenth century all had a bearing on their economic fortunes and eventual social position. The period before the plague was one of economic difficulty for many peasants. The bad years at the beginning of the century had brought many problems, which were compounded in England by a severe outbreak of disease among sheep. Losses of up to 50 per cent in some flocks are recorded. Heavy taxes for the wars in Scotland and in France were a further problem and in the 1330s prices of agricultural staples began to fall. Bolton sees this period as one in which *demesne* farming by the lords (the cultivation of the lords' lands on their own behalf using either customary or paid labour) was in decline and peasants were impoverished.[57]

After 1348 the situation hardly became easier for lords, though some historians have seen it as a golden age for the peasantry. One immediate effect was undoubtedly a determined effort by those in positions of power to control wages. The Ordinance of Labourers of 1349 was replaced by the Statute of Labourers in 1351. This legislation, described in its opening preamble as being, 'against the malice of servants who were idle and unwilling to serve after the pestilence without taking outrageous wages',[58] prescribed wage rates for agricultural workers, and those in the building trade. The prices to be charged by craftsmen like shoemakers or tailors were not to exceed those usual in 1346–7. Enforcement was in the hands of the justices of the peace and it is not true to assert that the law was completely ineffective. Justices did attempt to take action not only against workmen who were paid too much but also against those who enticed servants into their employ by offering them higher wages. Nevertheless, the pressure exerted by a fall in the supply of labour could not be resisted indefinitely and by the end of the fifteenth century both real and money wage rates had risen considerably. This is made clear by Figure 1, an index of wages and prices based on a basket of consumables, basic foodstuffs, fuel, drink and cloth.

The fortunes of landholders, whether peasants or lords, were perhaps more varied, dependent not only on the fertility of the land and its proximity to a market but also on the drive and energy of the farmer himself. On the estates of the bishop of Worcester, already mentioned, between 1395 and 1436 the bishop's

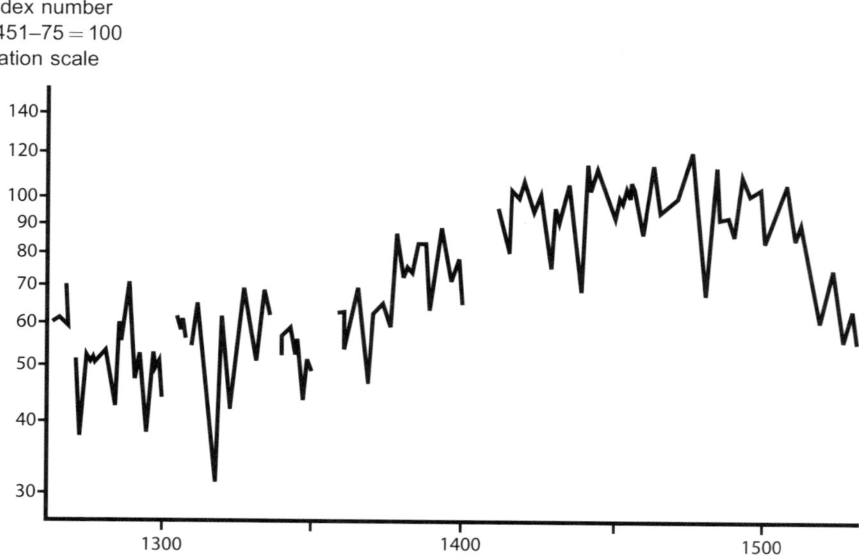

Figure 1 Building workers' wages, 1264–1532

officials managed to preserve the level of income usual in the fourteenth century with a fair degree of success. By 1410, however, most of the *demesne* lands had been leased out. The bishop's income was kept up by the success of his managers in extracting servile dues and taxes from his tenants. By 1433–5 arrears had begun to accumulate, with tenants refusing to pay what was due, citing the recurrence of pestilence or their own poverty. A survey in mid-century showed the bishop's estates to be mismanaged, neglected and discontented.[59] Mills and other buildings were in ruins and free tenants, gentry families like the Throckmortons, were out of the bishop's control and no longer paid him any dues at all. At Bredon peasant tenants had built up rent arrears reaching £63 5s 4d in 1476, and dues like that of £1 annually for fishing in the Avon could not be collected. By the end of the century, however, there were signs that things were getting easier for landlords. Revenues were rising on the estates of the archbishop of Canterbury. The raising of cattle and sheep on the rich pastures of the Romney marshes was prospering, with a healthy export trade to feed the garrison and merchants at Calais. The Knatchbulls, who leased some two thousand acres from the archbishop, took fresh options for land on the marsh in 1500 to be used for sheep.

An impression of the fortunes of a less eminent lay landowner and his tenants during the fifteenth century can also be gained by examining the affairs of John Hopton, a member of the lesser gentry. Hopton came originally from Yorkshire, but by a series of fortunate deaths and the lack of direct heirs he came to inherit in 1430 the fortune of his father's half-brother Sir Roger Swillington. This included a series of manors in Suffolk and it is some of these that will be considered in more detail. Hopton was not a magnate nor especially involved in public life. He had the misfortune to lose his sight in later life. Knowledge of his activities as a landowner come from the manorial accounts, *extents*, and other documents relating to his possessions, which allow us to look more closely at two of his manors. The first, Blythburgh, was on the Suffolk coast with heath and marsh as well as arable land, and also included the little port of Walberswick. The *demesne* lands were mostly leased out in the early part of the fifteenth century. Between 1477 and 1485 the land was directly exploited by the Hopton family as a sheep farm, with as many as 728 sheep grazing on the pastures and the marsh. After this date the land was again leased, with the sheep flock gone. The Hoptons also had a large rabbit warren on the property, which was highly profitable, producing over a thousand rabbits per year, which were sometimes sold locally or to London dealers. Not far away was another Hopton property, Easton Bavents. John Hopton bought the reversion of this estate (to come to him when the current holder died) in 1435 from one Ela Shardlow; in 1451 he acquired the property outright, although it was burdened with the payment of a pension to Ela. The Shardlows had largely used Easton Bavents to supply the needs of their household, with some success. By the 1460s, in Hopton's ownership, the property was almost entirely leased out as sheep pasture. John Deynes rented the former arable land, the manor house, the heath and the rabbit warren and was also paid £3 per annum for pasturing 300 sheep belonging to Hopton. Held on a separate lease was a swannery on the mere. We can see that the estate documents in general are concerned with rents, leases, and the exploitation of monetary fees and dues. The issue of labour services or the legal status of the tenants is hardly discernible in accounts by the end of the fifteenth century, probably because it was no longer of any practical concern to the landowner.[60] Hopton's actions are motivated by the desire to make his property profitable and exploit the available commercial opportunities. Active management of his lands was essential to achieve this aim.

If we consider the way in which things changed for both landowners and villagers in our period on both sides of the Channel we can see both important similarities and differences. First of all, any generalisations must remain tentative: local conditions whether climatic, topographic or political could exert great influence. This is particularly the case in northern France, where the devastation wrought by the wars could ruin a neighbourhood for many years. Rural life for both the English and the French, however, was changed by the demographic collapse in the later fourteenth century. The effects of the first visitation of the plague may have been overstated but the continued decline of the population over the remaining years of the fourteenth century strengthened the position of rural tenants, whatever their legal status, and undermined the economic position of large landowners. The recovery of population levels from the trough of the 1430s to 1440s happened sooner and was much faster in France than in England. The influence of market forces, Britnell's 'commercialising economy', can be seen in both realms. We can cite such examples as the need to supply towns with foodstuffs, especially a metropolis like London or Paris, or the wool market in England, or a more specialised factor like the success of woad growers around Toulouse in the late fifteenth century. England had also followed France in seeing the virtual end of serfdom.

The Empire

The lack of estate papers or manorial court rolls similar to those which exist for England, or legal records like those in France, makes it very difficult to provide comparable accounts of the fortunes of the peasants or the rural economy in general in Flanders, the northern Netherlands or the lands of the Empire. We can re-emphasise the point that conditions were often decisively influenced by local factors, by such matters as soil types, the nature of the terrain, nearness to large towns and the legal basis of land tenure. In the Netherlands as a whole, as we have already mentioned, the incidence of flooding was a further factor which must be taken into account. In the fifteenth century, floods on a large enough scale to cause widespread damage occurred in 1421, in 1446 on Palm Sunday, in 1467 and in 1477. The Flemish countryside, despite the effects of plague and the highly disruptive 'War of Ghent', the civil war which caused great destruction in 1379–85, was generally considered by contemporaries to be densely populated throughout our period. Serfdom had long ceased to be an issue. The counts had removed the legal restraints on their unfree tenants during the thirteenth century. Many burghers from the towns had bought up land in rural areas but many small peasant holdings remained. Figures from land confiscated from rebels after the Battle of Cassel in 1328 reveal that holdings were often less than ten acres. By the middle of the fifteenth century, despite the effects of plague and civil war, they do not appear to be any larger.[61] This fragmentation of holdings, in a society where partible inheritance (division in equal shares among all, or all male, surviving children) prevailed, is a good indication of a densely settled countryside. The peasant farmers concentrated more on the production of dairy produce, including cheese, meat and the breeding of horses, than on the growing of grain, which could be imported more cheaply by the cities from Germany or northern France. They also grew industrial crops like dyestuffs, including madder for the red *scharlaken* fabric made in Ghent and Bruges, flax for the linen industry, and hops for beer. Although times were harder for large landlords, faced with higher wages and lower prices for some produce, those whose records still exist – mainly the religious houses of the cities, like St Bavon's in Ghent – remained wealthy and powerful institutions.

Further to the north in the county of Holland research concentrating on one small area has shown a diverse pattern of development. The most easily cultivable lands, which had long been settled, were mostly divided into large estates where the income came from the proceeds of leases, not cultivation of the *demesne* by the lord. The less attractive peaty land was almost entirely in the hands of peasant farmers, perhaps the descendants of the original colonists of the eleventh and twelfth centuries. These farmers tended to concentrate on stock raising, therefore growing mainly fodder crops, especially oats. Small farms using only the labour of family members, raising stock or growing specialised crops, could be profitable despite the low prices of grain and the high wages of labourers.[62]

In the German lands of the Empire, intensely local factors could influence the fortunes of both the lord and the peasant family. There is, however, also a new factor to consider; that is, the difference which has often been claimed to exist between developments to the west and to the east of the River Elbe. The land to the east had been settled largely as the result of a deliberate colonisation process begun in the twelfth century. Peasants from German-speaking areas or from the Netherlands had moved east to new villages, often encouraged by a 'settlement planner' known as a *lokator*. He was employed by the lord to whom the 'new lands' had been assigned and was authorised 'to assign standard size holdings to a set number of settlers' on the lord's behalf.[63] Others moved to pre-existing Slavic villages, which then adopted German law. In both cases the peasants had larger holdings than they could have hoped for in their place of origin and an enhanced legal status with secure property rights.

In these areas especially, for example, Silesia and Prussia, the fifteenth century has often been described as the moment when a harsh regime of labour services was first enforced on the previously secure and free peasantry. The term *Gutherrschaft* (large estate lordship) was often used, with a clear contrast drawn with the *Grundherrschaft* (lordship over land) of the west. The latter is used for the system whereby a peasant owes dues and rent to a lord but does not work on his land. In 1978 Hans Rosenberg denounced the noble landowners in the east, claiming that they had risen to power at the cost of 'the legal and social degradation, political emasculation, moral crippling and destruction of the chances of self-determination of the subject peasantry'.[64] According to this view, in eastern Europe the nobility, unrestrained by weak princely powers, took over land unworked after the decline in population caused by the plague, and compelled the peasants to work it, often at the cost of neglecting their own holdings. The peasants were deprived of all personal freedom and became almost the chattels of their lords. The stimulus for this appropriation of the produce of the land was the growing market for cereals in Scandinavia and the Netherlands. Lords became large-scale agricultural entrepreneurs producing for the market.

To the west of the Elbe, peasants and landlords had much more varied and complex relationships. In general in the west the decline in population had in many ways strengthened the position of the peasants against their lords, as had been the tendency in England and in France. Large-scale *demesne* farming had more or less totally ceased. Many villages had already had, before the calamities of the fourteenth century, assemblies that were communal rather than seigneurial institutions. All those with full property rights in the village were members, and were involved in such matters as the organisation of the farming of the common fields and the enforcement of village by-laws (the *Weistümer*). These assemblies, in Upper Germany, might on occasion negotiate with the lord concerning their various dues and obligations, drawing up 'treaties of lordship' binding on both parties. Overall in the west, it was claimed that, as before the turmoil of the later fourteenth century, lords drew a large portion of their income from rents paid by a relatively secure and personally free peasantry.[65]

Recent research has modified these rather starkly contrasted views. It has been pointed out that conditions were not uniformly the same to the east of the Elbe. Some lords were, in Scott's description of the landlords in Mecklenburg, little more than 'aristocratic gangsters out of princely control'.[66] In other areas, however, as in the west, lords had to negotiate with the village commune, and in Brandenburg, for example, the peasants had access to the princely courts and fought hard against the demands of the landlords. It is also clear that the increased powers of lords in the east preceded the spread of the large-scale commercial growing of cereals. The crucial factor was often the assumption of full jurisdiction by the lords over their tenants, cutting out the role of princely courts. It is in any case plain that this process was only in its early stages by the end of our period and the most onerous forms of personal bondage only became commonplace after the Thirty Years War in the seventeenth century.[67]

In Germany to the west of the Elbe the fortunes of lords and the conditions for villagers varied much more widely than the traditional view allows. Some contemporary writing described lords who had fallen into such deep poverty that their only recourse was to take to crime. A Carthusian monk spoke of knights who ran 'the risk of the gallows or the rack simply to avert misery and hunger'.[68] It is not clear, however, that this is more than conventional preaching at the moral failings of those in power. Scott points out that landowners in these areas had other ways of maintaining their economic position apart from receiving rents. Many gained both influence and wealth by assisting their local prince to build up his territory, as the power of the Emperor decreased. Others benefited from the spread of craft working into the countryside or the growing of specialist crops. Some, especially religious houses, re-imposed a kind of serfdom on their peasants. This was generally intended to prevent the villagers abandoning their holdings for some better prospect in the years of the greatest falls in population, or from marrying without permission; it did not often involve labour services. Developments of this kind make it clear that it was not only in the east that lords wished to extend their powers over the villagers. It was also the case that it was possible for one peasant to have more than one lord. This arose because land was inherited from the father but personal status (which might still include serfdom) was inherited from the mother.[69] Scott's conclusion has much to recommend it: that neither arguments based on the primacy of demographic factors, nor those positing a 'crisis of feudalism', give enough weight to matters like the balance of power between the ruler and the lords in a particular locality.[70]

There were also within the Empire communities that had escaped almost entirely from the lordship of the nobility in fifteenth-century Europe. The most prominent of these were the forest cantons of what became known as the Swiss Confederation, whose independence was acknowledged in the course of the century. Less well known perhaps is the peasant republic of Dithmarschen. This grew up on marshy lands north of the Elbe. The need to co-operate to build dikes to drain the land perhaps increased the strength and unity of the peasant community. In 1283 the local administrators in the service of the archbishop of Bremen (who had had lordship over the area) were thrown out and power passed into the hands of two clans, the Wollersmannen and the Vodiemannen. A rough, violent society of pirates and brigands developed, living precariously in an area which was often in danger of flooding by the North Sea. The two clans feuded with each other at first but by the fifteenth century had settled their differences and established a stable society with a written constitution. Power was in the hands of 48 regents but there was also an assembly of all men of the 'country', meeting in the open air at Heide. Laws, publicly agreed and accepted, regulated their lives, even setting out the penalty 'when one man intentionally pours a glass of beer onto another'. This incurred a fine, and an oath that this had been paid and the insult cleared. The king of Denmark was a threat to their independence but this was successfully maintained till the middle of the sixteenth century. Life was harsh but the laws were their own and their freedom was valued and fought for. As they declared in one battle song:

> Now and for ever more
> we will risk our lives and goods
> and we are all ready to die
> before the King of Denmark
> should destroy our beautiful land.[71]

Any consideration of the condition of rural life as a whole in our study area should, in fact, emphasise the enormous importance of local factors, political and social as well as economic, in an evaluation of change. At the same time it would be foolish to deny that the steep decline in population, beginning in 1348 and lasting till about 1450 in some areas and the first years of the sixteenth century in others, did have important effects. Hatcher and Bailey have argued powerfully for a more integrated approach to the issues we have been discussing, one that is neither wholly Malthusian nor wholly Marxist. As they point out, any better explanation of the great changes which took place in the course of the Middle Ages 'will require the abandonment of restricted agendas and the quest for simple answers'.[72]

(iii) HOUSEHOLDS AND FAMILY LIFE

The peasantry

If we wish to look more closely at the daily lives of peasants and their standard of living, we are again faced with the fact that there is a much greater variety of detailed evidence in English sources than in those for either France or the Empire. We can, however, get some idea of the layout and comfort of village houses, particularly in the colonised areas of eastern Europe, through archaeology. A settlement in Pfaffenschlag in Moravia has been excavated. This was rebuilt in the thirteenth century with houses on stone foundations and there were similarly stoutly constructed barns and stables. One feature of the houses of the wealthier peasants in this village, which was also found in Upper Bavaria and elsewhere, was the *Stube*. This was a stove stoked from the back so that the parlour into which the front of the stove projected was completely free of smoke and also well heated.[73] English village houses of the same date had no chimneys so that the smoke of the fire had to make its way out through any available opening. Another impression of village houses, this time in northern France, comes from the scene for February in the *Très Riches Heures* of the Duc de Berry (see Illustration 2). This prayer book, with an illustration for every month of the year, was made some time between 1412 and 1416. The February scene shows a peasant family happily warming themselves by their fire on a very cold and snowy day.

2 February from *Les Très Riches Heures*

This image for February from the calendar in the magnificient Book of Hours made by the Limbourg brothers for the Duke of Berry, shows a peasant family in winter in their apparently cosy hut. Note the bee skeps in the garden, the sheep in the fold and the granary or grain store on the right of the image.

The house is wooden but with a fair degree of comfort; single storeyed but with a smoke hood and flue for the fire. The farmyard, with a wattle fence enclosing a covered sheepfold, some bee skeps and a granary, implies a modest prosperity.

Excavation of several houses at Caldecote in Hertfordshire has also provided some more information about the dwellings of late medieval villagers. One fourteenth century croft has a house and a barn; a later croft from the fifteenth-century has a house of much the same size as the earlier one but also two large barns (with a corn drier), and a dovecote. A toft at Grenstein in Norfolk of much the same date had a small house behind an earth bank and at least six outbuildings, one a byre, arranged around a cobbled yard.[74] Although the evidence must be treated with great care, it has also been suggested that the varied quality of the pottery found on fifteenth-century sites indicates a rise in the standard of living among villagers. From early in the century what are known as 'Tudor Green' vessels, a form of high-quality tableware, can be found quite widely. From after the 1450s, imported German stoneware jugs can be found some distance from port towns, for example in Wiltshire and the north-west.[75]

It is hard to find unambiguous evidence for the size and make-up of the families who inhabited these houses and tilled the lands beyond their fences. Most sources speak of households rather than families, a concept that includes not only those who are relations by blood or marriage but also living-in servants. We have already argued that the most successful peasant farms were those that were worked as a family enterprise, relying not only on the labour of husband and wife but also that of their children, perhaps from as early as the age of six. It was not uncommon for children as young as this to help the family economy by doing such things as fishing or herding animals.[76] Does this imply that adult children would remain under the parental roof even after they had married? The answer seems to be 'no', at any rate in the greater part of the area with which we are concerned.

The factors that have to be considered include inheritance customs. Was the family inheritance treated as *partible* or *impartible*? If *impartible*, did this mean that the heirs worked the land as one unit in common or did it mean that the eldest son (or even sometimes the youngest) inherited all the land, although some effort would be made to provide for other children from other possessions? What also was the attitude of the lord to the division of holdings, for usually his approval would have had to be sought? Another factor is the general availability of land. Even if they did not inherit, was it still easy for children to acquire a holding that would enable them to found a family? Finally there is the issue of life expectancy. How frequently might parents or grandparents survive for some time to share a household with their adult children? Certainly the fall in population made the acquisition of land by the survivors easier. Life expectancy was such that it was probably relatively uncommon for parents to survive for very long after their children came to maturity. It has been calculated that in Kibworth Harcourt in Lincolnshire male peasants could expect to survive for a further 28 years after they took over a holding at the age of 25.[77] This would give an average male life expectancy, for those who survived the multiple perils of infancy and childhood, of 53.

Rösener, in his full discussion of inheritance patterns, sees these as varying widely across Europe but with a tendency to favour the indivisibility of holdings. In his view small nuclear families were more common where holdings could be divided. Large households, including siblings with their families, were more characteristic of impartible holdings.[78] Le Roy Ladurie suggests in *Histoire sociale et économique de la France* that while, in the north of France, family structures were similar to those of England, the Netherlands and northern Germany, with small family units the norm, in southern Europe large complex households, including three generations and collaterals, were frequently established. He describes households in the Nivernais where something not unlike a modern commune can be found. The fieldwork of the whole interrelated group was organised by an elected 'master' while a similarly elected 'mistress' (who must not be the 'master's' wife) looked after the care of the household, all the family's clothing and the poultry yard.[79] English evidence reinforces the view that nuclear families were most common in northern Europe. Households do not seem to have averaged more than four or five persons at the most. In Halesowen in Worcestershire, after the plague, the average for all peasant families from the richest to the poorest was only 2.1 children. In the period worst affected by plague, 1350–1400, nearly 40% of the tenants on the manor died childless. Older people seem to have quite frequently come to agreements either with family members or with neighbours whereby they would be maintained and cared for in old age while their land was handed over to their younger relations or to new tenants.[80] In some cases a small house might be built for them near the main one or they might retain the right to a room in the main house.

Many of these maintenance agreements include details of the food to be allowed to the pensioner, which give some idea of the usual diets of peasants. Emma del Rood of Cranfield in Bedfordshire made an agreement in 1437–8 which allowed her 12 bushels of wheat , 2 quarters of malt and a peck of oatmeal per year. This would translate into 2 lbs of bread and $2\frac{1}{2}$ pints of strong ale per day, with the oats for pottage. No meat is mentioned although in 1347 John Stappe of Blackwell in Warwickshire received an allowance which totalled one pig and a quarter of an ox carcass per year, which would have produced him about half a pound of meat on all non-fast days (on fast days only fish or dairy produce could be eaten). Another source that gives an idea of how peasants ate, is the meals provided for harvesters as part of their payment. In the fourteenth and fifteenth centuries harvesters no longer expected to be given mostly bread (probably made of barley rather than wheat) and a little cheese and ale. They were now provided with good wheaten bread, fresh beef and fresh fish and a quantity of strong ale. When these peasants returned home after the exhausting work in the harvest fields, their houses also provided greater comfort than before. The inventory taken of the goods of Richard Sclatter of Elmley Castle in Worcestershire, a relatively poor peasant, on his death in 1457, lists a spade, shovel, spinning wheel and other tools, kitchen stuff, at least one bed with coverlets, sheets, pillows and a mattress, and furniture including three chests for his 'hall'.[81] Sclatter, like many smallholders at this date, was also a craftsman, a tiler, an occupation that did not require much expensive equipment.

In France and Germany information about diet comes from similar sources listing the diets of harvesters and the like. We need also to remember climatic differences. Olive oil was used in areas bordering on the Mediterranean and wine was much more widely available than in the British Isles, where it was found only on the tables of the nobility. Particularly in the Netherlands and in southern Germany, beer flavoured with hops replaced ale or mead as the normal drink of the majority. In the earlier medieval period the staple foodstuff of peasants was gruel or porridge made with oats and millet, called either *Mas* or *Brot*. Bread as now understood, made of wheat and raised with yeast or sour dough and then baked, was for the lords. By 1497, however, the archbishop of Mainz ordered that, 'every labourer no matter whether he works in the fields or elsewhere, shall receive soup with bread [a baked loaf is implied] in the morning, stew with meat and vegetables and half a pint of table wine for lunch and a meat dish with bread or stew with bread for supper'. A rather earlier (1483) diet for workers on the estates of Erasmus von Erbach laid down a very similar regime with two meat dishes and half a jug of wine a day. He also provided 'generous portions of bread and meat, in addition to half a jar of wine on Sundays and other holidays'.[82] The menu apparently provided for the workers in the vineyards of the duke of Bavaria, also in 1483, was even more elaborate. It extended to white bread, barley, oatmeal, millet, salt, lard, butter, meat for both roasting and boiling, cheese, milk, cabbage, turnips, eggs, semolina, fish, *stockfish*, herrings, onions, apples, cooking pears, and spices.[83]

Before, however, we get the impression that peasants at this time were uniformly well fed, it is as well to remember that these diets could only be provided in good years. Grain could not easily be transported over long distances, except by sea, so that severe local shortages could follow any downturn in the harvest yield and more widespread dearths and famines were not uncommon. In contemporary eyes, large quantities of meat and wheaten bread were the basis of the diet of prosperous people, Sir John Fortescue, an English judge and political theorist, wrote contemptuously in 1471 of the French peasants who had no stomach to rebel against their rapacious king because, 'they drink water, they eat apples with very brown bread made of rye, they eat no meat other than very seldom a little bacon or the entrails and heads of beasts slain for the nobles and merchants of the land'.[84] A diet like this was not only a mark of the poverty of France compared with England but, in his view, led to a lack of manly valour.

A further aspect of the life of the peasantry, which is of importance, is the position of women. There was no doubt in the minds of many contemporaries that women were, by their very nature, subservient to men. Wife-beating aroused no comment. A custumal from the German-speaking lands dating from 1424 laconically stated, 'A woman must do what a man wants.'[85] This does not mean, however, that marriage was regarded lightly or that women were not fully involved in very nearly all the activities associated with peasant life. The choice of a marriage partner involved considerations of family advantage regarding landholding in villages almost as much as among the nobility. There was the further complication that the lord's interests might also be involved; he usually had the right to the payment of a due on the marriage of a tenant on his estate (*merchet* in England), which might be increased if one partner was from the manor of a different lord. The legal status of any children also concerned the lord, intent on maintaining control where possible over 'his' serfs.[86] Once married, however, women were not necessarily confined to household tasks or to activities nearby like the care of poultry. Illustrations in books of hours, psalters and the like show women doing all manner of work including harvesting, trapping rabbits in a warren, or haymaking. A fifteenth-century English poem includes a description of a ploughman and his wife working as a team. The ploughman is dressed in old ragged clothes as he follows the plough.

> He wading in mud, almost up to his ankles,
> And before him four oxen, so weary and feeble,
> . . . his wife walked beside him, with a long ox goad,
> In a clouted coat cut short to the knee,
> Wrapped in a winnowing sheet to keep out the weather.[87]

As well as this often very heavy work, a peasant woman might also follow a craft, most often spinning or the brewing of ale, and she would have much of the responsibility for the care of any children. Barabara Hanawalt's use of the Coroner's Rolls (which are concerned exclusively with the causes of sudden deaths) has unearthed a grim picture, in some ways, of medieval standards of childcare among the peasantry. Babies and toddlers fall from their cradles into the fire, are savaged by wandering pigs, drown in puddles or are crushed by carts in the roadway. Children as young as four or five are left looking after their still younger siblings and disaster follows.[88] We must remember, however, that there was another side to life that is not recorded in this source. The cult of the Virgin Mary, which became much more popular and widespread during this period, elevated and idealised the relationship of mother and child. Parents suffered greatly at the loss of children, despite the views of historians like Ariès.[89] One father explained how his wife had been sick for 'half a year following' when his son had drowned.[90]

Finally, how did writers in our period see the peasantry? In many ways the most common view of this group in society, which in fact constituted the overwhelming majority of the population in virtually all areas, was decidedly ambiguous. Clearly the rest of society depended on the success of their labours in the fields and such work was virtuous, but peasants were often seen as by nature brutish, docile and stupid. Early writers, including Stephen Langton, had forcefully criticised the way in which the lords exploited the peasantry. Stephen of Fougères had expressed similar views in his *Livre des Manières*:

> We have the best grain
> The most pleasant and sound
> The dross is left for the villein.[91]

Serfdom, however, was not usually seen as oppressive by contemporaries of higher social standing. It was often explained on the grounds that serfs were the descendants of the cowardly, who had not resisted invaders in the period of barbarian incursions. In the fifteenth century when, as we have seen, the lot of peasants did improve a little there was, particularly in Germany, some violently hostile writing on this topic. Peasants had no religion, they were extraordinarily hairy, almost bestial in appearance. The Peasants' Revolt in England, of 1381, left a legacy of fear and distrust of the peasantry among their so-called betters. An anonymous poem of the 1390s about the revolt has the refrain, 'This was a warnyng to be ware.'[92] On the other hand, Langland in *Piers Plowman* pointed out that:

> The poor may plead and pray in the doorway
> They may quake for cold and thirst and hunger
> None receveth them rightly and relieves their suffering.[93]

A portrayal like that of the Ploughman in Chaucer's 'General Prologue' to *The Canterbury Tales*, a gentle saintly man working for the benefit of others as well as himself, raises questions. This character has been interpreted both as an exemplar of the fundamental divisions of society along with the Knight and the

Parson, and as satire, something perhaps more clearly evident in the picture of the Reeve. This wealthy and crafty peasant, acting as the landlord's agent, has no compunction at enriching himself to the detriment of both his lord and the rest of the village.

Those peasant communities who had managed to hold onto, or who demanded, real independence saw themselves in quite another manner. The well-known couplet asking who was a gentleman when Adam tilled the soil and Eve span can be found all over Europe, in versions in Swedish, Dutch, Czech and Polish as well as English. The leaders of the free peasant county of Dithmarschen, at a crisis point in their affairs, gave full expression to their deep desire for freedom: 'Even those who are born serfs long to be free. Are we who are born free to subject ourselves to servitude without resisting?'[94]

The demographic disaster beginning in the middle of the fourteenth century impacted severely on the lives of peasants; whether the results were beneficial or not might depend ultimately on local factors. It does seem, however, that as villagers became more self-conscious and aware of their inferior status, they also had a greater desire for change. This might happen gradually, due to economic pressures as in England, or it might be articulated more forcefully, as in the Bundschuh conspiracies in Upper Germany in the opening years of the sixteenth century. The password of one set of conspirators, 'In all the world the common man can find no comfort', may have been imprecise but did reflect a mood of restlessness among many.[95]

The nobility

In much the same way as there were both wealthy and poor peasants, so the term 'noble' includes, in all the areas we are considering, both families whose claim to be noble was perhaps the only thing which distinguished them from their peasant neighbours, and great lords of enormous wealth and power. On what basis was this all-important claim to be a noble made? The origins of this social rank lay, in the thinking of most contemporaries, in service to the prince as a warrior. In France moreover, while the concept of honour was closely associated with noble status, there was also an increasing legal element in the definition of nobility. The most obvious legal proof of nobility was being summoned to the French royal army as a mounted warrior or a knight; 20,000 individuals were summoned to his forces on this basis by Louis XI in 1468. If immediate family members were also included this would have implied a total of perhaps 80,000 persons. It has been suggested that nobles constituted 1% of the population in 1328 and much the same proportion over a century later in 1470.[96]

The status of nobility, however, could be acquired in various ways besides being a member of a lineage long connected with military service to the Crown. The nobility was not a closed group. There were, for example, in France, as well as families who acquired noble status through the lengthy occupation of a high judicial office, others who had bought land and seigneuries and paid a due known as *franc-fief*. This was payable since they were not themselves of sufficiently noble birth to perform the military service due. In 1470 Louis accorded all families in Normandy in this position noble status on payment of a further fee. This ensured their exemption from the *taille* (direct personal tax) but in return they were obliged to live nobly. This was a somewhat elusive concept but was agreed to be an essential mark of the true noble. Certainly it usually entailed the possession of land and seigneurial rights, the enjoyment of the chase, whether using dogs or hawks, the playing of suitable games like chess, and the avoidance of direct involvement in trade. It did not necessarily entail wealth or a lavish lifestyle. Jeanne de Chalon was in charge of a small, impoverished estate in the Tonnerrois at the end of the fourteenth century. She could not afford fresh meat but normally ate fat bacon instead; she had little in the way of furniture except beds. She held what wealth she did possess, apart from her lands, in the form of silver plate rather than coin but she managed to hang on to the core of the family lands and hand on the inheritance to her heirs.[97] In contrast the duc de la Tremoille had an average income from 1486 to 1509 of the enormous sum of 27,600 *livres tournois*, which ensured that he lived in splendour surrounded by retainers and could afford the lavish displays of hospitality and generosity expected of someone of his status.[98]

In Germany nobility was more clearly defined. The higher nobility, or *hochadel*, included margraves, electors and dukes who ruled as territorial princes under the Emperor, and *graffen* (counts) and *herren* (barons) with lesser powers. The *niederer adel* (lower nobility) or *rittern* (knights) held land from their superiors. Again it was the possession of land and the rights of lordship that marked them out as a group. In Bavaria their status (as *Turnieradel*) was also linked to their right to be invited to participate in the lavish tournaments arranged by the duke. The rules could be bent however: even though those nobles who married beneath them into wealthy bourgeois families were in theory excluded from these tournaments, in 1485 it was agreed that if the bride had a dowry of at least 4,000 *gulden* her lowly status would be overlooked.[99] On the other hand, in Flanders, despite the fact that its rulers were princes of the Empire, by the fifteenth century the nobility had more or less merged with the upper bourgeoisie. They lived in the towns, often in magnificent houses, intermarried with bourgeois families and had long ceased to have any realistic links with military service to the duke or count. The foundation of the Order of the Golden Fleece in January 1430 and the lavish ceremonies associated with it increased the prestige of those among the nobility who were members, but Charles the Bold's attempts to resuscitate the idea of military service was not received well. They might enter the ruler's service as a counsellor or the like but their way of life was much more urban than that of most nobles. Indeed Nicholas has claimed that 'its very existence as a separate group was becoming blurred under the impact of the towns and the Burgundian house'.[100]

In England the upper levels of society were divided between a very small group who could claim the status of peers (on the basis of a summons by an individual writ to meetings of Parliament, or by royal creation) and a much larger, ill-defined group who, by the fifteenth century, were usually described as 'the gentry'. The peerage, most of whom were wealthy with extensive landed estates, numbered no more than around fifty families. The gentry were usually distinguished by their right to a coat of arms or by their eligibility for knighthood; but in many cases the true test of gentility was acceptance by neighbours of the same rank, and a certain style of life. This involved the possession of land but did not exclude the pursuit of a profession or links with merchant families. The fortune of the Paston family of Norfolk was founded by William Paston I (reputedly the son of a villein), who:

> learned the law and there begat much good: and then he was made a serjeant, and afterwards a justice and a right cunning man in the law. And he purchased much land in Paston.[101]

His grandson was a knight and a member of the king's household, who eventually made good his claim to the large estate in East Anglia, formerly owned by Sir John Fastolf, a prominent military commander. The Stonor family, who lived on the borders of Oxfordshire and Buckinghamshire, had long been accounted gentry but, in 1475, William Stonor married Katherine Ryche, the daughter of a London alderman and the widow of Thomas Ryche, the son of a wealthy mercer. The marriage helped the Stonors do well out of the wool trade since the union linked them with the Staple in Calais.[102]

The choice of a husband or wife was of paramount importance to the nobility in all of our study areas. Marriage to an heiress could transform the fortunes of a noble family. It has often been argued that the earl of Warwick became increasingly disenchanted with Edward IV because the Queen, Elizabeth Woodville's relations were monopolising the marriage market in the 1460s.[103] Although free consent was essential for a valid marriage in canon law, a great deal of pressure might be brought on a young girl to marry the partner selected by her parents. Some couples were betrothed when both were very young. In a well-known case, Richard, earl of Arundel, and Isabella le Despenser claimed that they had been betrothed at the ages of 7 and 8 respectively. When they reached maturity they were forced to cohabit despite having no wish to continue the relationship; after a long legal process (and after Isabella had borne a son) the marriage was eventually annulled for lack of informed consent.[104] Christine de Pizan put forward a very practical view of noble marriage in her *Treasury of the City of Ladies*. She points out that noblewomen 'spend much of their lives in households without husbands. The men are usually at court or in distant countries.'[105] In these circumstances it was the lady's duty to understand the legal complexities of running an estate, direct the agricultural operations, watch for lazy workmen and in fact, 'keep her eyes wide open'.

The survival of personal letters as well as estate papers, accounts and wills increasingly gives us access to intimate information as well as other details of the lifestyle of noble or gentry families. Sir John Fastolf, for example, lived in style in the castle at Caister in Norfolk that he had built for himself from the proceeds of his campaigning in France. This had over fifty rooms including 28 bedrooms with 39 beds. His ample household of servants, advisers, estate managers and even paying guests easily filled the available space. His own suite of rooms included a bathroom or 'stew'. Outside there were stables, and a bakehouse and a brewhouse.[106] Many of Margaret Paston's letters to her husband are full of details regarding the management of the household, much as advised by Christine de

Pizan; she writes about the difficulties in getting suitable cloth for the servants' liveries in Norfolk, 'As touching your liveries, there can be none got here of the colour that you would have neither murrey nor blue nor good russets.' On occasion she was faced with more dramatic events, like the time when she was besieged in their manor house at Gresham. The ownership of this land was disputed by Lord Moleyns. He sent:

> to the said mansion a riotous people to the number of a thousand persons arrayed in a manner of war . . . they drove [Margaret and her servants] out of the said mansion and mined down the walls of the chamber wherein [she] was and bare her out of the gates and cut asunder the posts of the house and let them fall and broke up all the chambers and coffers in the said mansion and rifled . . . and bare away stuff array and money to the value of £200.[107]

Another Norfolk neighbour, embroiled in a dispute over possession of the manor of New Buckenham, one Alice Knyvet, had no compunction in confronting a group armed with a royal commission who had come to evict her from her house. She barricaded herself and her servants into the building and shouted from the roof of a turret on the gatehouse:

> if you begin to break the peace or to make any war to get the place of me, I shall defend me, for lever [I would prefer] I had in such wise to die than to be slain when my husband comes home for he charged me to keep it.

The party of JPs and the Sheriff of Norfolk then hastily withdrew.[108]

Noble households often also entertained on an enormous scale; this was not mere ostentation but part of the imperative to live nobly. This emerges particularly clearly from the survival of the Household Book or steward's account book for the year 1412–13, of Alice de Bryene. She was a wealthy widow living in Acton near Sudbury in Suffolk. During that period, over 16,000 meals were served to the household, an average of 45 per day. Her table was amply provided for with fresh meat of all kinds except on fish days. Fish was often salted or dried but included 14 different kinds of fresh fish, oysters, crabs, mussels, and shrimps. Spices were very important although expensive; these included saffron, cinnamon, pepper, ginger, cloves and mace. Each person in the household would also have expected to have a 2 lb loaf and three pints of ale at every meal. Wine was provided only for the gentry.[109] The provision for the chamberlains and courtiers of Charles the Bold (some ten in number) was considerably more lavish. Their daily rations included, on meat (non-fasting) days, the following: 'a piece of beef, two saddles of mutton, a leg of beef, a boiled capon or veal, chitterlings, sausages, tripe, small black puddings' and also soup, milk and other drinks.[110]

Even this pales beside what was served at a public feast like the one to celebrate the enthronement of John Chandler as Bishop of Salisbury, *c.*1417. There were three courses consisting of many dishes. The first course (which all present would have) included boiled meats. On this occasion it also included *frumenty* (a kind of rich porridge seasoned with sugar and spices) with venison, swan, peacock, and *Pomys en gele* (mincemeat balls in jelly). The second course included roasted meat, and more elaborate dishes such as *Crustade ryal* (rather like a quiche) and *Blandyssorye* (white soup with almond milk and ground chicken). The third and final course had fried meats and such things as fritters, jellies and filled pastries.[111] In Scotland, enormous quantities of expensive spices were procured for the marriage of David II and Joanna of England in 1328, including 180 lbs of pepper, 55 lbs of mace, 10 lbs of nutmegs and 74 lbs of cinnamon. The total cost of the feast, including liveries for the retainers and large quantities of canvas and towelling, comes to £941 0s 6d, about a fifth of the total income of the Scottish Crown at the time.[112]

There is no doubt that most nobles were acutely conscious of their status and the need to defend it. The Pastons invented a suitable family tree for themselves going back to Norman times, quite ignoring their villein progenitor. The Scropes of Bolton and the Grosvenors, both fairly new recruits to gentry status, fought a case in the Court of Arms for many years over the right to bear a particular set of armorial bearings. French nobles had every reason to maintain their right to their privileged status since, as we have seen, it brought with it exemption from tax. Louis XI also instituted a process known as *recherche* in an endeavour to deprive those not truly entitled to noble status. This caused such an uproar in Normandy in 1461 that it had to be abandoned.[113] In one case, Jean Barbin argued before the King's proctor:

> that the late Nicolas Barbin [his father] was in his lifetime a nobleman, born and descended of a noble line, and as such held and reputed publicly and to the knowledge of all.[114]

To maintain the lifestyle of a noble in a time of falling revenues for many landlords was a continual struggle. It is not surprising that many found the solution to their economic difficulties in the quest for royal favour or honourable employment in service to the Crown or dependence on a local prince.

CONCLUSIONS

Despite the apparent similarities in the organisation of rural society in our chosen study area in the period after the first advent of the Black Death, it would be clearly unwise to venture too far in attempting to find generalisations that have widespread validity. We can say only that in all these areas society was essentially hierarchical, with the great mass of country people, called here the peasantry, dependent to some extent on landowning lords. Beyond that there is not only great variety in the detail of the bases of village life but also considerable change over our period. The sudden fall in population following the first advent of the plague and its subsequent recurrences is undeniable but the effects of this collapse are controversial. This factor altered the balance of economic power within rural society. Even if we are cautious about accepting in full Bois's idea of a 'crisis of feudalism', we might suggest that villagers found their bargaining power strengthened as the effects of a labour shortage began to bite, while lords were faced with much more difficult circumstances than had been the case in the '*monde plein*'[115] of the late thirteenth century.

How this situation was dealt with in practice varied considerably from place to place. Some landlords persisted in attempting to run their estates as they had done in the past, until economic disaster was staring them in the face. This seems to have been the case with the bishop of Worcester. Others adapted much more easily to changes in the expectations of villagers and also, significantly, to changes in the market for agricultural products. This was the case with the counts of Tancarville exploiting their pasture lands, or Hopton actively managing his estates in Suffolk. In some parts of Germany and, for example, in the area round Toulouse, the market for industrial crops (dyestuffs, hops) created new opportunities. In the Empire the ability to provide loans for the ruling prince became an important strand in the economic success of a noble family. Similarly there were areas where the legal status of villagers improved markedly (the decay of villeinage or serfdom in England is the classic example here) and others where differing forms of servitude for peasants were re-imposed by more aggressive landowners.

In terms of the general standard of living, again individual circumstances varied widely. Certainly there is virtually no hint, at the highest levels, that the ostentatious display of wealth and magnificence declined. As will be shown in Chapter 6, this was for most rulers a political imperative. For villagers, if they could safely negotiate between the opportunities offered by rising wages and the effects of rising prices for manufactured goods, life did improve. How long this improvement lasted is a matter where regional differences are very noticeable. In France, population began to rise some time before the same effect is noticeable in England. On the other hand, the destruction and dislocation caused by war in the first half of the fifteenth century was much worse in some parts of France than in any part of the British Isles. An old Chinese proverb famously alludes to the disadvantages of living in 'interesting times'. This label could well apply to our period; but we also need to point out that opportunities for social advancement and economic success were there for those bold enough to take them. These opportunities might seem to herald the more individualistic world of the Renaissance. They certainly seem to deny the gloomy view put forward by Huizinga, and confirm the possibility of a commercialising society, advanced by Britnell. In Germany, Scott points to the importance of the 'uneasy balance between the separate, though reciprocal, interests of the state and the interests of the aristocracy', a conclusion which has application beyond the confines of the Empire.[116]

2

Townsmen, Traders and Unrest

INTRODUCTION: THEMES AND SOURCES

In this chapter we are concerned with what has often been considered the antithesis of the countryside and the slow rhythms of the agricultural year, the world of townsmen and of traders. Towns could be centres of activity carried out by craftsmen and women, important religiously because they were the seat of a bishop or contained a notable shrine, or important politically because the court of a ruler and his administration was situated there. Trade, however, whether local, regional or international, over long distances or in the immediate neighbourhood, was the lifeblood of most towns and the two topics of towns and trade are very closely related. Our first aim will be to look at the ways in which towns were ruled, the powers of their authorities and the extent to which this changed in our period.

Towns, of course, varied greatly: from the great trading and manufacturing centres of the Netherlands, which at times seemed on the verge of becoming fully independent city states like those in Italy, to very small towns in the more remote parts of England, France or Scotland. A major issue here is whether towns, or perhaps towns in particular circumstances, were declining in our period or not. There is also the issue of the possible political power of urban centres. Could a town, perhaps one which could be dignified with the name of 'city', carry real weight in a state and affect the outcome of events? Did the existence of powerful towns impede or accelerate the emergence of the idea of the nation state? Although we will look at towns across our chosen area, we will also examine in some detail case studies based on three notable towns, which will illustrate these points. Our first example is Cologne, a trading city, the seat and part of the lands of a Prince-Archbishop of the Empire; the second, Ghent, an industrial and trading city in Flanders, from 1385 part of the Burgundian Netherlands; and the last, London, the capital of England, a city of merchants but also closely linked to the king and the court. The question of whether there was a distinctive urban culture at this time, which compensated in part for the often squalid and crowded living conditions in many late medieval towns, will be considered in Chapter 6, where the question of possible cultural change in our period is in the forefront.

The second section of this chapter looks at trade more generally. What commodities were the most valuable or the most commonly exchanged? What routes were normally followed? How did merchants arrange payments? What was the importance of bullion on the one hand and credit in various forms on the other? The question of the so-called bullion crisis of this period, which has been much debated by Spufford and Munro, will be addressed.[1] Since trade transcended national boundaries, we will at times be discussing developments outside our chosen areas of France, the British Isles and the Empire but the focus will be primarily on these realms and not on more southerly states. A second group of case studies will be introduced here to take a close look at two differently organised associations of merchants; one, the Hanseatic League, was a loose confederation of trading cities in northern Europe and the other, the Company of the Staple, was a company of English merchants in control of the export of raw wool. Both had considerable political as well as economic importance though exercised in very different ways and will thus serve to highlight how a ruler might want to intervene in economic matters to advance the interests of his people and his realm.

The third section of the chapter will move on to a different aspect of town life; the possibility of disorder and riot. Although, in some cases, problems originated in the countryside they caused greater alarm to rulers when they also erupted in towns. The economic aspects of urban life were seen as beneficial to a realm but the potential for violent dissent among large gatherings of people, many excluded from power, was feared in our period as in later times. The main theme here will be an attempt to isolate the reasons behind urban riots and more general rebellions like the Jacquerie of 1358 in France and the Peasants' Revolt of 1381 in England. Guenée, for example, tends to discount specific social and economic conditions in favour of the idea that uprisings occurred 'not because things were intolerable but because they seemed so'.[2] The concluding section will attempt to pull these diverse ideas together into an overall view of the ways in which towns contributed to the pattern of life in our period.

The primary sources for our inquiry survive in large quantities in many places. Once a town achieved corporate status, enshrined in a charter, with some sort of a council, financial administration and courts, records were made and kept. Their survival to some extent depends on the vagaries of later events like war damage, or the continuing prosperity of the place, but in many instances municipal archives are very rich. Sometimes, as in Ghent, records will exist not only of the ruling council but also of other bodies like guilds or religious houses that flourished in the city. Friedrichs has pointed out that virtually all German cities have records, including tax records and records of property transactions, which allow a clear picture to be built up of urban society.[3] Knowledge of trade comes from princely as well as local sources. The idea of Customs duties was well established in our period and the records of taxes of this kind make it possible to get some idea of the value of trade and the routes followed. Legal records can throw light on the way trade was financed and directed. In a few cases, by the fifteenth century, some at least of the papers of individual merchant families survive, allowing an understanding of urban life on a more personal level. Riots are often recorded not only in national chronicles but also in others written for a particular town and its people. For example a whole series of London chronicles exists for the fifteenth century; similarly there are town chronicles in Lübeck and other Hanseatic towns.

(i) TOWNSMEN

Urban organisation and government

How does one define a town at this period? Barrie Dobson felt that no more precise definition could be offered than that of St Augustine in his *De Civitate dei* (Concerning the City of God), written in the fifth century: 'a city is a multitude of men bound together by a certain bond of society'.[4] Christopher Dyer has provided a more complex definition: a town was 'a permanent settlement in which a very high proportion of the population lived by a variety of trades, crafts and other non-agricultural activities'. A town would also have 'a distinct appearance', being compact and densely built up, 'with building plots arranged closely in rows along streets and around market places'.[5] One of these definitions sees the essence of a town in its corporate existence, the other focuses more on its physical appearance and on its economic function.

It is quite clear that the size of a settlement is of itself not a reliable guide to the difference between a rural village and a town. Some of the towns discussed by Dyer in the article already cited had no more than 300 inhabitants. To modern eyes this would be a small village. On the other hand, in 1300, before the famines of the early fourteenth century and the onset of the Black Death, the possible apogee of the population of most medieval towns, Nicholas has calculated that Paris, the largest town in western Europe, had some 200,000 people;[6] Granada, 150,000; Venice, 110,000; Genoa and Milan, 100,000; Florence, 95,000; Seville, 90,000; Ghent, 75,000; and Cologne, 55,000. Other towns in Italy and Spain had *c.*50,000 inhabitants while London, Bruges, Montpellier, Saint-Omer and Rouen had between 35,000 and 25,000. From this list it is easy to see that the majority of the largest towns were all situated in southern Europe but that there were, even so, some considerable cities in the north. To contemporaries, again in Dyer's view, a town would have been unmistakable in other ways, apart from its appearance: 'by its feel, sounds and smells'.[7] A town was crowded and had a stir in the streets quite unlike that of an agricultural village; the houses would be packed together. In the centre of Winchester in 1400, there were 81 persons per acre, a greater density than in almost all modern cities. Moreover, this business and commercial activity of all kinds was not confined to market days nor to the period of a fair but was the usual state of affairs. Scribner and Scott, however, found so many exceptions if a definition of towns in Germany was attempted by either economic or legal criteria that they largely abandoned the attempt in favour of merely stating that many different criteria could be used. What was more important, in their view, was how towns related 'one to another as part of a general urban landscape'.[8]

In the period with which we are dealing, towns in northern Europe faced serious problems. The explosive growth of urban settlements in the eleventh and twelfth centuries was over. New towns were rare and mostly founded in special circumstances; for example, mining towns in Saxony, which date from the late fifteenth century, were founded to exploit newly discovered silver ore deposits. The advent of the Black Death and its later recurrences had disastrous effects on many urban communities. We have already said something about death rates in

Chapter 1 but should emphasise here that these were probably higher in towns than in the countryside because of the over-crowded housing and the lack of even the most basic aspects of public hygiene. The sources from which population figures can be estimated are not easy to use, the data usually being collected for quite other purposes, but, for example, it has been calculated that the population of Narbonne had fallen by over 50% in 1366 and continued to decline to less than 25% of its peak level by 1378. Toulouse shows a much gentler fall with around 80% of its peak level recorded in 1385 and about 70% in 1420. In England it is generally agreed that, for most towns, figures based on the 1523 tax show little difference from those based on the 1377 poll tax. This is, of course, after the mortality of the first visitations of the plague and the effects of nearly 150 years of immigration from rural areas. Two notable exceptions are Norwich, which shows an estimated gain of about 2,000 persons (8,000 to 10,000), and York, which reveals a fall of 6,500 people (14,500 to 8,000). There is also the suggestion that while it is indisputable that many towns had declined considerably in size, the proportion of urban dwellers in the shrunken total European population in the late fourteenth and fifteenth centuries had actually risen. A consequence of this, it has been suggested, is that towns played a greater not a lesser role in national life, in particular the most powerful cities in many areas often controlled, whether formally or informally, quite large territories outside their walls.[9]

In certain areas, particularly northern and western France and the Netherlands, towns also had to face the problems caused by intermittent but destructive warfare. The need to build fortifications and walls to keep attackers at bay was a heavy expense in many communities, particularly during the Hundred Years War. At times, suburbs (areas outside the walls which could provide a base for a besieging army) were deliberately cleared. The *faubourgs* or suburbs of Paris were seen as very vulnerable to attack and had little more, as in the case of St Germain, than wooden barriers to protect them. The walls of the city themselves had fallen into disrepair by 1441. There was even a report that in the winter of 1440 fourteen people were killed by wolves within the walled centre of Paris. Anne Curry has also given a graphic account of the reaction of the people of Mantes (at that time in English hands) to the realisation in August 1449 that the forces of Charles VII were about to lay siege to the town. The most prominent *bourgeois* gathered in the town hall and decided that since there was little prospect of the English forces doing much to defend the town they should submit to Charles at once rather than face bombardment with cannon.[10] In England, one of the reasons for the success of early French raids on the south coast was the fact that most of the towns, notably Southampton, had no walls at all on the waterfront. Efforts to remedy this in Southampton were made after 1338 but the circle of fortifications was still not complete in 1386. One reason for this was undoubtedly the expense, which did fall largely on the unfortunate townspeople. We have, in fact, much better knowledge of Southampton in the fifteenth century than of many comparable towns because of the survival of the *Terrier* of 1454. This document recorded every property within the walls and its ownership to remove doubts about the size of the occupiers' liability to pay for the repair of one or more *loupe*, or sections of the town wall.[11]

We should not, however, paint too gloomy a picture of town life at this time. Many had acquired a privileged form of government from the local ruler, though this varied considerably in detail from place to place. The overall effect, however, was to allow townspeople, particularly the most prosperous, a degree of independence not to be found in the countryside. The usual way in which these privileges would be codified was by means of a charter establishing the place as a borough, although, in many cases, the town as a settlement would have come into existence before the charter was granted. By the thirteenth century there was a degree of uniformity across western Europe in the rights included in town charters. It was expected that burgesses would be free (i.e. not subject to the constraints of villein status); that they would have rights over their property in the town; that they would be free of most feudal dues; that the town would have a degree of financial autonomy and that it would have the right to a degree of self-government. The usual form taken by urban government (though the names for, and powers of, the various component parts might vary from region to region) was that of a council headed by a mayor. The council or corporation would usually have two levels of membership: in England, aldermen being the higher rank and councillors the lower.

Some have suggested that towns sat uneasily within feudal society because of these rights. Where did townsmen or merchants fit into the contemporary stereotype of a threefold division of society into priests, warriors or nobles, and labourers or peasants? Surely the aspirations of the *bourgeois* were anti-feudal in character and hostile to the power of kings or princes? Hilton does not accept that view but sees the granting of chartered status to towns as a move sometimes initiated by lords or rulers because it was to their benefit and made for ease in the collection of taxes or other dues. He also points out that within a town or city the same kind of social pyramid existed as in the non-urban world. 'The hierarchical structures of town and country even though not identical were part of a single system.'[12] Nuremberg, for example, had no fewer than five categories of citizen ranging from the patricians, via the members of craft guilds (classified by the degree of skill required in their trade), to the poor and the so-called 'marginals' (*Randgruppen*), which included prostitutes, beggars and vagrants. The most elaborate expression of this was probably the so-called Nuremberg 'dance statute' of 1521, which laid down precisely which categories of citizen could dance with each other at the balls held by the town council.[13]

By our period, power in many chartered towns was firmly in the hands of an oligarchy composed of members of the leading merchant families. Artisans or craftsmen, although they might be burgesses or citizens, were often excluded from positions of power. The whole question of trade will be discussed fully below but at this juncture we can point out the social prestige which attached to what we would call 'wholesale' trade. These merchants owed a major portion of their wealth not to a shop or stall in the market but to trade in commodities in bulk, whether on a local, regional or international scale. This was the case in York, in London and in many French towns. Christine de Pizan defined the *bourgeois* as 'those who are of ancient descent belonging to the families of the cities and have their own surname and ancient arms' (usually marks of noble status). These families distinguished themselves from mere citizens and did not pay taxes (like nobles in France outside towns), and often monopolised the town government, vacant places being filled by co-option. In Le Puy, where the oligarchs were also darkly suspected of fraud against the people, unrest in the city did eventually force a widening of the ruling group, at the end of the fifteenth century. Those, however, who benefited were not the citizens as a whole but the next rung down in the social hierarchy, the *maîtres* or mastercraftsmen of the trades or *métiers*. In York the procedure for the choice of mayor was fairly simple in the later fourteenth and early fifteenth centuries but clearly kept a great deal of power in the hands of an elite group. The mayor was elected by all the burgesses but the choice was restricted to two or three aldermen nominated by the outgoing mayor. After riots in 1464 a new procedure was introduced; according to this the nomination of the two aldermen to stand as mayor was made by the members of the craft guilds, but the election was confined to the outgoing mayor and council. For a brief period from 1473 to 1489 the craftsmen were allowed the choice of one candidate only for the mayoralty, but since it was still essential for him to be an alderman it was hardly an open election.

It has been suggested that to use the term 'oligarchy' for this kind of town government is anachronistic. The townspeople of this period did not see political life in their town in terms of conflict but according to an ideal of 'harmony and civic unity'. It was strongly believed that the rich had a duty to undertake civic responsibilities, as they would discharge them to the benefit of the community. Sentiments like this can be found, for example, expressed in mayoral oaths and in commissions for elections. Rigby has argued that:

> York may have been ruled by a mercantile plutocracy yet the commonalty could still justify its participation in political life on the grounds that, 'we be all one body incorporate, we think we be all in like privileged of the commonalty which has borne none office in the city.[14]

He also points out that the charters granted to towns in the later Middle Ages lay as much emphasis on the way a town is to be governed internally as on the relations between the town and the Crown. This not only served to make town government much more uniform throughout England but it also tended to increase the power of elites, favouring co-option over election. It also made it appear that power was delegated from the centre rather than based in the community, another aspect of the growing power of national monarchies. Some English towns in the late fourteenth and fifteenth centuries were given the same power as counties, for example, Bristol, York, Newcastle, Norwich and Lincoln. This again emphasised royal power, and town corporations as agents of central government. In Scotland most towns were royal foundations, often with a single parish with uniform law and customs. The ability to reach more specific conclusions is hampered by lack of records: the only significant medieval borough archive is that for Aberdeen, which begins in 1398; otherwise there are only fragmentary records of the merchant guilds of Perth and Dunfermline. The records for Edinburgh do not begin until 1580. Using Scots royal records, however, Michael Lynch has felt able to conclude that during our period a 'new urban aristocracy', composed largely of merchants, took control in the larger towns (Edinburgh and Aberdeen),[15] mirroring developments in England.

The situation in France, particularly in the fifteenth century, shows quite marked differences from those in the British Isles. In particular the group of towns called *bonnes villes* had obtained charters from the king which granted them certain privileges. Citizens of these towns (some 226 in 1538) did not pay the *taille*, though they were often required to contribute to subsidies (royal taxes). Though the commune (council) would have powers to administer the town, it might have to share these with the king (as in Paris) or with a bishop or local lord. The possible complexities of this situation are demonstrated in Beauvais and Tours, where power was divided among 'the bishop, the cathedral chapter, several monasteries and the commune'.[16] In Paris the division between the Hôtel de Ville, the base for the elected provost of merchants, and the Châtelet, where the royal officials were housed, was clearer. The Hôtel looked after the walls and bridges and was consulted on taxes; the Châtelet had the basic task of keeping order in the city by, among other things, making sure that the food supply was adequate.

It seems to be the case that the merchants, who had largely held the reins of power in French communes in the fourteenth century and earlier, gradually yielded their influence to royal *officiers*, lawyers and churchmen in the fifteenth century. Some might, of course, be members of the same families who had held municipal office previously but the important point is that, at this later period, a mercantile career no longer also generally carried the possibility of authority within the town government. The example can be given of Tours, where the proportion of lawyers on the council increased from 26 per cent in the fourteenth century to 47 per cent in the mid-fifteenth century. In Poitiers two-thirds of the mayors after 1414 were royal officials: in most cases this would have meant that the mayor was simultaneously a member of the royal financial or legal administration in the town. Perhaps even more notably in Lyon, which was a centre of international trade, nearly a third of the 184 consuls were lawyers between 1430 and 1450.[17] This had quite considerable effects on the independence of towns and the power of the Crown within them. Both these groups, lawyers and officials, were members of the *noblesse de robe* (that is, enjoying the status of nobility by reason of their office rather than by birth) and were unlikely to reject royal commands outright or even offer much opposition to them. They were therefore quite prepared to accept the encroachment of the state in the shape of the desire of Louis XI for greater control over municipalities. They were also very sensible of the residual power that the king had and how any sign of rebellion could lead to very severe sanctions against the town. As Louis announced in 1464:

> Because of our sovereignty and royal majesty the general government and administration of our kingdom belongs and pertains to us alone in matter of offices or jurisdictions or otherwise: and also of all of our *bonnes villes*, *lois* and *échevinages* [corporate towns, laws, administrative areas], we may renew, create and ordain at our simple pleasure and will: and all anyone can do about it is simply take notice of the fact.[18]

Not all rulers in northern Europe in our period, however, felt able to ignore so completely the pretensions of urban communities to independence of action. Particularly in the territories of the Empire, some towns were able to act independently and even confront princes with some success. The towns which had been part of the old Imperial domain could claim the status of *Reichsstädte* (imperial cities). They had more or less complete control over their internal affairs and often also had power over quite large areas outside the city walls as well. There was, of course, a considerable difference between the power and status of cities like Ulm or Nuremberg in the south, with populations of around 20,000, and some of the more obscure places like Warburg or Lemgo in northern Germany. A league of ten imperial cities in Alsace, known somewhat pretentiously as the Decapolis, had as members towns varying in size from 5,000 to around 1,000 inhabitants. A town's degree of control over surrounding territory and its extent could be an important factor in its political importance since this could be a source not only of tax revenue but also of manpower for the urban militia. Another factor was the practice common in many imperial towns, both in the Netherlands and in the German lands, of having a class of citizen known as out-burghers. These people were resident in the countryside outside the city walls but had many of the privileges of those inside the city. Their existence greatly helped a city's dominance of its immediate hinterland.

The so-called free cities (*Freie Stadte*) had in many ways similar ruling bodies and similar powers but had largely managed to extricate themselves from the control not of the Emperor but of an ecclesiastical ruler, a bishop or archbishop. It was not uncommon in the Empire to find churchmen ruling as princes with all the powers of their secular counterparts. At the end of our period representatives from both imperial and free cities formed part of the Imperial Diet or *Reichstag* but, in the opinion of Scott, their power as a group was greatly diminished by their reluctance to co-operate with each other.[19] The economic rivalry between cities was too intense to be abandoned in favour of concerted action. At the end of the fifteenth century the one group of cities which not only asserted its independence but also co-operated successfully with the more rural populations of the forest cantons was the city states of northern Switzerland. In the case of Bern in particular there is a valid comparison to be made with the city republics of Italy. Bern was fully self-governing, a prosperous trading centre, making alliances and entering group compacts as it alone saw fit.

The most thoroughly urbanised area in north-western Europe, however, was Flanders. Here the three major towns, Bruges, Ghent (which will form one of our case studies) and Ypres, had sufficient economic and cultural dominance to challenge the authority of the Count and to attempt to follow their own policies in external affairs. The cities, especially Bruges and Ypres, had been instrumental in ensuring the defeat of the chivalry of France at the Battle of Courtrai, also known as the Battle of the Golden Spurs, in 1302. This victory did not prevent France attempting to foist the treaty of Athis-sur-Orge on Flanders in 1305, which required the Flemish cities to demolish their fortifications and pay an enormous indemnity to the French king. It is characteristic of the power of the cities, especially Bruges and Ghent, that these terms were not accepted and many of the succeeding years were occupied in tangled negotiations during which the representatives of the cities played the count of Flanders (Robert of Béthune, 1305–22; Louis of Nevers, 1322–46) off against the French king, always with the intention of securing their own advantage. At stake was not only the ability of the towns to run their own affairs but also the health of their economies, closely bound up with trade in raw wool with England. In the first half of the fourteenth century, Flanders and its major cities can be represented as suffering considerably from natural disasters (like the famines of 1315–17), the effects of rebellions (like that of 1328, and of Jan van Artevelde in Ghent in 1338–46), and the efforts of the king of France, Philip VI, and Count Louis of Nevers to control the region. The cities survived them all. In 1343 they made their domination of Flanders clear by dividing the county into so-called quarters. Ghent controlled all the land east of the River Leie; Bruges, and its hinterland the Franc, constituted two separate quarters; and Ypres, its own *castellany* and the Westland made up the last. Even when Flanders was absorbed into the Burgundian lands in 1384 they were still a restless and fractious part of the duke's dominions. Although they never gained full independence it would be the end of the fifteenth century before a duke of Burgundy could take their loyalty for granted.

In 1405, when John the Fearless made his *Joyous Entry* (a ceremony usually marking the beginning of a ruler's reign) to Ghent, he was met by the representatives of the Four Members of Flanders (Ghent, Bruges, Ypres and the Franc, or county, of Bruges) with a list of their demands, all intended to further their interests rather than those of the duke. John hoped to build up support for himself among the leaders of the Four Members by extending favours to them. This had only limited success and he found himself faced with further demands in 1414 and 1417 when his attention was focused on the situation in France. The points at issue varied little; the towns wished to retain control over their own affairs and to ensure that obstacles were not placed in the way of trade with England.

John's son Philip finally managed to enforce ducal control over Bruges in 1438 and Ghent in 1453. When Bruges rebelled against the duke in 1437, Philip very nearly lost his life in a skirmish at one of the city gates and was forced to flee in ignominy. When he returned with larger forces in 1438 the city was compelled to come to terms, which included not only the payment of a heavy fine but the demolition of the gate and the building of a chapel as a symbol of their submission, on its site. Philip did not move against Ghent until 1451 when he seems to have almost provoked the city to rebel by a deliberate campaign against its privileges. The city's forces were finally defeated in 1453 at Gavere. Again an enormous fine was imposed; as much as the tax raised in the whole of Flanders from 1440 to 1443.[20] The duke also ensured that the humiliation of the city was complete by forcing all the leading citizens and guildsmen to come before him barefoot, bareheaded and in the robes of penitents to present to him the banners of the guilds, around which the city militia had mustered before setting out to do battle. As Blockmans and Prevenier point out, the subjection of Bruges and Ghent was intended as an example. If these cities submitted the others would remain docile. If we ask how these cities grew so powerful, the answer was perhaps provided by the Four Members themselves in 1473: 'Flanders is a sterile country, infertile in itself, completely founded on the fact and course of merchandise, densely populated with foreigners, merchants and others.'[21] The wealth of these cities, created by trade, was the source of their power and influence.

In the English realm as a whole, no city could approach the political importance and capacity for independent action of the Flemish cities. The influence of the king and royal policy largely determined a town's fate. In Wales, towns had largely been originally established by the invading Norman colonisers and legislation in the time of Edward I forbade native Welshmen from becoming burgesses. During Glyn Dwr's rebellion, towns suffered particular damage becauseof their association with the hated English. Griffiths estimates that forty out of a total of one hundred boroughs in Wales (some of them very small) were sacked by the rebels. Even Conwy, which was protected by one of the most impressive of the Edwardian castles, later claimed that damage valued at £16,000 had been inflicted. Some little towns, like Holt near Wrexham, never really recovered; as late as 1473 it was said that houses still lay unrepaired because of the lack of townsmen and their poverty.[22] In Ireland, in our period, Swanson sees colonisation taking a rather different course. She argues that towns became increasingly 'Gaelicised' with Irish becoming the most common language and Irish law and customs also adopted. This did not apply so obviously in Dublin and the Pale (the area around Dublin where English rule was strongest), but is clearly related to the looseness of English control over Ireland for much of the period *c.*1340 to *c.*1470.[23]

In England itself, London loomed over all other towns in population, size and wealth, and we will consider its importance separately in one of our case studies. Other towns were clearly significant economically but had little ability to challenge royal authority or to assert their individuality in the political sphere. Some had the right to send burgess members to Parliament but there was, as a rule, no specific 'urban' interest in that body. On one occasion in 1372, the Parliament Rolls record the burgesses meeting on their own after the shire members had gone home, to extend the grant of an extra subsidy on the duties on imported wine and exported general goods. However, this was represented by the 'prelates and great men' to be in their own interests since it was intended 'for the safe and sure conduct of the ships and merchandise coming to this land by sea and passing from it'.[24] Later, in 1472, there is some evidence of the local gentry exerting their influence to obtain borough seats in Parliament but this, of course, was not primarily for the benefit of the borough concerned. Friends of Sir John Paston hoped to secure his election for Malden in this way, assuring the bailiff of the town that 'such a man of worship and wit' and 'such a one as in favour with the king and of the lords of his council' was what was needed as MP for the town; a description which Paston apparently fitted admirably.[25] This is, however, evidence of the links based on patronage and personal standing which were so important at this time, rather than of urban independence.

York, the base of royal government in the north of England, the seat of the archbishop and a wealthy and ancient town, did gain a degree of political importance in the reign of Richard III. The civic records reveal the support that Richard of Gloucester received from the town both before he seized the throne and when he toured his realm in August 1483 after his coronation. Richard was undoubtedly appreciative of this, his secretary writing of the 'entire affection that his grace bears towards you [the mayor] and your worshipful city for your many kind and loving deservings shown to his grace heretofore'. In 1485, however, following the Battle of Bosworth, after some initial horror at the news of Richard's defeat, the mayor and corporation made as much haste as possible to repair relations with the new king, Henry VII, offering his representatives 'two gallons of wine at the [council] chamber's cost'.[26]

Much more controversial has been the question of the economic fortunes of English towns in our period. Many towns complained bitterly, at the time, of their inability to pay the dues owed to the Crown because of their poverty and the decay of trade. This might, of course, have been special pleading but studies like Phythian-Evans's *Desolation of a City*, looking at Coventry, have strongly argued in favour of a prolonged and serious urban crisis in fifteenth-century England.[27] Britnell's work on Colchester lays emphasis on the way in which the town suffered both ups and downs in our period even if, by the beginning of the sixteenth century, it is clear it was 'a larger and in aggregate a wealthier town' than it had been before the advent of the Black Death.[28] Alan Dyer has also been concerned to point out how varied the fortunes of English towns seem to be. In some cases large towns suffered more than small ones, but on the other hand, London, the largest town of all, expanded throughout the period. Perhaps of most interest is his conclusion that there is 'little trace of that conspicuous urban decline which the pessimist finds in England', in continental Europe. Most opinion favours the idea that European towns were subject to fluctuations in their fortunes, sometimes because of changes in local conditions (the experience of warfare, for example), sometimes because of more widespread problems (like the shortage of labour resulting from the general fall in population).[29] This seems to be the most satisfactory general explanation of the economic health of towns in our period. In the political sphere, we can conclude that only in realms with a lack of centralised government or where that government was weak could towns profitably assert their independence.

Case studies

The towns chosen for the case studies strengthen these conclusions. Cologne was a member of the Hanseatic League and largely controlled trade up and down the Rhine. Its nominal prince, the archbishop, although not only a spiritual leader but one of the Imperial Electors, had little power over the town. We have already said something of Ghent's position, the weak counts of Flanders of the fourteenth century giving way to the more forceful dukes of Burgundy after 1384. London was the capital city of England but not the site of the court, which had settled just up the river at Westminster. Their economic fortunes varied in our period but none could be said to experience real decline. These studies will allow comparisons to be made and help to understand what made these cities successful even in the difficult fifteenth century.

Cologne

Cologne was the largest and probably the richest city in the German lands of the Empire for much of our period. Its commercial success was built on firm foundations, the town being well situated on the Rhine at the point where overland trade routes from the south and the east met the route up the Rhine from the North Sea. Although two hundred miles from the sea, its wharves were a major factor in its development, with cargo being loaded and off-loaded from river craft. It was also an important religious centre, being not only the seat of the Prince-Archbishop, with a large and splendid cathedral built in the thirteenth century, but also connected with the major pilgrimage shrine of the Three Kings and the dramatic story of St Ursula and the eleven thousand virgins.[30] The city was firmly under the control of the archbishop and his officials, the *Burggraf* (equivalent to a mayor) and the *Stadtvogt* (judge in the town court), until the thirteenth century when the richest patrician families of merchants took power in the town government. This was confined to a small group of families who were members of the *Richerzeche*, a term which translates as 'Rich Club' and neatly encapsulates their status and qualification for office. By the end of the century the archbishop had retired to live in Bonn and had only the most vestigial authority over affairs in the city. This was not the case in the lands surrounding Cologne, and here the archbishop kept control over the *Kölner Bucht* (the plain around the city). Cologne, unlike many other German cities, had no political power over its immediate hinterland although its economic dominance of this area was complete.

By the fourteenth century, Cologne's ruling oligarchy governed through the *Rat*, or small council of fifteen members, and eventually also a large council of eighty-two members. The stable and somewhat cosy world of the Rich Club, however, was challenged by the weavers guild, the *Wollamt*, who mounted something rather like a coup against them in 1371. Their aim was to abolish the dominance of the Rich Club and transfer power to the craftsmen and artisans of the trade guilds. This first attempt ended in violence the following year, but in 1396 a new system of government for Cologne was established and recorded in the *Verbundbrief* (literally, the letter of union), whose provisions lasted for as long as Cologne's independence. All citizens (this did not mean all inhabitants but only those who had purchased this status) were members of a *Gaffel*. This was originally a trading or craft group like a guild, but soon any real connection with a particular activity was lost. These *Gaffeln* controlled membership of and election to the council itself.

Economically Cologne was a regional centre of great importance throughout our period. It had had from the twelfth century a close connection with England, merchants buying raw wool there to feed the cloth industry in the town. Cologne merchants had their own base in the city of London, on the south side of Dowgate, from the time of Henry II. Later, *c.*1260, all the German merchants in London, mainly from Lübeck and Hamburg as well as Cologne, seem to have come together at this site, which developed into the Steelyard, the base of the Hanseatic League in England. Cologne gained great advantage from its membership of the League, as the terminus of a trade route beginning in Novgorod which fed the highly desirable and also very costly furs from Russia into the European luxury market. The town was less happy about League policy in the fifteenth century with regard to England, since this disrupted the wool trade (see the case study on the Company of the Staple, below), and it tended to pursue its own interests rather than those of its fellow members. By the fifteenth century also, Cologne had become a successful manufacturing centre; it produced a special form of mixed linen and wool textile known as *turtey*. This was a cheap cloth but the city was also well known for the skill of its silk workers, and those in associated trades like the making of gold thread and embroideries and ecclesiastical vestments. One

3 St Ursula arrives at the Cologne waterfront

This image from a shrine for St Ursula's relics painted by Hans Memling shows the arrival of the saint and her companions at the waterfront of Cologne. The cathedral and other buildings in the background are an accurate representation of the city at this time.

matter of some note is that women were heavily involved in these trades and could join the appropriate guilds in their own right irrespective of their marital status. Metal workers were also prominent in the city, making items like locks, tools, weapons and armour.

Thus, on the banks of the Rhine, Cologne was a thriving city with its fate largely in its own hands or at least in the hands of the most prominent members of the *Gaffeln*. It undoubtedly had pride in itself and its achievements. Its university, founded in 1388, was unusual as being the result not of a ruling prince's initiative but that of the citizens, helped by the Dominicans who had run a school there since the middle of the thirteenth century. To gain some impression of the appearance of the city at this period, we can look closely at the background images in Memling's decorations of the reliquary of St Ursula, now in Bruges (see Illustration 3). The cathedral rises over the town, its walls and towers and its impressive gateway, while the saint and her companions disembark at a busy riverside. A series of paintings of the Rinke family who became burgers of Cologne in 1432 and traded with Danzig and England also exists to help us picture the townspeople. They show us determined, unostentatious figures soberly dressed and in the case of one, Herman Rinke, clutching what looks very like an important contract.[31]

Ghent

In some ways the origins of Ghent mirror those of Cologne. It was probably the most populous city in Flanders, though Bruges may have outshone it in wealth. It was well placed to profit by trade, being at the confluence of the rivers Leie and Scheldt. It had to assert its independence, however, not against a churchman in the Empire, where central government was weak, but against a count who was a vassal of the king of France, like Louis de Nevers, or who combined this status with that of duke of Burgundy. The counts were in general French speaking and often French in sympathy – something which caused difficulties in Flanders, increasingly aware of its own culture and language. Flanders, in general, and particularly trading towns like Ghent, tended to be pro-English for commercial reasons and thus very wary of their counts' desires to support France in its hostility to England. We have already seen how this led to rebellions and open warfare between the Flemings and their overlords. What we will discuss here is the way in which Ghent was governed internally, its economy and the kind of life led by its burghers.

Till the end of the twelfth century, town government had been firmly under the control of the count and his bailiff. Count Philip of Alsace had built the imposing castle of Gravensteen in the late twelfth century, within the city walls to overawe the burghers. By the late thirteenth century a group of patrician, landholding, elite town families had emerged and taken control, known as *viri hereditarii*; they were called this because of the terms on which they held land, not because they were hereditary town officials. From 1228 these families completely controlled the XXXIX: a system of three councils of 13 members each, which co-opted new members when necessary but which otherwise formed a closed oligarchy. This did not mean they were without public spirit. The town had been involved in early projects for draining land in the vicinity by building dikes, and in 1251 constructed, at the public expense, a canal from the Leie to Damme to secure Ghent a clear passage by water to the coast. Other benefactions included a leper hospital, founded in 1146, and a system of 'Holy Ghost Tables', run by the city parishes, which provided food for the destitute. The records of the parish of St Nicholas in the centre of Ghent show that shoes and pork as well as grain were distributed to those without sustenance.

The principal features of the public policy of Ghent in the fourteenth century seem to be restlessness and aggression, often but not always aimed at the count who was, as we have said, by the end of the century also the duke of Burgundy. (see Section (iii) below). During the ascendancy of Jacob van Artevelde, on 2 May 1345, internal tensions between the weavers and the fullers (usually employed by the wealthier and more skilled weavers) led to a bloody battle in the Friday marketplace. The chronicler gives the cause as, 'the fullers wanted to have four grooten more than the weavers wanted to give them',[32] but the city was also deeply divided between those in favour and those hostile to Artevelde. Artevelde himself some two months later had a deep disagreement with the dean of the weavers' guild over the direction affairs were taking. The chronicler goes on to describe how van Artevelde went home to dinner and was then attacked and killed by a mob incited by the weavers. The volatility of Ghent and the relative ease with which its people could be roused to action is also shown by the way in which the destructive conflict of 1379–85 broke out. The ostensible cause here was the discovery that Bruges was digging a canal to link the Leie with the network of waterways around Bruges which led to the Zwin. It was clearly feared in Ghent that this would allow Bruges to 'steal' the Gentenaars' trade. A gang from Ghent, known as the White Hoods, attacked the workers and the disturbance developed into a rising against the count, Louis of Male, who had authorised the work. We cannot even say that the submission of the city to Philip the Good in 1453 put an end to its tendency to take up arms since at the very end of the century it went to war once more against the new Habsburg duke, Maximilian.

The system of government was, however, widened from that of the XXXIX in 1360. The constitution introduced at this date divided citizens into three 'Members': landowners, weavers, and members of the small guilds. The councillors now came from these groups and involved a greater range of people than before. The prominence of the weavers was at first a reflection of the importance of the cloth trade and cloth manufacture to Ghent. It was undoubtedly the foundation of its prosperity. During the fifteenth century this trade declined because of competition from English cloth and the problems over the supply of raw wool. Ghent now became much more reliant on its control of the trade in grain. This was based on its staple rights, which required all cargoes of grain using its waterways to pay a toll and grant the city a proportion of the cargo. With the income from this and diversification into other crafts such as leather working, Ghent recovered from the decline in cloth working. Wealthy burghers could continue to adorn the city by commissioning art works, for example the great altarpiece donated to St Bavo's cathedral by Joos Vijd and his wife Elisabeth Borhuut. This picture, the Adoration of the Lamb, as well as being a magnificent example of the work of

Jan and Hugo van Eyk, also allows us a clear impression of the clothing, jewellery and love of display of the Gentenaars in the picture of the donors included on the exterior 'doors' of the altarpiece.

Another example is the account of the arrangements made in 1458 for the Joyous Entry of Philip the Good to this fractious city, which now finally wished to make a good impression on its ruler. The town council arranged a competition for the best display, with silver dishes as prizes. In response there was a re-creation of the Van Eyk altarpiece with living actors, and dramas in French and Dutch telling suitable stories, like that of the Prodigal Son or the meeting of David (symbolising the duke) with Abigail (symbolising the city). There were rich tapestries on display, paintings of Alexander, Caesar and Pompey, and in fact the duke was (according to a contemporary) 'most outstandingly joyously and richly' applauded.[33] In the face of this it is as well to remember Nicholas's final verdict on Ghent and its rival Bruges. He characterises them first of all as 'twin pillars of egotistical privilege that had constituted the singularity of medieval Flanders', and then sums up:

> Unfortunately the greatness of Ghent and Bruges was achieved only through monopoly privileges that caused problems for the smaller communities and ultimately for the entire Flemish state and economy.[34]

In his view the dominance of these two cities did not work to the advantage of Flanders as a whole but rather left it vulnerable to the ambitions of the dukes of Burgundy and their need for money to achieve them. It also curtailed the development of a more broadly based economy by the exercise of their quasi-monopolistic trading powers.

London

London, as the capital city of a kingdom with, at this date, a relatively fully developed system of government, was obviously in a different position from those of our other examples. Its aim perhaps as a city was not to cherish dreams of independence but to defend as far as possible its right to internal self-government from royal interference. At the very end of our period, a visiting Venetian reported to his employer on London's importance in the realm. He mentioned the convenience of the site for trade. Although sixty miles from the sea, because of the tidal River Thames, 'vessels of 100 tons burden can come up to the city and ships of any size to within five miles of it'. He is also amazed by the amount of gold and silver ware displayed in London goldsmiths' shops. 'In all the shops in Milan, Rome and Venice and Florence put together I do not think there would be found so many vessels of the magnificence that are to be seen in London.' He then gives a clear and largely accurate account of the way the city was ruled at that time. The city was divided into wards for elections but real power was in the hands of twenty-four aldermen. From this group, one was elected every year to be mayor and he 'is in no less estimation with the Londoners, than the person of our most serene lord' (the Doge, the head of the Venetian republic). He was not, it seems, aware of the fact that by this period only those who were freemen of the city, that is were full members of one of the livery companies or guilds, were able to participate in ward elections.[35]

Henry III had confirmed London's early charters despite the fact that London had supported the rebel barons against his father King John at the time of the drawing up of Magna Carta. Its capacity to rule itself was, however, still very much dependent on the will of the king despite the granting of charters. Edward I fined the city heavily for its support for Simon de Montfort, the leader of a rebellion against him, and suspended all charter rights between 1285 and 1298, ruling the city via royally appointed wardens. Edward II granted a new charter in 1319 and it was this which was the basis of London government for the remainder of our period. This confined many benefits to those who were freemen or burgesses of London. Only they could open shops in the city and the status of freeman could only be gained by membership of a guild. Behind these provisions lay the same tensions and hostilities between the craftsmen of the guilds, or *misteries*, and the elite families of the merchant aldermen, which we have seen in other cities. Elections to the Common Council, the lowest rung of the city government, were confined to guildsmen but were organised on the basis of wards, divisions of the city linked to the aldermen.

London was, of course, in a peculiar position as far as its relationship with the Crown went. It was not the site of the king's usual residence nor of the royal courts, including Parliament, nor of administrative offices like the Exchequer. These were all to be found just up river at Westminster, outside the bounds of the City itself. The Tower of London, the fortress in the eastern corner of the city wall on the riverfront, was the most important expression of royal power within London itself (see Map 2). It was used as a royal residence on occasions but was also the storehouse of the Royal Ordnance and, at times, a prison. The city was, however, as we have said, by far the largest and wealthiest in England. The Italian quoted above in fact thought there were only two in the country worth mentioning apart from London: Bristol and York. Its share of England's overseas trade grew during our period to the detriment of places like Boston in Lincolnshire. Within its walls was the greatest concentration of financial expertise in the nation. The king was increasingly reliant on the ability of London merchants to lend money to the Crown, especially in time of war. At the same time, London merchants gained considerably from supplying the court with both luxuries and necessities, and needed royal support when conflicts arose with merchants from other states.

London was often at the centre of events even if the leading citizens had little control over them. Thus we can take the example of the fierce quarrel which broke out between London and Richard II in 1392. Richard was infuriated with the City because his requests for loans were not being met. Leading merchants in London, the usual source of money for the Crown, were deaf to his pleas because they believed that foreign merchants in the wool trade were being given unwarranted privileges. The king took the extreme step of suspending the charters to put pressure on the city, and the conflict was only resolved some two years later largely by the intervention of Richard Whittington, much of whose considerable fortune had come from supplying the needs of the Royal Wardrobe.

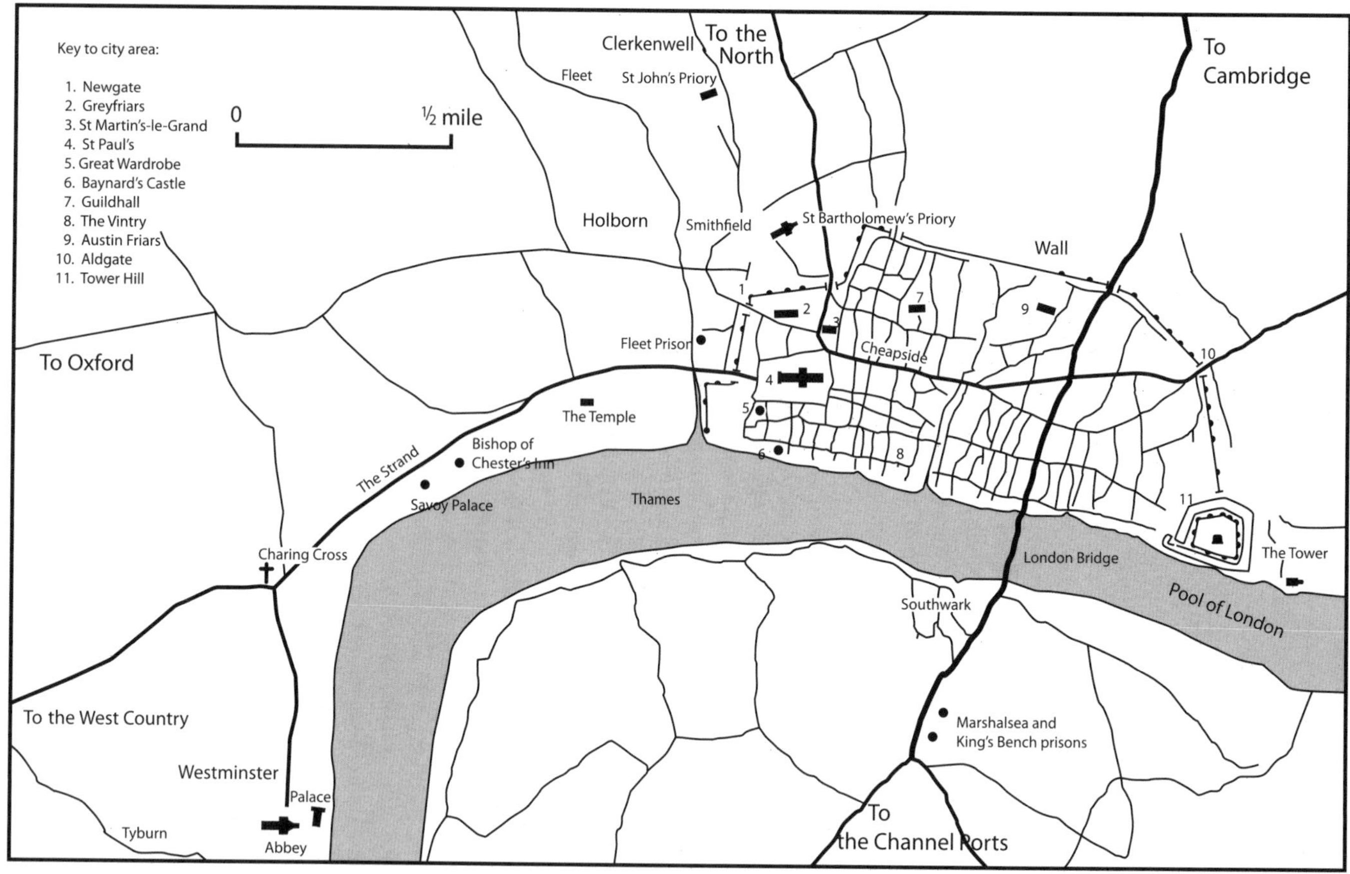

Map 2 London in the late fourteenth century

The city's role in more general public affairs took various forms. After Agincourt, Henry V was welcomed back to England by an enormous display of triumphant patriotic pageantry. At the gate on the south end of London bridge,

> the tower was adorned with spears bearing the royal arms projecting from the battlements and trumpets and horns sounded in manifold melody: spread across the front of the tower was this elegant and convenient inscription, 'The City of the King of Justice'.

At the cross in Cheapside a wooden castle had been built with many adornments and when the king's procession came into sight, 'a chorus of beautiful girls dressed in virgin white' came out playing on tambourines and singing, 'Welcome Henry V, King of England and France.' Boys meanwhile, on the turrets, dressed like angels, threw 'gold coins and laurel leaves' and 'as a sign of victory all sang together . . . "we praise thee O God we acknowledge thee to be the Lord" '. It's not surprising that we are told that the streets were thronged and all the upper windows filled with spectators to watch the king pass by, as he did, 'in a purple robe not with a haughty look and a pompous train . . . but with a serious countenance and a reverend pace'.[36]

The atmosphere would have been quite different when, over fifty years later during the crisis of 1471, when Edward IV was on the verge of recovering the throne, Henry VI was paraded through the streets of London by the Lancastrians. The Great Chronicle of London describes how he was led by the hand of the archbishop of York, with a 'small company of gentlemen going on foot before, one on horseback carrying a pole or long shaft with two fox tails fastened on the end'. The king was wearing 'a long gown of blue velvet as though he had no more to change with'. It is not surprising that the chronicler feels that the whole event was 'more like a play than the showing of a prince to win men's hearts'. The event demonstrates, however, the accepted need to get the support of Londoners, and that it could not be taken for granted.[37]

The self-confidence of the city is shown not only by the fact that the keeping of its own record of events, as in the chronicle above, was no novelty by this time but also by the amount of new buildings that were erected within the walls in our period. The Guildhall with an adjacent chapel and library was built between 1411 and 1455. The problem of a supply of good water was alleviated by the renewal, at the cost of over £5,000, of the conduit from Tyburn. The livery companies, especially the most powerful merchant guilds, erected company halls like that of the Grocers. This was built on the site of a house belonging to the Fitzwalter family near Old Jewry, up a narrow lane from the Poultry, bought in 1426. The building of the hall, parlour and other facilities took some years but it was near enough to completion for an inaugural feast to be held there on 1 July 1431. This must have been quite an occasion since apparently 210 gallons of wine and nine barrels of ale were drunk by the Grocers and their guests. The city records also illuminate less savoury aspects of London life in the later fifteenth century. Attempts were made to close all the latrines over the open Walbrook ditch in the centre of the city; entrails of slaughtered animals were not to be thrown into the

Thames, since victuallers and others used the water. A certain William Campion, who had been unlawfully tapping the public water supply for his own use, suffered the bizarre punishment of being put on a horse with a vessel like a conduit on his head with water running out of it and thus promenaded through the city.[38]

Overall, London as a capital city was near to the heart of events but cannot be seen as having more than a limited amount of power on its own account. This did not prevent it from being both a lively and a self-confident community with a keen sense of its own worth. To the Crown it was an indispensable source of the loan finance essential to sovereigns in emerging nation states; to its people it was a city to be honoured. When the mayor dealt firmly with a suspected slight in 1464, the chronicler wrote approvingly, 'And so the worship of the city was kept and not lost for him: and I trust that it never shall be by the grace of God.'[39]

All three of these towns were important politically in the life of their respective realm. They each seem to have had the ability to adapt successfully to changing economic circumstances, perhaps because of their size and their dominance in their region. All possessed a rich and varied culture and could count on the loyalty, even the affection of their citizens. What was much less uniform was the true extent of their freedom of action politically. This depended much more on the power of the central authority in the realm than on their own efforts.

(ii) TRADERS

From what we have already said about towns and their place in late medieval society in our study area, it is clear that trade was an essential element in their growth and development. It is also clear that trade linked to the making of woollen textiles was the most important and widespread. If we think of the realms with which we are principally concerned, all had a deep interest in this aspect of commerce. England had been a major source of raw wool to feed the spinning wheels and looms of Flanders since the twelfth century. The fortunes of the Four Members of Flanders, especially the cities of Bruges, Ghent and Ypres, were dependent to a large extent on the health of this trade until at least the last quarter of the fifteenth century. Merchants from further south, especially those from Italy and its great trading cities of Florence, Genoa and Venice, primarily came north in search of wool and cloth. At the same time, their fleets of galleys and *carracks*, bringing luxuries to northern Europe, were also laden among other things with the fine products of Italian weavers. Cologne participated in the same trade along with the other cities of the Hanseatic League. Vessels coming into Bristol from Irish ports, principally those in the south-east of the island but also including Galway, carried cargoes which included, among the more valuable items, checked Irish cloth and Irish mantles. In this section we will examine this and other trades, trying to assess their importance for the states concerned. We will also look at the way in which commerce was organised. How important was the supply of bullion, or alternatively, did exchanges commonly take place on a credit basis? To what extent was trade regulated by rulers and affected by their political actions? Finally we will look at some further case studies; this time concerned with two quite different groups of merchants, the Hanseatic League of towns and cities mostly based around the Baltic, and the Company of the Staple, the organisation of English wool merchants.

Trade routes and commodities

The lure of international and long-distance trade has led to this topic dominating much of the discussion of trade in our period. It is easy to romanticise the exploits of Venetian or Genoese merchants in the eastern Mediterranean, or to concentrate on some major figures like the French financier Jacques Coeur, the directors of the Fugger Bank in Augsburg, or some of the major merchants in the city of London. Most trade, of course, was conducted on a much more local basis between villages and small market towns. We will discuss this here first before moving on to the longer routes and more exotic commodities usual in trade between states.

In both England and Germany historians such as Keith Lilley, Heather Swanson and Tom Scott have made use of 'central place theory', developed by urban geographers to make sense of the way in which trading links developed. This theory is based on the idea that there are regional centres, inevitably large towns, which are involved in long-distance trade. They will have a favourable location, on a river crossing or with a good harbour, for example, and will not only trade in high-value goods over long distances but will serve as distribution centres, sending out goods to smaller towns or intermediate markets. These towns in their turn will serve a somewhat similar function for small village markets. Swanson has pointed out that the theory, originally developed in the context of the well-established borders of modern nation states, does not always take into account the changing national frontiers in our period. Thus, in the British Isles we find that the 'regional centre' for Irish trade was in fact Bristol, while the greater part of the hinterland of both Carlisle and Berwick (even after 1333 and its capture by Edward III) was in Scotland.[40] Bristol's role as a distribution centre for Irish towns in fact emerges very clearly from the Customs accounts of the later fifteenth century, which record a wide range of manufactured goods of all kinds being exported to ports like Wexford and Cork.

In relation to German towns, discussion has centred on the idea of market zones. There is an immediate market zone very near to a town in which people come to the market frequently for everyday needs. Beyond this is the intermediate zone, in which the major centre is the dominant economic influence, selling its manufactures within this area and bringing artisans and traders into the centre for special purposes. The widest zone of all will be that of international or long-distance trade, which may stretch for more than a hundred kilometres. These zones will, of course, be modified by the existence of other towns nearby, or by natural features such as navigable rivers or mountainous areas, which will control the ease of access to the market. In Germany also, towns might face stiff competition for trade from village craftsmen, leading to attempts by town authorities to suppress local markets. Augsburg, for example, attempted to bring all the textile trade in eastern Swabia under its control. Scott also points out that these 'zones' could differ markedly for different commodities. In the case of Cologne, furs were supplied to the market from a much wider area than copper or iron, while hops for the brewers came from a relatively small area to the east of the city.[41]

The local trade of Southampton, a good example of a medium-sized port, can be examined in detail, in the fifteenth century, because of the surviving local records. Southampton had a system of local tolls and Customs on traffic arriving in the port which was quite separate from that of the king. Moreover, although all Southampton burgesses and those from quite a large number of other towns in the vicinity, for example Winchester and Marlborough, were exempt from these Customs, the passage of goods consigned to them was still recorded in the Port Books. There was also a toll which was payable on all carts, with the same exceptions, going through the Bargate; this was the main route out of town and thus the Brokage Books, the records of this toll, record most inland trade leaving the town. Books survive for only a limited number of years but this is still sufficient to understand the pattern of Southampton's trade.

The Port Books, which deal with seaborne trade, tend to deal separately with goods belonging to 'aliens', mostly Italians from Genoa or Venice, and those belonging to 'denizens' (Englishmen). If we concern ourselves only with the latter in detail here, we find ships and their cargoes mentioned from all the small creeks and harbours along Southampton Water from Christchurch to Pagham. There are also vessels from places like Lyme, Dartmouth, Chichester and Winchelsea. Their cargoes vary: on 23 December 1439, a vessel from Winchelsea left the port with wine. On 4 January, another from Lowestoft came in with a mixture of red and white herring. This ship later left to return to its home port with fruit from Spain.

Through the Bargate carts left for a wide range of local places and also those further afield. In the Brokage Book for 1443–4 the most usual local destinations were Winchester (370 loads), Romsey (213 loads), and Ringwood in the New Forest (30 loads); occasional carts went to places like Bishop's Waltham and Alresford. These local carts might carry goods like woad, a dyestuff needed for the cloth industry, or more specialised needs like the roofing tiles which were sent to Hyde Abbey in Winchester in December 1443. The more distant places served by overland traffic from Southampton included Salisbury, the most important (861 loads), London (535 loads), Oxford (54 loads), and Coventry (59 loads). In the majority of cases the carters were distributing raw material for the cloth trade, some imported by Italians, including soap for washing wool, dyes and fixatives like alum, and also wine, mainly from Guyenne. Luxury items like dates, pepper, aniseed and rice often went to London too. The commonest 'inward' load was wool and various foodstuffs like corn or salmon. From this we can see that Southampton was on the one hand linked into the international trade of major players like Venice, and on the other linked to most markets of any significance in southern England (see Map 3). We can also see that the commodities of greatest importance were either basic foodstuffs or necessary for the wool trade or for the making of cloth. Trade in manufactured items other than cloth was still limited.[42]

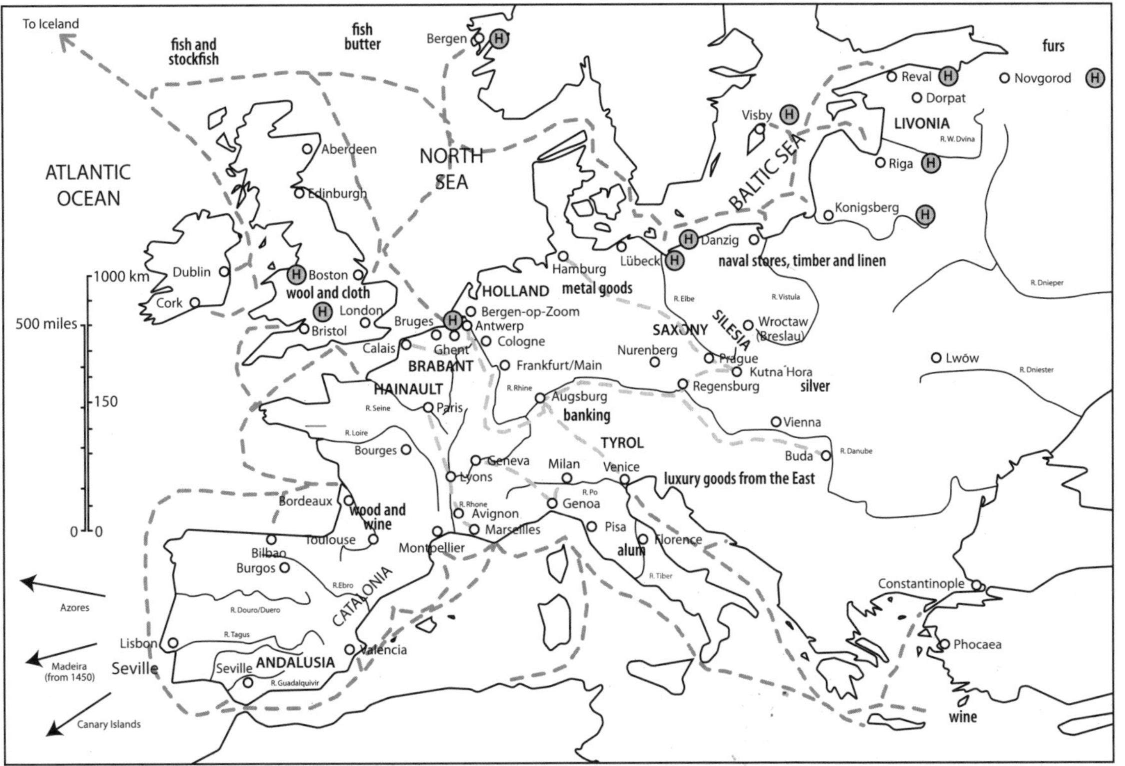

Map 3 Major trade routes in late medieval Europe

The Italians who off-loaded their galleys or *carracks* in Southampton were part of a trading network which stretched from the Black Sea to Bruges. From 1347 the Venetians made regular voyages from their city, through the Mediterranean and up the Atlantic coast of Iberia to the Channel and eventually their final destination, Bruges. The state galley fleet began calling at Southampton on a regular basis from 1384. The Genoese followed much the same route but by the reign of Richard II used, not the oared galleys with their large and expensive crews, but *carracks*, sailing vessels with much lower running costs. Florence did not become involved with state galley fleets on the model of the Venetian ones until 1422 after her capture of Pisa and its port, Porto Pisano. The first Florentine voyage to Bruges took place in 1425. By 1436 the galleys were sailing to Bruges on a regular basis, usually with an intermediate stop at Southampton. The final voyage of these state fleets on this route took place in 1478, brought to an end by a combination of economic difficulties in Florence itself and the curtailment of the privileges of foreign merchants in England by Edward IV.[43]

The prime motivation of all these merchants was to purchase raw wool. We have detailed knowledge of an early Florentine voyage, that of 1429–30, because the diary of Luca di Maso degli Albizzi, the captain of the galleys, has survived. From this we can estimate that the return cargo of his galleys included 1026 *pokes* of wool (a defined amount equal to half a sack); 63 large bales of cloth including 670 Guildford cloths and 630 others; 130 *pieces* of tin and 120 *pieces* of lead, 7 beds (probably feather beds or the woollen coverings and curtains for a bed), 5 pieces of *worsted* (a tightly woven cloth on which the nap had not been raised), and 5 dozen 'hairy caps'. The Royal Customs accounts also show very similar cargoes for galleys freighted in 1439 and 1444. Their outward cargoes from Florence, which were often sold in Bruges rather than England, consisted of general Mediterranean goods, madder, almonds, raisins, rice, wax, saffron and silk. Most of this was bought in Spanish ports on the galleys' way north. Often little was unloaded in Southampton except small quantities of fruit and spices. Alum only became an important item in the cargoes of these vessels on their outward voyage when Florence got control of the alum mines at Tolfa in the early 1460s.[44]

Bruges was in fact the most important trading centre in northern Europe until the last quarter of the fifteenth century, when much of its trade seeped away to Antwerp. Its rise to prominence was primarily due to its position at a point where routes from the Baltic and as far east as Novgorod in Russia intercepted sea routes along the Channel which led eventually to the Mediterranean. A key factor in its early prosperity was access to the sea by the estuary of the Zwin. The continually shifting sandbanks and coastline and the rapidly silting waterways of this area threatened to eliminate this advantage in the twelfth century but a canal was dug along the line of the River Reie to the new port of Damme. This served Bruges throughout our period and allowed reasonable access to the city by sea. The final factor in its emergence as the leading commercial city in northern Europe in our period was its role as a centre of banking and financial expertise. By the end of the thirteenth century the fairs of Champagne had ceased to be the places were most international transactions in this region were finalised and this role was now adopted by Bruges. Here, as we have said, was the terminus of the

Italian trading fleets. Here the towns of the Hanseatic League had their most important *Kontor*, or trading centre. Here came ships from all the east coast and southern ports of the British Isles and from the Channel ports of France. From this centre luxury goods coming from Italy itself and from the trading contacts of Italian merchants in the Mediterranean were redistributed: dyestuffs, cotton, spices (a term which included not only things like pepper and cinnamon but also as many as 288 different items, according to a list in an Italian merchant's handbook[45]), dried fruit and sweet wines and much else besides. The Hanseatic merchants traded in bulky goods like *stockfish* from their *Kontor* in Bergen in Norway, but also in furs from Russia (these were greatly sought after in a period when most houses were very poorly heated), amber from the Baltic and silver ingots for minting into coins and for the workshops of silversmiths.

Bruges was also accessible overland or along inland waterways in the Rhine valley. Similar spiders' webs of trading routes spread out from other regional centres, Paris, Lyon, Toulouse, Bourges, Cologne, London and ultimately linked them together in a trading world which, to almost the end of the fifteenth century, must have seemed stable and successful. Merchants were well aware of the problems that could be caused by wars and other political interventions but must have been ill-prepared for the re-orientation of routes and the appearance of new commodities which were among the results of the opening of trade directly with the East by the Portuguese and the exploitation of the Americas by the Spanish in the sixteenth century. The wealth from this source was perhaps instrumental in providing a new power base and financing the courts and the wars of sixteenth-century princes.

Merchants, money and the bullion crisis

Even from the relatively brief description of the commodities and trade routes of north-western Europe above, it can be appreciated that in our period trade was no longer a matter of simple barter or even of markets where all transactions were in cash. The dangers of carrying large quantities of gold or silver coins from one city to another were no new thing; at sea, shipwreck or piracy threatened; on land, roads led over mountain passes or through forests where brigands might lurk; in towns, simple robbery was as much a problem in late medieval times as it is today. Italian merchants had developed various financial arrangements to facilitate trade as early as the twelfth century. One was the *commenda* contract. This allowed an investor to provide some or all of the capital for a voyage in return for a proportion of the profits. The voyage itself would be undertaken by a partner, who would also share in the profits but often at a lower rate. For example, in 1163, two Genoese made such an agreement for a voyage to Tunis; one put up two-thirds of the money needed and the other (who went on the voyage) put up one-third. If it was profitable they would split the proceeds equally between them.[46] Much more widely used than this type of agreement, by the fifteenth century, was the bill of exchange. The essence of this is perhaps made clear by this example from Marseilles:

September 26 1381

To Madonna Thomasa Lhatauba, greetings and good love from me, Barthouieu Guiber.

Donna by this letter give to Sen Antonio Pomier 32 florins of 12 groats each and 3 groats because I have received them here. Therefore make good payment to him in eight days after seeing the letter.[47]

A payment could be made in another city by a merchant, without transporting the cash there or being there himself, by drawing on credit balances with other merchants in that city, instructing them to pay by means of a written instrument. From this kind of transaction banks with functions very like those of modern merchant banks developed. The best known was probably that of the Medici, the virtual rulers of Florence by the middle of the fifteenth century, which had branches in both Bruges and London at this time. These and the 'head office' in Florence were linked by a regular courier service carrying reports of commercial and political developments as well as the all-important letters of credit. Then as now, good intelligence could be vital to commercial success.

There were, however, problems with the use of these letters and similar credit instruments. First of all the taking of interest, usury, was forbidden by the Church as sinful. This prohibition could be and was enforced in the Church courts, troubled the consciences of many merchant bankers and was an obstacle to the growth of credit and banking. Hunt and Murray have suggested that since many of these bills of exchange involved international trade and complicated exchange rate calculations, interest could be disguised by the way the exchange rate was manipulated.[48] Peter Spufford has drawn attention to the difference between loans for consumption (which were completely against Church law) and productive loans, which were acceptable. This difference was certainly appreciated in Italy by the thirteenth century.[49] There is, not surprisingly, little evidence to support these arguments, but other disadvantages need to be noted. There was often no way of enforcing payment of the debt except through the honour of the individuals concerned. It worked most effectively in close-knit groups of friends or relations, or fellow townsmen. There was no collateral, no supporting value (like the value of the property which is the security for a mortgage), behind the transaction. Moreover the system depended on there being a reasonable balance of trade between the areas involved, as we discuss below. If this was not the case, bullion still had to be transported form place to place despite all the dangers involved. Furthermore, some authorities actively discouraged agreements like this, for example the dukes of Burgundy in Bruges.

The reason for this hostility lies in the attitude of most rulers in this period to the notion that international trade could lead to bullion (gold and silver) draining out of a country and thus impoverishing it. Bullion was conceived of as the wealth of a state and thus efforts had always to be made to prevent it leaving the country. Taking currency abroad with the intention of buying goods was the most obvious way in which this could happen, especially if the trade was unbalanced (where one area had goods much in demand by its trading partner but this partner area produced little that was wanted or needed by the first partner).

Hunt and Murray point out that the only way to meet the continuing demand for oriental merchandise in the West was 'by the only commodities assured of ready acceptance in the East – precious metals'.[50] Spufford suggests that even in 'the most important centres in western Europe', while individual merchants might use bills of exchange, ultimately imbalances had to be settled by the movement of bullion. In trade like that between central Europe and northern Italy payment was expected to be in gold and silver.[51] This perception has given rise to controversy over whether there was in fact a severe shortage of bullion, a bullion crisis, in our study area in this period, which severely impeded trade. Silver had been the precious metal of choice in European mints until the beginning of the fourteenth century, with supplies coming from mines in Bohemia and Slovakia. Gold, however, in quite large quantities, was discovered at Kremnitz in 1320. When coined as the Hungarian ducat this became the preferred currency in central Europe. Gold from this source, and that brought across the Sahara to the North African ports, ensured that there was no real lack of gold for currency in our period. Silver production, however, fell off very rapidly around the mid-fourteenth century. Even the very productive Bohemian mines at Kutna Hora were exhausted and finally closed after being sacked during the Hussite rebellion in 1422 (see below, Section 2(iii)). It has been suggested that the depression visible in much of our study area in the 1460s was largely caused by an acute shortage of money. The upturn in trade did not begin until new mines opened in the Tyrol and in Saxony; a better way of extracting the metal from the ore also allowed some of the old mines to re-open.[52]

In Munro's view, historians who agree that there was a late medieval bullion famine have accepted the collapse in the output of the silver mines as a major factor. They also blame 'wear and tear' affecting existing coins, as well as losses by shipwreck and other means. Supply was also affected by a reduced inflow of gold from trade with North Africa, and more bullion drained away because of the increase in trade with the East. He himself lays greater emphasis on the effects of war, trade embargoes and the ravages of undisciplined soldiers together with the 'bullionist' hoarding policies of many rulers in this period.[53] The extent of state intervention in trade is not in doubt. All rulers attempted both to use trade as a source of revenue and to regulate it and control it. The tangled story of the relations between Flanders and England over the wool and cloth trades exemplifies this well. The Flemish cities needed English raw wool for their textile industry but regarded English cloth as an unwelcome intruder in markets rightfully theirs. The way in which the marketing of English wool intended for the Low Countries market was controlled and manipulated by the Crown through the Company of the Staple will be looked at below, but here we can note that the sale of English cloth was forbidden in Flanders in 1346, though it was apparently smuggled in via Sluis. By the Partition and Bullion Ordinances of 1429, the English Crown tried to insist that wool could only be sold in Calais for full payment in gold or silver coins, with no credit allowed. This ruined many smaller traders and led to political difficulties with Burgundy. Burgundy also banned the import of English cloth from 1447 to 1452, and 1464 to 1467. In 1493–6 Henry VII, in his turn, banned the export of cloth to Burgundy for political reasons. In this case the pent up demand when the ban was lifted caused the total amount exported to surge from around 60,000 cloths per annum before the ban to 70,000 in 1499–1500 when it was lifted.

The trade in wine was another area which suffered badly from the effects of war. Almost all the wine exported from the Bordeaux region went to England when Gascony was a possession of the English Crown. Much of this came into the ports of either Bristol or Southampton in English ships. The dangers of the voyage during the war years had already pushed the trade into decline (30,000 tuns in the 1360s, 10,000 in the fifteenth century). It was more or less completely interrupted after the French capture of the Bordeaux region in 1453 and did not revive till after the Treaty of Picquigny (see Chapter 4). After this date too, virtually all the ships used were Breton or Spanish because of French hostility to English traders. The effects of royal policy could be as devastating for an individual as for a particular trading area. Here we can cite the example of Jacques Coeur. He was a native of Bourges, the town which served as a capital for Charles VII in the dark days of the 1420s. He began his rise to wealth by becoming involved in the minting of money for the king. He then became a leading financier involved in royal loans and by 1441 was a collector of the *taille* in Languedoc. In the South he was soon involved in a wide range of trading, mining and manufacturing enterprises, accumulating a truly colossal fortune. His influence seemed boundless as he increased his loans to the Crown, now in the final stages of the reconquest of northern France from the English. His large and elegant house in Bourges, decorated with elaborate and beautiful sculptures, symbolised his importance (see Illustration 4). He had, however, risen too fast and too far; his enemies spread rumours of his involvement with Agnes Sorel, the king's mistress. In 1451 he was arrested, accused of poisoning her, and all his possessions, worth the huge sum of 400,000 *écus*, were confiscated by the Crown.

Wendy Childs, however, sees Coeur's spectacular career, which occurred in a period usually seen as one of recession, in a country in the final stages of a very destructive war, as evidence of the 'essential soundness of the traditional European commercial structure'.[54] Despite all these disadvantages a skilled trader could turn a good profit and use his wealth to rise in the world. The continuing development of commercial practices, as for example in southern Germany, could help in this process. Here a trading company known as the Great Ravensburg Company had been established in the 1380s. This traded solely in linen manufactured locally but lasted until 1530, employing capital of 130,000 florins put up by its two dozen shareholders, at its peak in 1500. Another successful company between 1400 and 1450 was the Diesbach-Watt company from St Gallen, which traded between Poland in the east and Catalonia in the west, exporting linen, and brass and iron ware, in exchange for furs and wax in the east and saffron in the west. There had also been early banking firms in Nuremberg but all these were overshadowed by the Fugger Bank, which was founded in 1486 in Augsburg. This was headed by a family who had come to Augsburg as peasants from the Lech valley. They used the capital accumulated from successful investment in the mining enterprises in Silesia to lend to rulers, especially Maximilian of Habsburg. By the middle of the sixteenth century they had branch offices all over Europe and were as powerful financially, if not politically, as the Medici a century earlier.

4 The house of Jacques Coeur at Bourges

This magnificent mansion was built by Jacques Coeur for his own use at Bourges. It is perhaps not surprising that he thus incurred the envy of Charles VII and eventually was deprived of all his possessions.

Case studies

Traders in late medieval Europe operated in an uncertain climate in some respects. A change in ruler or in a ruler's policy might have a sudden and unforeseen effect on their fortunes but the strong and commercially minded princes of later medieval Europe could be the source of opportunities for bold merchants.

Despite the dangers, profits could be made by those determined to exploit some of the openings on offer. This is well evidenced in our two case studies, first looking more closely at a league of trading cities and secondly looking at a company of merchants closely controlled by the ruler.

The Hanseatic League

The Hanseatic League has already been mentioned several times in our discussion of trade and merchants. We now need to consider how and why it came into being, and how and why it came to exercise so much influence in our study area in this period. Up until the twelfth century the Baltic region was remote from many developments in western Europe; there was little trade outside the region itself and many of those living in Livonia and other areas in the east were not Christian and thus were cut off from the main source of European unity. The gradual extension of Germanic settlers into this region brought it to the attention of the Empire, promoting trading relations and the founding of towns. Lübeck was founded between 1143 and 1159, and Riga, much further to the east, on the river Dvina in 1201. It was not unusual for merchants from the same nation trading overseas to form associations to treat with foreign rulers or for their own protection. This kind of thing can be found in, for example, Alexandria in Egypt, where the Genoese and Venetians formed organised groups, as well as in northern Europe. Traders from Cologne, as we said above, formed a group like this in London in 1157, and four years later German traders visiting the island of Gotland off Sweden did much the same thing. These two associations proved to be the beginnings of a trading league which, by the time of the first general *diet* or assembly in 1356, included virtually all the towns of any note in the northern Netherlands, the Empire and the Baltic coast. It is hard to compile a complete list since some towns were members for only short periods but the most important included Cologne, Deventer, Kampen, Bremen, Hamburg, Dortmund, Münster, Osnabruck, Brunswick, Lübeck, Wismar, Rostock, Danzig, Breslau, Cracow, Riga, Stockholm and Visby. Dollinger in fact lists a total of 199 towns as at one time being part of the League and sharing in the privileges granted to its merchants.[55]

These privileges were, of course, in many ways the *raison d'être* of the organisation. By banding together, these towns had managed to conclude agreements with foreign rulers which placed them in a very favourable position in the local market. In London the Steelyard was the Hanse base or *Kontor* but merchants from these towns could be found in most of the east coast ports. The foundation of their privileges lay in charters concluded with English kings from the time of Henry III onwards. One of the most valuable was freedom from general arrest, conceded by Edward II in 1314. This meant that an English merchant who had suffered some loss in a Hanse town or at the hands of its townsmen could not get recompense in England by asking the courts to arrest or impound goods to the same value from the possessions of merchants of that city based in England. They also gained exemption in 1347 from the extra subsidy on the export of cloth imposed by Edward III to pay for the war, a privilege which left them paying less in Customs duties than Englishmen. The merchants of the Steelyard and their associates were valued customers for English wool and cloth but also had virtual monopolies of imports greatly desired in London: metalwork and armour from Cologne, furs, wax for church candles, and more mundane articles like the so-called 'Prussian deal' needed for shipbuilding, and hemp for ropes.

We can see similar privileges leading on occasion to the virtual monopolising of a trade route in other areas. One of the most notable is the hold that the Hanseatic merchants achieved over trade with Norway through the town of Bergen. There was a *Kontor* here, and less important centres at Tönsberg and Oslo. Trade with Bergen was entirely in the hands of merchants from Lübeck, and at the other two centres largely in the hands of those from Rostock. The so-called *Bergenfahrer* (voyage to Bergen) was organised so that around twenty vessels from Lübeck sailed to Bergen every year with cargoes of grain and flour, hops and malt for beer, salt and linen. There they loaded large quantities of *stockfish*, air dried cod caught off the Lofoten Islands on the west coast of Norway. The only other exports were small quantities of salmon, cod liver oil, furs and butter. Virtually no other merchants visited the port and the complaints of the Norwegian king Haakon VI at abuses committed by the Hansards in 1370 have a plaintive tone: they allow no Norwegians to ship goods in their ships; they have caused trouble in Bergen so that some of the king's subjects have been killed. A particular incident complained of consisted of the Hansards going to the monastery of Bergen, there capturing one of the servants and cutting off his head. They then, according to the king, demanded absolution for this murder from the bishop of Bergen and threatened to burn down the bishop's palace and the whole town of Bergen if this was refused. Beside events like this, the merchants' refusal to accept Norwegian coinage, demanding instead that of Lübeck or Stralsund, seems quite minor.[56] The Hansards had also taken over all trade between England and Norway, with some vessels in the fourteenth century operating a kind of triangular trade, taking flour from Lübeck to Bergen, then *stockfish* from Bergen to Boston and finally cloth from Boston to Lübeck. In the fifteenth century, English mariners from the east coast ports and Bristol were infuriated by the strenuous efforts of the Hanse to prevent English ships becoming involved in direct trade with Iceland, a Norwegian dependency.

The members of the League situated further to the east on the Baltic coast profited from trade with Prussia and Poland or with Russia and Livonia. Danzig was the centre of the Prussian trade, which grew explosively in the fifteenth century with 1,100 ships leaving the port for Flanders with grain in 1481. Trade with Russia and Livonia fared less well. In the thirteenth century, German merchants had gone regularly to Smolensk and Vitebsk; from the fourteenth they went no further inland than Novgorod and Polotsk. By the middle of the fifteenth century the Muscovite conquests in the region ensured that all trade was henceforth confined to the Livonian towns, which gradually excluded the merchants from the more westerly towns from their markets.

A trading group of the strength and wealth of the Hanse at its peak also had, of course, considerable political influence. In the third quarter of the fourteenth century a trade dispute with Flanders and open war with Denmark were the stimuli to transform an association of German-speaking merchants into a league of towns which had many of the characteristics of a state. Dollinger goes so far as to claim that for the ensuing 150 years the Hanse was a 'great power' in northern

Europe.[57] The dispute with Bruges centred on the absolute priority which the Hansards placed on the defence of their privileged position in the largest and most important of their *Kontors*. In the course of the negotiations the position of Lübeck as the head of the League was made clear, with authority to control the activities of merchants in the various distant centres. An interdiction of trade between Flanders and the League from 1358 to 1360 served in many ways to remind both parties how much they stood to lose if relations were broken off. Bruges's need of grain from Prussia in the spring of 1360 after a bad harvest the year before was acute. The League's ships blocked the Sound (the narrows between Denmark and Sweden) so that even smuggled grain could not get through. Within weeks new agreements were reached and the Hansard merchants returned to Bruges. The League had emerged with its privileges intact and the advantages of unity among the cities clearly demonstrated.

The Danish war perhaps posed even greater problems for the League. Denmark, which from 1360 also ruled Scania, the southern province of modern Sweden, was in a position itself to close the Sound. This was the only exit from the Baltic to the North Sea and closing this strait to Hansard shipping would strangle their seaborne trade. When relations between Denmark and the Hanse towns worsened, this threat became a reality. In the face of an attack on its commercial fortunes of this magnitude the League sought to raise special monetary levies from its members and organise a naval force. Although the process severely strained the cohesiveness of the League it was finally successful in 1370 after Copenhagen had been attacked by a fleet from Lübeck and the Netherlands, together with operations on land in Scania. The Treaty of Stralsund was signed, and made clear Hansard domination of the region; all their old privileges were confirmed, while their possession for fifteen years of four castles on the Sound together with two-thirds of the tolls paid by passing ships made it impossible for Denmark to close the strait.

The League thus created in this region a special kind of society of self-confident urban trading communities. Some were cities of the Empire, others further to the east were part of the territories of the Teutonic Knights, but this was of far less significance than their membership of the League. It would be hard to argue that their merchants were popular in other cities but it is equally clear that few wished to sever connections with them completely. There was too much to lose economically and commercially, something which remained the case to the end of our period. The eventual decline and breakup of the League in the sixteenth century would not have been apparent to an observer in 1500. With the benefit of hindsight we can perhaps conclude that this kind of semi-state, held together only by commercial considerations, was very vulnerable to the growth of strong centralised monarchies and to the beginnings of national feeling based on common languages, laws and customs.

The Company of the Staple

The idea of a staple town or a staple commodity was not unusual in our period. We have already met it in connection with Ghent, which had staple privileges with regard to the grain trade down the River Leie. This meant that all grain coming through the town had to pay a toll, while some remained in the town for its own use. Wool was so valuable a commodity to the authorities in England, because of the relative ease with which it could be burdened with dues and taxes, that it is not surprising that the idea of establishing a staple town in order to control its sale came to the fore quite early. Staples, with the monopoly of a trade or other privileges, were not unwelcome to those who were, as it were, 'on the inside'. They were, however, unfavourable to the interests of 'outsiders' or small traders excluded from the privileged group. The real beneficiary was usually intended to be the prince or other authority which established the staple. A staple town was designated for the conduct of business in English wool from the beginning of the fourteenth century. St Omer was used for this purpose in 1313 but the Staple was later moved briefly to Antwerp (1315–17) and Bruges (1325–6), largely for political reasons.

Establishing a staple overseas, however, depended to some extent on the consent and co-operation of the local ruler, whose interests might not be best served by the arrival of a group of foreign merchants wishing to regulate a trade which was often of great importance to the host nation as well as to the alien merchants. Staples were often moved from one place to another in order to profit from the best terms obtainable or to escape onerous obstructions. So-called home staples were in fact set up in England, Wales and Ireland after 1326, although the richer merchants still favoured an overseas base.[58] Their preferred location was Bruges. The strains of the opening years of the Hundred Years War caused wool merchants great problems, not the least of these being the king's attempts to milk the trade for war finance or to use the Customs receipts as collateral for loans. The war itself also interrupted trade and led to political considerations influencing commercial relations; whether or not Edward III was on good terms with the Flemings or their Count was often the deciding factor.

In 1363 the staple was established in a more regulated fashion at Calais. This had been, of course, an English town since 1348; it was very well placed for merchants from the Flemish cloth towns and but a short sea passage from London. A statute was passed in the Parliament of October 1362 reaffirming the rights of denizen merchants to export wool but making no mention of Calais in this connection. Calais's position as the staple town was established by entries to be found in the French Rolls for 1363.[59] The Staple was not thereafter always at Calais nor did denizen merchants have monopoly rights. During Richard II's reign, for example, the Staple was removed from Calais between 1369 and 1376 and again in 1384 when French action made it impossible for Flemish merchants to reach the market. It settled in Calais permanently in 1399, however, and it is from this period that the Fellowship or Company itself begins to appear more frequently in the records. The Staplers appear as a wealthy and well-organised body of merchants, 'reputed and taken to be the most worshipful company of merchants subject to a king that any prince in Christendom hath had'.[60] We do not have precise details of their membership or of their statutes dating from their period of greatest power and influence. This is because their records were kept in the Place (as Staple Hall, their trading centre in Calais, was generally known) and were all lost or destroyed when Calais fell to the French in 1558. There is a later set of their statutes from 1565 which, it is thought, mirrors many of their earlier practices;[61] other sources are the frequent mentions of Staplers in royal records or the records of London, or in family papers, most notably those of the Celys.

The dual role of the company in controlling the greater part of the export of wool from England and as a means for the Crown to tap mercantile wealth became clear as soon as it was firmly established in Calais. The Staplers were concerned to strengthen their monopoly in the export of wool and frequently complained of the fact that northern wool from Newcastle did not have to go via Calais to Flanders, and that Italians could export directly from English ports to Italy via the Straits of Gibraltar (i.e. by sea not overland). The Crown saw the company as a source of loan finance, particularly for the purpose of paying the expensive garrison of Calais. Despite this the Crown provoked a crisis in the wool and cloth trade in Flanders and England by the Partition and Bullion ordinances of 1429. The Bullion ordinances laid down that all wool sold at the Staple had to be paid for in gold or silver coins, not by credit instruments, and that one-third of this bullion had to be handed over to the Mint in Calais to be coined. The partition ordinance insisted that all the wool coming to Calais should be graded by the Company at the Place and then sold in parcels made up there at controlled prices. The profits would be divided among the various merchants, in proportion to the wool they owned, after the sales were completed. The Flemish towns (the usual customers of the Staplers) and their overlord the duke of Burgundy were so infuriated by this highly restrictive system that it undoubtedly influenced the breakdown of the Anglo-Burgundian alliance in 1434–5 and led to an attack on the town in 1435.

The ordinances were withdrawn in 1444 but the Company, the town and its trade were still very much affected by the political situation both in England and, until 1453, in the other French possessions of the English Crown. Edward IV, however, reached an agreement with the Company which, to a modern reader, seems analogous to the privatisation of the defence of Calais. It was agreed by an Act of Parliament passed in 1466 and renewed in 1473 that the 'said mayor, fellowship and merchants of the said staple of Calais' will not pay customs on their exports to the town but shall

> have and retain all customs and subsidies of wools and wool fells ... and that £10,022 4s 8d of the said sums of money ... to be applied contented and paid yearly ... for and upon payment of the said wages fees and rewards of the captain or the King's lieutenant and other lieutenants and soldiers.[62]

The king would have the right to any 'surplusage' once the outstanding loans from the Company to the king had been paid off. Furthermore the Company was also to have the right to the income from royal property in the town, to apply to the repair of the defences and artillery of the town. This did not prevent further disagreements between the Crown and the Company. Because of the sometimes baleful effects of differing exchange rates between Calais and London there were often arguments about the details of the garrison's pay. The king was inclined to demand his 'surplusage' whether it existed or not, but the system worked reasonably well until the sixteenth century.

What, however, about the individual members of the Company and their lives and business activities? It is here that the Cely letters are an invaluable source, giving us a way into their lifestyle. The Cely family was based in London but also had a country estate, Bretts Place in Aveley, Essex. Much of the correspondence is between the family in London and their factor or agent in Calais. It was a peculiarity of the Company that its mayor (its highest official) was always based in London while the business of the Company was carried on at the Place or Staple Hall in Calais.

The trade itself was in many ways complex and demanding for an individual merchant. The Celys would normally buy their stocks of wool from a 'gatherer' in the Cotswolds. He would have brought wool from various growers into a central place, usually Chipping Norton or Northleach, where Cely or his representative would view it and agree to buy it if satisfied. The Celys normally dealt with a gatherer called Midwinter. On 15 February 1487 George Cely noted,

> we made a bargain with William Midwinter of Northleach for 50 sacks wool good and middle of Cotswold. The refuse to be cast out by the wool-packer. The said William to have for every sack 14 mark. To be paid at Midsummer next £100 and at Midsummer come twelve month the rest of the same wool.[63]

This contract makes clear some of the features of the trade. Wool was carefully graded by quality, with that from the Cotswolds acknowledged as the best. It had to be professionally packed before being transported to London and then eventually to the Calais mart. Credit terms were the usual basis of payment. At Calais buyers would be sought and enormous complications arose over exchange difference and the reliability of currencies. The Place had displayed in its lower hall a table of the current valuations of all the coins used in the mart. George once drew up an account for his brother of the coins he had in England; he had at least seven different kinds, which had to be separated into 'good' groats and 'evil' groats. Credit sales were often on the terms that the balance would be paid at one of the seasonal fairs or marts, Pask mart (Easter) at Bruges, Cold or Winter mart at Bergen-op-Zoom, or the Antwerp Whitsun mart (Sinxen mart). Bills of exchange were not often used and George had to make the journey himself to collect the money owing. He would sometimes take advantage of the other traders frequenting the mart to buy a wide range of goods, including girdles and pillowcases, and luxuries like coral beads and lute strings.[64]

It is hard to assess the profit that the Cely family partnership made from this trade because of gaps in the records and the complexities of their accounting system. We can say that exports of raw wool had declined from over 25,000 sacks in the 1370s but had settled at around 8,000 to 10,000 sacks after 1459. In the trade, that was the basis of their fortune; however, membership of the Company of the Staple was essential. Its regulations might at times be onerous but a wool merchant had no option but to accept them.

The future for merchant associations perhaps lay neither with town leagues like the Hanse, which was vulnerable to attacks from local monarchs, to its demands for privileged status for its members, and to the general growth of national feeling, nor with Crown-regulated companies like the Staple. The trading companies of south Germany were one way ahead, being structured not unlike modern limited companies. Another could be that followed by the Merchant Adventurers in London, a purely voluntary association. These merchants dealt in cloth, not wool: their trade was expanding, not contracting, and they were not burdened with the cumbersome rules of the Company of the Staple. An individual merchant would still often be faced with interference from meddling rulers but he was much freer to run his own business as he chose.

(iii) THE BREAKDOWN OF CONSENT

Popular unrest and rebellion

The concept of popular unrest and rebellion is a slippery one, difficult to separate from other political factors and hard to tie into a series of firm conclusions. Much of it had an urban setting, which is why this section concludes the chapter on townsmen and traders, but in some cases unrest originated in the countryside. To Marxist historians in the second half of the twentieth century it seemed to be a manifestation of a sort of class war: the just reaction of the common people to their feudal oppressors. Although most contemporary commentators were hostile to insurgents they did at least relate some sentiments which voiced the genuine views and aspirations of those people. The court records of the indictments, fines, imprisonings, mutilations and executions that inevitably followed such events provided further evidence. The difficulties of isolating the phenomenon of popular revolt and the progress of revisionism have perhaps diminished interest in the subject: during the last decade, for example, no special sections were devoted to it in the recently published volumes of the *New Cambridge Medieval History*. Yet there unquestionably were riots and rebellions that were not instigated by the upper orders and much can be learnt about contemporary society from studying them.

A possibility suggested by Rodney Hilton[65] was that the incidence of revolts, particularly high in Europe between 1378 and 1385, may have been linked to each other in some way. Why should people as diverse as the *ciompi* (textile workers) in Florence, English and French peasants and artisans, and burghers of Flanders all revolt at the same time? Michel Mollat and Philippe Wolff were also inclined to see a connection, and quote a contemporary chronicler, the monk of Saint-Denis:

> Nearly all the people of France had rebelled and were agitated with great fury and, according to general rumour, they were excited by messengers from the Flemings, who were themselves being worked upon by the plague of a similar rebellion, stimulated by the example of the English.[66]

The phenomenon of popular unrest and rebellion, from the mid-fourteenth century to the end of the fifteenth century, will be considered below by looking at the three main areas in which historians have felt the explanations for them are to be found. These are social and economic factors; disastrous events such as plague, famine and external wars; and political and religious factors. These areas cannot realistically be further subdivided, and even then, when particular examples are considered, it will usually be clear that other issues than those chosen for more detailed discussion were involved. The possibility of collusion between groups of insurgents in different countries in the late fourteenth century looks increasingly unlikely as particular examples of unrest are examined. The conclusion will address another question raised by Mollat and Wolff: were any of the uprisings sufficiently planned to count as revolutions?

Economic and social factors

Chapter 1 described the decline in population that brought about radical changes in the economies of European states. Phrases such as 'the crisis of feudalism' or 'the Agrarian crisis' have been used to typify the pressures on society. The description 'crisis' applies not just to the sufferings of the common people and the anxieties of their lords but also to internal unrest. This often culminated in the refusal to pay taxes, riots, attacks on urban elites, and on the unpopular representatives of landowners and princes, or rebellions that defied the rulers themselves.[67] The economic components of the 'crisis' were assembled in the late thirteenth and early fourteenth centuries. The consequent disorders were manifested most frequently in the second half of the fourteenth century.

Marxist historians such as Rodney Hilton and Robert Brenner have suggested that the main cause of the 'crisis' was the increasing gap between what the peasants could pay their lords from the yield of their lands and what the lords considered to be a sufficient income. This problem was compounded by the expansionist ambitions of states such as England, France and (later) Burgundy, which had to be funded by increased taxation. In France, clerics had total exemption from taxation and nobles, depending on the region in which they owned land, also enjoyed varying degrees of exemption. This made the burden fall more heavily on peasants, artisans and the increasingly influential bourgeoisie. Guenée has remarked on the frequent references made by Pintoin, the monk of St Denis, to the injustice felt by the people at this situation.[68]

A good example of this kind of grievance would seem to be the brief revolt which shook the countryside in northern France in May and June 1358. It was known as the *Jacquerie*, from the familiar name of 'Jacques' attributed to peasants: the common people attacked castles and manor houses, some ladies were raped and some nobles were killed. The king of Navarre and the nobles of Picardy quickly crushed the rising and punished the ringleaders severely. There certainly was great resentment at the high taxes that were being exacted to pay for the ransom of John II, recently captured by the English at Poitiers. The people blamed the cowardice and incompetence of the lords and knights who had allowed such a disaster to happen, rather than holding their king responsible. This feeling may furnish an explanation of the vicious treatment of the nobility in 1358. Raymond Cazelles makes a further rather surprising point: of those subsequently indicted a large number were rural artisans, shoemakers, masons and sellers of foodstuffs, rather than peasants.[69] There were also some priests, minor royal officials and burgesses: an altogether different body of insurgents than has traditionally been depicted. Peasants were unlikely to have chosen the season when their crops were reaching fruition as a time to revolt. Allowing for the impact of the war, the machinations of the king of Navarre and the simultaneous uprising in Paris led by Etienne Marcel, there seems to have been political as well as economic motivation behind the *Jacquerie*.

Since 1356 there had been a movement for reform in Paris led by the bourgeois Provost of Merchants (the chief municipal office), Etienne Marcel. His rise certainly exemplifies the growing power of his class but it cannot be described simply as the result of a conflict between citizens and nobles. Some of the latter supported him when he tried to enlist the help of the Estates General in subjecting the monarchy to its control. He had a strong following amongst the common people but some of his order, including members of his own family, disapproved of his ambitions. He believed that he could browbeat the Dauphin Charles, who was Regent in France during his father's captivity, led 3,000 artisans to the royal palace in the centre of Paris and murdered two royal marshals in the presence of the prince. Marcel over-reached himself in the following months: he became associated with the *jacquerie*, alarming many moderates, and ignored the grievances of those who were close to him. In July he was assassinated by a kinsman and the Regent was soon able to restore order in the capital. As with the *Jacquerie*, social and economic grievances seem to have combined with the volatile political situation to provoke disorder.

The closely inhabited areas of the Low Countries, and particularly of Flanders, had for a long time defied their rulers if they felt that their customs and privileges were being threatened. The cities of Bruges, Ypres and Ghent dominated Flanders: Ghent enjoyed a higher annual income than did the count himself. As a poet sympathetic to the dilemma facing the count put it in the 1380s:

> He could not render sentence
> For whatever judgement he rendered
> Another would allege that it violated
> The content of its franchise.
> Everyone wanted to acquit
> Criminals of their misdeeds
> On the basis of the liberties of the city.
> This happened more than a thousand times
> And especially in Ghent ...[70]

The cities derived much of their prosperity from the woollen cloth trade with England and took its part in the Hundred Years War. In 1369 the last count of the house of Dampierre had married his only child, Margaret, to Philip of Burgundy, the brother of the French king. When the count died, Philip would succeed him and Flanders would become a French sphere of influence, and this prospect unsettled the population. Added to this were long-standing tensions between the various trade guilds; the weaker ones resented the dominance of the textile workers. These problems had led to a series of disorders in the middle years of the century orchestrated by Jan van Artevelde, a citizen of Ghent (see above). He had eventually been murdered but his son Philip assumed his mantle, becoming captain of Ghent in 1382. In the following year he too was killed, in a battle between the Flemings and French royal forces. Even Ghent could not long defy the power of the new count, Philip of Burgundy, and it made a treaty which left it with a decent degree of control over its own affairs. Ruled by a strong and competent French prince, Flanders became part of an expanding and powerful duchy and did not seriously defy its ruler again for over half a century.

The fourteenth century had been a period of unremitting internal violence in Flanders. The Belgian historian Henri Pirenne and his followers had seen this in terms of the conflicts between the different orders employed within the textile industry.[71] But David Nicholas does not believe that class conflict provides a satis factory explanation since workers were grouped within guilds that cut across several levels of income and status. He also suggests that family rivalries, such as those that troubled the van Arteveldes, could affect the parties to disputes. Combined with political considerations such as the war with England, loyalties to different popes during the Schism, and the change of the ruling dynasty, the motivation for the disturbances in the 1380s looks complex.

The unrest in German towns during the 1370s and 1380s may be attributed primarily to social and economic causes. Originally they were mainly under the control of patrician oligarchies but, during the previous century, there had been increasing pressure from the craft guilds to be given a share in municipal government. The situation was further complicated by the rivalries between the greater and lesser guilds. In Brunswick in 1374, for example, there was a revolt of craftsmen against locally imposed taxes in which several councillors were murdered or banished. A few years later a conspiracy by the butchers of Lübeck to install a government that was more favourable to them was discovered and the ringleader committed suicide. Although such urban violence was widespread throughout Europe the right conditions could ensure that it was largely avoided. The prosperity of great mercantile cities such as Nuremberg and Bordeaux brought social stability to their inhabitants.

Calamitous events

Whilst it would be ridiculous to suggest that people would rise up against their rulers simply because they had been afflicted by flood, famine or plague, historians have frequently cited such disasters as contributing to the long-term causes of unrest. Apart from the social, economic and political impact of disasters, the religious psychology of late medieval people must be taken into account. A natural disaster or the depredations of an invading army was probably sent by God to punish them for their sins. One reaction was to repent and do good works but another was to blame those who might be responsible for attracting divine wrath. Jews, heretics and lepers often suffered for this reason (see below, Chapter 5: iii), but local lords or royal servants could also attract reprisals. Princes were seldom held responsible; they might be old (Edward III of England), mad (Charles VI of France and Henry VI of England) or minors (Richard II of England) when rebellions occurred, so their ministers took the blame.

Probably no disaster had such a traumatic impact on the consciousness of late medieval people as the Black Death. Chapter 1 has described its devastating effect on population levels, agriculture and the capacity of landowners to employ labour. The response of the government in England was to introduce the Statute of Labourers in 1351, restricting the levels of wages that could be paid and prices that could be charged, and it also attempted to control the movement of workers. Many peasants were still technically *villeins*, tied to the manor where they had been born and obliged to give their lord a proportion of the produce from their farms and to render him free labour services for part of the year. These obligations varied from manor to manor and region to region but, by the second half of the fourteenth century, when the plague had made labourers much in demand, they were bitterly resented. Barbara Harvey sees the pressure from lords and the desire of the peasants to avoid excessive labour services as a key factor in the growing crisis.[72]

The final years of Edward III's reign saw the French territories bleed away through the skilful campaigning of Charles V and du Guesclin. The English nobility became factious as the authority of the ageing king declined, giving the common people an example that they followed in 1381. There had already been sporadic outbursts of resentment against the Statute of Labourers, in Middlesex (1351), Lincolnshire (1352) and Northamptonshire (1359). The death of the old king and the succession of the youthful Richard II, who inherited his grandfather's advisers including the hated John of Gaunt, seemed to offer an opportunity for radical reform. The imposition of a poll tax, apparently to pay for the foreign ambitions of such princes, sparked off the rebellion.

The poem *Piers Plowman* was probably written in the 1370s by John Langland: it voices a disillusionment with church and state that was widespread amongst the politically aware lower orders. The priest John Ball, one of the leaders of the Revolt, had been calling for reform in his sermons with such vehemence that he had several times been sent to prison. Such factors justified the opponents of change in linking *Lollardy* with sedition (see below, Chapter 5: iii). The actual revolt lasted no longer than the earlier *Jacquerie* in France, from late May to June 1381. Bands of armed peasants from the counties surrounding London, especially Kent, marched on the capital. Apart from John Ball, Jack Straw and Wat Tyler were amongst those who led the rebels, but little is known about them. The peasants and townspeople who had suffered from the domination of the great abbey of Bury St Edmunds and the University of Cambridge rose up in East Anglia to secure their liberties and a similar movement occurred against the abbey of St Albans. Risings also took place in the north, in 1380–1, in York, Beverley and Scarborough.

The rebels, or at least their leaders, may have prepared a manifesto of demands before they took to the field. They were admitted to London; a few citizens seem to have been active supporters and others were sympathetic. Richard II was in the comparative safety of the Tower but he consented to meet Wat Tyler at Mile End on 14 June. Four main demands were presented to him: serfdom (*villeinage*) should be abolished; all tenants would pay a uniform rent of fourpence per acre; all restrictions upon buying and selling were to be lifted and a general amnesty was to be proclaimed. The king accepted these demands and returned to London, where there had been pillaging and the unpopular Chancellor, Simon Sudbury the archbishop of Canterbury, and some other royal servants were murdered.

The following day Richard had another interview with Tyler and the rebels at Mile End. This time a more elaborate and radical manifesto was presented; Tyler's demands included:

> no lord should have lordship in future, but it should be divided among all men, except for the king's own lordship. He also asked that the goods of Holy Church should not remain in the hands of the religious [monks], nor of parsons and vicars, and other churchmen; but that the clergy already in possession should have a sufficient sustenance and the rest of their goods should be divided among the people of the parish. And he demanded that there should be only one bishop in England and only one prelate.[73]

Those who framed these demands seem to have given no thought to the needs of townspeople or to how royal government, without its traditional support, would work. The fact that they were made at all and that some sort of negotiation took place over several days implies a degree of political maturity on the part of the rebels. This broke down at Smithfield, however, when Tyler became involved in a brawl that was probably deliberately provoked by the king's followers. He was killed and Richard prevailed upon the rebels to disperse and return to their homes. Despite promises of amnesty the usual executions and fines punished the ringleaders and some of their followers.

Steven Justice in *Writing and Rebellion: England in 1381* rejects some earlier portrayals of the rebels as essentially lawless and uneducated people who were only seeking redress for immediate economic concerns, especially the abolition of the Statute of Labourers and the poll tax.[74] Leaders such as the priest John Ball had developed a reform agenda by the summer of 1381 and their followers were acting in its spirit by making their own law. This came from traditional customs and practices: the burning of legal records was linked to the fires lighted at Midsummer on the eve of the feast of the nativity of St John the Baptist in late June. At St Albans the people forced their way into the cloister and lifted some stone handmills from the parlour floor, they broke them into small pieces and distributed them amongst the insurgents. The mills had been placed in the Abbey to commemorate its victory in an old dispute with its *villeins*. Chapter 5 describes the custom of distributing bread that had been blessed, to congregations after Mass. Justice believes that the rebels were adapting this practice to make a legal point. All the pieces of stone were carefully preserved by the recipients since they were returned to the Abbey as part of the reparations that followed the end of the Revolt.

The Revolt of 1381 almost certainly can be attributed in part to the long-term effects of the social and economic devastation caused by the Black Death, although political factors also played an important part. It can be compared with the almost contemporary disturbances that broke out in France. The Languedoc had been troubled by the lawless *Tuchins* (so-called from the wild country in which they operated) since the 1360s. In 1380 just before he died, Charles V cancelled the unpopular *fouages*, or hearth taxes, and this apparent weakness has sometimes been seen as the reason for the escalation of social unrest during the next two years. Henry Miskimin disputes this, claiming that the royal finances were sound after a lull in the war with the English and a long period of high taxation.[75] It was the harsh governance of one of the uncles of the young Charles VI, Louis I of Anjou, and his attempt to impose more taxes, which led to the *Harelle* (from 'Haro', a cry of protest) in Rouen and the rising of the *Maillotins* (people armed with mallets) in Paris. The disorders, which did not claim many lives, were eventually put down but French society continued to be unstable for the rest of the reign. From 1399 to 1402, for example, there was a serious outbreak of plague, the king suffered regular bouts of insanity and the violent rivalry between the dukes of Orleans and Burgundy commenced.

Whilst the motivation of the French riots was partly to resist unreasonable levels of taxation, the conflicting ambitions of the king's uncles and the removal of the revered figure of Charles V were also important factors. *Villeinage* was not such an issue for French peasants as it was in England: most were free by the middle of the fourteenth century and working as tenants on land leased from their local lords. The rebels seem to have had no programme, and no charismatic leaders emerged. Conversely, in England Caroline Barron suggests that, despite the fact that the Peasants' Revolt was suppressed, the political nation had expanded by direct action rather than through parliamentary representation, and the ruling classes had learnt a lesson that they would not forget.[76] *Villeinage* declined during the remainder of the late Middle Ages in England and some orders in society, prosperous peasants, the bourgeoisie and minor gentry, played a greater part in political life. The institutions of local government in the towns, the expanding duties of the office of Justice of the Peace and the Lower House in Parliament offered such opportunities. The Black Death and the social unrest that culminated in 1381 arguably played an important part in bringing about these changes in England. In France the Hundred Years War and the princes' campaigns for personal aggrandisement did not promote a politically active minor nobility and bourgeoisie.

Political and religious factors

None of the causes of popular uprisings discussed above disappeared in the fifteenth century: the plague recurred throughout Europe with gruesome regularity, harvests failed, taxes were perceived to be excessive and their gatherers to be corrupt, and conflicts in the towns centred on inter-craft rivalry and the disaffection of poorer citizens. Yet religion and politics became more central to many of the rebellions. The great *Hussite* movement in Bohemia changed the premises on which many revolts had previously been based, and the abortive uprising of the *Lollard* Sir John Oldcastle, in England, attempted to achieve the same result. National loyalties were another element in the Hussite movement and these can also be discerned in the Welsh rebellion, in the support given to Owain Glyn Dwr (see Chapter 3). Other risings in England, Flanders and France seem to have been primarily motivated by political considerations.

The Hussite and Lollard movements are discussed in more detail in Chapter 5, and the focus here is on the aspect of popular unrest that characterised them both. John Wyclif was an Oxford don whose ideas later formed part of the reform agenda of the Lollards. At the same time that he was writing, in the third quarter of the fourteenth century, preachers such as John Ball and visionaries such as the author of *Piers Plowman* were drawing similar conclusions about the need to purify the Church. The Revolt of 1381 probably occurred too early to have been influenced by Lollardy, yet the programme of the rebels included radical reform of Church property holdings. Wyclif kept himself aloof from lawless agitation but his scholarly followers were to preach defiance of the existing order and Lollardy was to be linked with sedition by its opponents until the time of the Protestant Reformation. Margaret Aston and Anne Hudson have shown that there was an appetite for Lollard literature, especially for vernacular bibles and sermons, amongst townsfolk and the gentry in the fifteenth century.[77] Yet it was usually humble people who were prosecuted and even burnt from time to time for their heretical beliefs. The Oldcastle Rising of 1415 was not really a popular revolt as it was led by a knight and was poorly supported. The importance, however, of an undercurrent of disaffection with orthodox religion in England should not be discounted: by the middle of the following century a substantial proportion of all orders of society were prepared to embrace Protestantism.

In Bohemia and Moravia a radical programme of religious and social reform was successfully introduced and maintained by the *Taborites* (see Chapter 5) for several decades. The way had been prepared by the inflammatory sermons of preachers like John of Zeliv and by popular songs that such ideas inspired:

> Had the masters been really wise, they would have counselled God to arrange things thus: that the poor should never eat nor drink, that they should go naked, that they should sleep neither by day nor night, but work constantly for the lords, and constantly pay them dues. The lords, counselled by the priests, would become harder still and would command that still more should be paid to them. When they can no longer obtain payments, they turn the poor man's body into a beast of burden and subject him to forced labour, which was never instituted by God nor by any valid authority. Such is the torment of the poor in all countries and especially of the Czech, thanks to the arrogant clergy.[78]

The Taborites were mostly led by priests and knights and, eventually, had to compromise with their king to achieve peace and stability. Yet there can be no doubt that the movement drew its strength from the great support it enjoyed from the common people. There is some debate over the degree to which it was nationalist, a Czech and Moravian reaction against the German population and the predominantly German character of the Empire. This was certainly an important motivation for many, but it also answered the genuine dissatisfaction that was felt with the hierarchy of the Church, and offered a means of escaping the constraints of feudal economic and social relationships.

In France there was no comparable interest in reforming the Church in the early fifteenth century. This may largely be accounted for by the distressing consequences of the Hundred Years War, which were compounded by the weakness of the monarchy and the conflicts between the royal princes of the houses of Burgundy and Orleans (supporters of the latter were called *Armagnacs*). The interests of the common people, especially in Paris and other towns and cities, were involved in these disputes. The duke of Burgundy, John the Fearless, used the people of Paris against the *Armagnacs*: Guenée has shown him to be 'a truly modern prince who understood the importance of public opinion and manipulated it'.[79] The *Cabochins* (as the rebels were called, after their leader Simon Caboche) became increasingly violent in 1413, pressing demands for administrative reform, and the alarmed duke distanced himself from them.

The weakness of the monarchy and the depredations of the English caused continuing disorder that culminated in another uprising in 1418 led by Capeluche, the public executioner. Bronislaw Geremek has investigated these disturbances to discover what part was played by the very poorest and lowest orders of society: vagabonds, criminals and paupers.[80] The war had caused an influx of unskilled people into Paris who could not fit into the hierarchical structure of the trade guilds and had difficulty in finding employment. These 'marginal people' seem to have taken a leading role in looting and massacring prisoners who were believed to be *Armagnacs*. Again the duke of Burgundy saw matters getting out of control and managed to persuade many of the rioters to go to Montlhéry to beseige the *Armagnacs*. In their absence, Capeluche, whose office made him both revered and abhorred by the people, was seized and executed together with other ringleaders. The duke and citizens of Paris, rather than the 'marginal people', had retained the initiative and eventually restored order. Further studies would probably show that their role in the French disturbances was typical of the part they played in other European uprisings. Her energies consumed by the war with the English, France did not experience serious popular disorder again until the following century.

England had its share of politically motivated revolts in the fifteenth century, provoked, in the first instance, by the dubious legality of the change of dynasty. Simon Walker has observed that this generated an atmosphere of social unrest that led to many specious claims that Richard II was still alive.[81] The deposed king was not a very promising figurehead for rebellion as he had been neither popular nor charismatic during his reign. People probably perpetuated the myth of his survival more as a means of protesting against the control that the new king was attempting to exert over their lives than out of loyalty to the memory of Richard. In the early years of his reign, Henry IV felt obliged to extend the definition of treason (to include treason by words) to counter the rumours, but became more relaxed about them as the security of his dynasty seemed assured. Clerics and humble people were involved in most of the charges of spreading such rumours that are recorded but the actual rebellions were led by nobles.

Towards the end of the Hundred Years War, in 1450, Jack Cade's Rebellion erupted in Kent and other areas of southern, eastern and western England. It was partly provoked by disgust at the loss of the French territories. The identity of the leader is uncertain although Isobel Harvey suggests that he may have been a Sussex yeoman who had been forced to flee the country two years earlier for some kind of criminal activity.[82] In early June the rebels followed the same programme that had been initially successful in 1381, by marching to London. There was a difference, however: the king and Parliament were absent in Leicester. The hapless citizens of London had to deal both with the commissioners sent by the king and their armed retinues and with the demands of the rebels for supplies, so they strengthened the City's fortifications.

King Henry VI came to London but did not speak directly with the rebels, who presented at least three petitions. The first dealt extensively with the economic grievances of Kent as well as making more general demands, for example, that Henry should be advised by lords of the royal blood rather than by 'persons of lower nature'.[83] He sent a delegation of lords and prelates to the rebels on 16 June and it was probably then that they received the third of the three petitions. It addressed issues that the ruling classes would have believed to be beyond the competence of humble folk, and gave tacit approval to the recent murder of the duke of Suffolk and support to the duke of York, who was estranged from the king (see Chapter 3):

> desireth the captain of the said commons the welfare of our sovereign lord the king and all his true lords spiritual and temporal. Desiring of our said sovereign lord and of all the true lords of his council he to take in all his domains that he may reign like a king royal according as he is born our true christian king anointed, and who so will say the contrary we all will live and die in the same quarrel as his true liege men.
>
> Item, desireth the said captain that he will avoid all the false progeny and affinity of the duke of Suffolk, the which been openly known, and they to be punished after the custom and law of this land. And to take about his person the true lords of his royal blood of his realm, that is to say the high and mighty prince the duke of York, late exiled from our sovereign lord's presence by the motion and stirring of the traitors and false disposed the duke of Suffolk and his affinity, and the mighty princes and dukes of Exeter, Buckingham and Norfolk and all the earls and barons of this land, and then shall he be the richest king christian.
>
> Item, desireth the said captain and commons punishment upon the false traitors the which contrived and imagined the death of the high and mighty excellent prince, the duke of Gloucester.[84]

These demands were, unsurprisingly, not granted and the rebels dispersed for a few days when they were threatened by a royal army. The depredations made by some of the king's retainers in Kent and some kind of internal mutiny amongst his nobles and servants led him to retreat to Kenilworth, and encouraged the rebels to return to their London encampment on Blackheath, probably on 29 June. The basis for their demands seems to have been a longer version of the petition presented to the royal delegation in the middle of the month. At the same time, risings occurred in Wiltshire, where William Aiscough, bishop of Salisbury, was murdered, and in Colchester. On 3 July, Cade and his followers managed to enter London: there was a good deal of looting and extortion over the next few days and two royal servants, some of their followers and a few others were killed. Between 5 and 6 July, Cade and his men fought a vicious battle with the Londoners, who managed to prevent him from re-entering the City from Southwark. The archbishops of Canterbury and York brokered an agreement by which the rebels would return home with general pardons. Most did so but Cade, rightly distrusting the efficacy of any pardon for himself, fell back on Kent with his booty and a small fighting force. On 12 July he was apprehended and mortally wounded in Sussex. His dead body was taken to London where it was beheaded, and quarters were sent to centres of the rebellion as an awful warning. Other leaders found that their pardons were ineffective and were severely punished, but many of the obscure thousands who had participated in some way in the risings got away with fines or no penalties.

Harvey concludes that a social group below the nobility and gentry, the people who counted in village life, found a voice in Cade's rebellion of 1450.[85] Their leader may well have been an ex-soldier and much of the discontent was certainly caused by the loss of the lands in France, but the petitions addressed both local and national issues. Most of the looting and killing (which was on a small scale apart from the battle on 5 to 6 July) that took place in London and elsewhere was specifically directed against unpopular royal servants with deplorable records of abusing their positions for private gain. There even seems to have been some sympathy for the rebel cause within the royal entourage for the petitions were inherently conservative. No radical changes comparable to the programmes of the Taborites in Bohemia were requested. What was really wanted was a return to the sound governance of the days of Edward III and Henry V. During the remainder of the century the English Commons were to support the causes of the various factions that fought in the Wars of the Roses. They were usually motivated either by loyalty to a local magnate or by a search for stable governance but it was the lords and gentry rather than the lower echelons of the political nation who made the running.

After the end of the Hundred Years War and for the remainder of the century the French were not involved in serious internal popular revolts. The monarchy had emerged from the war with its prestige and power enhanced and the people were generally contented with the peace and relative prosperity brought by the royal victory. It was otherwise in the Low Countries: the people of Ghent were expressing the widespread disgust felt at their count's desertion of the English alliance in favour of France when they revolted in 1452–3. Philip of Burgundy had recently demanded a salt tax but this immediate cause was probably less important than the resentment felt at his desire to reduce local privileges. The rest of Flanders withheld its support from Ghent and the city was crippled by a massive fine. Thirty years later, after the death of Charles the Bold in 1477, it had its revenge by exacting substantial privileges from Mary his daughter, the new duchess. In 1482, after her sudden death, Ghent rose again together with other Flemish towns and parts of the Low Countries, such as Brabant, against Mary's widower, Maximilian of Austria. The issues were again the enjoyment of local privileges but also the question of who should have custody of young Philip the Fair, the son of Mary and Maximilian, the new duke of Burgundy. After several years of sporadic fighting they were forced in 1492 to submit to the loss of some of their privileges. The absorption of the Low Countries as a satellite of the Habsburg Empire put an end to their aspirations for political semi-independence until the issue of religion revived them during the following century. The Habsburgs and other princes only exercised a precarious control over their German towns and the great mass of peasantry. Yet it was not until the 1520s that they were to rise up against princely authority, stirred by the dissolution of religious certainties and the challenge this posed to the existing social order.

CONCLUSION

Christopher Dyer's contention, mentioned at the beginning of this chapter, that a town was recognised as such not by its size but by the bustle on its streets and 'its feel, sounds and smell' is in many ways very persuasive. The more sophisticated but also more fragile economy of north-west Europe in our period allowed some towns to prosper while others suffered various levels of decline. None would have grown, or escaped dramatic falls in population, if they had not had a steady flow of immigrants from the countryside, something which presupposes the existence of a strong 'pull' factor in the eyes of contemporaries. Much attention has been focused on the idea of a general depression in the fifteenth century, reaching its peak probably in the 1450s and early 1460s. This has been linked to the idea of a 'bullion famine' or, to use modern terminology, severe deflation. The explanations for this decline in economic activity have focused on extraneous factors like the prevalence of war, the policies of princes and the genuine shortage of precious metals caused by the exhaustion of mines. These probably had some effect on the margins or for brief periods. We can cite here the disastrous effects of the Bullion Ordinance on the wool trade between England and Burgundy. Much more important may have been the general imbalance of trade between Europe and the East.

Although the application of the terminology of modern business studies to late medieval history may at times seem bizarre, Hunt and Murray do make some useful points. For example, it is valuable to be reminded that economic life in our period was not characterised by stagnation but by volatility, requiring frequent adaptation in order for a town or an individual to be successful.[86] It is also important not to overlook the existence of credit instruments and the beginnings of banking despite the attention focused on the role of bullion. The Celys may have settled their accounts in cash but at the same time in Antwerp the first steps were being taken towards the founding of the Bourse, a true capital market and a driving force behind the expansion of European trade in the early sixteenth century. It is notable that Antwerp based its rise to pre-eminence as a trading centre on the 'old' trade in textiles. It was, however, able to combine that in the new century with the great success of its role as the distributor of Eastern products for the Portuguese, after they had opened the Cape route to the Indies.

By the end of our period the possibility of towns escaping from the authority of the prince to become independent city states was no longer a realistic prospect. At the same time the political and economic importance of towns and cities within states had probably increased. In London the greatest peers and bishops had town houses; it was essential for them to have easy access to the machinery of government at Westminster and the financial resources of London itself. Feeding and supplying the other needs of a large city could stimulate agriculture and other trades and crafts over a wide area. Spufford has shown how the demands of the Parisian market dominated the economy of most of northern France.[87] Against these benefits rulers had to balance the inherent potential for revolt when a large and volatile population, many only surviving with difficulty, were gathered together in one place.

A number of social, economic, natural and religious reasons for popular revolts have been suggested above. Some, such as the disinclination to pay high taxes or the quest for civic freedoms, had long been at issue between rulers and ruled. The conclusions of Philippa Maddern's study of *Violence and Social Order* in early fifteenth-century England can be applied throughout Northern Europe to explain how rulers and their officials successfully used moderate violence or just the threat of it to stabilise society.[88] They could normally deal with what were essentially revolts against local grievances. The radical programme of the *Taborites* in Bohemia and Moravia and the demands of the English rebels in 1381 and 1450, however, moved their whole agenda into a revolutionary context. But whilst the former, at least temporarily, constructed a new social order, the latter were searching for a means to restore good governance through existing institutions. Due weight should also be given to Guenée's explanation of popular unrest, mentioned in the Introduction to this chapter: sometimes situations that had been tolerated just became intolerable for no rational reason. When discussing the turmoil that arose in France during the strife between Burgundians and *Armagnacs* he ascribed it to 'hatred, unforgiving hatred, inveterate hatred, mortal hatred which cut the realm in two'.[89]

Part II
Sovereignty and Warfare

3

Princes: Ideal and Reality

INTRODUCTION: THEMES AND SOURCES

So far we have discussed both rural and urban society in northern Europe and looked at the economic conditions that supported it. This chapter concentrates on those who ruled Britain, France, Burgundy and the Empire: kings, princes, nobles, knights, gentry, their administration and the assemblies which could voice the grievances and aspirations of politically conscious subjects in those states. 'Sovereignty', the right to exercise supreme power, was claimed by the kings of Scotland, England (the latter also ruled Wales and parts of Ireland), France and the king of the Romans. This last title was given to the ruler of the Empire when he was elected; he only gained the title 'Emperor' if and when he was crowned by the Pope. All the cities, bishoprics and princely states in the Empire were subject to the Emperor but in practice they could often act independently. The dukes of Burgundy technically owed allegiance to the king of France and to the Emperor for different parts of their lands but their power and wealth led them to behave as if they enjoyed full sovereignty.

From the early fourteenth century to 1417 the Papacy (including some schismatic popes) was often resident in its small enclave of Avignon in Provence. When it returned to Rome it remained an important factor in affairs throughout Europe. Its organisation as a kind of princely state, its central role in the religious life of Christendom, and the crises that rocked it, will be discussed in Chapter 5. The late Middle Ages saw a fundamental change in papal power: in previous centuries popes had claimed, with varying degrees of success, to be the worldly (temporal) as well as the spiritual superiors to the princes of Europe. This claim was progressively eroded by the growing powers of the secular states, and by the Great Schism of 1378 to 1417 and the Conciliar Movement. The princes of Europe seemed to support the Pope in Rome, or in Avignon, for reasons of political expediency rather than from religious conviction and they exacted concessions from the Papacy when it was at its weakest.[1] The subsequent attempt permanently to limit papal powers by a series of General Councils of the Church failed but it was another symptom of a decline in spiritual authority.

During our period the princes in France, England, Scotland, Burgundy and Germany increased their control of justice, taxation, and appointments to high ecclesiastical office and were often advised by assemblies that represented the upper orders of society. By 1500 the nobility and great prelates of the Church were seldom able to defy their princes, except for the greater German secular rulers, since the powers they had enjoyed in the heyday of feudalism had declined. As was the case with the princes themselves, the powers and expectations of the nobility varied considerably in the constituent parts of northern Europe. The princes had established that their sovereignty was limited only by the laws and customs of their lands. These lands, as in the case of mainland Scotland, might represent a fairly coherent nation state. Others, such as the areas ruled by the duke of Burgundy or the Emperor, included a number of different and even mutually hostile nationalities. This led to problems that had been less apparent when the universal authority of the Papacy offered at least a psychological protection to minorities. The modern nation state, which some would claim was a phenomenon of the Renaissance and the sixteenth century onwards, was already emerging by the fourteenth century. Jean Philippe Genet has shown that it was equipped with a political language in the following century, supplied by lawyers, humanists and poets to ensure that the aims of good government could be properly articulated.[2]

The first part of this chapter addresses a topic that has attracted a considerable amount of interest in recent decades: the ideal of good princely conduct. This involved not just a simple desire that rulers should respect the highest standards of Christian morality. Unless they were prepared to conform (at least outwardly) to those standards their power and prestige would be undermined and they might even be deposed. Some of the ablest writers of the time were anxious to offer their rulers treatises containing good advice as to how they should govern. Initially these 'mirrors for princes' adhered to the conventional view of the virtues that a good ruler should possess. During the horrors of the Hundred Years War, the Bohemian Hussite rebellion and the English Wars of the Roses, however, the tone and content of political poems, manifestos and treatises became far more pragmatic. The sources for these ideas are plentiful in western Europe since scholarly works were prized, held in libraries for later generations and later published by modern historians. The ideas of writers in the eastern parts of the Empire are not so readily available although some recent work on them has been done in English, French and German. For centuries the pamphlets, songs and poems that often expressed popular political ideas were not valued and their survival has been largely fortuitous.

The second part of this chapter discusses the various dynasties that ruled during the period and analyses the bases for their power: the essential link between the successful exercise of princely authority and the support it enjoyed from the leaders of society will be emphasised. An increasingly important means by which that support was expressed or withheld was the formal bodies of nobles, clergy and rich commoners that could be convened by the princes. In addition to royal councils, there were parliaments in the British Isles and assemblies (or *Estates*) in France and the Empire. During the 150 years that are considered, there were signs that the countries were adopting more of the characteristics of modern nation states. The chapter ends with an assessment of how the ideal of kingship interacted with reality during the later Middle Ages.

The area of northern Europe to be discussed, with its princes, nobles and assemblies, comprises the British Isles, France, the Empire, Burgundy and the Swiss Confederation (which came into existence during our period). With the exception of the Empire, where the Emperor was elected, and the republican Swiss

Confederation, succession in all these states was normally determined by primogeniture: the heir should be the eldest son of the previous prince. Problems arose if a prince had no sons, or if they were minors or proved incompetent. When a male line failed, should the right of succession then go to the nearest male relative through the female line or, if not, how should it be determined? French writers developed the *Salic Law*, which, they claimed, enshrined the practice that women could neither inherit kingdoms nor pass on the right of inheritance to their male heirs. These questions were to cause a great deal of bloodshed in the fourteenth and fifteenth centuries.

The sources for information on the government of the countries vary widely in their quantity and quality. Despite the French Revolution when they were deliberately destroyed between 1789 and 1794, the records of central government in France are extensive. By the fifteenth century it was an administrative policy to make copies, summaries and reports, which has been a godsend to historians. English and, to a lesser extent, Scots records are also generally good although much detailed work still needs to be done on legal archives. The dissolution of the Burgundian principality and its subsequent merging into France and the Empire, and later, the emergence of Holland and Belgium, makes the task of tracing its records challenging but not impossible. The many changes and traumas suffered by the Empire and its constituent parts make the survival of legal and administrative records very patchy. Such records are well supplemented in all parts of northern Europe by both local and general chronicles. These were increasingly kept by lay people, often townsmen, as well as by monks. They are most useful when more objective forms of evidence – legal, fiscal and administrative – are available, since no one had told medieval writers that they were meant to be impartial.

(i) MIRRORS FOR PRINCES: THE IDEAL OF KINGSHIP

If anyone had asked them what they expected of their prince, most people in the late Middle Ages would probably have replied that he should defend their lives and property and support the Catholic Church against heretics and infidels. Today, when states tax their citizens by up to 50 per cent or more of their incomes, and many religions and much unbelief flourish, only the first purpose of government is immediately recognisable. Princes and their subjects agreed that the institution of monarchy had a sacred origin and this was traced back to the Old Testament of the Bible, in which God instructed his prophet to anoint Saul and then David as kings of Israel. The words of Jesus Christ, 'render unto Caesar the things that are Caesar's', could also be interpreted as a sanction for monarchy.

Monarchs in the Middle Ages were presented allegorically as wielding a sword and a sceptre. The sword was to bring swift retribution to enemies, traitors and malefactors within their country and to adversaries abroad. The sceptre signified the other royal duty: to give impartial justice tempered with mercy. Most coronation ceremonies included an oath in which the king swore to uphold the Catholic Church and the rule of law in his realm (see Illustration 5). The French kings,

5 The coronation of Charles VI of France in 1380 in the cathedral of Notre Dame, Rheims

The king is crowned by two prelates, one of them the archbishop of Rheims, and surrounded by the peers of France, older knights and young men (facing him) who have just been knighted for example, first promised to protect the bishops and their churches and then, turning to the laity swore:

> Also, that I shall forbid all rapacities and all iniquities of all degrees;
> Also, that I shall enjoin justice and mercy in all judgements in order that a clement and merciful God may grant his mercy to me and to you;
> Also, that in good faith to all men I shall be diligent to expel from my land and also from the jurisdiction subject to me all heretics designated by the Church.[3]

These promises were not empty clichés for we should not be misled by the great deference paid to princes, nobles and prelates, into thinking that it was acceptable for them to threaten the 'common good' (a phrase often used in Britain and France by the fifteenth century to describe the protection of peoples' rights) by unreasonable behaviour. Richard II of England (see Section (ii) below) probably came the closest to claiming that he could ignore the laws and customs of his kingdom, and he was deposed.

By the later fourteenth century all orders of society and especially the clergy, lawyers, educated merchants, bailiffs, knights and nobles recognised standards by which they could judge royal conduct. These were to be found in the scriptures, the writings of the fathers of the Church and the many learned commentaries on them that had been produced since antiquity. Until the late Middle Ages these were almost entirely the preserve of educated clerics: the same people who administered the king's government. The complex arguments of the *scholastics* (highly educated churchmen who preserved the traditions of Christian learning) were beyond the comprehension of most of the laity. So a series of handbooks or 'mirrors for princes' ('prince' is used in this context to mean any kind of ruler) were produced by clerics, from the thirteenth century, to mediate this wisdom and make it accessible. Much of the material on which these 'mirrors' drew had recently been made available by a flurry of translating activity. During the thirteenth century many of the treatises of ancient authorities, notably of the Greek philosopher Aristotle, were rendered into Latin for the first time. Some academics were suspicious of these texts, fearing their pagan origins, but the great intellect of St Thomas Aquinas and the industry of his followers demonstrated that their ideas could be subordinated to the service of Christian ethics.

Some of the 'mirrors' were translations of ancient texts or amalgamations of the wisdom of antiquity with more recent learning from the Islamic kingdoms of the Arab world and from Jewish scholarship. The most widely used book of the latter kind was the anonymous *Secret of Secrets* (*Secreta Secretorum*), which purported to have been sent by Aristotle to Alexander the Great. It was a mixture of practical advice, for example, about behaving in a dignified manner and eating sensibly, and magical formulae, such as how to make an amulet which would give the owner superhuman powers. There was also a section on physiognomy: how a prince might tell the characters of those he encountered, from their features. Books of this kind were not the exclusive property of kings and princes: wills, inventories and inscriptions in manuscripts show that they were owned by a variety of people.

Giles of Rome (Egidio Colonna), a renowned bishop and *scholastic* philosopher, presented the most influential handbook of all to Philip IV the Fair of

France. *The Government of Princes* (*De Regimine Principum*, *c.*1277–9) drew on ancient wisdom, especially on Aristotle's *Ethics* and *Politics*, but its structure and argument were the creation of Giles. The three sections into which the work was subdivided dealt respectively with the government of oneself, one's household and one's city or realm. Again, despite the fact that the text presupposed a princely reader, many others owned and cited this book. The first part of Giles's book concentrated on the qualities that a good prince should possess: Christian writers called them the four 'cardinal virtues'. A sense of justice, courage (fortitude), prudence and temperance, and other lesser virtues such as magnanimity (generosity of spirit), were thought to be particularly princely. In Section (ii) below, the careers of a number of late medieval princes are examined and it will be suggested that the most successful were those who displayed at least some of these qualities. This leads to the question of whether they deliberately behaved in such a manner to impress their subjects and fellow monarchs or whether they were genuinely devout individuals who were simply obeying the precepts of their Christian consciences. This is a question that has recently been discussed by Peter Lewis in relation to political ideas in France.[4]

One explanation for the fact that some princes did seem to exemplify the virtues recommended in the 'mirrors' lies in the strong hold that conventional Catholic beliefs had upon them and upon most of their subjects. Even rulers who were powerful enough to exercise their will, unconstrained by the advice of their ministers or councils or by the wishes of assemblies of their subjects, believed that one day they would have to answer to God for their conduct. Quentin Skinner has proposed another reason why most princes tried to rule according to the accepted precepts of morality.[5] A prince who failed to observe the precepts that constituted the 'normative vocabulary' of good political conduct would be diminished in the eyes of his subjects. In some cases, and these will be discussed below, princes were rendered ineffective or even deposed because they failed to observe the code of conduct which was expected of them.

The manner in which a prince chose his servants and advisers, his treatment of his family and the way in which he governed his realm, the subjects of the second and third parts of Giles's *The Government of Princes*, also showed how far he possessed royal virtues. Wisdom and honesty were the qualities he should look for in his ministers, and flatterers were to be avoided. He should ensure that his wife, children and servants were given every opportunity to live good lives. Aristotle had defined the three main forms of government in his *Politics*: monarchy, aristocracy and democracy. By the last he did not mean 'one person, one vote' but the rule of citizens; men of foreign origin, slaves and women were excluded. Giles adopted these definitions of government and also those of their perverted forms: tyranny, oligarchy and anarchy. He came down firmly in favour of monarchy, as would be expected of an adviser to the kings of France, but this did not mean that monarchs could act as they pleased.

Apart from the constraints of the coronation oaths that princes made to God, writers on politics in the late Middle Ages agreed that the divine law imposed further limitations on their freedom of action. Nothing could be done which violated the natural law, which was itself a reflection of the divine law as it operated on earth. A mother, for example, could never lawfully marry her own son even if the Pope gave her a dispensation to do so. Any king who colluded in violations of the natural law was a tyrant and if he persisted in such wickedness, theologians such as St Thomas Aquinas claimed, he could be deposed. So if he was bound to observe the laws and customs of his realm and the divine law, what powers were left to the prince? He could make new laws and later change or abolish them and, in practice, he often controlled the judges and other lawyers who interpreted the laws and customs of the past. It was also generally accepted that in special circumstances some parts of the divine law could be set aside. It was forbidden to kill, for example, but the prince was allowed to order the execution of criminals or to send his soldiers into battle.

By the end of the fourteenth century a combination of greater economic freedom, wider literacy and challenges to the authority of religion was to introduce new, more pragmatic strands into the advice which was offered to princes. Members of the laity joined the clerics who had traditionally done so, whilst popular songs and poems, which were invariably anonymous on account of their inflammatory contents, contained ideas about the government of princes. The latter were frequently connected with great popular upheavals such as the Peasants' Revolt of 1381 in England and the Hussite movement a few decades later in Bohemia (see below, Chapter 5).

Members of the laity might feel impelled to advise their princes for other reasons, for example, Philippe de Mézières in his *Dream of the Old Pilgrim* (1389), exhorted Charles VI to make peace with England and to reconquer the Holy Land. Later he addressed a letter pleading for peace to Richard II of England. Christine de Pizan, the loyal servant and admirer of Charles V, probably felt that his son was in danger of falling short of the high standards of the previous reign. She presented her *Life of Charles V* (1404) to Charles VI and also composed *The Body of Policy* (*c.*1407) for his son the dauphin. The latter work followed a literary tradition in treating the state as a human body in which all the parts had to act well to achieve stability. The king was the head, the nobles and knights the upper torso, and the Third Estate (Commons) the stomach, legs and feet.[6] But Christine also contributed to what is described as 'the French Renaissance of the fifteenth century': it was characterised by a new openness to early humanism, based on the better knowledge of classical texts that was developing in Italy, and a willingness to explore new arguments. She wrote frankly, for example, about the injustices suffered by the Third Estate:

> rich people and great office holders of the king and princes who could well bear the cost [of taxes] are exempted and the poor who receive no income from the king have to pay.[7]

In about 1470 George Ashby, a minor English civil servant, dedicated his poem *The Active Policy of a Prince* to Edward of Lancaster, the son of Henry VI and Margaret of Anjou. It was divided into discussion of the past, present and future and was mostly dependent on traditional ancient, Arabic and scholastic books of advice. Yet Ashby also clearly wished the prince to avoid the mistakes of his incompetent father and urged him:

> There was never yet fall / of high estate,
> But it was for vices / or negligence,
> Were he never so high / or elevate,
> Without he would attend well by prudence
> To his charge / avoiding from his presence,
> Men vicious / and namely covetous;
> Where they abide they destroy every house.[8]

Sir John Fortescue had also served the house of Lancaster as Lord Chief Justice of the Court of King's Bench and he acted as their Chancellor in exile during the 1460s. He had received plenty of opportunities to observe the weaknesses that had plagued the government of Henry VI. In about 1470 he also wrote a handbook for Edward of Lancaster to introduce him to the common law, *In Praise of the Laws of England*. He feared that the prince would be seduced by the authoritarian laws and social structure of France, where he was exiled, and fail to understand the nature of the country he would one day rule. Fortescue developed his theory about the superiority of the English polity in his *Governance of England*, which he probably presented to the Yorkist king Edward IV, in the 1470s (after he had been pardoned for his Lancastrian past). He praised the political and regal form of government in England that meant that the king did not impose extra taxes on his people except by the consent of Parliament. He also urged the king to rule with the consent of a wise, well-paid council, which would only serve him: the previous reign had been bedevilled by over-powerful, greedy nobles and royal servants. Fortescue compared the limited rule of the English kings very favourably with the authoritarian French government and social structure. Not only were the English more contented as a result of the country's prosperity, they were also braver than the French.

In Burgundy two treatises on good government, written in the late 1430s, were addressed to Duke Philip the Good; their authors were probably members of the noble house of Lannoy. The duke was urged to make peace with England, live economically, avoid demands for heavy taxation and rule with the advice of a council of wise men. In 1468 the Chapter of the Knights of the Golden Fleece (an institution similar to the Order of the Garter in England) showed signs that they were apprehensive of the overweening ambition and desire for mastery displayed by the new duke, Charles the Bold. They advised him to be temperate and just in his dealings and to consider the interests of his subjects before committing them to more wars. The same cautionary note was struck by the historian Georges Chastellain, who prayed:

> God . . . confirm your rule on your throne without any unrest in the kingdom. Do not be like Rheoboam [an Old Testament king] in whose hands all was scattered and destroyed through turmoil.[9]

Traditional advice literature in Bohemia stressed the Christian virtues of St Wenceslas, an early medieval king; later the chivalric ideal of a warrior monarch was also adopted. The Emperor Charles IV seemed to embody all the attributes of a good prince and he left his son Wenceslas a *Mirror for Princes* (*c.*1377), which he hoped would recommend these virtues to him. When he succeeded, the young king proved to be lazy, self-indulgent, lacking in martial skills and prone to favour followers drawn from the lesser nobility and bourgeoisie, who were thought to encourage his bad traits through their flattery. The *New Advice*, probably written in the late 1370s by Smil Flaska of Pardubice, the nephew of Archbishop Arnost (see Section (ii) below), attempted to rectify those faults. Cast in the guise of a bestiary it depicted a young lion king who was advised by noble animals, such as an eagle and a swan, to avoid the influence of evil creatures, for example, a fox and an owl. These came from the forest (Wenceslas spent much time there hunting and drinking) and wished by their flattery and servility to encourage his bad habits for their own profit.[10]

Medieval writers on politics did not concern themselves exclusively with the rule of princes; the conflicts between the Papacy and the Empire, which often involved the Italian city states, generated some republican literature. 'Republican' in this context did not mean a form of government that necessarily excluded princely authority. Rather, writers envisaged a polity in which the interests of citizens were paramount irrespective of who might claim sovereignty over them. Marsiglio of Padua was teaching at the University of Paris when he wrote *The Defender of the Peace* (1324), which supported the Emperor against the aspirations of the Papacy to hold supreme temporal power. He claimed that the functions of lay government should be exercised by the highest civil authority, not by the Popes. Theoretically the Emperor could claim sovereignty over large parts of northern Italy but, in practice, the ideas of Marsilio legitimised the independent rule of the city states.

The influence of Marsilio, and other writers who supported some form of popular sovereignty, on secular polities was to be limited but they made an important contribution to the ideas which underpinned the Conciliar Movement within the Catholic Church (Chapter 5). The Swiss Confederation was the only state that had a republican form of government in northern Europe during our period: even the strong cities of Germany and the Low Countries recognised the sovereignty of the Emperor although they chafed against it. The Swiss had gradually secured their independence and a distinctive government structure by a long and difficult series of wars and pragmatic decisions but it is unlikely that the outcome was much influenced by the ideas of writers on politics.

The second part of this chapter looks at the careers of princes, their families and their interaction with the nobility and other major property owners in the states of north-western Europe during the late Middle Ages. The success or failure of individual rulers will be shown to be due, to a considerable extent, to the way in which they were viewed by their subjects. Those flourished who seemed to possess the traditional virtues of courage, prudence and temperance, who in their dispensation of justice observed the laws and customs of their land and who conquered or outwitted external enemies. Princes who were defeated by their adversaries or who appeared to disregard the 'common good' were either deposed during their lifetimes or have been condemned by posterity.

(ii) THE EXERCISE OF SOVEREIGNTY

Scotland

The kingdom of Scotland defended its independent status throughout this period despite the attempts of various English kings to subjugate it. The Lowlands shared a common language with England, and some institutions, such as Parliament, were similar to those south of the Border, but many Highlanders still spoke only Gaelic. In political terms, Scotland had more in common with the Empire or France, since it lacked the centralising processes of government which had been set up by the Anglo-Norman kings of England. The northern parts of the kingdom and the islands were fairly inaccessible; in the west and the islands the principal power was the Lord of the Isles. He was, on occasions, prepared to make separate agreements with foreign powers and exercised many of the rights and functions of a king:

> the great Macdonald, ruler of the Western Highlands, was installed in a ceremony which imitated the ancient installation of the kings of Dalriada [Gaelic kingdoms in Scotland and Ireland]. The new lord, clad in white, put his foot in the hallowed footstep in the special square stone, and received a white rod and a sword to symbolize power and protection. At least one bishop, and if possible two bishops and seven priests, attended, as well as all the leading chieftains under him. Mass was said, the new ruler was blessed, gifts were given to monks and bards, and everyone feasted for a week.[11]

The problem of powerful lords who ignored royal authority and pursued their own interests regardless of the realm as a whole has been portrayed as particularly acute in Scotland at this time. Jennifer Brown has put forward a different view: Scots kings, although lacking the administrative machinery of larger states, possessed great residual powers. She points out that 'a weak nobility was of little use to a king'; particularly a king who relied on the co-operation of his most powerful subjects, to rule.[12] It was still considered imperative for a king to be personally involved in the leadership of his army and in the dispensation of justice. The army, however, would be composed entirely of the retinues of the magnates, with no question of payment involved. This did place power in noble hands but it was power they held at the royal pleasure, as the fate of the Douglas family in 1455 was to demonstrate (see below). Even the lay judges (who were not necessarily professional lawyers) in the court of session, which was established in the fifteenth century, the first Scottish central court, served 'of their own benevolence', that is, voluntarily.[13]

For those of lesser degree it was almost essential to have the support of a lord who offered effective protection; to be numbered among his 'kin, friends, allies partakers, tenants, servants and dependants'. The 'kin' included all those related in the male line, often expressed as all those who shared the same surname. The 'friends' were men of equal rank linked by written bonds of friendship. The 'allies partakers' were men of lesser rank who had sworn a bond of 'manrent', as the Scottish phrase went: it imposed an obligation of lifelong or even hereditary personal service to the lord. The last three categories were tenants and members of the household, whose loyalty to their lord is easier to understand. In some ways this is similar to the patronage systems to be found in other realms, particularly England, but it does have particular features such as the emphasis on the overwhelming importance of the 'kin' group. Often no direct material incentives were involved; the bond was one of mutual advantage. Kinship groups often had the responsibility of bringing wrongdoers to justice and of finding ways to resolve the feuds which could otherwise destroy the peace of a whole area. When the balance between royal authority and a magnate's local power was correct all would be well.

King Robert I, 'the Bruce', had confirmed Scotland's independence from England by his victory at the Battle of Bannockburn in 1314 and initiated its emergence as a nation state. In the subsequent Treaty of Northampton of 1328 he was recognised as king of Scotland. By 1346, however, his son David II was in captivity in England following his disastrous defeat at Neville's Cross, near Durham. The wrangling over the precise size of the enormous ransom that would secure his release went on for another seven years and it was only settled when France too was defeated at Poitiers. The French invariably supported the Scots during the Hundred Years War, a policy that came to be known as the 'auld alliance' and which continued until the mid-sixteenth century. Writing of the earl of Mar's visit to Paris in 1408, the chronicler Andrew of Wyntoun smugly commented on the noble's preferential treatment compared with that given to the earl of Warwick:

> The Duke of Burgundy then in France
> Took him in special acquaintance.
> In Paris he before him found
> The Earl of Warwick of England,
> That there was treated honestly [decently]
> As a stranger; but specially
> This Earl of Mar was treated there
> As a household familiar
> Special to the King of France.[14]

David returned to in 1357 to a country that had been governed in his absence by his nephew and heir, Robert the Steward. After a thorough audit of royal resources, large amounts of revenue had been raised to pay off the English ransom demand and this put the king in a strong position for he was in control of a good income that he continued to collect after he was liberated. Parliament was generally complacent, falling in with the policies of the most powerful in the land. Unlike the English body it was only composed of one chamber and the landowners, clerics and burgesses who sat in it were mainly concerned to preserve the peace and safeguard their property. Disputes about aspects of the treaty with England meant that by no means all of the ransom money was eventually paid. It had been set at 100,000 marks – £66,666 – and was to be paid in ten yearly instalments; these were guaranteed by a number of noble Scots hostages who were sent to England.

Ranald Nicholson believes that, despite his long exile and the financial burden of the ransom, David II ruled Scotland well and safeguarded its independence.[15]

One unforeseen by-product of the ransom taxation, however, was the deteriorating relationship between the Lowlands and the Highlands. The chieftains and the Lord of the Isles had been lightly governed by the laid-back Steward and were more resentful of the new taxes than the Lowlanders. David was childless and he was succeeded in 1371 by his nephew, the Steward, who became Robert II (see p. xx, 'The Rulers of Scotland'). He had several children and they all needed lands, titles and marriages suitable for members of the royal house and this was to lay up trouble for the new Stewart dynasty. The conflicts between various noble families, their attempts to gain influence over the monarchy, and the growing antagonism between Lowlanders and 'wild, wicked Highland-men' were to plague political life for the next two centuries.[16]

Robert II has been portrayed as a weak, easy-going man who, as he aged, showed little inclination to rule, although Alexander Grant has suggested that the uneventfulness of his reign proves that he was an effective monarch.[17] Robert's second son, another Robert, later duke of Albany, became Guardian (or Lieutenant-General, or Governor) of Scotland, exercising authority on behalf of the king and this was resented by the king's eldest grandson, David, later duke of Rothesay. The situation deteriorated further on the king's death in 1390 and the succession of his lame son, Robert III. He equalled his father in poor health and lack of vigour: the *Chronicle of Moray*, for example, recorded the disorder created by Alexander, earl of Buchan, 'the Wolf of Badenoch':

> There was no law in Scotland but whoever was the stronger oppressed the weak and the whole kingdom was one den of thieves. Murder, plundering, burning and other crimes were unpunished and justice was exiled from the kingdom.[18]

Robert III tried to placate the Guardian and his own son David by making them both dukes but this did nothing to end their feud. In a violent encounter in 1402 Rothesay fell into the hands of Albany, where he died in suspicious circumstances. This escalation of violence was to involve the royal family in all manner of mayhem in the future. The king feared that Albany would destroy his next son, James, too, so he decided in 1406 to send the twelve-year-old to the safety of France.

The boy was intercepted on the sea by the English, who kept him in custody for the next eighteen years. He soon became titular king of Scotland as his fragile father was said to have died of shock at the news of his capture, but t. The country was actually ruled by the duke of Albany, who was in no hurry to secure the release of James I. Lawlessness and corruption are often said to have characterised that time, as Albany worked primarily to secure his own family's interests. Grant, however, believes that it was to his credit that his was 'one of the least eventful regencies in Scottish or English history'.[19] After his death, followed closely in 1422 by the death of Henry V of England, the prospects for the release of James I improved. Three years later he was allowed to return to Scotland after marrying Joan, the niece of Cardinal Beaufort (great-uncle to Henry VI and strongly influential in the minority government), and promising to pay £40,000 to cover his 'living expenses' while he was detained in England. Grant describes this phase in Anglo-Scottish relations as one of 'Renaissance diplomacy'.[20]

The simple confrontational model was replaced during the reigns of James I, II and III by a 'complex quadrille' involving Scotland, England, France and Burgundy, and there was a readiness to deal with more remote powers in Italy, Spain and Scandinavia. This was eventually to culminate in the establishment of peaceful relations between England and Scotland when they both experienced a Protestant reformation in the mid-sixteenth century.

Once he had been crowned at Scone, James I took stern measures against the lawlessness and corruption that he claimed had flourished under Albany: 'throughout all the realm I will make the key keep the castle and the bracken bush the cow.'[21] He disposed of the leading members of the Albany family on trumped up charges and used their confiscated estates to supplement his meagre revenue. Most of the rest of the nobility submitted to him, although he only achieved partial success in the Highlands. The downfall of James I was associated with his resumption of war with England in 1436, when he was soundly defeated. This destroyed his reputation for invincibility and the following year he was murdered by some disaffected nobles, although they were not representative of general opinion and were hunted down and executed.

Despite the achievements of his father, the minority of James II proved as lawless and faction-ridden as had previous reigns when the king had been weak or in captivity. Three centres of power and influence emerged: the Douglas family (called the 'Black' Douglases), the Livingstons, who amassed considerable wealth as they occupied key posts in the administration, and James Kennedy, bishop of St Andrews. By 1449 the king was prepared to make independent decisions: in taking Mary, the daughter of the duke of Guelders, as his wife, and by the foreign marriages of four of his sisters, he firmly allied Scotland to the pro-French, anti-British powers of Europe. He then turned on the Livingstons, executing two and forfeiting much of the family's property. In 1452 he invited the 8th earl of Douglas to dinner and murdered him – Parliament promptly exonerated the king from all possible blame. Three years later a rising by the surviving Douglases and their supporters gave James the excuse to execute those he caught, and the rest, including the 9th earl, fled into exile. The lands that fell to the Crown through the destruction of the 'Black' Douglases could be used to attract the loyalty of other nobles and chieftains. Their demise of the Douglases saw the end of the great families that had dominated politics in the fourteenth and early fifteenth century, although other noble dynasties such as the Campbells and the Gordons would eventually take their place.

Bishop Kennedy had survived the king's resentment against those who had exploited his minority, and he came into his own in 1460. James II, an enthusiast for modern technology, was killed by an exploding cannon during the siege of the English-held castle of Roxburgh. Another minority ensued since James III was only eight years old and the government divided into factions. One was led by his mother, Mary of Guelders, the other included Kennedy; but both died before the king became of age. By 1469 James was ready to emulate his father and grandfather and exercise his sovereignty effectively. He married Margaret of Denmark who, as part of the settlement, brought Orkney and Shetland under Scottish rule. The Boyd family, who had dominated the government in the late 1460s, then fell victims to a process described by Nicholson:

> the cyclical pattern during the reigns of most of the Scottish monarchs of the fifteenth and sixteenth centuries – a royal minority, or its equivalent . . . was followed by an attack led by the king upon those who had hitherto ruled in his name.[22]

James III was not so martially minded as his immediate predecessors, loving music, the arts and fine jewellery. He was predisposed to keep the peace with England and spent much futile energy in trying to marry his young son to a daughter of Edward IV. He had inherited his forebears' distrust of the nobility and this led him to surround himself with obscurely born courtiers or 'familiars', although Norman MacDougall has suggested that this tendency was exaggerated by later writers.[23] He also undermined the Lord of the Isles and accused his own brothers of treason; one was killed, and the other, the duke of Albany, fled to France. These vigorous measures were not, however, accompanied by a capacity to enforce general law and order.

In 1482 the nobility rose against James III; he became a virtual prisoner and Albany returned. The rebels found (as Warwick and the duke of Clarence had discovered in similar circumstances in England twelve years earlier) that it was difficult for others to exercise sovereignty if the king was still alive and present in his realm. By the following year the king had re-asserted his authority and Albany fled to England. The succession of a Tudor, Henry VII, who replaced Richard III (a formidable leader of Border skirmishes), brought a peace-loving monarch to the English throne who shared the wish of James to continue friendly relations. Yet the king could not, despite all his precautions, ensure peace within Scotland. Hostilities were exacerbated by the mutual distrust between the Highlands and the Lowlands and his own son was drawn into a noble faction, which again wished to deprive him of power. James III was killed at the battle of Sauchieburn in 1488 and his son, another minor, succeeded as James IV.

James soon proclaimed that he would rule in his own right and set about reconstructing the authority his father had struggled to maintain. He assembled a new circle of familiars and finally destroyed the power of the Macdonalds as Lords of the Isles. His victory was largely due to his superior navy and particularly to the guns that were mounted on his ships. In Renaissance states, where princely authority was being enhanced, it was normally only rulers who had the resources to deploy such expensive and complicated weapons and they also needed to exact higher taxes to pay for them. Yet James only achieved royal mastery of the Highlands by entrusting their rule to two other potentially troublesome families: the Campbells and the Gordons. This bears out the general point made by Norman MacDougall about an underfunded, de-centralised state such as Scotland:

> there was no question of the crown having the wealth to pay judges or lawyers, or even give proper remuneration to important officials such as wardens of the marches. The answer . . . was delegation of authority to responsible magnates who alone could represent central government effectively in the localities.[24]

The marriage of James IV to Margaret, the elder daughter of Henry VII, in 1502 would belatedly fulfil the aspirations of James III and ensure that peace with England was maintained. It was also eventually to make the kings of Scotland the heirs to England, Wales and Ireland. Despite the vicious feuding and chronic shortage of revenue which had characterised the rule of the kings of Scotland, in capable hands the monarchy could profit from the new opportunities offered by the mastery of Renaissance learning and technology. James II in particular, despite his premature death, grasped the essential qualities required for effective rule: a ruthless determination to be obeyed and the need to amass sufficient wealth to be able to govern. He ensured that even his most draconian deeds had some shreds of legality attached to them and the people, through Parliament, were prepared to accept them as justified even by the ethical standards set by the 'mirrors for princes': painfully Scotland was emerging as a nation state.

England, Wales and Ireland

The kingdom of England differed from other north-western European countries in the late Middle Ages because its political and legal institutions had developed and become centralised to a unique degree: two of the characteristics of a state as opposed to a realm. Anglo-Saxon England had been conquered and subjugated in the late eleventh and twelfth centuries by a vigorous and able dynasty of Normans. It was then ruled by the French Plantagenets, who grafted civil laws (derived from the ancient Roman Empire) and administrative practices onto existing native customs. These included the right of the nobility to be consulted as a formal body when major new taxes were to be raised and for freemen only to be arrested and tried when good cause could be shown.

By the middle of the fourteenth century the English legal system could exercise a high degree of control over the population. The central courts of Chancery, King's Bench and Common Pleas met in the Palace of Westminster and the highest judges in the land, the Lord Chancellor and the two Lord Chief Justices, assisted by others, presided over them. They dispensed the common law: a mixture of custom, statutes and Roman law, a system based on precedent, which had been developed over the centuries. The general eyre, a formal annual visit by the king's justices to each region, had largely been replaced by commissions of the peace. Special commissions of *oyer et terminer* (to hear and decide), composed of king's justices, nobles and local dignitaries, were still sent out in troubled times from the central courts to ensure that the king's law was observed. Justices also held assizes (court sessions to deal with the most important cases) in county towns at least once a year. But by 1350 the enforcement of the criminal law at local level was largely in the hands of the commissions of the peace. This was formalised eleven years later by the passage of a statute that gave them power to try 'all manner of felonies and trespasses'. These commissions, one for each county with six and then eight justices, including prominent members of the local gentry, usually supported by lawyers or nobles, met once a quarter to deal with civil and criminal cases. Gradually petty offences that had traditionally been dealt with by lords in their manor courts passed to these justices of the peace. They also had to enforce the Statute of Labourers: in 1371, for example, there were 192 breaches in Kesteven, Lincolnshire. Amongst those indicted were a fisherman who had sold herrings at six for 1d instead of eight for 1d, the controlled price, and a roofer who had demanded an excess wage of 4d a day and his dinner. Not all those appointed to commissions of the peace were themselves of good character: Sir Gilbert Denham of Little Wenham, Suffolk, for example, routinely took bribes, intimidated royal officials and was involved in riots. He was not removed from the commission until he was over seventy and even then no action was taken against him. Despite such cases Guenée suggests that by means of the commissions of the peace a dialogue was 'established between king and country which was continued in Parliament and on which English democracy was gradually founded'.[25]

Apart from the rents from its own domains the English Crown derived revenue from various indirect taxes such as Customs dues, *scutage* (payments by knights in lieu of military service) and legal fines. There was also the feudal tradition that subjects should pay aids (taxes) when the king's oldest son was knighted, when his oldest daughter was married, and if he was imprisoned and needed to raise a ransom. As administration became more complex and England was embroiled in a series of costly wars with Scotland, Wales and France, even more revenue was required. From the later years of Henry III in the thirteenth century, the king's practice of consulting leading magnates and clergy when he wished to raise extra taxes had been formalised by the institution of Parliament. It differed from the earlier bodies since non-noble landowners from the shires and burgesses from the larger towns joined the nobles and prelates and formed a separate chamber: the Commons. It has been suggested in Chapter 1 that the Black Death had a major impact on socio-economic relations in northern Europe. In England it produced a less deferential artisan and peasant class; the more articulate members of these orders were conscious of their rights as well as their duties. Merchants, priests and farmers emerged from their ranks with aspirations to participate in the government of the country. A poem written early in the reign of Henry V gives voice to this feeling:

> When all a kingdom gathered is
> In God's law, by one assent,
> For to amend that was amiss
> Therefore is ordained a parliament.
> Truth with glad cheer thither went,
> And falsehood stands ever in dread
> For fear of righteous judgement,
> For to be deemed according to his deed.[26]

Allegiance was due to France for Aquitaine, which Henry II of England had acquired in the middle of the twelfth century by his marriage to its duchess, Eleanor. English monarchs had a lower income than the kings of France and dukes of Burgundy, although they were usually wealthier than the German Emperors and kings of Scotland. The problem in England was that the extra taxation required to conduct war effectively was voted by a parliament composed of property owners who had a vested interest in making it as low as possible. They were then responsible for collecting it and the yield regularly fell well below the estimated revenue. On the other hand, increasing prosperity meant that income from indirect taxes such as Customs dues rose from the second half of the fourteenth century.[27] The relatively centralised nature of the administration and their capacity to work in partnership with the magnates and their retinues made monarchs such as Edward III and Henry V formidable opponents in the Hundred Years War with France. It was from members of their own families that the Plantagenet kings were to experience the greatest threats to their authority.

The English coronation rite, in comparison with the French, laid less emphasis on the divinely appointed role of the monarch. Instead the contractual nature of the oath, which stressed the king's obligation to uphold the laws and customs of his people, was central to the ceremony. He had to agree to four requests:

> Sire, will you grant and keep and by your oath confirm to the people of England the laws and customs granted to them by the ancient kings of England . . . ?
>
> Sire, will you observe to God and Holy Church and to the clergy and people peace and accord in God entirely, according to your power?
>
> Sire, will you cause to be done in all your judgements equal and right justice and discretion in mercy and truth, to your power?
>
> Sire, will you grant to hold and keep the rightful laws and customs that the commonalty of your realm shall choose, and will you defend them and strengthen them, to the honour of God, to your power?[28]

A fifth request, that the king should protect the rights of the Church, was only added in 1485 at the coronation of Henry VII.

Edward III succeeded without question in 1327 despite the fact that his father, Edward II, had been deposed and probably murdered in a nobles' conspiracy led by his own wife, Isabelle of France, and her lover, Mortimer. The Plantagenet dynasty had been shaken by numerous noble factions over the previous two centuries but their sovereignty had, if anything, become stronger as the institutions of government had developed. During his long reign Edward III enjoyed the effective support of his sons, most notably the Prince of Wales Edward, 'the Black Prince', and John of Gaunt, duke of Lancaster. The king also benefited from the allegiance of members of the old nobility, such as the earls of Warwick and Arundel, and newly created earls. Chris Given-Wilson points out that the king avoided arousing enmity between the old and new peers by promoting well-born and worthy knights and by endowing them with lands, by marriage and grants, in ways that did not impoverish other nobles.[29]

During this time the old feudal ties of lords to vassals were being replaced by a system of patronage in which lesser nobles, knights and gentry would look to one of their superiors to be their 'good lord'. This meant that the patron would speak for his clients, perhaps even to the king, and support their claims for land and positions. In return he would expect their loyalty and even armed assistance: they were known as his 'affinity'. These arrangements could be informal but the greatest lords, men like John of Gaunt or Edward IV's friend Lord Hastings, had large retinues of indentured retainers who were bound by contract to serve them and, in return, expected fees as well as their good will. A nineteenth-century historian called this system 'bastard feudalism' and it has been blamed for much of the unrest in the late middle ages.[30] This is to misunderstand the nature of society in this period: patronage networks could exercise a stabilising influence. Trouble arose not from the existence of the system but in times when it was not controlled by a strong monarch.[31]

A wrangle over the nature of the homage Edward owed to the kings of France for Aquitaine, and the subsequent penalties that were exacted on his French lands, persuaded him to press a claim to the French throne derived from his mother Isabelle (a princess of the house of Capet – see p. xxii, 'The Rulers of England'). During the early years of the ensuing conflict he achieved an encouraging series of victories, the capture of more French territory in the South and, in 1347, Calais. The transfer of some of this land to successful English captains made the war, and the king who led it, popular. In the long term, however, discord arose between Edward and his subjects, caused by factors such as his incapable old age, the illness and eventual death of the Black Prince and the realisation that the financial burden of the wars fell on many who did not benefit from them.

The inheritance of Richard II, the son of the Black Prince, in 1377 was consequently more problematic than the glorious reputation of his grandfather would lead one to expect. Four years after his succession, when he was fourteen years old, he showed fortitude and sound judgement in the way in which he dealt with the rebels during the Peasants' Revolt (see above, Chapter 2). No formal minority had been established at his accession so, as Nigel Saul remarks, it is difficult to be precise about when Richard assumed the full responsibilities of government, which had been initially exercised on his behalf by the royal council.[32] The king's early view of his prerogatives, however, was probably influenced by his success in dealing face-to-face with the rebels. It increased his optimistic faith in the sanctity of monarchy and belief in his own omniscience at a time when increasingly large and influential groups of gentry and merchants were becoming less deferential and aspiring to economic and political power.

Whilst Richard II has frequently been condemned as one of England's least successful kings, viewed from a European perspective he achieved peace, prosperity and cultural distinction. He had been born in Bordeaux in his father's duchy of Aquitaine and had a more cosmopolitan outlook than was usual in English princes: it was further promoted by his first wife, Anne of Bohemia, daughter of Charles IV, the Holy Roman Emperor. Charles had established a magnificent court at Prague and patronised many French and Czech artists both to celebrate the glory of his dynasty and to stress that it was inseparable from devotion to Christianity. His policy was intensely appealing to Richard, who also became a patron of art. The significance of the design of the Wilton Diptych (a small painting of the Virgin and child, Richard II, saints and angels, intended to stand on an altar) has recently been discussed in the context of representations of majesty.[33] Richard had commissioned a painting of his own image endowed with all the trappings of monarchical splendour, receiving the sanction of Heaven.

By 1388 a powerful section of the nobility, the Lords Appellant (so-called because they 'appealed' or prosecuted the king's friends), supported by their allies in the 'Merciless Parliament', had threatened Richard's exalted view of his status. They executed or disgraced his closest advisers and restricted his power to act independently. Yet it was extremely difficult permanently to constrain the sovereignty of a ruling monarch. During the next few years, by a combination of appeasement and ruthlessness, Richard managed to recover the use of all his prerogatives. He confirmed his renewed authority in 1394–5 by a vigorous campaign to subdue Ireland to obedience.

The Plantagenet kings had claimed to be overlords of Ireland since the twelfth century but had only enjoyed limited success in exercising their sovereignty. The position of Dublin, close to a port on the eastern coast, made it feasible for them to dominate the immediate area that surrounded it. That was also where the Parliament met but its influence was extremely limited. Beyond 'the Pale' (as it came to be called) the kings were dependent to a large extent on the good will of the Irish nobility. Some were of English origin (such as the earls of Desmond, Ormond and Kildare) and had been rewarded for their service by Henry II with lands; others were native Irish chieftains. Until the middle years of the reign of Edward III the Dublin *justiciars* (the chief representatives of the king) had successfully managed the colony by a series of alliances with both nobles and chieftains. This stability was progressively undermined by the absenteeism of many of the major English landowners and by the generally poor calibre of royal officials appointed during the later years of the century. An appeal for aid against the lawlessness of the colony had been made to Edward III from the council of Kilkenny as early as 1360 but little had been done. Ireland had formerly been a profitable source of income for the English Crown but, by Richard's reign, it was proving expensive to administer.

Richard II made a bad start in developing his Irish policy when he appointed his favourite, Robert de Vere, earl of Oxford, to be marquis of Dublin with lordship over the whole of Ireland. This was counterproductive as it alienated both the English and Irish magnates, de Vere had no power base from which to operate, he could only acquire lands by conquering them and this he was quite unfitted to do. He fell victim to the Lords Appellant in 1388 and Ireland was left in limbo. In 1394, soon after the death of his first wife, Richard crossed to Ireland at the head of a well-equipped army, which was strengthened by a household contingent of 4,000 to 5,000 men. He received the submission of many of the chieftains since they hoped that he would protect them from the depredations of the English landowners. The following year the king returned to England leaving the young earl of March as his lieutenant, but there were still many outstanding disputes over land to be settled and the situation soon deteriorated.

Richard's apparent success in Ireland probably enhanced his belief in his God-given status as king, in his military capacities and his infallible judgement. His rule became more arbitrary and his personal behaviour more unreasonable. He distanced himself from the nobility, including his royal uncles, and increasingly relied on his household men, especially on his archers from Cheshire (their leader was allowed to address this most formal of kings as 'Dykun').[34] Richard persecuted the former Lords Appellant including his uncle, the duke of Gloucester, who was murdered on the king's orders whilst he was in custody on a charge of treason. The Parliament of September 1397, which colluded in these actions, was composed of a large proportion of new, inexperienced MPs and managed by loyal followers of the king. Richard's marriage to Anne of Bohemia had been childless and his cousin Roger Mortimer, earl of March, and John of Gaunt, duke of Lancaster, his oldest surviving uncle, were his closest heirs. In 1396 Richard took Isabelle, the seven-year-old daughter of Charles VI of France, as his bride, setting aside the view of many nobles, gentlemen and merchants that the war should continue to protect English conquests. Despite Richard's peace policy, however, England continued to support the Roman popes in the Great Schism, principally because France was loyal to those based in Avignon. The marriage consolidated his policy but meant that any possibility of a direct heir being born was postponed for several years: a dangerous situation when his subjects were becoming increasingly restive under his harsh rule.

In 1399 Richard mounted another expedition to Ireland hoping to build on his earlier success to bring permanent order to its government. Before his departure from England he had seized the enormous estate of the recently deceased John of Gaunt. This arbitrary act, which disinherited Gaunt's son Henry Bolingbroke, duke of Hereford (known as Henry of Lancaster), alarmed the nobility for it seemed to undermine the security of their tenure of property. Lancaster had been exiled the previous year after a dispute with another lord and there was a perception that his punishment was unjust. When he returned to England in the summer of 1399 many people were sympathetic towards him. There has been much debate as to his intentions: initially he proclaimed that he was coming to recover his inheritance yet it soon appeared that the king was unpopular, and he claimed the Crown as well. Richard on his return from Ireland seems to have been unprepared for the seriousness of the situation, few magnates were ready to fight for him and he soon fell into Lancaster's hands. It is impossible to know what proportion of the population wanted him to be deposed; decisions were taken by a small group of nobles who remembered that it had been impossible to control the king after the crisis of 1388.

The disparity between how the king viewed his role and what many of his subjects thought of him by 1399 is demonstrated by an extract from the poem *Richard the Redeless* [Ill-advised]. The author wished to advise the king:

> to know him better,
> and to move him away from misrule,
> his mind to refresh,
> for to praise the prince
> that paradise made,
> to fulfil him with faith, and fortune above.[35]

Richard was eventually prevailed upon to renounce the crown, was kept in close confinement and died mysteriously, probably murdered, early in the following year. Saul graphically described the gap between the aspirations of Richard II and his capacities as king:

> in the theatre of medieval monarchy there was no keener actor than Richard. His tragedy was that he mistook the illusion of the stage for the reality of the world around him.[36]

The speeches delivered by Henry IV, as Lancaster had now become, to his first Parliament contrast the fantasies of his predecessor with his own practical grasp of what his subjects expected of him and of the language in which to communicate with them:

> In the name of the Father, Son and Holy Ghost, I, Henry of Lancaster, challenge this realm of England and the crown with all its members and appurtenances, as I am descended by right line of the blood coming from the good lord king Henry III, and through that right that God by his grace has sent me, with the help of my kindred and my friends to recover it; the which realm was on the point of being undone for default of governance and undoing of good laws . . . it is not my will that any man should think that by way of conquest I would disinherit any man of his heritage, franchise, or other rights that he ought to have, nor put him out of what he has and has had by the good laws and customs of the realm; except those persons that have been against the good purpose and the common profit of the realm.[37]

Henry IV still faced daunting problems in making good his hold on the kingdom. Richard, before the sudden collapse of his power, had at least been at peace with his neighbours, he enjoyed high revenues and the support of a loyal following of retainers. Nineteenth-century historians believed that the new house of Lancaster depended on a parliamentary support in 1399 for its legitimacy, leading them to conclude that the role given to Parliament in determining the succession enhanced its importance and laid the foundations for the development of a constitutional monarchy. The body was not strictly a parliament since it met between the fall of Richard and the coronation of Henry but it was perceived to hold parliamentary authority. In more recent times the interpretation has been questioned: Parliament's role has been described as essentially reactive, giving retrospective sanction to changes in the succession.[38] This rejection of the idea that an initial consensus existed in favour of the new king also explains the many difficulties he was to encounter in the early years of his reign.

King Henry had to struggle with internal and external enemies who were swift to exploit the dubious nature of his claim to the throne. Edmund Wright has described the crisis of 1406–7, when Parliament expostulated against his demands for high taxation and demanded that tight controls should be exercised over expenditure.[39] This seems to have coincided with a breakdown in the king's health, for the subsequent measures that were taken to redress the situation were initiated by the council. The origins of these financial problems can be traced to the high cost of the royal household, and the depredations made by the French on the English lands in France. Then there was the expense of suppressing the Percies' (the earl of Northumberland and his son 'Harry Hotspur') rebellion against what, they claimed, was the usurpation of Henry IV, and another noble rebellion in which Archbishop Scrope of York was implicated. There were also the £20,000 worth of pensions that Henry was obliged to pay out each year to enlist support for his regime, and the cost of the Welsh campaigns to quell the revolt of Owain Glyn Dwr (Glendower).

Wales had never experienced a unified government either under its native princes and chieftains or under Plantagenet rule, divided as the country was into North and South by ranges of hills and mountains. When Edward I finally subjugated the country (much of which was already dominated by Anglo-Norman marcher lords) his armies penetrated along the river valleys which ran from west to east. He then built a series of great coastal castles, such as Beaumaris and Harlech, which could be supplied from the sea. The common people of Wales were probably treated no differently by their own lords than by their English equivalents, but they were expected to pay large amounts to the largely absentee landowners: these amounted to about £60,000 per annum before the Black Death. The native gentry had lost some of their lands to the invaders and were often treated with contempt, as second-class citizens, by the English. They were needed at local level, however, to ensure the administration of justice and the collection of revenue. Extensive marcher lands belonged to the Crown, both to the King and to the Prince of Wales. Edward of Caernarvon (later Edward II) had been given the principality by Edward I as part of a policy to tie it more closely to England. There seems to have been no particular reason for the revolt to break out when it did apart from the impact of the recent, violent change of monarch in England.

In the summer of 1400 a squire, Owain Glyn Dwr, proclaimed that he was the true prince of Wales as he was descended from three ancient Welsh dynasties. Geoffrey Hodges has suggested that the timing of the revolt was associated with the Lancastrian 'usurpation' in England: Henry of Monmouth (later Henry V) had no legitimate claim to the principality, so this was a war of succession like the Hundred Years War in France.[40] Conversely it could be claimed that Glyn Dwr was an opportunist taking advantage of English dynastic preoccupations. During the next few years, largely because the Lancastrians were tied down elsewhere by English revolts and French attacks, Owain was successful and attracted many of the Welsh to his cause. He established a base in the north-west, called several parliaments, forged links with English rebels and made a treaty with France; in many areas tenants stopped paying rents to their marcher lords. Owain's plan to make a Celtic alliance is recorded by the chronicler Adam of Usk, in a letter he sent as early as 1401 to the king of Scotland and the Irish chieftains:

> Cadwallader ... was the last crowned king of my people ... from whom I, your simple cousin, am descended in direct line; after whose decease, I and my ancestors and all my said people have been, and are still, under the tyranny and bondage of mine and your mortal enemies, the Saxons. ... And from this tyranny and bondage the prophecy saith that I shall be delivered by the help and succour of your royal majesty.[41]

After a few years, when events had favoured the rebels, prince Henry based himself on the borders of Wales and he and his lieutenants started the slow process of bringing the principality back to obedience.

As part of its reaction to the revolt, the English Parliament had passed a series of statutes and ordinances prohibiting Welshmen from occupying many administrative and legal posts. These measures were renewed several times during the following decades. They were largely disregarded as the English simply could not govern Wales without the co-operation of the leaders of the indigenous population, yet the laws tended to reinforce the perception that they were second-class citizens. Owain failed in the end because of superior English military strength and because many of the Welsh decided that their English lords could better guarantee their safety and the security of their property. In the long term, however, the revolt changed the future for Wales: R. R. Davies has identified a 'crisis of lordship' when the tenants of the marcher lords refused to pay their rents. In many areas they were not held at previous levels or even paid at all after the revolt finished, and seigneurial authority would never be the same.[42] Owain had also voiced the aspiration to achieve 'an independent Wales governed by its own native, legitimate ruler', which would remain as part of the Welsh psyche to the present day.

Despite the great difficulties of his reign, Henry IV possessed an asset denied to his predecessor – four sons: Henry, Prince of Wales, Thomas duke of Clarence (who was killed in France whilst still a young man), John, and Humphrey, who were later to be made dukes of Bedford and Gloucester. The existence of a vigorous young heir may have seemed a mixed blessing to the ailing king. There were rumours concerning the wildness of Prince Harry and he was certainly perceived as an alternative source of power and patronage during his father's lifetime, but at least it ensured a smooth succession in 1413. Gerald Harriss suggests that from the beginning of his short reign Henry V used his sovereignty strongly yet fairly to avoid the problems experienced by previous kings. In his relations with his magnates the faction caused by Richard II's partisan rule was terminated and 'confidence in the right exercise of royal authority was reborn'.[43] The king had bonded with some members of the nobility, such as the earls of Warwick and Arundel, during his campaigns in the Welsh marches in his father's reign. He gradually restored the lands and titles of the noble families that had opposed the Lancastrian succession, rewarding proven loyalty and good service.

Henry's most spectacular achievement was the renewal of war with France because this enabled his nobility and gentry to work off their aggression abroad and fulfil their ambitions by acquiring land in the newly conquered territories. In 1417, two years after his victory at Agincourt, he undertook the conquest of Normandy. The king was, however, careful not to alienate the resident French population: if they were prepared to swear oaths of fealty to him their lives and property were protected. The *Norman Rolls* record the enormous volume of administrative, commercial and military business controlled by this industrious king and his officials. Here is an extract from 1420 when he was based in Normandy:

> March 21, Rouen, Mandate to all captains and other officers not to detain the vessels 'Le Marie' of Wrangle, and 'Le Trinite', of London, laden with iron.
>
> Mandate to William Bourghchier, captain of Eu, to exact fealty from Thomas, Abbot of the Convent of S. Mary of Eu.
>
> March 27, Evreux, Commission to Henry, bishop of Chichester, William Phelip, and Roger Waltham, to array the men of Thomas Duke of Clarence.
>
> The same to Henry Fitz Hugh and Philip Morgan to array the men of Humphrey Duke of Gloucester and William Earl of Suffolk.
>
> Mandate to John Golafre to receive the homage of Louis de Breville knight.
>
> April 6, Vernon, Mandate to John Assheton, bailiff of Cotentin, to receive the homage of Isabel de Brully, widow of William de Gesthebert.
>
> April 10, Vernon, Mandate to the bailiffs of Rouen, Caen, Cotentin, Alençon, Evreux, Caux, and Gisors to make proclamation forbidding any soldier or other person, in the castles, towns and garrisons within their bailiwicks to take provisions, or horses, without payment for the same.[44]

Henry V was fortunate as well as efficient: the quarrel between Philip the Good, duke of Burgundy, and Charles, the Dauphin, over the murder of Philip's father threw England and Burgundy into each other's arms. That circumstance, together with Henry's military victories, was the origin of the extraordinary Treaty of Troyes, in 1420, which delivered the crown of France to him on the death of Charles VI. It also gave him a wife – Katherine, the king's daughter, and she duly presented him with a son. It would be this infant rather than his vigorous father who would be crowned 'king of France', and the successes of Henry V left an inheritance that would ultimately contribute to the downfall of his dynasty: 'It was the very grandeur of his aims which proved fatal for Lancastrian kingship and for the good governance which had become its justification'.[45]

Henry died of battlefield dysentry in France in 1422, leaving behind him a stable and united realm and a formidable reputation as a strong and victorious king, which even the most able successor would have found it hard to equal. The government of the infant Henry VI, king of England and France and Lord of Ireland, was conducted by his council, led by the Protector, his uncle Humphrey of Gloucester. The parts of France, including Paris, which were occupied by the English were ruled by Henry's other surviving uncle, John of Bedford, as Regent. He was advised by a separate council that he wisely ensured was mainly composed of Frenchmen. He was an able leader who inspired the same kind of confidence in his followers as the late king had done and his marriage to Anne, a Burgundian princess, confirmed the alliance that had made the Treaty of Troyes possible (see Illustration 6).

There were many difficulties to surmount for the cost of defending so much territory beyond the sea was enormous, especially as Bedford conquered new areas: yet the French lands had been intended to be self-financing. Considerable numbers of nobles, gentry and even yeomen had been given land and property in France and some had settled there, but from the 1430s the English Parliament had to find most of the money to defend them. Humphrey of Gloucester was a proud, ambitious man, at odds with other members of the council, especially Cardinal Beaufort, the enormously wealthy bishop of Winchester. He was the head of the family that John of Gaunt had fathered by a mistress: after the death of his second wife, Constance of Castile, they had married and their offspring were declared legitimate by Parliament but excluded from succession to the throne. Humphrey's ill-advised dabbling in the Low Countries, in an attempt to secure himself a power base by marrying the duchess of Hainault, threatened to alienate the duke of Burgundy, thus endangering the stability of the situation in France.

While Bedford lived, and the council governed on behalf of the young king, English political society remained reasonably stable. A great deal of discussion has taken place in recent decades about the interaction of royal, noble and gentry power and what bearing this might have had on the great crisis which afflicted the monarchy in the middle years of the fifteenth century.[46] It has been suggested in the first part of this chapter that it was important for the public actions of princes to conform to the ethical standards expected of them by clergy and laity alike. The career of Richard II demonstrates how quickly a king who was perceived to be acting in an arbitrary, unjust fashion could fall from an

6 Anne, Duchess of Bedford, at prayer before St Anne, her daughter the Virgin Mary and the infant Jesus

Anne was the sister of Philip, duke of Burgundy, and her marriage to John, duke of Bedford, consolidated the alliance between England and Burgundy. This Book of Hours was produced in Paris between 1422 and 1430.

apparently powerful position. Some would argue that Charles VII of France was only able to extend his authority beyond the kingdom of Bourges when his claim to be the rightful ruler of France seemed to be vindicated by heaven via Joan of Arc in 1429 (see below). To a lesser extent society had the same expectations of nobles, gentry and clergy. The strongest states were those where the leaders of society, from the king downwards, seemed to conform to traditional, Christian patterns of good behaviour, observe lawful customs and dispense good justice.

The death of Bedford in 1435, closely followed by a peace treaty between France and Burgundy at the Congress of Arras, marked a decline in English fortunes. As Henry VI grew older it became clear that he had inherited none of his father's martial qualities or ruthless good judgement: a pious disposition and great generosity to those who served him were inadequate to deal with the growing crisis. Despite his good intentions, Ralph Griffiths has shown that his childhood dependence on advisers continued into adulthood and that he lacked the discrimination to choose them well.[47]

Two factions within the royal council had alternative remedies for settling the French problem. Humphrey of Gloucester wanted to wage war vigorously, Cardinal Beaufort and the king's most powerful favourite, the earl of Suffolk, wished to make peace. Their policy prevailed when Henry VI married Margaret of Anjou, daughter of King René, head of a cadet branch of the Valois family. The English suspected that the marriage treaty was accompanied by a secret promise to cede the county of Maine to the French and it was, indeed, surrendered to them in 1448. In the previous year, probably through the machinations of Suffolk, Gloucester had been arrested and died in custody under suspicious circumstances. The French conquests bled away to the alarm of the nobles, gentry and yeomen who had been rewarded with land for their service across the Channel. Aquitaine was also attacked by the forces of Charles VII so effectively that by the early 1450s, of all the French territories, only Calais remained in English hands.

The crisis of confidence in the regime of Henry VI resulted, in 1450, in strong parliamentary censure, the murder of royal advisers including Suffolk, and Jack Cade's revolt. It was a precursor to a troubled decade in which the mantle of opposition to royal policies fell on the shoulders of Henry's cousin and heir, Richard, duke of York. Historians have often characterised York and the nobles and gentry who supported him as self-seeking. More recently writers such as John Watts have argued that their attempts to limit royal power and subject the king to some kind of tutelage were more public spirited, aimed at ensuring peaceful and stable government, the 'common good'. In the mid-1450s two events changed the situation: the king was totally incapacitated for eighteen months by a mental collapse, and his wife bore him a male heir, Edward of Lancaster. The duke of York ruled as Protector during Henry's illness and after the king recovered the duke tried several times to regain the political initiative. Both sides, called respectively 'Yorkists' and 'Lancastrians', were increasingly resorting to the use of armed force – 'the Wars of the Roses' (a term coined by nineteenth-century writers, they are now sometimes called the 'civil wars') had started. York's peaceful attempts to dominate the royal government were always frustrated by the fact that sovereignty was vested in the king and those he chose as advisers.

York's 1460 victory over Henry VI and his supporters at Northampton, won with the help of the earl of Warwick, seems to have convinced him that the only way in which the issue could be resolved was to claim the throne for his own line. When his title to the crown was presented to Parliament it was based on the fact that he was descended from the daughter of the second surviving son of Edward III. Henry VI was the great-grandson of John of Gaunt, the third son of Edward III. There was little taste amongst the politically conscious orders to dethrone the inadequate but pious king. The fact that he had been anointed with holy oil and had received oaths of allegiance from the nobility, including York, was important in an age when the ideals of religion and of fealty were taken seriously. The same compromise which had been concluded with France at Troyes forty years earlier was agreed: Henry would remain king but when he died York, or one of his sons, would succeed. The settlement soon unravelled when York was defeated and killed by the Lancastrians at Wakefield at the end of the year. The eldest son of the dead duke, Edward, earl of March, continued the war and was proclaimed king as Edward IV. His victory at Towton near York in March 1461 confirmed his hold on the kingdom. London was well-disposed towards him as someone capable of restoring order; the support that the Lancastrians were receiving from the Scots was to prove a gift to Yorkist propaganda. Henry VI and Margaret of Anjou had plotted that:

> our said outward enemies in great number shall in all haste to them possible enter into this our realm of England to make in the same such cruel, horrible and mortal war, depopulation, robbery and manslaughter as here before hath not been used among Christian people.[48]

During the next few years the supporters of Henry VI and Margaret of Anjou, who were based in Scotland, made sporadic sorties south of the border where they held a few castles. This only served further to alienate English property owners who had to pay for the costs of defence, and to associate the unpopular French queen with the 'auld alliance' of Scotland and France. Burgundy was well-disposed towards the new Yorkist dynasty and neither Scotland nor France felt it worthwhile to continue to pour money into the Lancastrian attempts to achieve a restoration. By the end of 1463 both countries had made truces with Edward and promised to give no more aid to Lancaster. Henry VI was captured and imprisoned soon afterwards by the Yorkists as he wandered around the north of England while Margaret of Anjou, her son Edward of Lancaster, and a small following went into exile in one of her father's castles in Bar, in eastern France.

For a time it looked as if the new, vigorous young king would put an end to the turmoil of the last decade. Parliament was amenable to the change of dynasty and several prominent Lancastrians, potential leaders of rebellion, had been killed in the conflict. Yet while Henry VI and his son still lived, loyalty to the Yorkists was provisional since sound finance and stable government by men 'of worship' was required to consolidate the dynasty. Edward IV was a highly eligible bachelor, sought after by the princes of Europe as a husband for their sisters, cousins or daughters. Instead he chose in 1464 to marry Elizabeth Woodville, the beautiful widow of a Lancastrian knight. Opinions differ as to how far this served to alienate the king from his most powerful supporter, the earl of Warwick, who had been negotiating for a French bride: Michael Hicks plays down its significance.[49] There were certainly other factors which were distancing them from each other: Warwick's disappointment about the paucity of extra lands and offices he and his family had received as a reward for service, and his alliance with Edward's brother, the duke of Clarence, who was also discontented. The need to provide for the new queen's large and impecunious family by lands, offices, marriages, ennoblement and pensions caused scandal in a society where everyone was thought to have their 'place', and deprived the nobility, including Warwick's family, of potential wealth. The breakdown of Edward IV's authority and the temporary restoration of Henry VI, from October 1470 to April 1471, is described below in the section on France. Had Edward's brother-in-law, Charles the Bold, not supported him he might never have regained his crown. He was also fortunate that his brother Clarence had become disillusioned with his alliance with Warwick and the Lancastrians and was ready to change sides again. Edward also seems to have been a more effective general than Warwick or the group of Lancastrian leaders who faced him at Tewkesbury.

Edward's second reign was more authoritarian than his first: he was well served by his friend the Chamberlain, Lord Hastings, and by his younger brother Richard, duke of Gloucester. Richard married Anne Neville, an heiress of Warwick and the widow of Edward of Lancaster, the son of Henry VI and Margaret of Anjou. He consolidated an extensive property holding in the north of England with the lands she inherited, which gave him great influence in the area. Gloucester, Hastings, the earl of Northumberland and a few other loyal magnates could enforce royal authority over huge stretches of the country. When Edward IV's oldest son, Edward, the Prince of Wales, was old enough to leave his mother, his household was established at Ludlow, a good base for controlling the Welsh marches. From the late nineteenth century some historians saw this as an aspect of a 'New Monarchy'. The authoritarian government of Edward certainly anticipated the early Tudor regime in some respects: the employment of non-noble, professional administrators, careful accounting to conserve income and limit expenditure, all kept directly under the king's control, and the avoidance of dependence on Parliament. Yet Charles Ross in his biography saw novelty rather in the degree of self-interest which the king displayed in promoting the fortunes of his family: the generally proclaimed purpose of medieval monarchs had always been to serve the 'common good'.[50]

The irony was to be that Edward's attempts to shore up the strength of his dynasty by appointing Woodvilles to strategic posts as well as allowing his brother Gloucester and Hastings to retain great power were doomed by these same measures to failure. Gloucester and Hastings both detested the Woodvilles and, when Edward died unexpectedly in 1483, initially co-operated to remove the young Edward V from their custody. This achieved, Gloucester turned on Hastings and had him summarily executed for 'treason'. Edward V and his younger brother were declared illegitimate because their father had been betrothed to another lady before his marriage (the Church regarded betrothal as having the same binding quality as marriage).[51] They disappeared into the Tower and were never seen again. A group of amenable Londoners and nobles proclaimed Gloucester as Richard III and Parliament colluded in the usurpation. Anne

Sutton has made a convincing case for the new king's attempt to rule as a 'good prince'.[52] She cites evidence of his piety and 'good lordship' before he seized the throne, deducing that they were genuine, rather than assumed as has often been alleged. Nothing, however, could erase the shock to contemporaries of his treatment of his nephews – a negation of the trust imposed on him as their uncle and Protector and of all Christian values. The last author of the *Crowland Chronicle* tried to write impartially but several times in his narrative of the reign he presented Richard as inherently immoral and stated that on the eve of the Battle of Bosworth he was plagued with dreams full of ill omens.[53]

Despite his energy and apparent commitment to the ideals of good kingship, Richard was conquered and killed by his cousin Henry Tudor, earl of Richmond, in 1485. The king had certainly lost much public support through his perceived immorality (some thought he intended to marry his own niece, Edward IV's daughter Elizabeth). Colin Richmond suggests that there were other factors at work as well: Henry landed in Britain in early August and Richard had insufficient time to muster his forces for the Battle of Bosworth at the end of the month.[54] Many of the nobility, made wary by decades of civil warfare and the consequent loss of lands and lives, preferred not to fight on either side until they could predict the outcome. Southerners were alienated by the continued favour that Richard showed towards his followers from northern England. The result was that a young man, the grandson of a Welsh squire, who had lived mostly abroad and who claimed the throne through his mother, Margaret Beaufort, a descendant of the originally illegitimate line of John of Gaunt, was proclaimed king as Henry VII.

The new king established his power effectively despite frequent uprisings in his early years. He married Edward IV's daughter Elizabeth, so at least their children would have a respectable claim to the throne. He retained elements of the so-called 'New Monarchy' that had been developed under the Yorkist kings. In particular he kept a very tight control on finance, avoiding unnecessary wars and bringing most receipts and payments into his own chamber. It was a positive advantage to him that he had few close relations, as over-ambitious royal princes had been the bane of previous recent reigns. He was also very economical in making new peerages, preferring to reward royal office holders with gifts and expecting them to enforce his authority in the provinces. Parliament, full of gentry who had deplored the instability of recent decades, gave Henry its support; this enabled him to quell the uprisings against his perceived usurpation that plagued the first fifteen years of his reign.

Ireland was punished for the support it gave to the most dangerous rebel, Perkin Warbeck. Sir Edward Poynings, made Lord Deputy (an office which had replaced that of *justiciar*) in 1494, was responsible for the infamous 'Poynings' Law' which brought the Irish Parliament firmly under the control of the English king and his council. Reforms in taxation were intended to make Ireland self-supporting. These measures brought more orderly, controlled government to the Pale but beyond, English authority was limited. Henry VII recognised this in 1496 when he replaced Poynings as Lord Deputy with the powerful Irish noble Gerald Fitzgerald, the earl of Kildare. The king was a realist and recognised that English control over most of Ireland would remain limited: his main concern was that it should not be used as a base by his enemies.

Another means by which the king increased the security of his dynasty was by an extended use of the system of bonds. These were written guarantees of good behaviour exacted from nobles, gentry and clerics whom Henry had reason to suspect of disloyalty. They either paid, or promised to pay (if found to be culpable), sums of up to £10,000. The threat of such fines, sufficient to ruin many families, usually proved effective in curbing potential dissidents.

The bishops who were appointed by Henry VII tended to be lawyers, able administrators rather than the men of learning who had often been favoured by his predecessors. Yet he was no enemy of scholarship and patronised a number of the writers who praised his regime. The Italian humanist Polydore Vergil rendered great service to Henry's dubious dynasty by writing a favourable account of it in his *History of England*. English, Italian and Scottish poets produced laudatory verses, although not all were prepared to ignore the negative aspects of the court and the system of patronage it fostered. John Skelton wrote an English version of Alain Chartier's condemnation of the French Court, in which those seeking patronage beg Fortune for favour:

> They throng in fast and flocked her about,
> And I with them prayed her to have in mind.
> She promised to us all she would be kind;
> Of Bowge of Court she asked what we would have,
> And we asked favour, and favour she us gave.[55]

Despite his inclination to conserve as much treasure as possible, Henry VII also knew how important it was for a king to be magnificent. His patronage of writers was one aspect of this policy; he also expanded the royal library, commissioned tapestries and pageants and kept companies of minstrels and players.

Queen Elizabeth produced two sons and two daughters; the Prince of Wales was given the unusual royal name of Arthur, which was likely to attract the loyalty of Henry's Welsh subjects.[56] When he died in 1509 Henry VII left behind sound royal finances, a peaceful country where the law could be administered effectively and a nobility who were obliged to accept royal authority. The essential components of a strong, centralised nation state were all present: the issue that was to cause major disruption to the polity during the next century was to be religion.

France and Burgundy

In 1364 Charles V of France was crowned at Reims with ceremonies which emphasised the liturgical aspect of his kingship, making 'overwhelmingly clear the obsessive concern with the divine source of kingship, triumph over enemies and peace'.[57] The house of Valois was a comparatively new royal dynasty, only dating from 1328, and their succession was being hotly contested by Edward III of England (see p. xxiii, 'The Rulers of France and Burgundy'). The father of Charles V, John II, had been captured by Edward's son and heir, Edward the Black Prince, at Poitiers in 1356 and spent most of the remainder of his reign in captivity waiting for the enormous ransom of 3,000,000 gold crowns (£500,000) to be paid. John has attracted generally unfavourable verdicts from historians, who felt that he was unintelligent in the manner in which he waged war against the English. R. Cazelles, however, has given a more positive account: his possession and patronage of books show intellectual interests that had not previously been credited to him. John was also something of an innovator, remaining in Paris for longer periods than had been customary for his predecessors, bringing much needed stability and personal involvement to the administration.[58] The period of John's captivity had been trying for his son Charles, who as Regent had to deal with fractious subjects, resentful of the taxes they had to pay to accumulate the ransom money, and disorderly nobles.

Charles V was to prove much more adroit than his father had been in dealing with the English claims. His coronation sent out an unambiguous signal that he was above and apart from even the most powerful of his subjects (including Edward III, who by feudal law had to pay him homage for Aquitaine). The most important element in this process of distancing the king was his anointment with holy oil from the *ampulla*. This was a flask that was reputed to have been brought down from heaven by an angel or a dove for the baptism of Clovis, king of the Franks, when he was converted to Christianity. Charles V made much of the claim that the touch of an anointed French king could heal scrofula (a nasty deficiency disease). By linking his line with Clovis he could also establish some kind of continuity with the Capet monarchs, who had ruled for centuries before the dynasty ran out of direct male heirs in the early fourteenth century.

The warlike presence of the English in France was only the greatest of the problems that P. S. Lewis has characterised as the 'political crisis in French society'.[59] In addition to English-held Calais and the duchy of Aquitaine, members of the royal family were dukes of Anjou, Berry, Orleans and Burgundy. The duke of Brittany also possessed a large area of territory, and Provence remained a separate county within the kingdom, ruled by the dukes of Anjou. All these magnates owed homage to the king of France but, in practice, there were endless possibilities for them to treat independently with other states and to de-stabilise the French government by their internal disputes. The feud between the dukes of Orleans and Burgundy in the early fifteenth century, for example, was exacerbated by attempts to get their own clients appointed to posts in the service of the Crown. Since its purchase in 1344 the heir to the throne was always given the Dauphiné, hence his title of 'dauphin'; so this area, in addition to their ancestral lands in Normandy and the Ile de France around Paris, was directly under the control of the Valois.

In the fourteenth century the great semi-independent duchies had their own law courts (the *parlements* were usually the highest) where a mixture of local custom and Roman law determined their decisions. As the duchies were brought under the French Crown during the following century the *parlement* of Paris claimed supreme jurisdiction, but the provincial courts continued to flourish. A great deal of the task of governing France was still left to the *seigneurs* or lords. Many had powers to administer not only 'low' justice relating to petty offences but also 'high' justice dealing with what would be felonies in England, cases only to be heard in royal courts. The very greatest nobles, the princes of the blood and families such as the counts of Foix, operated in their *apanages* (large areas of territory where they had extensive jurisdiction) an administrative system that in many respects mirrored that of the Crown but was independent of it. An enormously wealthy prince like John, duke of Berry, had the *baillages* (administrative areas) of Berry, Auvergne, the Montagnes d'Auvergne and the county of Poitou as his *apanage*. To serve him he had twenty-one chamberlains, more than twenty *valets de chambre* (squires) and other household servants as well as a chancery, a *Chambre des Comptes* and a corps of lawyers and local officials. The elegant and expensive lifestyle depicted in the illuminations of the *Très Riches Heures* (Very Fine Hours), made at his request, reflects no more than the reality (see Illustration 7).

Did the employment of many *seigneurs* in the roles mentioned above increase royal control? 'Yes' and 'No'. The system of the sale of offices that was to become so important a feature of political life in the sixteenth and seventeenth centuries had already started. In 1413 the Cabochian ordinance listed the office holders 'who are accustomed to sell . . . their offices and in this way abandon them to other people and to take a profit from the transaction' (see above, Chapter 2).[60] Like subsequent measures the ordinance did little to halt the abuses: the revenue raised by sales was too important to the Crown and its servants even if they did lose control of parts of the administration.

Tension between the centre and the regions may be discerned in the case of the assemblies or *Estates* but, in this instance, it was the monarchy that preferred to divide and rule. The areas that had been governed directly by the French Crown for centuries did not have the right to hold these assemblies. The regions, such as Dauphiné, which had been recently united with France were more likely to have their own Estates. Although they could present their grievances and ask for reform, their principal function was to vote extra taxes when they were needed. They were composed of the three orders or 'estates' of society: the nobility, the clergy and the third estate (prosperous merchants and lawyers were its representatives). It was easier to persuade the smaller, weaker Estates such as Provence or Picardy to comply with the royal will than if they were combined into a national *Estates General*. When one met in 1484, during the minority of Charles VIII (when the monarchy was unusually vulnerable), it was critical of the ruthless policies that had been pursued by his father, Louis IX. It demanded that all three estates should be represented on the royal council and that it should be convened again within two years. But these reforms were not implemented as the institution was inherently powerless: it could only be summoned by the king and he had other ways of raising the revenue he needed.

The king appointed large numbers of civil servants both to the *parlements* and to fiscal offices, some of which were subsequently sold by their holders. The *Chambre des Comptes* had subsidiary offices: the *Trésor* for non-tax revenue and the *Généraux des finances* for taxes such as the *fouages* (hearth taxes) and *taille* (personal taxes). *Seigneurs* not only enjoyed their own powers and privileges as office-holders, they were also involved in patronage networks which were not unlike the affinities that were prevalent in England and Scotland. Indentured retinues could be found in France, but in many cases the ties were more informal, based on feelings of loyalty to a superior lord (*fidélité*) or a relationship based on reciprocal support, that of client and patron. This is exemplified in the affairs of the Murol

7 October from *Les Très Riches Heures*

This shows peasants engaged in harrowing their fields and sowing seed but in the background can be seen the walls of Paris and the Palace of the Louvre rising from the banks of the Seine. The image of the Louvre is so precise that it enabled a modern model to be made of the palace.

family in the Auvergne. Guillaume de Murol left legacies to two of his clients, one a tenant on his estate who acted as his agent, the other with less formal ties and no post. The Murols in their turn were clients of the counts of Auvergne, receiving benefits such as lands and offices. When the counts lost influence the Murols transferred their loyalty first to the Pope at Avignon and eventually to the duke of Berry and the sires of Latour. So in the late fourteenth century an apparent national system of administration, a characteristic of a developed state, was actually overlaid on regional power networks still firmly in the hands of the nobility. The lever in the hands of the monarchy was that it could and did place resources in the hands of favoured members of the nobility by means of its control of offices, pensions, lands and other gifts.

Throughout his reign Charles V fully justified his sobriquet 'the Wise'. He managed to prevent his three brothers from disrupting his careful reconstruction of the status of the Monarchy and reformed the central administration to achieve more efficient government. A pious king of irreproachable private life, he attracted artists and scholars of distinction to his court. Christine de Pizan the poetess and political theorist enhanced his reputation by writing a highly favourable account of his life. Charles avoided the pitched battles with the English that had proved so disastrous for his predecessors. He felt that he might legally ignore the terms of the Treaty of Brétigny (1360) (including the obligation to keep paying his father's ransom) when war resumed with England in 1369. Since Edward III had never observed the undertaking to renounce his claim to the French throne, Charles stopped the payment of instalments of the ransom. The extra taxes that had been raised to pay it, especially the *aides* and the *gabelle* (a salt tax), were eventually to become a regular part of the revenue. Later a *fouage*, fixed according to the householder's income, was imposed to pay the nobility to fight for the Crown. This was eventually to be replaced by the *taille*, which was to last until the French Revolution.

Edward III was unable (and probably unwilling) to control the bands of freebooters (*routiers*) who remained in France after the Treaty of Brétigny had been signed and who continued to live off the land. Captains loyal to Charles V, most notably Bertrand du Guesclin, started to play the English at their own game, devastating areas that were then unable to support marauding soldiers. Charles detached a useful ally from the English in 1369 by allowing his brother, Philip the Bold, duke of Burgundy, to marry the daughter and heiress of the count of Flanders. The commercial links between England and the Flemings had predisposed the great towns of Flanders, which were Imperial fiefs, to support Edward III in the early stages of the war. Their formidable new lord would prevent such independence in the future: yet the proximity of so powerful a duchy was to prove a serious threat to the French monarchy for much of the next century.

The administrative structure of Burgundy, during the century in which it enjoyed quasi-independence of France and the Empire, was determined by the fact that it was an *apanage* of a French prince (see Map 4). The government of the Burgundian state was essentially personal: everything was in the hands of the duke, and the organs of central government were concentrated around him.[61] Philip the Bold already held the French duchy of Burgundy when he acquired Flanders and, like the French kings, he used his Great Council of

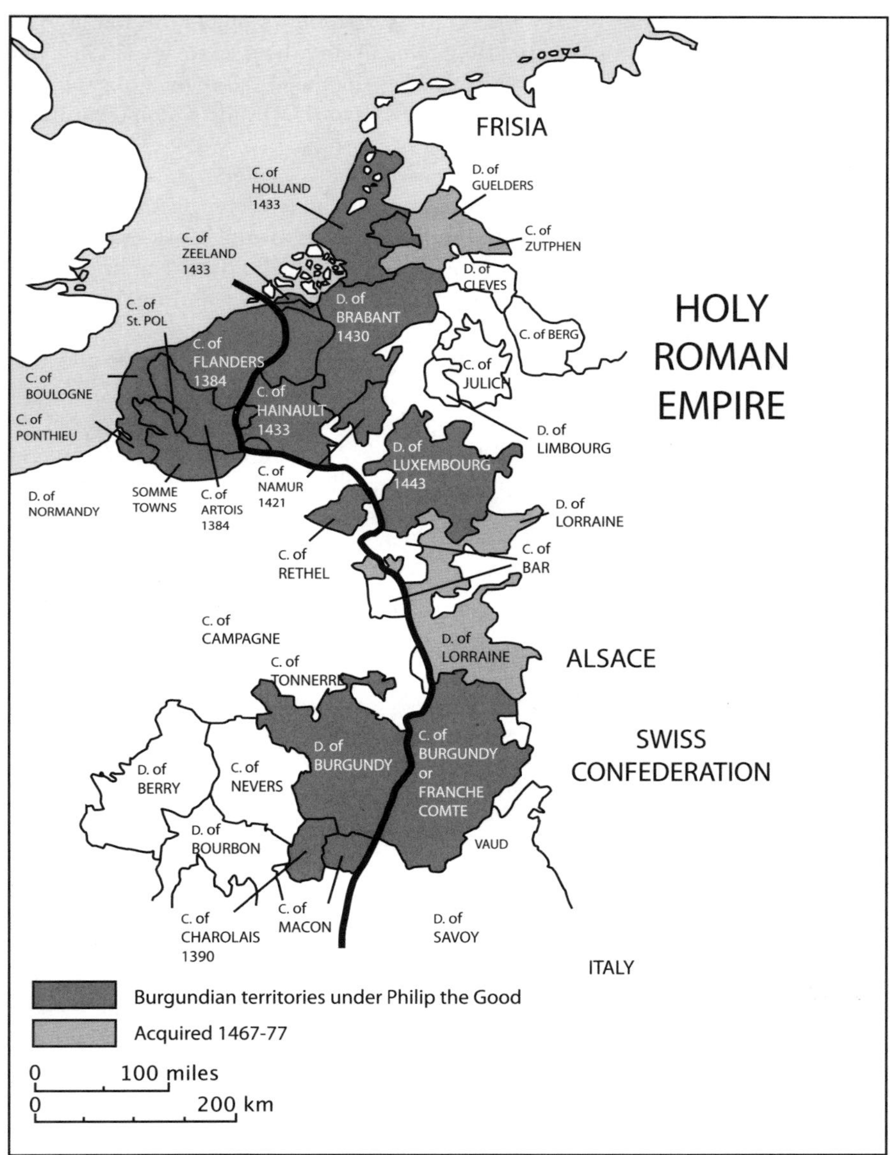

Map 4 The growth of the Burgundian domains

ministers and civil servants as a high court of law. Appeals could still be made to the *Parlement* of Paris: an unwelcome reminder to Philip and his successors that their sovereignty was shared with the king of France. In the following century Brabant, Holland, Hainault and Luxemburg were incorporated into the duchy. Each of the regions of this sizeable and prosperous state had its own local laws and customs and on the whole the dukes were successful in accommodating them without allowing their central authority to be undermined. In Burgundy, as in

France, local interests were often asserted by assemblies or Estates made up of representatives of the most politically powerful members of society. They had the function of voting *aides* to pay for expenses such as warfare or, after the capture of John the Fearless by the Turks (in a disastrous Crusade which terminated in the defeat of Nicopolis in 1396), a princely ransom.

Several of the duchesses of Burgundy were effective rulers, Isabelle of Portugal, the wife of Philip the Good, was a diplomat who worked incessantly for the benefit of her family and her adopted country. Margaret of York (the sister of Edward IV), the wife and then the widow of Charles the Bold, had an implacable enmity towards the new house of Tudor in England and several times this had an impact on European politics.

The English nobility and their retinues had come to regard northern France as a source of rich pickings: they wanted booty and, if possible, property. During the 1370s, when it was clear that the English would get nothing more out of the Treaty of Brétigny, they conducted *chevauchées*, extended raids that ravaged #the country through which they passed. They caused only inconvenience to the French king and nobility as no permanent gains were made, but they inflicted terrible suffering and long-term economic damage on the peasantry. The threat to France was considerably diminished in 1376/7 by the deaths of the Black Prince and his father, Edward III, who was succeeded by a child, Richard II. He proved in adulthood to be inclined towards peace with France and was also deeply involved in conflicts within the British Isles.

Lewis wrote of the Valois kingship:

> Although he appeared to rule the game his wits were constantly stretched to keep the upper hand. And although God may have given him authority, God might not have provided him, poor human, with wits enough.[62]

It was Charles VI (who succeeded his wise father in 1380) that Lewis had in mind when he anticipated the disasters that were to befall France during his long reign. He was a healthy and active young man but after a series of accidents he had become subject to fits of insanity. These became worse after 1393 when in a court fête he was nearly burnt to death in a hairy, waxed costume: some of his friends, who were chained with him for a parade, died horribly. The early years of his reign had benefited from the legacy of stable government bequeathed by his father and by the disinclination of Richard II to resume hostilities. This had enabled the Crown to defeat a popular rebellion in Flanders, which threatened its recent pro-French alignment.

The vacuum left by the incapacity of the king was filled by the ambitions of his brother the duke of Orleans, his ally Queen Isabelle of Bavaria, and of the other magnates. Most damaging of all was the feud that broke out between Louis of Orleans and his cousin John the Fearless, duke of Burgundy; it culminated in 1407 when the latter arranged for the assassination of Orleans. Rivalry between the Burgundians and the *Armagnacs* (as the followers of Orleans were called) simmered on for twelve more years. Then the assassination of John with the complicity of the dauphin Charles in 1419 threw the new duke of Burgundy, Philip the Good, into the arms of the English. Henry V was in the process of conquering large tracts of northern France, a sequel to his victory at Agincourt four years earlier. Isabelle was prevailed upon to declare that her own son, the dauphin Charles, was illegitimate. By the 1420 Treaty of Troyes, Henry V, based in Paris, was to rule France as co-regent with the duke of Burgundy and when the incapable Charles VI died he was to become king. The French court poet, Alain Chartier, described his country's predicament in the *Quadrilogue Invectif* (Invective in Four Parts). In a dream, Lady France reproves her children, a knight, a cleric and a peasant, for bickering amongst themselves when they should be uniting to save their king and country, like the bees which:

> In their swarm keep their order and risk their lives to keep and defend their assemblies and little policy and for to keep the lordship of their king, which reigns among them under a little hive, that at sometimes when he is hurt in battle ... they bear him up with their wings and suffer death for to keep and maintain his seigneury and his life.[63]

When the dauphin, Charles VII, succeeded his father in 1422 he came into an unenviable inheritance. Paris was closed to him so he had to establish a temporary capital at Bourges. In a number of areas, such as Guyenne (part of Aquitaine, what remained of the duchy which had originally been inherited by English kings in the twelfth century) and Brittany, the people gave their allegiance to their own duke rather than to the king. In others the local lords would sell themselves to the highest bidder. Charles was not physically prepossessing or a natural military leader and wisely left most of the fighting to the Constable of France (the general of the highest military rank) and his captains. The common people in the royal lands of north, central and southern France were prepared to obey him if he could demonstrate that he was their legitimate king. It has traditionally been claimed that it was the achievement of Joan of Arc, in inspiring the troops to raise the siege of Orleans in 1429 and then persuading Charles to be crowned at Reims to confirm that legitimacy. The fortunes of the Valois started to revive and Charles VII could exercise his kingly virtues of prudence (i.e. patience and persistence) with growing success.

The work of scholars such as Françoise Autrand and Roger Little on the records of the *parlements* of Paris and Poitiers have assigned a more proactive role to the king in the recovery of the French Monarchy. Between 1418 and 1436 there were two sovereign *parlements*: one under Burgundian and English control in Paris and the other created by Charles in Poitiers in the kingdom of Bourges. Many of the personnel who staffed the latter had fled from Paris and this gave continuity to the royal government and assisted in the development of French consciousness and a national state. Roger Little points to the adroitness with which Charles managed the conflicts between rival nobles within the narrow confines of Bourges. He may also have manipulated Joan of Arc for her propaganda value rather than submissively following her agenda. When she was captured, tried and burnt he distanced himself from her since he did not wish to be associated with a convicted witch.[64] This may do him little credit on a personal level but puts him at the head of the league of wily state-builders such as Philip the Good of Burgundy, Henry VII of England and his own son, Louis XI.

Charles was not a robust man but he survived until 1461. His pious and prolific wife had presented him with fourteen children and enough of them survived to ensure that he had a male heir and to provide princesses for useful diplomatic marriages. His comparative longevity enabled France to avoid the evils of either a minority regime or a disputed succession. By the end of 1453, with the exception of Calais, the English had been defeated and excluded from France. Yet Charles was to encounter other troubles: he had to deal with treacherous nobles especially in the *Praguerie* of 1440. Led by the dukes of Alençon and Bourbon they suborned the dauphin, Louis, into supporting them. The revolt seems to have been a response to the king's attempt to reform the companies of soldiers led by nobles, to bring them more directly under royal control. Charles took prompt action against the rebels, the dauphin was returned and Alençon and Bourbon submitted, with the admission that:

> all the war of the said kingdom belongs to the king and his officers, . . . and there is no one so great in the said kingdom that he can levy war nor retain troops, without the authority, commission and command of the king.[65]

But the dauphin and his father proved irreconcilable and they did not meet during the last fourteen years of his life. 1458 marked another stage by which the king reduced the power of the nobility: Alençon was brought to trial for treasonable contacts with the English and was imprisoned for life. Malcolm Vale's biography anticipates the work of Autrand and Little in giving a more positive account of Charles VII than those of earlier historians. He suggests that some of his characteristics, such as duplicity, were advantageous to France in dangerous and uncertain times.[66]

The reputation of Louis XI has also benefited from some recent revision. To romantic writers and some historians he was 'the universal spider' who caught up all his enemies in a web of intrigue. Yet even when castigating his ruthlessness and lack of principle these writers could not dispute his formidable intelligence and industry. This they counter-balanced by suggesting that all his achievements were for reasons of personal ambition and avarice. Yet Emmanuel Bourassin has claimed that his strong kingship brought great advantages to his subjects; when he died in 1483; 'he left an enriched kingdom, flourishing commerce, agriculture, despite the heavy charges which weighed upon the peasants, renewed by long years of peace'.[67]

The 'long years of peace' had not been easily achieved. The reign of Louis XI coincided almost exactly with that of the new Yorkist king of England, Edward IV, and from 1467 Charles the Bold was duke of Burgundy. Charles, just before he became duke, had participated in the 'league of public weal'. It was an alliance of disaffected French noblemen including the king's brother Charles of France (he led the dissidents; his main grievance was that he should have been given more lands) and the duke of Brittany, which was intended permanently to reduce the capacity of Louis to take independent action. He fell into the power of the leaguers but managed to extricate himself by making promises of political concessions and territory to its most powerful members: dividing and ruling by playing on their self-interest. Once he was free again he was able to go back on most of these promises: Charles the Bold and his other adversaries discovered that an unscrupulous anointed king was almost impossible to control, for the location of sovereignty in his person was unquestionable.

Louis inclined in his early reign to sympathise with the exiled house of Lancaster, although he also saw them as pawns in an elaborate network of alliances. His main purpose was to keep the threat of a Lancastrian invasion hanging over Edward IV and thus deter him from supporting the expansionist aims of Charles the Bold of Burgundy, who wished to make an independent kingdom out of his domains. In 1468 this policy seemed to have failed when Charles married Edward's sister to consolidate an alliance with England. Yet this contributed to the process by which the earl of Warwick ('the Kingmaker'), who seems to have had a personal antipathy to Charles the Bold, was alienated from Edward. In 1470 Warwick left England and made a treaty with the Lancastrians, led by Queen Margaret of Anjou and her teenage son, prince Edward. With French assistance Warwick was to restore Henry VI of Lancaster (currently Edward's prisoner, languishing in the Tower of London) to the throne. Margaret would allow Prince Edward to marry the earl's daughter and reward him and his followers with many lands and high offices, and: 'From henceforth to treat the said earl as true and faithful to king Henry, her and the prince. And for the deeds past never hereafter to make him reproach.'[68]

In return for his aid, Louis expected Warwick and the Lancastrians to support him in an offensive war against Charles the Bold, and Henry VI and his son were to stop pushing the English claim to the French throne. The first part of the plan went smoothly: Warwick bested Edward IV, who fled to Burgundy, and replaced a dirty and demented Henry VI on the throne. Louis pressed the earl to fulfil his promises but the English had no wish for war with their major trading partner, Burgundy, and Parliament refused to withdraw the English claim to the French throne. Early in 1471, with Burgundian assistance, Edward invaded England and defeated and killed Warwick at the Battle of Barnet. A month later Margaret of Anjou, who had been unable to join forces with Warwick, was defeated at Tewkesbury. Her only son and various Lancastrian lords were killed during or after the battle and Henry VI died mysteriously in the Tower of London a few days later. The diplomacy of Louis XI was in ruins: four years later Edward, in alliance with the dukes of Brittany and Burgundy, invaded France to exact revenge.

Charles the Bold was unintentionally to undermine the success of this anti-French alliance. By involving Burgundy in a debilitating war with the Swiss, he put at risk his long-term aim of rendering France incapable of denying him full sovereignty. In 1475 Edward IV was not, as he had expected, met by a Burgundian army; Parliament had voted him limited funds and his soldiers were poorly prepared for a long campaign. These factors made him amenable to conciliatory overtures by Louis XI, which culminated in the Treaty of Picquigny. This gave some trading concessions to England but little else: Edward was to be paid an annual pension of £10,000 (which the English called 'tribute') and his daughter was to marry the dauphin. Compared with the cost of prolonged warfare both sovereigns seemed to have got a good bargain, but Louis could and did renege on the agreement. In 1482 he promised to marry his son to the daughter of

Maximilian of Austria and he also stopped paying the pension. Charles the Bold had been killed in battle with the Swiss five years earlier, his daughter and heir had married Maximilian, whilst France seized the French lands of the disappearing Burgundian state. Louis could safely realign his foreign policy, forging a new friendship with the Austrian Habsburgs and ignoring English indignation.

Bourassin expressed surprise that the Italian political theorist Niccolò Machiavelli never mentioned Louis XI as a master of statecraft: some examples of his inspired duplicity have been cited above.[69] His unscrupulous political manoeuvres were combined with a strong and publicly demonstrated piety: his successes ensured that his subjects would not murmur against a prince who so evidently observed the precepts of religion. Louis was certainly lucky as well as clever, for the internal divisions in England, the premature death of Charles the Bold and the fact that he only left a female heir greatly assisted in the maintenance and extension of royal power in France. In less capable hands, however, it is unlikely that the Monarchy would have been left in such a strong position that it survived unscathed the potentially catastrophic reign of Charles VIII. The new king was to exemplify the enduring power of the ideals of chivalry, as Huizinga remarked, it was: 'the great source of tragic political errors, exactly as are nationalism and national pride at the present day'.[70]

Charles was only thirteen when he succeeded to the throne in 1483 and for several years his much older sister, Anne of Beaujeu, ruled on his behalf. The last Angevin king of Naples had died two years earlier leaving his claim to the succession to that kingdom (which was actually ruled by Ferrante, an illegitimate son of the house of Aragon), and to the duchy of Provence, to the French Crown. In 1491 the government reneged on the promise that Charles would wed Margaret of Austria and instead he married Anne, the heiress to the duchy of Brittany. Three large areas of France – Anjou, Provence and Brittany – were thus peacefully brought under direct royal authority. Anne of Beaujeu died in the following year and it may have been the removal of her prudent influence that led to the king's involvement in an enterprise which many historians have believed was to prove disastrous for the Crown and the people of France and Italy for the following half-century. Like many of his noble contemporaries Charles was captivated by chivalric romances: tales of the victories of Charlemagne, Arthur and his Round Table and Godfrey of Bouillon's conquest of Jerusalem.

'A young army, a young king who, in their perfect ignorance of themselves and of the enemy, crossed Italy at a gallop.'[71] This was J. Michelet's withering verdict on the first French campaign in Italy. Charles revived the Valois claim to the throne of Naples and in 1494, apparently with the support of most of the Italian states, invaded the peninsula. Huge taxes, which were mainly raised from his non-noble subjects, were needed to pay the cost of the invasion force. At the head of the army of about 31,000 soldiers, supported by a large navy and baggage trains, Charles swept down to Naples. His rapid success alarmed the Papacy, several of the initially friendly Italian states, and Maximilian of Austria, who had his own claims to Italian lands. Spain (recently united by the marriage of Ferdinand of Aragon and Isabella of Castile) regarded the kingdoms of Naples and Sicily, ruled by a junior branch of the house of Aragon, as its dynastic preserve.

Charles VIII left an occupying force in his new 'kingdom' and retreated up through Italy with a dispirited army weakened by disease. He was met by the allied forces at Fornovo and was fortunate to keep most of his army intact after a drawn battle. The French were soon afterwards to be expelled from Naples by the Aragonese ruler and his supporters. Charles was planning a new campaign in 1498 when he died after an accident, without leaving a direct heir. His cousin, the duke of Orleans, became Louis XII: he was descended from the Visconti dukes of Milan and was anxious to continue the Italian ambitions of the French Crown.

English historians, bemused by two centuries in which a Plantagenet sovereign rarely died peacefully in his bed, wonder at the manner in which the French kings emerged from the Hundred Years War and the Italian Wars. Their authority and the power of the state were greater than they had ever been. Their belligerent foreign policy, supported by heavy taxation, helped to keep their subjects under control. The institutions of the *parlements* and the Estates, used as arms of the royal administration, contributed towards the development of a nation state. Lewis also suggests that the king's subjects believed the rhetoric of their coronation rites and court ceremonial:

> Nobles, churchmen, oligarchs accepted the myths of monarchy. In this sense at least there was an absolute monarchy in France, an absolute monarchy by 'divine right'.[72]

The public Christian piety of all the French kings, the military and diplomatic successes of Charles VII and Louis XI and the chivalric aspirations of Charles VIII and Louis XII accorded well with the received image of a 'good prince'.

The Empire and the Swiss Confederation

The history of Scotland, France, Burgundy and England in the late Middle Ages reveals four states and their rulers becoming progressively stronger. The administrative structure of the first two might have been relatively loose and they suffered great political trauma. Scotland's series of prisoner or child kings, the Hundred Years War in France, and in both, conflict within the nobility, presented great dangers, yet they emerged into the early modern period led by formidable, authoritarian kings. England also needed to fund years of expensive external wars, followed by decades of civil war, and yet Henry VII was better placed to enforce his will than any of his predecessors had been. The relatively centralised nature of the state and the sophisticated legal framework that had developed during the previous two centuries, made his achievements possible. The Holy Roman Empire, on the other hand, was an inherently de-centralised state, dependent on the co-operation of the princes who ruled its constituent parts. Two new states also emerged during this period which technically owed allegiance to the Emperor: the dukes of Burgundy (for part of their territories) and the Swiss Confederation.

By the late thirteenth century three Swiss forest cantons, Uri, Schwyz and Unterwalden, had banded together to resist their Habsburg overlords. Their successful defiance attracted other cities and the surrounding countryside: Lucerne,

Zurich and Berne, and two more forest cantons, Glarus and Zug. As Denys Hay has observed, the towns were dominated by patrician oligarchies whilst the rural cantons had a more popular form of government and this led to early tensions.[73] A series of agreements between the first Swiss cantons did, however, lay the foundations of federation. Especially important were the Priests' Charter (1370), which defined the ecclesiastical autonomy of the region, and the Charter of Sempach (1393), which provided a common military discipline. The Confederation has been defined by Roger Sablonier as one of a series of alliances between various states existing within the Empire, with, until 1500, no clearly defined territory.[74] It was able to grow and expand without serious interruption partly because of the difficult nature of much of its terrain and also because the Swiss were formidable soldiers, both defending their land and hiring themselves to foreign princes to fight as mercenaries.

The Confederation managed to produce a few national institutions that improved its chances of survival. In 1481 a Diet at which each canton was represented produced the Charter of Stanz, laying down provisions to avert rebellions and forbidding unauthorised armies. More areas joined the Confederation, including Basle in 1501; they were attracted by the high prestige of its military prowess (especially the defeat of Charles the Bold in 1477) and the wealth they could accumulate as mercenaries. Members of the Confederation were probably wise not to press for closer political integration as local interests would have proved too powerful for it to be successful. They had the distinction, apart from some Italian city states, of being amongst the few people in Europe who did not owe obedience to a prince: by 1500 the Habsburgs had given up trying to enforce even a theoretical sovereignty. The peasant republic of Dithmarschen, the only other area with this distinction in northern Europe, has beeen discussed in Chapter 1.

Western European historians generally find it difficult to analyse what was going on in the Empire in the later Middle Ages. It is hard not to describe it as a failing institution if the meagre authority exercised by the Emperors and their pitiful revenues are compared either with the glories of Charlemagne and the Ottonian Emperors or with contemporary monarchs like Charles V of France or Henry VII of England. Yet it was imperial authority which terminated the Great Schism and forced the Hussites to become an embattled minority in the fifteenth century. Two hundred years later it was still strong enough successfully to defend Catholic orthodoxy in Germany and Bohemia. So why did the Empire seem to be so fragile and what ensured its survival?

The map of the Empire explains one of the main problems faced by the Eemperors and their ministers in attempting to develop coherent policies (see Map 1). It covered a huge area bounded on the east by Poland, and further to the south by Hungary, and by various Italian states that owed a shadowy form of allegiance to the Emperor. The western borders of the Empire, including by the late fourteenth century the new state of Burgundy, were co-terminous with France, and to the north lay the countries of Scandinavia. There was scope for involvement in all manner of territorial disputes, especially as the constituent parts of the Empire were so varied. They ranged from big principalities like Austria and Saxony to towns and bishoprics such as Lübeck and Cologne. Most of the inhabitants of the states were of Germanic stock but there were also Slavs, Magyars, Flemings,

French and many other ethnic groups: in Bohemia, Czech Slavs formed the majority of the population.

For minority groups, to live under the sovereignty of an emperor was an advantage for he gave them some protection. Bernard Guenée, on the other hand, has recorded the reservations of some German historians about the institution.[75] The existence of the Empire may have prevented Germany from developing into a unified state similar to those that were emerging in England, Spain or France. Much debate has taken place about when the peoples of Europe became conscious of their national identities and whether they were manifested at the same time in all parts of the Continent. Phenomena such as the Hundred Years War and the Hussite revolution do seem to have fostered nationalist feelings but they should not be exaggerated. Older loyalties – to the Catholic Church, between knights who belonged to the same order, to fellow guildsmen, to one's own town or village – might cut across newer allegiances.

The Empire contained thirty-odd major principalities, ninety ecclesiastical states, approximately a hundred countships and a mass of minor lordships, knights' fiefs and independent towns. Many once powerful families had been weakened by the custom of dividing inheritances, leading to the creation of some of the small states. At times the *Rittern*, or knightly class, seemed able virtually to ignore the demands of their supposed superiors. The seven electoral princes, who alone had the right to chose each new Emperor (see below), and of whom three were ecclesiastics, had their privileges endorsed by the Golden Bull in 1356. They were in a stronger position than the lesser princes, but their lands were often not a homogeneous whole but a mixture of tenures with different customs and powers. Where they had authority their style of government, however, had some similarities with French models.

In the Rhine Palatinate, for example, members of some 600 noble families were closely involved in the administration of the state, often as officials or *Amtleute*, trained in the law and receiving salaries from the Elector. He was invariably impecunious and their ability to lend him money further entrenched their position. Yet the terms on which they held their lands seem curiously outdated when compared with such arrangements in England or France. The feudal bonds were retained by the Elector: he had a new register drawn up in 1471 to avoid any inadvertent loss of his rights. Lands were still regarded as fiefs and they could revert to the Elector if heirs failed; any alteration in the way in which they were held also required his consent.[76] Many of the larger states that made up the Empire also had their own assemblies. Tom Scott suggests that the extent of their power often depended on whether or not their prince received substantial revenues without the need to summon the assemblies to vote taxes. Assemblies could assert themselves during minorities or if their prince was suffering some form of pressure; at other times they had limited opportunities to press their interests.[77]

There were other political forces for the Emperor to recognise: the Hanseatic League, the association of Northern trading cities, which has been discussed in Chapter 2, for example, was a potential ally. According to Dollinger, Emperor Charles IV seems to have hoped to strengthen bonds with it in 1375 when he visited Lübeck.[78] Sigismund was later to act as an arbitrator between the Hanseatic League and Lübeck, but there does not seem to have been much interaction beyond these minor events. Neither of the imperial dynasties that ruled during our period had vital interests involved on the German seaboard. The towns of the Hanseatic League probably felt that the best thing that the Emperors could do for them was to abstain from interfering in their activities.

The Teutonic Knights had been founded with a monastic discipline at the end of the twelfth century. They were similar to the crusading orders of Palestine in that their principal objective was to convert the heathen to Christianity. Their base was the great fortress of the Marienburg between Prussia and Pomerania just outside the eastern limits of the Empire. Their main enemies were the Lithuanians, who were only converted to Christianity in the late fourteenth century, and the Poles, who resented their expansionism. The knights were defeated by an alliance of the Poles and Lithuanians at the Battle of Tannenburg in 1410. This marked an important stage in their decline and they eventually recognised the king of Poland as their overlord – a conflict of allegiances as some of their lands formed part of the Empire. Their fortunes had little direct impact on the Empire in the late Middle Ages but, together with the margraveate of Brandenburg, their lands were eventually to form the militaristic state of Prussia. In common with the other great German principalities, such as Saxony and the Palatinate, the new state was to modernise its finances and administrative institutions to enable its rulers to enjoy unchallenged authority.

In the middle of the fourteenth century the German Emperor was Charles IV, who was a member of the house of Luxemburg and also king of Bohemia. He had spent his youth at the French court and retained a considerable affection for its culture: his tutor had been Pierre de Rosiers, who later became Pope as Clement VI. Their friendship continued and probably accounts for the fact that Prague was made into an independent archbishopric in 1344. In partnership with Arnost of Pardubice, the first archbishop (who had studied law and the classics in Italy for fourteen years), Charles encouraged artists, scribes and illuminators to produce both devotional and humanist works. The Emperor continued the rebuilding of the cathedral of St Vitus and other churches and monasteries and founded a university in Prague. The magnificent, cosmopolitan court enjoyed a high reputation throughout Europe. The Italian humanist Francesco Petrarch visited it on a diplomatic mission and subsequently wrote a flattering letter to Archbishop Arnost (who had protested that Petrarch would find it to be barbaric), claiming that the Emperor and his companions were worthy of great honour: they were 'so mellow and urbane that one would think that they were Athenians born and bred'.[79]

In 1356 Charles IV promulgated the Golden Bull which laid down the rules for the election of future emperors. Seven princes formed the College of Electors: the king of Bohemia, the count Palatine of the Rhine, the duke of Saxony, the margrave of Brandenburg and the archbishops of Cologne, Mainz and Trier. On the death of an emperor they would normally meet in the church of St Bartholomew in Frankfurt-am-Main and choose a new one by a simple majority decision. He would be known as the 'king of the Romans' unless he gained the imperial title by receiving coronation from the Pope. During the late fourteenth and early fifteenth centuries papal coronation was a problematic business since the Great Schism produced two or even three rival popes and the choice of one would set off a diplomatic reaction from princes who supported rival candidates. In practice the Golden Bull had marginalised papal influence in the matter since the Electors made the choice, and, even without a coronation, their candidate exercised full powers.

The Emperor had two administrative structures to support him: the royal servants, lawyers and clerics carried on the government in his own lands. These were the Luxemburg domains in the fourteenth and early fifteenth centuries, the Habsburg territories for most of the fifteenth century. There was also the Imperial Chancery, which was charged with the government of the Empire as a whole. This consisted of a Chancellor, who presided over a hierarchy of officials and clerks, a Treasurer and an Imperial Court of Justice. This Court did not function very effectively in the fourteenth century as most of the princes, often the main offenders against the peace, claimed exemption from its jurisdiction. Those who staffed these bodies were few in number but they were professionals, and, considering the perennial shortage of cash, the system seems to have functioned reasonably well. Even the Imperial Court was to become more effective from the early fifteenth century. From the time of Charles IV, German was used instead of Latin and this went some way towards confirming a national identity for the Empire. The Imperial Diet or *Reichstag* was less effective than the Chancery. It was composed of the College of Electors (except the king of Bohemia), the major princes and nobles of the Empire, and representatives of the towns. There were no hard and fast rules about who could attend and the number of participating members varied. The Diet was summoned by the Emperor yet he seldom presided over it in person, his place being taken by the Chancellor. The Diet could draft ordinances but it was so difficult to get everyone to agree to anything of any consequence that the assembly was little more than a debating chamber.

The Emperor, advised by the administrators from his ancestral lands and from the Imperial Chancery, formulated internal and external policies. As far as the German lands were concerned, he had to rely on a combination of persuasion and pressure to keep the peace between his many subjects, who often had conflicting interests. If he could placate the greater princes, who wielded considerable political power, and the bishops, who had moral authority, he could usually deal with the knights (many of whom were lawless) and the towns. There was a tendency for the small states and associations of knights to band together in leagues or 'circles', but the difficulty they had in agreeing to co-operate usually made them ineffectual. The Emperors themselves were not dedicated to the disinterested pursuit of the common good: most of their policies were intended to benefit their own dynasties. Robin du Boulay, for example, praises Charles IV for avoiding expensive and futile Italian entanglements but suspects him of aspiring to rule a huge northern empire including Lithuania and Rus, the nucleus of modern Russia.[80] Charles was also short-sighted in selling so much imperial land to pay bribes to the electors to choose his son Wenceslas as king of the Romans, as Wenceslas turned out to be a poor bargain for the dynasty. He presented a stark contrast to his able and pious father, lacking the qualities contemporaries expected in a prince. The perennial problem of raising adequate revenue became acute during his reign and his attempts at tax-gathering made him very unpopular. The process of alienating land continued: Eberhard Isenmann estimates that between the reign of Charles IV and that of Frederick III, a hundred years later, revenue fell from about 130,000 florins to between 2,000 and 5,000 a year.[81]

The Hussite revolution (see below, Chapter 5) would probably have occurred irrespective of who was reigning but a stronger monarch might have limited the damage it did to imperial authority. In 1400 the electors deposed Wencelas, replacing him with Rupert of Wittelsbach, count palatine of the Rhine, but he was no more effective, in imposing his authority than his predecessor had been. The house of Luxemburg regained the imperial title in 1411 with Sigismund, king of Hungary and younger brother of Wenceslas (although he was not crowned Emperor until 1433). Despite the continuing problem of inadequate revenue he proved reasonably effective, presiding over the re-unification of the Church after the Great Schism, defending Hungary against Turkish expansion and regaining some authority in Bohemia. For many years he clung to the delusion that he could suppress the Hussites by force, and launched a series of ineffectual crusades against them. Eventually he embraced the realism that successful princely state-builders were displaying elsewhere in Europe and exploited their internal divisions to make a settlement with the moderates.

The failure of male heirs saw the end of the house of Luxemburg in the middle of the fifteenth century. Sigismund's daughter had married Duke Albert V, the Habsburg duke of Austria. He soon died campaigning against the Turks in Hungary and was succeeded as Emperor in 1440 by his cousin Frederick of Styria. Hungary and Bohemia fell under the control of members of the local nobility during the next few decades but the king of Bohemia retained his electoral seat. Hungary was not part of the Empire but it bore the brunt of defending Germany from the Turkish onslaught until they conquered most of it early in the next century. This was one of the factors that probably ensured the survival of Frederick III and his son, Maximilian. They remained chronically short of revenue but, if they had been obliged to sustain a continuous war in south-eastern Europe, they could have been ruined: as it was, Frederick could seldom afford to venture beyond his ancestral lands.

The marriage of Maximilian to Mary of Burgundy, soon after the death of her father Charles at Nancy in 1477, changed the fortunes of the Habsburgs. The wealthy Flemish towns, which he now ruled directly, showed Maximilian scant respect and were unwilling to see their resources being squandered on imperial projects. They had always been technically under Imperial sovereignty but, since 1369, had been ruled by the able and martial dukes of Burgundy. Now they presented a challenge to the authority of Mary and her husband that proved difficult to resolve. Yet under him the whole orientation of the Empire was to change, especially after his son, Philip the Fair, married Joanna the Mad of Castile in 1496. Philip did not live long enough to succeed his father as Emperor but his inheritance and the kingdom he gained by marriage gave him and his son Charles (later the Emperor Charles V) great wealth and power. Under his rule the Empire survived the religious conflicts which plunged Europe into warfare within and between states, and the Turkish onslaught, which was intensified after the defeat of the last king of Hungary.

Even allowing for the enhanced power achieved by Habsburg marriage policy, in lazy or incompetent hands the dynasty was unlikely to have prospered.

Maximilian initiated some reforms to the imperial administration; for example, he strengthened the Imperial Court of Justice and managed in 1495 to raise an effective tax, the 'common penny', to pay for his wars. He was also very active in making alliances although he avoided the expense of warfare except when it was absolutely necessary. During his long reign (he was elected king of the Romans in 1486 and died in 1519) he established the Habsburgs as the major European power they were to remain until the early twentieth century. Sigismund had already defined their principal mission: to defend the Catholic faith against heresy within the Empire and externally against the Turks. These were objectives that contemporaries would recognise as worthy of the greatest of the Christian princes in Europe.

CONCLUSION

The exercise of sovereignty in Britain, France and the Empire in the late Middle Ages has been considered along with the relationship of the princes to the nobility and to the assemblies of their subjects, discussed in the context of developing administrative institutions and the emergence of nation states. There should now be sufficient evidence available to address the question posed in the Introduction to this chapter about how the ideal of kingship interacted with reality during the period.

The first section suggested some criteria by which princes were judged to be effective or ineffective by contemporaries. Even the most authoritarian rulers bound themselves to certain undertakings in their coronation oaths. The most universal of these was to respect the Catholic Church, both its clergy and the orthodoxy of its beliefs, and on the whole, the clergy got off pretty lightly where taxation was concerned. Apart from Bohemia, where clerical property was at risk from the Hussites, in material terms the Church prospered under devout and orthodox monarchs. Chapter 5 will discuss how the Lancastrian kings of England and the German Emperors were punctilious in moving against heresy.

Another regular element in the coronation oath was a promise to do justice: an activity that was open to various interpretations. As Sir John Fortescue remarked:

> For nothing may make his [the king's] people to arise nor make insurrection but lack of goods or lack of justice, but yet certainly when they lack goods they will arise saying that they lack justice.[82]

He was certainly correct in his analysis that the most common cause of unrest was linked to the exaction of revenue. But while there were revolts against heavy taxation during the early years of Richard II and in 1450, as the French lands were being lost, people paid equally hefty sums under Henry V and Henry VII with scarcely a murmur. In France, Charles VIII and his successors involved the country in expensive and unprofitable wars without any serious defiance being offered to their authority. There were other elements in the rule of Richard II and Henry VI that cast them in the role of bad or ineffective princes. The former was perceived to be behaving unjustly towards members of his family and the nobility, flouting both the laws and customs of the realm and Christian morality. The latter was widely praised for his piety and virtue but he lacked the decisiveness of an effective ruler, was dethroned twice and eventually murdered. Reliance on unsuitable counsellors, foolish generosity and a complete lack of martial skills progressively lost him the loyalty of his people.

Temperance was one of the four 'cardinal virtues' but it was of small value to the subjects of a prince if he lacked prudence, military ability and the resolution to enforce the rule of law. Wenceslas lost his Empire because he was unable to quell the early Hussite movement or remedy the great social upheavals that were under way. This was in direct contravention of his coronation oath to protect the Church, and a mistake that his eventual successor, Sigismund, was determined not to repeat. Military prowess and the maintenance of the law, however, were insufficient if a monarch was thought seriously to have violated the code of Christian ethics. Richard III was an enthusiastic and experienced warrior and anxious to rule the kingdom well but his violation of the law by the execution of Hastings and (it was believed) the murder of his nephews alienated opinion. A later rumour that he intended to marry his own niece, after the suspicious death of his wife, helped the invasion by Henry Tudor to achieve unexpected success. Louis XI of France flagrantly broke his word on several occasions and harshly imposed his will upon the nobility but his opponents were mostly unpopular foreign princes and he brought peace and stability to the country, so his subjects continued to obey him.

The spread of education and economic prosperity amongst the laity meant that more people were prepared to comment on the strengths and weaknesses of princely rule and to offer advice. Christine de Pizan, the Lannoys, Alain Chartier, Smil Flaska of Pardubice, George Ashby and John Skelton were all loyal courtiers but they dared to draw attention to weaknesses as well as virtues in the rule of their princes. The anonymous authors of songs and manifestos were less deferential as they fulminated against their rulers for their heavy taxation, reliance on flatterers and neglect of religion and justice. These views were held by some members of the nobility, knights, clergy, lawyers, merchants and, increasingly, politically aware members of the lower orders of society. Many of the attitudes expressed by political commentators and activists harked back to traditional Christianity and to the concept of 'the good prince' as it had been developed over recent centuries in the 'mirrors'. A new, more pragmatic element was also being introduced: a feeling that subjects were not pawns in some princely game but citizens possessed of rights as well as duties. During the early Renaissance the city states of Italy harked back to the republican ideals of the ancients, and these ideas spread to northern Europe to a limited extent. During the Reformations religious conviction was directly to involve all orders of society in political activity: the foundations of these attitudes had been laid in the late Middle Ages.

4

Waging War

INTRODUCTION: THEMES AND SOURCES

To most commentators in our period war was the proper occupation of princes. Sir John Fortescue, for example, stated categorically:

> All the power of a king ought to be applied to the good of his realm, which in effect consists in the defence of it against invasions by foreigners and the protection of the inhabitants of his realm and their goods from injuries and rapine by the native population.[1]

The most important and basic obligation on any government was to defend its territory and people, using such force as might be necessary. It is not surprising, therefore, given the pre-eminence of warfare in the rule of princes and the fact that acting as a warrior was the basis of the privileges of those claiming noble status that there was, in our period, a body of writing addressing issues related to warfare. This will be discussed in the first section of this chapter, looking not only at the moral basis of the just war but also at what contemporary theorists had to say about the best way to conduct a war. Most writing on the conduct of a war in the late Middle Ages was based on the views of Vegetius, whose book *Epitoma de Re Militari* was originally produced between the late fourth and mid-fifth centuries AD.[2] Writers like Giles of Rome in his *De Regimine Principium*, or Christine de Pizan in her *Art de Chevalrie*, either directly copy his work or follow it closely. As Contamine has pointed out, there are 'dozens of MSS' still extant of Vegetius and it was frequently listed among the books belonging to notable warriors, for example, not only Edward III but also Sir John Fastolf. There were even 'pocket sized folding editions' of the work,[3] perhaps for use on campaign.

Another aspect of the conduct of war and the attitudes of those engaged in it, which has provoked much discussion, is chivalry. Here we will be concerned to assess whether this concept had a noticeable effect on the conduct of war or whether it belonged solely to the realm of romances and stories. Phillipe Contamine, Maurice Keen, Richard Barber, Michael Prestwich, and Richard Kaeuper have all contributed to the discussion of this topic. There are plentiful contemporary texts; not only chronicles or biographies intended to laud the achievements of individuals (here we might mention Froissart's *Chronicle*, Chandos Herald's *Life of the Black Prince* or Jean de Bueil's *Le Jouvencel*). There are also manuals for knights (almost 'how to' books), like Ramon Lull's *Book of the Order of Chivalry* (*Libre del Ordre de Cavayleria*), originally composed probably between

1263 and 1276, but printed and translated into English by Caxton at the end of the fifteenth century. Geoffrey de Charny, who was killed at Poitiers in 1356, wrote the *Libre de Chevalerie*, another very popular text.

We will then attempt to analyse the strategy and tactics used in a sample of well-known campaigns and battles to try and determine what principles seem to have been guiding commanders in the field. This will bring us up against the idea that there was a 'military revolution' in the Middle Ages. This interpretation has arisen from the efforts of some historians to push the beginnings of the military changes that have been described as characteristic of the seventeenth century and the major wars of that period back in time to the later Middle Ages. Broadly speaking, the most important elements of this so-called revolution are said to be the growing reliance on infantry rather than heavy cavalry (mounted knights) in battle; the increasing importance of guns and gunpowder weapons of various kinds and the noticeable growth in the size of the armies which could be put in the field. These ideas have been discussed by, among others, Clifford J. Rogers, particularly in *War Cruel and Sharp*, Michael Prestwich in *Armies and Warfare in the Middle Ages: The English Experience*, and in Ayton and Price's *The Medieval Military Revolution: State, Society and Military Change in Medieval and Early Modern Europe.*[4]

The second section of this chapter will look at the logistics of warfare. Fighting a war has always been an expensive and complex operation. How did rulers at this time finance their military adventures? How did they raise armies and navies? How did the effort involved affect other aspects of a ruler's regime and the lives of his subjects? Did the growth of the administration necessary for success in these logistical aspects of conflict also have an impact on the growth of a more centralised state and perhaps contribute to the creation of a nation, the subject of our last section? The sources for an inquiry of this nature can be found in the archives of the government concerned; not only those explicitly dealing with the mechanisms of fighting a war but also those dealing with taxation and other aspects of state finance. The discussion of what it meant to be French or Scots, so that loyalty to a ruler or a nation seemed more important than loyalty to a town or a *pays* or region, will also be based on less formal personal and literary sources and the unspoken assumptions underlying official documents.

(i) LESSONS FROM HISTORY

Theories of war

Although the Middle Ages are often portrayed as violent and lawless, with might constituting right, in most cases war was not seen as the inevitable answer to all conflicts between the powerful. The idea of the 'just war', which had first been propounded in the period before the First Crusade, was still very influential. War should not be used as a tool of naked aggression; it must in some colourable way involve the assertion of rights that had been infringed, or be fought to protect those in danger or to punish those who had acted treacherously or rebelliously. If opportunity offered, within these constraints, a prince might seek to extend his lands and increase his power. He should not, however, acquiesce in the loss of territory or seem unwilling to fight to protect what was rightfully his. Warfare between Christian states particularly needed some kind of justification. Civil wars or 'private wars' (those between nobles rather than princes) could never be seen as 'just' according to the usual criteria. These ideas were set out in Gratian's *Decretals*, a collection of canon law dating from the mid-eleventh century. As summarised by an Italian civil lawyer in the fourteenth century, a just war was fought by laymen, in self-defence or to right a wrong, by the authority of a prince and activated neither by hatred nor by greed.[5]

Even in the later Middle Ages, warfare against non-Christians in the eastern Mediterranean was still seen in the context of the Crusades. Acre, the last remnant of the kingdom of Jerusalem, had fallen to the Mamluks of Egypt in 1291, yet the Crusading ideal still had considerable support in our period. The rapid advance of the armies of the Ottoman Turks into Anatolia and the Balkans, particularly after the Battle of Maritsa in 1371 had given them control of Bulgaria and Serbian Macedonia, gave urgency to the need to defend Christendom against the attacks of infidels. A Crusade was not only the supreme example of a just war to contemporaries, but participants also gained merit from their involvement; the Indulgence granted to crusaders absolved them from the consequences of all their sins. This kind of war was in itself a religious act. Men like Phillipe de Mézières, the tutor of Charles VI of France, campaigned tirelessly for new expeditions to the eastern Mediterranean, dreaming of the recovery of Jerusalem. Crusades were, in fact, mounted in our period against the Turks in the Balkans but the first came to a disastrous conclusion at the Battle of Nicopolis (1396). A second, led by Ladislas of Hungary, resulted in an equally total defeat of the Christian forces at Varna in Bulgaria in 1444. Crusading also flourished in eastern Europe, directed against the pagan Lithuanians both in Pomerania and in the northern Ukraine. The Teutonic Knights, a military order whose purpose was warfare against unbelievers, were based in this area and attracted crusaders to their banner from all over western Europe (see above, Chapter 3: iii). They included well-known figures like Henry Grosmont, earl of Lancaster; Henry, earl of Derby, the future Henry IV of England, and Duke Albert of Austria. Their so-called *reysen*, or expeditions, against the heathen enemy were to some extent glamourised with chivalric feasts and other trappings[6] and it was not until the fifteenth century that they finally ceased. Lithuania was by then controlled by Christian Poland and the rationale for Crusading no longer held good.

Once war had begun, general principles (sometimes called the laws of war) governing the behaviour of the combatants were usually accepted, even if they were not always observed. Again there are contemporary collections of these precepts, often with comment. A typical and admired example is Honoré Bouvet's *Tree of Battles*, completed in 1386–7. To some extent these principles were closely connected with the ideals of chivalry but they also had a separate existence. It was generally accepted that religious sites, property and persons should not be molested. Prisoners should not be slain but ransomed. The actions of the Turks in killing most of the prisoners taken at Nicopolis in 1396 have been held to be responsible for the belief in Turkish cruelty current in western Europe in the fifteenth and sixteenth centuries.[7]

In sieges particular conventions applied. Once a siege was under way, no-one might enter or leave the town or castle. This might lead to scenes of desperation like that at Rouen in 1417 when the poor were turned out of the town because supplies were nearly exhausted, but were not let through the English lines, leaving many to die miserably in the town ditch. Of greatest practical importance were the rules governing the surrender of a besieged town. Often a period was set by the besiegers in negotiations with the besieged; if help had not arrived by the end of that time the town would surrender and would escape the horrors of a sack. If no agreement was reached, the town or castle could be taken by storm and the lives and property of all the inhabitants were at the mercy of the besiegers. This was the case at the end of the siege of Limoges in 1370; in the eyes of contemporary English chroniclers like Walsingham the Black Prince's army had every right to slaughter the defenders. Froissart found the massacre distressing;

> there is no man so hard-hearted that, if he had been in Limoges on that day and had remembered God, he would not have wept bitterly at the fearful slaughter which took place. More than three thousand persons, men, women and children were dragged out to have their throats cut.[8]

It was, however, justifiable according to the laws of war.

Similar examples can be found from other campaigns: rape was common and sometimes those on the losing side might become slaves. To those on the winning side, other well-known rules governed the division of the spoils, whether property or the ransom of prisoners. By the time of the Hundred Years War these conventions can be found written into the indentures under which armies were recruited. In April 1415 before the Agincourt campaign, Thomas Tunstall contracted with the king to supply six men at arms and 18 mounted archers. The indenture set out that if they took any captives, 'the lord king shall have the third part of the gains of Thomas as well as a third of a third part of the gains of the men of his retinue'.[9] Disputes easily arose in the field over who had made captive an important prisoner and thus could claim the ransom, leading to lawsuits that could drag on for years. The case over the division of the ransom of the count of Denia, captured at the Battle of Najera (fought by the English, led by the Black Prince, in Spain) in 1367 lasted for over a century.[10]

If we move on, to the way in which war was conducted in our period, some commentators have remarked on an alleged dislike of pitched battles among medieval commanders. Historians like Charles Oman, writing in the 1920s, attributed this to the incompetence of medieval generals or their inability to control ill-disciplined and ill-trained troops. Later writers have tended to emphasise the influence of Vegetius's views. He pointed out the perhaps obvious fact that the outcome of a war is difficult to predict. Rather than risk the perils of the battlefield it was better to 'secure plenty of provisions for yourself and to destroy the enemy by famine'. The reluctance of medieval generals to indulge in battle was due to an acceptance that a war of attrition, with many sieges and the laying waste of the countryside, might be slower to produce a result but was also much less risky than chancing all on the battlefield. Vegetius explained that 'good officers decline general engagements where danger is common'. They were well aware that 'fortune often has a greater share than valour' on the battlefield.[11]

This point of view has been strongly argued by John Gillingham in particular, who also sees the *chevauchée*, or raid, causing the maximum amount of devastation to the enemy's towns, villages and agriculture, as part of the same strategy.[12] Gillingham's views have been disputed by Rogers but both see medieval commanders as following another of Vegetius's principles, 'all that is profitable to you is noxious and unprofitable to your adversary and all that is helpful to him is harmful to you'. Vegetius also laid stress on preparing a campaign carefully. Intelligence should be gathered from spies about the enemy's forces and his dispositions. Late medieval military leaders, usually either monarchs or noblemen, did not go to war lightly, but when it was necessary they acted with at least some idea of the appropriate strategy and a modicum of forward planning.

We should, however, beware of seeing all violent encounters in our period as following this pattern. Stephen Morillo has pointed out that wars on the Vegetian pattern, characterised by a very cautious attitude to battle, must have as their prime aim the acquisition (or defence) of territory: in effect they must be fought between rulers of settled societies.[13] A civil war, fought to gain possession of power rather than land, might result in a different pattern, with little raiding and fierce and frequent battles. This contrast can perhaps be seen between the first phase of the Hundred Years War and the Wars of the Roses. Crécy (1347) and Poitiers (1356) are so well known partly perhaps because such battles were rare occasions. Between December 1460 and March 1461, during the civil wars, however, no fewer than four field engagements took place in England, while in 1471 only three weeks separated the bitterly fought battles of Barnet and Tewkesbury.

The reality of chivalry?

The very idea of civil war is one that seems foreign to the ideals of chivalry as they are generally understood. The virtues of *prouesse*, *loyauté*, *largesse*, *courtoisie* and *franchise* (prowess in war, loyalty, generosity, courtesy and a free bearing) listed by Keen[14] seem to accord ill with the grubby reality of any kind of warfare, especially that between fellow countrymen. Huizinga's *The Waning of the Middle Ages* argues forcefully that by our period chivalry was no more than a convention found in romances or at most a polite veneer over the unpleasant realities of aristocratic life at this time. We can find similarly divergent views in interpretations of one of the best known portraits of a knight in English literature. To most readers Chaucer's Knight is a model of chivalry; but to one commentator, Terry Jones, the description 'he was a very perfect gentle knight' is heavily ironic. The Knight of *The Canterbury Tales* was in his view a vicious mercenary.[15] Admiration of the idea, however, that chivalry encouraged honour, the protection of non-combatants (particularly women), and feats of arms of almost reckless bravery is not hard to find in contemporary writings, some of which have been mentioned above.

The founding of Orders of Knighthood – the Garter in England in 1348, the Star in France in 1351 and the Golden Fleece in Burgundy in 1431 – can be seen as having the same dual character. On the one hand these Orders provided opportunities for feasts and festivals, both religious and secular in character, and could be linked either openly or by implication with knightly brotherhoods of legend. A link with King Arthur and the knights of the Round Table had obvious appeal, and as Keen pointed out, the story of Merlin coming to Arthur's father explaining how he would form a brotherhood of fifty noble knights provided the model for these later Orders.[16] On the other hand, the Orders were a very useful tool for forging close bonds among the political group around a monarch and rewarding good service with the coveted membership of an elite body. This did not preclude the members of these groups or individuals acting on occasion in ways which are reminiscent of those of the knights in romances. Virtually the whole membership of the Order of the Star fell on the field of Poitiers rather than abandon their king, John the Good. In 1370 John Seton, a Scotsman fighting in France with the English at a siege, challenged any Frenchman to single combat. He fought several bouts and then returned to his friends unharmed. While he was challenging them in this way, the French defenders of the town refrained from shooting him with a crossbow or other weapon as they easily could have done.[17] On an individual level we can also note the account of the beginning of his knightly career given in the diary of the German knight Jorg von Ehingen. He wrote:

> After this my father was much pleased and said, 'Dear son I will fit you out well and honourably for the expedition in such a manner as becomes a knightly man so that you may exercise yourself in all knightly matters and tournaments and be prepared to take your place among your equals and superiors who have been dubbed knights and so you shall return to your place.' Accordingly I was provided with armour and cuirass with stallions, horses, pages, clothes and other things and fitted out as a knight.[18]

On a larger scale, the Teutonic Knights, as we have mentioned, needed the help of warriors from across western Europe in their crusading wars. To encourage this they deliberately played up the chivalric aspects of their expeditions by establishing a special feast, known as the Table of Honour, for their guests. As described by a French chronicler, this had many of the features found in romances. For example, at the end of the feast: 'And then one of the knights of that religion (the Teutonic Order) gave to each of them a shoulder badge on which was written in letters of gold "*Honneur vainc tout.*" '[19] In this instance the secular, religious and 'play-acting' elements of chivalry seem inextricably mixed.

The fact that chivalry was a 'complex and often contradictory code' was what struck J. Barnie particularly when looking at some of the events recorded by chroniclers. He noted how, in an incident recorded in the Scots *Scalachronica*, when addressing a knight who wished to bring honour on his lady by performing great feats of arms in the Scots wars, the English commander agreed, 'where that is practicable'. The desire to do such things was not seen as entirely foolish but considerations of practicality had to be taken into account.[20] In his view chivalry, though it might at times seem hypocritical, did promote 'ideas and values' which did influence the 'the characteristic outlook and actions of the aristocrats and knights' who fought in France. To this group, the Black Prince as described by Chandos Herald was 'a near-perfect embodiment of the ideal they professed to follow'.[21]

> Those who dwelt about him esteemed him and loved him greatly, for largesse sustained him and nobleness governed him, and discretion, temperance and uprightness, reason, justice and moderation: one might rightly say that such a Prince would not be found, were the whole world to be searched throughout its whole extent.

At much the same period, however, Peter the Ceremonious of Aragon listed the qualities to look for in knights; as well as being hardworking and used to suffering, 'they should be cruel so as not to have pity in pillaging their enemies nor in wounding nor in killing them'. In this text, effective battle-hardened soldiers, not knights of romance, are the preferred model.[22]

Tactics and strategy in practice

The Hundred Years War

The major conflict in our period was the Hundred Years War, fought between England and France, though at times other princes, particularly the rulers of Burgundy and Scotland, were drawn into the conflict. From the English point of view the most prominent feature of the war was their three resounding victories over the French: Crécy 1347, Poitiers 1356, and Agincourt 1415. The French tend to think of the cunning and daring of Bertrand du Guesclin in the 1370s; the appealing legend of *La Pucelle*, the Maid of France, Joan of Arc; or their final crushing victory at Castillon in 1453. Our aim here is not to consider the causes of these battles or the politics involved, these has been dealt with in Chapter 3. Our purpose is to consider what events can tell us about the way in which war was waged at this time, and whether the idea of a military revolution can be sustained.

In any war the strategy of the attacking army may be hardest to discern. The aims of the defenders are usually simple; to rid their lands of their enemies and restore peace. If, however, we consider the aims of Edward III in the first phase of the Hundred Years War or of Henry V in the period from 1415 till his death, these are not so easy to ascertain. Did English kings take their claim to the French Crown seriously or was it an excuse for war, part of the justification needed for attacking fellow Christians? Was Edward III's real aim to restore, as far as possible, English rule to the territories of his great-great-great-grandfather Henry II? Did Henry V intend to conquer France or only to re-establish an English duchy of Normandy? Or did they have no overall view but a desire for military glory and the spoils of war, whatever these might turn out to be? It may well be the case that war aims changed as the situation developed. Once the Treaty of Troyes had been signed, making Henry V the heir of Charles VI of France, the English were in fact parties to a civil war between the Armagnacs and the Burgundians.

Looking at particular campaigns may help to provide some answers to these 'big'questions and also allow us to consider commanders' tactics. Our first example is the campaign of 1346–7, which includes the English victory at Crécy and the siege of Calais. One commentator has found Edward III's intentions on his landing at St-Vaast-la-Hogue in Normandy in July 1346, 'impossible to fathom'.[23] A more general view of recent writers has been that Edward embarked on the devastating raid across Normandy in order to wreak economic damage on the French but that he did not intend to fight a battle. In the best Vegetian manner he was anxious to avoid the dangers and uncertainties of a pitched battle but was trapped by the French on his march north towards Flanders and his allies, and forced to give battle.[24] It is Rogers' contention that Edward was not only using the economic weapon of a *chevauchée* but was also actively seeking to provoke his opponent to battle, but battle on his terms and in a place of his choosing. His aim in fact was to bring the war to an end by fighting and winning a decisive engagement. This was the purpose underlying his march north; it was expressed in so many words in his response to the challenge of Philip VI of France: 'we have come without pride or presumption into our realm of France, making our way towards you to make an end to war by battle'. The successful crossing of the Somme by the English at the ford at Blanchetacque ensured that the battle was fought in a position chosen by Edward, not Philip VI.

In the actual encounter, on 26 August 1346, the English deployed in three squadrons (confusingly know to contemporaries as *battles*). One remained in the rear; the other two consisted of men at arms on foot with archers on the wings. The French had a large force of Italian crossbowmen in the front ranks, with heavy cavalry (knights) behind. The crossbowmen were unable to match the rate of fire of the English archers with their longbows. When they began to give way the knights pressed forward but the sheer number of men involved and the confusion caused by dying and wounded horses led to the battlefield becoming a place of chaotic slaughter, with many Frenchmen smothered in the piles of the fallen. King Philip himself fought bravely but, unable to rally the remnants of his forces, slipped away to Abbeville leaving Edward to contemplate his overwhelming victory.[25]

Two days later King Edward led his forces north to lay siege to Calais, arriving there on 3 September. The siege would last eleven months and again his aims in spending so much time, energy and treasure in this way have been questioned. Perroy believed that the aim was only to capture a port from which the English could return home; but Le Crotoy was already in their hands. Others have seen it as almost an irrelevant sideshow and afterthought. Rogers, however, sees it as a further step on the way to ending the war for good; Philip had been defeated at Crécy but could still put an army in the field. He would be provoked to yet another battle by the siege of this strategic Channel port. This argument has cogency since it is hard to understand why otherwise so much was invested in this siege. It is also the case that the catastrophe of the Black Death, which struck just as the siege was ending, prevented Edward III from exploiting his two victories as he may have intended. The war was not ended but continued for many more weary years. If we accept Rogers' views, Edward III was not only a brilliant battlefield commander but had a sure grasp of strategy; the failure to realise his aims in this campaign was due to forces completely outside his control.[26] He, in fact, achieved almost all of these in 1360 by the Treaty of Brétigny. Edward III, by the determined use of devastating *chevauchées*, had provoked his enemies into chancing all on the battlefield, and at Poitiers had captured their king. This created a situation where the French were prepared to sign a humiliating treaty because, bad as the situation was, leaving things as they were was even worse.[27] Edward regained the bulk of his ancestral Angevin territories in full sovereignty (not as a vassal of the king of France) but promised to renounce his claim to the Crown.

Was his grandson Henry V attempting to repeat this strategy when the war against France re-opened with the siege of Harfleur and the Battle of Agincourt? Since, in negotiations with the French prior to the outbreak of hostilities, Henry had claimed that his aim was the full implementation of the terms of the Treaty of Brétigny, there is room for argument that this was his purpose.[28] He was, however, initially far less successful than his great-grandfather in putting his strategy into effect. His landing place, Harfleur, immediately involved him in a siege. It took him a month to take the town and when he left to march for Calais his troops were suffering from dysentery and were depleted by the number left behind to garrison the town. It was already late in the year for campaigning and the weather was very poor. The motive for this move is obscure; he had no need to take this route merely to return to England and he did not devastate the countryside on the line of march. His chaplain explained it by saying that the king felt he could rely 'on divine grace and the justice of his cause' and thus was prepared to take the risk of marching the length of what he called 'his duchy of Normandy'.

There is perhaps more justification for thinking that Henry, rather than Edward III before Crécy, had been trapped by the French when on 25 October, 14 days after he left Harfleur, battle was joined at Agincourt. The tactics of the battle itself, however, confirm Henry's skill as a commander. His manoeuvrings, which ensured that the small English army fought on a restricted site, the skilful deployment of his archers, and their use of pointed stakes to protect their position, all ensured that the battle became a blood bath for the French forces. There was little opportunity for the French to implement the plan drawn up before the battle, which involved cavalry attacks on the flanks of the English. Both Crécy and Agincourt have been used as examples of a new kind of warfare, with noble knights being defeated by archers of lesser rank. This seems to oversimplify the situation, with success being due to reasons peculiar to each encounter. At Agincourt, unlike Crécy, the vanguard of the French was composed of dismounted men at arms; the French cavalry attack on the English baggage train, in fact, caused real alarm. The firepower of the archers greatly helped the English victory but so did the careful disposition of forces, and extraneous factors like the softness of the ground, caused by days of rain.[29] In his next campaign, in 1417, however, Henry adopted a quite different strategy based on the slow and patient reduction of towns and castles by siege, which resulted in the English occupation of Normandy, and their ruling it much like a colony.

Border warfare

The need to adapt both strategy and tactics to the particular physical and social circumstances of the 'war zone' is made very clear in the case of the wars between England and Scotland on the Borders. In the first half of the fourteenth century the Scots both won a crushing victory at Bannockburn and were themselves defeated at Halidon Hill. Much more characteristic of the region was low-level raiding by both sides, with no decisive outcome. There were certain features of Scots society and of the manner in which war was waged in this area that made either victory or a lasting settlement hard to come by. Despite the often bitter and complex disputes within the Stuart family, the royal house of Scotland and between the Crown and the nobility, the captivity of both David II and James I in English hands, and the long minorities of David II, James I and James II (described in Chapter 3: i), the capacity of Scotland to resist the English was not severely impaired. The magnates, despite their feuding, could and would use their own forces to defend their lands and to raid into England. Specifically royal forces were often very small. English armies, though frequently many times larger than those raised by the Scots, often suffered from a lack of supplies or from an inability to cope with the terrain and the weather. Although writing of the 1327 expedition to Scotland, Froissart's description of its miseries would apply to other later incursions as well:

> Mounts and riders were tired out yet the men had to sleep in full armour holding their horses by the bridles since they had nothing to tie them to, having left their equipment in the carts which could not follow them over such country. For the same reason there were no oats . . . and they themselves had nothing to eat . . . they had nothing to drink . . . they had no lights or fires. They hoped for better things when day dawned, [but] . . . it began to rain so heavily and steadily all day . . . that by noon . . . The river . . . was too swollen to be re-crossed.[30]

It is also the case that neither side harboured cordial feelings for the other. The Scots boasted that they might 'enter England at our ease and ride far into the country without any hindrance from the sea'. The English saw them as savage perpetrators of atrocities against the innocent: in 1388 a chronicle records that they 'confined two hundred or more weak and decrepit old men in their dwellings with the doors shut . . . they unpardonably and without mercy burnt them to death'.[31]

This kind of warfare may have been a good training ground for individual commanders but demanded a different approach from that needed on major campaigns in France.

Burgundy

Our third example of the conduct of war is provided by Burgundy; more particularly the campaign against Swiss forces which ended with the death of Charles the Bold on the battlefield in 1477: a dramatic example of the unforeseen consequences of battle signalled centuries earlier by Vegetius. The Burgundian dukes had enjoyed a reputation as warriors since the end of the fourteenth century. John the Fearless as a young man was involved in the disaster at Nicopolis in 1396, during the Crusade led by the king of Hungary and later Emperor, Sigismund, and was one of the few prisoners to be ransomed rather than slaughtered by the Turks. The *podestá* (governor) of Lucca in 1407 had remarked,

> you may be sure that the duke of Burgundy will remain the most influential and powerful prince of this kingdom. His power is based on the troops which he can raise in his lands. He can muster so many that he fears no-one.[32]

We also know something of the organisation of these forces for war from the rich sources available in the Burgundian archives. A document of 1411 sets out how John dealt with preventing quarrels among troops raised from the many different lands of his domains. Since, on this occasion, troops from the *Franc* (county) of Bruges were in dispute with those from Ypres as to who should march behind the contingent from the city of Bruges itself, he laid down that they should do so on alternate days. In September 1417 when moving against the *Armagnacs*, he warned his forces to keep their distance from Paris since there, 'they [the Armagnacs] can easily and plentifully supply themselves with cannon and other similar armaments'. The baggage train should also 'be placed battened down behind the rearguard to fortify it'.[33]

John's grandson Charles the Bold became involved in more serious warfare from 1471. His almost obsessive interest in military matters had already been noted. An Italian ambassador described him on the march:

> The trouble he takes is incredible. He always rides in his cuirass. All his pleasure, his every thought is in men-at-arms, to make them look good and move in good order. He never dismounts until the whole camp is lodged and he has inspected all round the site.[34]

In 1476, however, things did not go his way. His overall intentions are clear enough. He wished to stabilise his eastern frontier against the Swiss, and especially the towns of Bern and Basle, and assert his control over the duchy of Lorraine. All this was probably related to his desire to create for himself an independent realm consisting of a coherent block of territory, owing fealty neither to the French Crown nor to the Empire. The previous year's campaign had not gone well. He had failed to take the town of Neuss by siege and had been defeated by the Swiss both at Grandson and at Murten. Now he was greatly outnumbered by the forces of the Swiss and their allies; he was not familiar with the difficult mountainous and wooded terrain, while his opponents were on their home ground. He had a large and well-served artillery train but the rate of fire of the guns was slow and moving them over the bad roads was extremely difficult. He was thus already in trouble when he laid siege to Nancy at the end of October 1476. Severe winter weather set in, leaving him and his soldiers with inadequate supplies. During December reinforcements, perhaps as many as 20,000 including about 6,000 experienced Swiss infantrymen, joined the opposing forces. Charles probably had about five and a half thousand demoralised, cold, hungry men facing a large force of fresh well-equipped volunteers. He decided to abandon the siege of Nancy and march out to confront his enemies. On 5 January, in heavy snow, he positioned himself across the road leading into Nancy but in such a way that he was unable to see his enemies outflanking his forces on his right wing. Within a relatively short space of time his forces gave way under the Swiss flanking attack; his artillery was overrun and the remnants of the army fled in disorder for Metz some fifty kilometres away. His own body was not found until two days later, stripped naked, lying in a frozen streambed.[35] With him fell the duchy of Burgundy.

This is, of course, only a very selective look at the warfare of a century and a half, but can we see any relationship between these sample battles and campaigns and the idea of a military revolution in the later Middle Ages, mentioned above? First of all, had infantry become of greater value to a commander than cavalry? The English victories in France have often been accounted for by the use of archers; the Burgundian army was destroyed largely by Swiss infantry. A cavalry charge can be a devastating weapon but can also lead to rapid disaster if misjudged. The catastrophic defeat of the crusading army at Nicopolis was the result of a cavalry charge over unsuitable ground against a well prepared enemy. We need, however, to beware of jumping to hasty conclusions. The most notable change in the armies engaged, during the Hundred Years War, was the increasing proportion of mounted archers; even if archers fought on foot, mobility before battle was joined was a precious asset. The terrain at Nancy and the weather conditions were both unsuitable for horses: Charles the Bold had nearly 3,000 mounted troops in his army and the combined forces of his opponents included 2,000 horse in the vanguard.[36] Moreover, Contamine has called our period 'the Age of the Horse' and has pointed out that it is not until the end of the fifteenth century that the number of true foot soldiers in armies begins to rise and to consist of well-trained men who could hope to resist cavalry.[37]

With regard to the use of guns, there is little evidence that cannon could decide the outcome of a battle at this period. Matthew Bennett argues that the English defeats at Formigny (1450) and Castillon (1453) occurred not because of the French use of field artillery but because the English commanders lost control of their forces and thus could not employ the tactics which had brought victory at Agincourt or Verneuil.[38] The only battles where the use of gunpowder weapons may have had a decisive influence on the result are those between the forces of the Empire and the Hussites in the 1420s and early 1430s (see below). Where the use of gunpowder was undeniably important was in the conduct of sieges. David Eltis has pointed out how towns in Germany frantically tried to remodel their fortifications to deal with the threat posed by siege guns to their old town walls. Some just piled up earth behind the walls to absorb the force of cannon shot but sometimes this made things easier for the attackers; 'the earth tumbles down with the masonry which makes it all the easier for the enemy to climb into the breach'.[39] By the end of our period, any army setting out on a serious campaign needed an artillery train and a corps of gunners for use in these circumstances but would not find that artillery did more than create confusion in a field engagement. The final characteristic of the so-called military revolution of the Middle Ages is the size of the armies that could be put in the field. This involves matters of supply and finance and will be dealt with in our next section.

(ii) THE LOGISTICS OF CONFLICT

England

The fact that a paid, at least quasi-professional, army was used in the Hundred Years War, not an army composed of those fulfilling their feudal obligations to an overlord, has been seen as a highly significant change in the nature of war. Attention has also been drawn to the ability of the English Crown to organise supplies.

Hewitt's work on the fourteenth century set out in detail the way in which Edward III's armies were supplied by the Crown.[40] Prestwich, however, has pointed out that this system was no longer used in the fifteenth century, when armies fighting in France were expected largely to survive by foraging.[41] Henry V's army, for example, suffered badly from hunger before Agincourt, and later English armies in France were not supplied from England but were expected to 'live off the country' using local resources.

Edward I had been able to raise the infantry element of the very large armies needed to fight in Scotland by the expedient of sending commissions of array out into the counties and offering pay to the men raised. The basis of these commissions was the widely accepted obligation that each able-bodied man had, to defend his country. The commissioners (local knights for the most part) expected each community to provide a certain number of men. These were intended to be those most fitted for war but there was no way of ensuring that they had any training or any real inclination to join an army. The cavalry for these expeditions was largely composed of those who had a duty to fight for their king. This might be expressed in the old feudal terms of knight service or it might be voluntary service offered by those nobles who accepted their role in society as warriors.

There is some evidence that earls and other lords were reluctant to accept paid service in a royal army, fearing perhaps a loss of their independence or their ability to benefit directly from booty or captured lands.[42] In 1327, for the campaign in Scotland, Edward III's army still contained a feudal element but this was small; it was clear that this system could not provide an adequate fighting force. In 1337, at the outset of the Hundred Years War, the army was wholly recruited by contract, often using indentures signed with individual captains, which obligated them to provide so many men, divided into the categories of bannerets, knights, men at arms and archers, at pre-determined rates of pay, at a certain place and at a certain time. (A banneret was usually of knightly status and was the equivalent of a modern army officer. He would be in charge of a section of the force and his presence on the battlefield would be marked by a banner; hence the name.) Once they were assembled, a muster would be taken and a roll drawn up of the names of those present. The men would then receive an advance on their wages, with the remainder to be paid at regular intervals during the campaign.

The earliest surviving indenture is from 1270 in connection with a proposed Crusade, but the concept soon became familiar. Those who were recruited by the captains would be volunteers in many instances; increasingly, as the war progressed, they would be experienced soldiers. Very often they would have some prior connection with the captain or lord, perhaps as tenants or the sons of tenants on his estates, or members of his affinity or retinue. Individual indentures between a member of a retinue and a lord would often refer to service in both peace and war, with an annual fee being paid. These private indentures have been linked to the idea of 'bastard feudalism' first put forward by Plummer in the nineteenth century, and since discussed by virtually all historians writing on the period. It was suggested that the retinues or affinities created in this way amounted to the 'private armies' of English nobles and were an important factor in the disorder of the second half of the fifteenth century. Michael Hicks[43] and others have tended to see the system more as the exercise of patronage in a way which could stabilise society (see above, Chapter 3: iii).

Certainly, despite the wording of many documents, only a minority of a magnate's feed retainers would be involved in overseas warfare under his command. Indentures for war – that between the duke of Bedford and Sir John Fastolf from November 1424, for example, – set out the terms of service of the captain of a military unit and his commander. Fastolf agrees to provide and lead 80 mounted men at arms and 250 archers for a year. They will be employed in the conquest of Maine. Wages will be on the usual scale: that is, 4s per day for a knight banneret; 2s per day for a knight bachelor; 12d per day for a mounted man at arms and 6d per day for an archer. If booty is taken, one-third of its value will be due to Bedford; Fastolf will have the right to the ransoms of any prisoners taken except those of very high rank, including the Dauphin himself, who must be handed over to Bedford. In this particular indenture a final clause also obliges Fastolf to protect 'the people and subjects obedient to the king' [Henry VI] 'from all force, violence, pillages, robberies, seizure of provisions, horses, cattle, and all other exactions whatever'.[44] A further element in the wages of most expeditions, from the 1340s, was a *reward* or quarterly bonus, often paid at the rate of 100 marks (£66 13s 4d) per hundred men at arms.

If the king himself was present on an expedition formal indentures were often not signed with individuals, since royal servants would handle administrative matters, but the 'terms of engagement' differed little from those set out above. The composition of an entire army can be grasped from the account of Walter de Wetewang, Treasurer at War for the forces besieging Calais in 1347. In this army there were 20,076 archers, 1,066 knights and 4,182 esquires and men at arms; 88 named captains were present with their men, their followings varying in size from the 1,376 with Henry, earl of Lancaster, to the three or four men with knights like Sir Rauf Ferrers or Sir William Marmion.[45]

While armies raised to serve in France and recruited in England used this system almost exclusively during the Hundred Years War, the idea of war service being linked to grants of land did not entirely fade away. On the Borders, landowners throughout the fifteenth century were still liable to provide armed men to serve against the Scots whether on small-scale raids or in larger forces. In Normandy, and in what was called the *pays de conquête* (conquered lands), grants of estates were made to English captains on terms very like those of knight service. Sir Gilbert Umfraville was granted extensive lands at Amfreville-sur-Iton in 1419 on the terms that he would provide garrisons for all the castles on his lands and also twelve men-at-arms and twenty-four archers for the royal army.[46] In England itself, the general obligation to defend the realm was also invoked, particularly from the late 1330s to the 1370s, to provide a militia to protect the towns on the south coast, which were vulnerable to French raids. The traditional lighting of beacons on high ground and the ringing of church bells were supposed to provide warning of an attack. Local gentry were commissioned as 'keepers of the maritime lands' to gather together a force to resist invaders and to make sure that warnings were given. When an attack did occur, like the raid on Winchelsea in 1360, the militia does not seem to have been of much use and the need to maintain vigilance caused considerable disruption and a climate of nervousness in these areas. Men with military capability were not supposed to move away from these districts and, for example, Bartholomew de l'Isle was severely rebuked by the Crown for leaving the Isle of Wight in 1339.[47]

We must also not forget all the auxiliaries who were included on many expeditions. Some were essential from the military point of view: miners from the Forest of Dean to make tunnels beneath the walls of besieged towns; chaplains, surgeons and farriers. Others perhaps had the purpose of enhancing the prestige of their lord. Edward III set out for France in 1344 accompanied by a band including five trumpeters, five pipers, three waits (playing wind instruments), two clarioners (playing small trumpets much like a bugle), one taborer (playing a small drum), one nakerer (kettle drummer) and one fiddler. In 1359 he is also said to have taken his falconers to France.[48]

Once an army had been raised, of course, it needed supplies both of arms and of food. Ways of providing these did change during the war and differed in the various theatres of war. A feudal knight had been expected to provide for himself all the equipment needed to make him an effective fighting man. The high cost of doing so perhaps contributed to the prestige that attached to knighthood by the later medieval period. Archers and foot soldiers recruited by commissions of array were supposed to be armed and clothed by their community. This could amount to a considerable sum: up to £2 per man in the early years of Edward III, when horses as well as arms had to be provided. Increasingly during the course of the war the Crown assumed responsibility for arming its forces. The Tower of London acted as the base of the Royal Ordnance and collected large quantities of arms, mostly longbows and arrows, when an expedition was being prepared. Orders would be sent out to sheriffs to assemble what was needed. The number of bows, some painted, some white, and sheaves of arrows which were received at the Tower between 1355 and 1360 have been described by H. J. Hewitt. The total of over 4,000 bows and 6,000 sheaves of arrows was collected from counties in the south and the Midlands. Some form of basic uniform (known frequently as livery) was also provided, often no more than the requirement that the sign of St George (a red cross on a white ground) should be displayed on clothing, but sometimes white coats were included. The most elaborate uniforms seem to reflect local rather than national pride. The Black Prince's Cheshire archers in 1355 had green and white parti-coloured hats and tunics; in 1463–4 Nottingham equipped a troop with red coats with a local slogan picked out in white.

The increasing use of cannons placed even more responsibility on the Royal Ordnance for the supply of suitable guns. The Tower had long been responsible for the production of 'engines', the large contrivances used at sieges to fling stones at or over the walls. They appear under various names, *springalds*, *mangonels* or *trébuchets*, and were certainly used alongside guns in the fourteenth centuries. Details of the work of the Royal Ordnance are hard to come by: we do not have certain knowledge of the design and manufacture of early guns or of how effective they were. Cannon for use on ships in the fifteenth century are always described as coming from the Tower but this does not mean that either they or the stone cannon balls that they fired were made there. What is clear is that these weapons were more costly than others previously known, and more complex to manufacture and to service.

Although the king had his own stud and bred horses for his own use, knights and mounted archers were expected to supply their own mounts. This was a considerable expense since a fully trained war horse was worth an average of £9 in the middle of the fourteenth century. An exceptional animal like that bought by Edward III in the Netherlands in 1337 cost the enormous sum of £168 15s. We have information about the worth of the horses used by knights and others because, although the king did not provide mounts, he did compensate their owners for their loss if they were killed or died in the course of an expedition. An elaborate system was evolved to value horses at the start of a campaign and then record the compensation paid for those lost. Each animal was described, 'a grey horse with one left foot white', 'a black *destrier* (a highly trained warhorse, always a stallion) with a white muzzle and left hind foot white',[49] and valued. All this took up so much time that when the war was renewed in 1369 the system (called *restor*) was abandoned and the *reward* was doubled.

We have already mentioned the commonly held assumption that an army would live 'off the land'; that is by seizing supplies from the enemy or even purchasing them locally. This could be unrealistic when a body of some ten thousand men needed to be fed, not to speak of their horses and all the assorted hangers on, in a poor and rugged land. Scottish campaigns in the late thirteenth and early fourteenth centuries had made the need to organise supplies clear. The abject failure of Edward II's 1322 expedition was put down to the fact that Flemish pirates prevented English supply ships getting through, while the Scots had destroyed or carried away all local food or fodder. When the foragers could only find one lame cow, earl Warenne is said to have remarked, 'this is the dearest beast I have ever yet seen: it must surely have cost £1000 or more'.[50] (At this date £1,000 was an enormous sum of money; greater than the yearly income of many lords.) The Scots, on the other hand, apparently needed no elaborate preparations nor were they in any danger of running out of supplies on their raids unto England. Froissart records in a kind of fascinated horror how the Scots:

> take with them no provision of bread nor wine. . . . They seethe [captured] beasts in their own skins . . . and behind the saddle they will have a little sack full of oatmeal and . . . make a little cake in manner of a cracknell or a biscuit and that they eat to comfort withal their stomachs.[51]

In the 1340s, the system known as *purveyance* was widely used. This involved the collection of foodstuffs from all over the country on orders sent to the sheriffs in each county by the Crown. It was much disliked since although the goods required would be paid for eventually, prices were often low and the delay considerable. Sometimes it was claimed goods were bought for the king but then reappeared on the open market at higher prices. On some occasions so much was required for the king's purposes that ordinary people suffered from shortages. The quantities demanded could be large: in 1340, 60,400 gallons of ale were to be purveyed for the crews of thirty ships serving for forty days, setting sail from Yarmouth. This amounted to no less than a gallon of ale per man per day. In 1346, the receiver of the king's victuals, William de Kelleseye, was supplied with flour, oats, salt pork, mutton, sides of beef, weys of cheese, and peas and

8 War at sea from the Warwick Pageant

This picture of a sea battle was drawn in the late fifteenth century. It purports to show an incident during the pilgrimage of Richard Beauchamp, earl of Warwick, to Jerusalem. Note the men in the 'castle' on top of the main masts hurling missiles, the use of both crossbows and longbows by armed men on the vessels and the cannon firing over the side of one ship. The streamer on the left-hand ship clearly shows the 'bear and ragged staff' badge of the earldom of Warwick.

beans from all the counties of eastern England. All this foodstuff had to be transported to Portsmouth, the muster point for this campaign, most of it going by water. By the time some of it got there it was rotten and unfit for use.

By 1415, however, the system of *purveyance* was little used because of its general unpopularity. The victualler of Calais, for example, was now expected to buy his supplies from contracted merchants. Later, in 1417, captains were expected to provide at least two months' supplies for their men at the beginning of an expedition and thereafter to rely on local supplies. In this aspect of the organisation of war, in Prestwich's opinion, efficiency had declined since the days of Edward I.[52] It is notable that Sir John Fastolf makes no mention at all of the need for supplies in his scheme for the future conduct of the war written in 1435.[53]

Naval forces were put together in a somewhat different way. The underlying obligation on all to defend their country, already mentioned, was used as the justification of the power of the Crown to arrest all shipping in English ports, including that owned by foreigners, in time of need. Commissions were issued to groups of local gentry and other worthies to achieve this; they generally laid down specific criteria on the size of ships required. As well as this source of shipping, both Edward III and Henry V owned quite large numbers of royal ships, which were crewed by mariners receiving the king's wages. The *Cog Thomas* was Edward's most prized vessel and the one on which he led the English into battle at Sluys, in 1340. Henry V built up a considerable base for his ships at Southampton. He was also responsible for the building of a group of 'great ships', larger and of a more sophisticated design than any seen before, intended to be able to take on and defeat any vessels likely to be in the service of the French king. His death led to the dispersal of his ships, sold to pay his debts, since they were considered as his private property. Their maintenance may also have seemed an unwarranted expense to Henry VI's government at a time when both sides of the Channel were in English hands. The illustration of a sea battle, drawn in the late fifteenth century clearly shows the vessels and weapons available at that date (see Illustration 8).

France

French methods of recruitment until about 1420 were in many ways superficially similar to those of the English Crown. The general obligation on all able-bodied men to defend the realm, which in England was the legal justification for the activities of commissions of array, was the core of the French system. Contamine has pointed out that it comprised three strands, a mass levy of nobles, a mass levy of the common people and a fiscal (tax) element. This was because those who could not or would not serve themselves, were expected to pay for a substitute. The *ban et arrière ban*, as this mass levy was called, was supposed to be used only in a dire emergency but was in fact called out seven times between 1338 and 1356. The terms of the levy could be varied; for example, in 1358 walled towns were expected to produce one man at arms for one year at a cost of 10 *sous tournois* per day for each group of 75 hearths (households); in an unwalled town each group of 100 hearths had the same obligation. The system was generally seen as hard to control and usually produced unwilling or inexperienced recruits. A variation on this system was the *semonce des nobles* (summons of nobles). This was used by John II in 1355 when he summoned all knights and esquires in his kingdom between the ages of 15 and 60 to meet him at Amiens because he wanted to fight the English. Individual nobles might have further obligations related to the terms on which they held land, service that could properly be described as feudal.

The French Crown also recruited, in the first period of the Hundred Years War, by means of what were called *lettres de retenue*, which corresponded almost exactly to the English system of indentures. The *lettres* themselves were, however, phrased differently and were less precise, in defining the length of service, for example. This was often taken to be equivalent to the amount of time covered by the *prest* (wages) mentioned; this sounds reasonable but meant that it was perfectly possible and legal for a captain and his men to abandon a campaign without notice if it lasted longer than originally envisaged. A great deal of concern was also displayed in France over the possibility that musters were fraudulent, with the number of combatants present inflated to the benefit of the captain. After 1369, Charles V used this system almost exclusively, relying on a small group of favoured captains who served him for long periods. Their followings were by this time divided into groups of one hundred men at arms, known as *routes*. It was widely accepted that recruitment was in each captain's hands but that his men had three overriding obligations: they must serve continuously; they must not abandon their *route* without permission; and they must not cause damage to the persons or property of the king's loyal subjects. If this did occur, liability for all damage caused lay on their captain. Charles VI, however, returned to the old way of the *ban et arrière ban*. The army that fought at Agincourt was composed largely of those fighting on the basis of their feudal obligation, not volunteers.

All those serving in French armies in our period received some kind of pay whether answering a feudal summons or recruited by *lettres de retinue*. There were, however, several ways this might be done. A very few highly privileged individuals had all their expenses met by the Crown: their horses, food, arms and clothing were all provided. The garrisons of the many castles or other fortified places were granted a total sum to be spent as the captain decided. The majority was paid a daily wage that varied according to their status. These wages were subject to deductions, the so-called *droitures*, but could be increased by a payment known as *venues et retours* for the days spent travelling to and from the muster at the beginning and end of a campaign. Like all payments due from the Crown, a long period often elapsed between serving in the army and receiving the wages due. These soldiers were expected to provide their own arms or receive them from their captain at his expense. Similarly it was hoped by the Crown that the army could live off the country and only the most intermittent efforts were made to victual the army centrally. The failing efforts of the foragers left the army at the siege of Castillon-sur-Dordogne starving even though parties scoured the countryside for food up to 12 or 15 leagues away from the siege. The French Crown could exercise the right of *prise*, an equivalent of the English *purveyance*, but this was also exceedingly unpopular. It was largely enforced against the stores of religious houses, and when a garrison received food in this manner the captain was expected to reimburse the Crown for the costs.

Superficially, with regard to naval forces the French, particularly at the beginning of the Hundred Years War, had a much more coherent and centralised approach than that for land forces. Philip IV had established a base for French royal vessels at Rouen as early as 1295. The *clos des galées*, as it was known, had facilities to build and repair galleys, probably modelled on the dockyards widely available in the Mediterranean at the same date. Quite extensive use was made of the yard and its ships in attempts to relieve Calais in 1347. After that date, however, it seems to have become almost abandoned. The ships that the French did use with considerable success against English forces – for example, at La Rochelle in 1372, and in raids on the English coast – were either arrested in much the same way as English ships in similar circumstances or hired from French allies. These were usually Castile in the fourteenth century and Genoa (which had developed large sailing ships called *carracks*) in the early fifteenth century. The yard was taken by the English and burnt when Rouen fell in 1417.

The complex and relatively inefficient systems, relating to the army, were all changed by the reforms introduced by Charles VII after 1445. From this time on, the foundations were laid for the forces that served the Crown of France, usually with great success, until the Revolution. A clear distinction was made between those groups which formed part of a permanent 'standing' army, serving both in times of peace and in times of war, and those which served only when needed. The permanent companies were known as those *de l'ordonnance*, that is they served as ordered by the king. From 1450 these companies were divided into those *du grand ordonnance* and those *du petit ordonnance*. The former were composed of heavy cavalry for field armies; the latter were garrison troops. The basis of both groups was what was called the *lance*. This was not a weapon but a group of armed men consisting, in field armies, of six men and six horses: one man at arms with a supporting *coutiller* (so-called because he was armed with a type of knife) and a page, and also two mounted archers with another page or servant. The size of a French army could now be estimated according to the number of *lances* it contained. Charles VII could command 1500 to 1800 *lances*; Louis XI at the peak of his armed might, when considering an attack on Burgundy in 1477, had 4,142 available. The garrison troops became known as *mortes-payes* and in this case a *lance* consisted of only four men and four horses. This number was soon reduced considerably since mobility was not needed for most of their tasks. Despite the view that the French Crown was particularly adept in the use of artillery in field armies (their master gunner Jean Bureau was well known), the number of artillery specialists recruited for the standing army was small, no more than about 297 in the reign of Louis XI.

The major part of the temporarily recruited members of the armies of France was provided by the system of *franc-archers*. These owed their origin to a decree of 28 April 1448. This laid down that in every parish in France, each group of 80 hearths would have to provide one armed man, equipped with armour (a protective coat either of leather or mail, and a helmet) and arms. Initially these were to be a dagger, sword and bow, most frequently a crossbow; by 1466, however, the requirement was for a pike or a halberd, reflecting changes in the way infantry were deployed in battle. Charles VII could raise 8,000 men in this manner while Louis XI doubled this to 16,000. The decree also made clear that the selected *archers* should practice their skill regularly; would be, in recompense, exempt from most taxes; and should swear an oath 'to serve us (the king) faithfully and loyally against all and everybody'.[54] To victual these forces the Crown also set up a rather similar system. Merchants might still be encouraged to sell food and other goods directly to the army but also communities now had to provide regular obligatory contributions. The city of Troyes had to provide each month specified quantities of breadcorn, half wheat and half rye, barley, and wine for the army. The whole country was divided into zones, each with the duty of victualling the soldiers within its area. In Contamine's opinion, this had the effect of ensuring that, 'instead of provincial or local loyalty the population gave their support to all military operations'.[55] These arrangements did not prevent the French Crown from also employing mercenaries; many were Scots in the first half of the fifteenth century while Swiss became more common at the time of the Italian campaigns at the very end of the century. It is thought that the French Crown had permanent forces of about 20,000–25,000 men at this time, maybe as much as 1 per cent of the male population between 18 and 45.[56] Forces on this scale do seem to constitute a new departure and make it easier to understand why Charles VIII was eager to invade Italy.[57]

The Empire

The raising of armies within the Empire during our period depended largely on the Emperor receiving the support of the princes, especially, of course, the Electors. The Emperor could raise troops from his own family lands using the feudal obligation on landholders to support their overlord but this would not on its own produce the forces needed in most circumstances. Among the lesser nobility of the Empire, many once powerful families had been greatly weakened by the custom of dividing inheritances, leading to the creation of small weak states. At times the *Rittern*, or knightly class, seemed able virtually to ignore the demands of their supposed superiors and were certainly unable to offer much in the way of military aid. The seven electoral princes were in a stronger position, but even so, their lands were often not a homogeneous whole but a mixture of different tenures with different customs and powers. Where they had authority, their style of government resembled that in France. In the Palatinate, for example, members of some 600 noble families were closely linked to the ruler, as we have said (see above, Chapter 3: ii). However, even if lands granted by the prince to a lord were still regarded as fiefs, military service in the princely army had ceased to be associated with the possession of particular estates. The Elector (and most other German rulers) had built up a network of *Diener* or retainers, who were bound to serve their lord either for life or for a term of years at his expense. They would normally be expected to produce an agreed number of horsemen when summoned to the prince's forces. Some might receive the title of *Rat* or counsellor as a sign of honour. The system developed in such a way that *Diener* became more akin to mercenaries than to the members of a noble affinity in England, since there was no obligation on them to live within the prince's territory, let alone be his close associates except in the context of war.[58]

Sigismund's attempts to crush the rebellious Hussites in Bohemia (see Chapter 5) provide an example of how the Emperor went about obtaining the support of forces like these. To obtain princely support, a *Reichstag* (assembly of princes) was necessary; this was held at Breslau in 1420. At this, a Crusade against the heretic Czechs was proclaimed by the papal legate. This served as the stimulus to spur the princes to action, and all the subsequent campaigns against the Hussites, which uniformly ended in disaster for the imperial forces, were conducted on this basis. Sigismund suffered from his poverty; attempts to raise an imperial tax that could be used to pay an army were made at an Imperial Diet (general assembly of the Empire) in Nuremberg in 1422 but this was not successful.[59] His forces had no overall commander who was respected by all those present. The soldiers themselves were frequently accused of showing a great reluctance to fight. They were faced with opponents who were not only fired with religious enthusiasm, with a strongly nationalistic element, but who were also well led and well equipped. The Hussites developed the tactic of using war wagons, which made them almost invincible to Sigismund's forces. The army's supply wagons were drawn up in a square formation protected by ditches, with artillery in the centre. The wagons protected the infantry but could be quickly moved aside to allow a counter-attack once the opposing army began to reel from the fire of the Hussite gunners. The infantry also used battle flails (weapons which resembled the flails used in threshing corn), highly effective in close combat; their discipline was reinforced by their strong sense of unity, expressed in such things as the singing of battle anthems. One, 'You are the Warriors of God', combined their religious idealism with good military advice:

> You must all remember the password
> As it was given to you
> Always obey your captain
> Each shall help and protect the other.
> Each shall look for and stay with his own battalion.[60]

Even the final Hussite Crusade of 1431, when the heretics were divided among themselves and no longer had the leadership of their original remarkable general Jan Zizka (he had died in 1424), ended in 'circumstances of paralysis and confusion' as far as Sigismund's army was concerned. J. Riley-Smith comments on the notable energy with which these Crusades were organised but he also characterises them as futile.[61] The kind of army which Sigismund could raise by appealing to the old idea of Crusading and by calling on the support of the princes of the Empire could not overcome the much more coherent forces of the Hussites.

Burgundy

Burgundian armies in the late fourteenth century had a large element of knightly cavalry but also included contingents of foot soldiers from the Flemish towns. They enjoyed a formidable reputation ever since they had gained an unexpected victory over the French king at Courtrai in 1302. Between 1471 and 1473, Charles the Bold is usually credited with introducing reforms as a part of his agenda for uniting his scattered and disparate territories. He issued a series of decrees that re-organised his army. In these decrees he apparently adopted a scheme very like that which had been in existence in France since the late 1440s, described above. Twenty companies *de l'ordonnance* were set up, each comprising 900 men. The basic unit was, as in France, the *lance*. In Charles's plan, however, eight rather than six men made up each unit, with a greater emphasis on heavy cavalry. He also established rules of discipline and systems of drill; regulations specified that there should be no swearing or blaspheming in his army, as well as requiring a uniform and methods of identification. W. Paravicini and Richard Vaughan both saw these decrees as setting up something very like a standing army, largely composed of mercenaries and very different from the forces of his father and grandfather. Bacharach, however, argues that the dukes of Burgundy had always employed mercenaries on quite a large scale and had also had a large military element in their households. He also points out that though Charles may have wished to recruit at least 10,800 men for his new companies he was unable to do so. His army was very like that of his predecessors, being made up of a mixture of mercenaries, often recruited under their own captain, along with nobles and units from the town militias.[62] Change might have become more visible if Charles's death at Nancy had not ensured the collapse of his army along with the unified duchy of Burgundy.

Routiers and *écorcheurs*

Apart from the 'official' armies of the French Crown and other rulers we also need to consider the problem of the bands of armed men usually known as *routiers* in the fourteenth century and *écorcheurs* in the fifteenth. It is very easy to find in the various chronicle sources accounts of the devastation that overtook extensive areas of rural France in the course of the wars. Some were the result of the deliberate tactics of royal armies, particularly those of the English in the course of a *chevauchée*. Jean de Venette paints a picture of utter desolation.

> The fields were not sown or ploughed. There were no cattle or fowls in the fields ... the wolf might seek his prey elsewhere. ... Houses and churches no longer presented a smiling appearance with newly repaired roofs but rather the lamentable spectacle of scattered smoking ruins. ... Every misery increased on every hand.[63]

Much, however, was the work of bands or companies of armed men who preyed on the wretched country people. The lack of royal funds and therefore the failure to pay soldiers properly and promptly was held responsible for the scourge of these 'unofficial' armed bands, which terrorised much of the French countryside during the Hundred Years War. Similar groups could also be found in Italy and in other theatres of war. Evidence of their depredations is not lacking. Froissart has tales of their activities in the mid-fourteenth century. One group would enter a town secretly by night, set five or six houses on fire and when the townspeople then fled in terror steal the abandoned valuables.[64] Later in the fifteenth century, court records have many instances of robbery and violence including the story of

Mathiot Rousell, a man of over eighty. He claimed that he lost a mare and her foal, grain, cloth and other possessions to soldiers. Later they took him away as a prisoner to the town of Lioffans, where he was beaten and held to ransom.[65]

The system of *appatis*, or protection money, demanded by armed bands from towns or whole districts, was also widespread and could lay a heavy burden on those least able to pay. Wright, in his *Knights and Peasants*, has studied this whole aspect of the wars and points out that some villages could protect themselves by building fortified places or by the villagers themselves becoming brigands. He also argues that much of what the *écorcheurs* demanded from peasants was similar to the demands of legitimate lords in time of peace. To a peasant family the difference may not have been very noticeable.[66]

Financing the wars

Clearly the issue of how war was financed was one which could have grave consequences for the people. How did realms like England or France find the resources to fight such prolonged and at times expensive wars? In some ways Edward III and his successors were better able to do this than their rivals in France. War was no new experience for the English, who had fought long campaigns in both Wales and Scotland as well as shorter conflicts in France under Edward III's father and grandfather. As well as direct taxation based on a proportion of the annual value of an individual's moveable goods (that is, not including land or buildings), usually at the rate of one-tenth for the property of townsmen and one-fifteenth for the property of country people, which had to be sanctioned by Parliament, there were indirect taxes on the export or import of goods. The most important of these was the Custom (dating from the reign of Edward I) and subsidy (dating from the reign of Edward III) on the export of raw wool, woolfells (sheepskins) and hides. An import duty was paid on other goods, paid according to their declared value (tunnage on wine and poundage on other goods). The advantage of the indirect taxes, particularly the wool taxes, was that they needed no special parliamentary sanction for collection; they were usually authorised for a term of years at the beginning of a reign. The yield was also elastic (it increased or decreased with the volume of trade) and to some extent it could be relied on, though the Commons did from time to time vary the rate at which both Customs and subsidies were to be collected.

Borrowed money was a very important feature of English war finance and these duties were very suitable as security for loans. Creditors had a visible source of repayment and the yield of the Customs in a particular port could be and was assigned to repay a particular loan. The Crown jewels might be, in effect, 'pawned' in a rather similar way. Even so the king's need for loans could outrun the resources of the wealthiest lenders. Edward III caused the bankruptcy of the Italian merchant houses of the Bardi and the Peruzzi in 1338–9. The merchants of the City of London, including the very wealthy and powerful Richard Whittington (in his case the fiction is not far from the truth), later became a source of loan finance for the Crown, as did churchmen like Cardinal Beaufort, the bishop of Winchester, in the 1420s and 1430s. The fact that direct taxes needed parliamentary consent placed power in the hands of this body, which it, at times, exploited effectively. It also meant that the war had to have a measure of support form the community at large. Efforts were made with little success to find better ways of taxing the people than the old fifteenths and tenths; the failure to devise an acceptable way of re-assessing the value of taxpayers' possessions made the yield of this tax fall steadily over the fourteenth century. The perceived unfairness of one new system that was devised, the poll tax, has been largely blamed for the Peasants' Revolt of 1381.

In the fifteenth century the enthusiasm generated by Henry V's victories at first meant that Parliament was willing to grant taxes more or less as requested, but in the reign of his son it became increasingly reluctant to agree. In 1433, the Treasurer Lord Cromwell drew up a balance sheet of royal income and expenditure that has survived. This came to the melancholy conclusion that expenditure exceeded revenue by £47,887 7s 4¼d, not counting debts. These debts comprised money borrowed in the past for the Calais campaign, and expeditions in the Marches of Scotland, Aquitaine, Fronsac and Ireland, which came to a further £110,584, 2s 6d.[67] The total deficit of the Crown was therefore nearly £160,000, and the Crown was experiencing difficulty in raising further loans. From these figures we can well understand why there were such great difficulties in sending adequate aid to France in the last years of the English occupation.

A close look at operations at sea in the same period also illustrates the financial difficulties of the English Crown and the ways in which attempts were made to tackle them. Henry IV spent very little on ships in royal ownership. The often anarchic conditions in the Channel, with frequent attacks on trading vessels, were met with little official activity apart from a rather half-hearted response to complaints by merchants. Henry V, on his accession, as we have seen, vigorously encouraged the building of royal ships including one, the *Gracedieu*, of truly exceptional size. His fleet had considerable success against the vessels hired by the French from the Genoese. By the 1440s there was nothing left of the former royal squadron and the House of Commons complained vigorously of the damage caused to trade by the attacks on shipping in the Channel. The members put together an elaborate scheme to raise ships to guard the seas, which would have cost over £4,500 a year. They showed no sign, however, of being willing to provide this money and the scheme was quietly forgotten. What defence there was at sea was left in the hands of individuals, with little public involvement. The earl of Warwick in the 1450s and 1460s had the most powerful force at sea, financed from his own resources.

The king of France had much larger funds from his 'ordinary' (non-tax) income than the English king, perhaps three to five times greater; speaking of the early fourteenth century it has been said that 'the French kings were rich without strain'. He had, however, at the beginning of the Hundred Years War, a much less developed tax system, no history of using credit for financing a war and no available source of ready cash like the English duties on wool. Various expedients were tried in the early years including the manipulation of the bullion content of the coinage, short-term taxes and the raising of loans, including a large one from Pope Clement VI. No expedient was really successful and all incurred a degree of unpopularity. The capture of John II by the English at Poitiers, however, created the necessity for money to be collected for his ransom. This was an obligation that no Frenchman could deny. It served the purpose of allowing the French Crown to gain public acceptance of the idea that tax should be due on a regular basis whether or not a war was, in fact, in progress. The ravages of the *routiers*, noted above, also created the need for money for fortifications and other defences, particularly in towns, although a truce was officially in operation for much of the 1360s. During this decade the *gabelle* (salt tax), *aides* (indirect tax on the sale of commodities like wine) and *fouage* (later known as the *taille*, a hearth or household tax due from those not of noble status) became permanent. The administration of these taxes was not uniform throughout France. A greater or lesser degree of consent or consultation was expected in different provinces. Certainly there were much greater numbers of tax officials in France, particularly in the later fifteenth century, than in England. It is also the case that during the reign of Louis XI the amount raised in taxation increased greatly. In 1482 the total reached some 5.4 million *livres tournois*. Because of the continual variation in the bullion content of the currency it has been calculated that taxes between 1461 and 1479 increased by 105.71% in terms of *livres tournois*, 57.71% in terms of gold and 71.42% in terms of silver.[68]

Protests and riots did occur, to little avail. The French king could afford to keep a permanent army in being, as we have seen; had the necessary bureaucracy to administer such a body; and, under Louis XI, had a clear idea of the way in which such an army should be used. In contrast to the more traditional view that foreign wars were a disaster for the state, P. Chaunu has also pointed out that the wars in Italy were much less of a financial burden for France, than the reconquest of English-held territory and all the devastation caused by war on French soil. In his view the Italian wars removed potential aggressive trouble-makers from France while most of the economic costs of the war were borne by Italy. It was even possible to assert that war, provided it took place outside France, brought not an increase but a decrease in taxes.[69] All this contrasts forcibly with the more leisured approach to war and finance in the fourteenth century in France and the much more straitened circumstances of the English king.

The relative financial security of French kings was also probably greatly envied by the dukes of Burgundy. The nature of their domain made it necessary to become involved in negotiations with Estates (assemblies) for the different territories, and the councils of the major towns, if any tax was desired. Philip the Good tried hard to get Ghent, as the forerunner for other areas, to accept the idea of a salt tax in 1447 but with no success. Charles the Bold set up a central Chamber of Accounts at Mechlen, which improved the financial administration, but it is till very hard to get a clear idea of how his wars were paid for. He certainly sold offices on the French model and he raised loans from his own subjects and from bankers like the Italian Tommaso Portinari. He devised new taxes, the most successful being one on lands acquired by religious houses in the recent past. Vaughan's final conclusion is that he 'was supremely successful in obtaining money from his subjects whether in the form of loans, *aides* (taxes) or otherwise'.[70]

(iii) WAR AND NATIONHOOD

The idea that nation states have been forged by conflict against their neighbours is not new, nor is the belief that the sixteenth century was marked by the clear emergence of such states in Europe. How does this perception relate to the wars we have examined above?

In some ways the Hundred Years War, the major conflict we have discussed, had an inconclusive end. There was no formal peace; in fact English kings continued to include 'King of France' among their titles until the first years of the nineteenth century. At the beginning of this chapter we suggested that rulers saw their most basic function as the defence of their realm and their people. How does this perception relate to this war? The English had, on the one hand, won a series of victories in pitched battles which had spread their fame throughout Europe; on the other hand, all they had to show for over one hundred years of conflict ostensibly in pursuit of their 'rights' to the French Crown, was a port (Calais) on the Channel coast and the surrounding area of marshy, sandy ground. The rich and fertile lands of Gascony had been lost, as had all hope of recovering Normandy. The English Crown was embroiled in civil wars even as royal power in France, especially in the outlying provinces, was increased. The French, on the other hand, had survived very difficult circumstances and had emerged with the power of the Crown greatly increased.

Barnie felt that the first phase of the Hundred Years War could not be said to have heralded the growth of nationalism in either England or France, but he was prepared to see 'the beginnings of a crude form of patriotism'.[71] Peter Lewis has pointed out that the war was 'bound to force men to think in terms of "French" and "English", to produce a semblance of "national sentiment"'.[72] There is a considerable amount of contemporary Valois propaganda denigrating the English and their allies. Christine de Pizan wrote sneeringly of the 'snotty-nosed rebels / who've sided with the English'. The Gascons of Bayonne were eventually convinced of the rectitude of French claims to their town by the convenient miraculous appearance of a 'cross crowned with a crown of blue and ... the crown turned into a fleur-de-lis', in the sky as the French troops approached.[73] There was similar jingoistic writing in England. One poem began:

> France, effiminate, Pharisaical, shadow of vigour,
> Lynx, viper, foxy, wolvish, Medea
> Sly, siren, heartless, repulsive, proud.[74]

Ormrod, writing in 1994, makes the reasonable point that even if most could only express their identity 'through an often obscene contempt for the lecherous and treacherous French', they did see the war as 'a form of national crusade'.[75] Allmand emphasises the role of deliberate national propaganda by both sides but stresses the importance of the war in the development of national consciousness only in relation to France. Symbols like the fleur-de-lis or the *oriflamme*, the sacred banner from St Denis, were more frequently displayed. Even more importantly, however, national institutions developed in France at this period, particularly a royal army and a national tax system.[76]

In England the development of Parliament as a powerful check on royal power to tax at will clearly owes much to the need for war finance. We can also cite matters like the way in which English became the normal means of communication for all levels of society. Exchequer documents may still have used a form of Latin for the accounts of the kingdom but they are full of latinised English terms, and families like the Pastons, Stonors and Celys all used English in their letters. A counter-argument to this might be that in Scotland the close links between their form of English and that used in England itself did not make for better relations between the two peoples. The Scots had made a ringing declaration of their desire for independence in the Declaration of Arbroath (1320). In a letter to the Pope from thirty-nine Scottish magnates 'and the rest of the barons and freeholders and the whole community of the realm of Scotland', they had claimed: 'It is not glory nor riches nor honours but liberty alone that we fight and contend for which no honest person will lose except with his life.'[77] This was, of course, in the context of war against the English.

The fact that the roots of national identity can be obscure is perhaps made clear in the case of a realm that did not successfully make the transition to become a nation state, the duchy of Burgundy. We have seen how this state fell apart into two sections after Nancy, one absorbed by France, the other becoming part of the Habsburg lands. Was this because Burgundy was a combination of the personal domains of its dukes, with no real coherence? Was it because Louis XI of France was only too ready to profit by the disaster that had overtaken his cousin's realm? Did the dukes not make strenuous enough efforts to unite all their lands? These questions cannot be answered easily but what is clear is that war could destroy realms as well as unite them. We have also pointed out that there was undoubtedly a strong element of national feeling among the Czech Hussite rebels in their wars against Sigismund. Yet neither the Empire nor, more obviously, the Czech lands emerged as 'nation states' until long after our period. Something as complex as the creation of a 'nation state' cannot be accounted for simply as the result of wartime patriotism.

CONCLUSION

This chapter has examined war and the conduct of warfare from several different angles. It has discussed contemporary views of the justification of war and looked at the theory of the conduct of war. On a more pragmatic level it has looked at the strategy and tactics of commanders of the period, exemplified in certain selected campaigns and the ways in which wars were financed and armies organised. One difference of interpretation among historians has received some attention: the question of whether there was anything that can reasonably be called a military revolution at this period.

On this it seems that the evidence is far from clear. Leaving aside the matter of whether 'revolution' is the right word to use in these circumstances (no-one really suggests that there were any sudden or violent changes), were there still substantial developments, particularly in areas which also saw changes in the sixteenth and seventeenth centuries? Here it seems that those in favour of this view have not really made their case. Knights or cavalry were still an important part of all armies. Despite the devastating impact of well-placed archers on a well-chosen site, no fifteenth-century army dispensed with cavalry and in some ways the need for horses increased. We might also question whether the cavalry charge, despite its terrifying potential, had ever been a common feature of pitched battles in earlier periods. The proportion of knights/men at arms to other men, whether foot soldiers or archers, changed over our period: but we are not looking at something like the armies of the Thirty Years War in the seventeenth century, with squadrons of well trained pikemen. In the same way cannon and other gunpowder weapons became more common over our period but they remained expensive, difficult weapons to deploy successfully, with their greatest use in sieges.

As far as the size of armies and their organisation goes, only in France after the reforms of Charles VII, extended by Louis XI, does something begin to emerge which was radically different from the armies of the fourteenth century. This was much nearer to a true 'standing army' than that possessed by any other state. The nature of French monarchy and the prosperity of France by the end of our period meant that it could even be financed without putting undue pressure on the remainder of society. This certainly placed a powerful weapon in the hands of French kings, which was put to the test in the Italian wars. Perhaps in this respect only, the change was dramatic enough to be called a revolution.

In other realms, much more gradual and evolutionary change is visible. Our final conclusion perhaps should be that over this period much had happened which, far from disproving the insights of Vegetius, served only to reinforce his view that 'fortune often has a greater share than valour on the battlefield'.

Part III

A Changing Culture?

5

The Church, Religion and Dissent

INTRODUCTION: THEMES AND SOURCES

The Catholic Church provided the only lawful religion in Europe during the Middle Ages for most of the population, from princes to peasants. Since the early schisms and heresies in the Church, Catholic doctrines had undergone few changes, although their interpretation had developed first with the writings of the early Fathers, saints Jerome, Augustine, Ambrose and Gregory, and later with the commentaries of the scholastics. By the fourteenth century many lay people and most clerics (the ignorance of parish priests was a problem in some areas) could give something approximating to the following account of their faith.

God the Father had created the first human beings, Adam and Eve, to praise him and live in the earthly paradise of Eden. Their disobedience when they listened to Satan (in the form of a serpent) caused their expulsion and the loss, for them and for all their descendants, of any means by which they would enter God's presence in heaven. The prophets whose words were recorded in the Old Testament of the Bible did, however, promise that a messiah would eventually come to rescue humanity from the consequences of the sin of Adam and Eve. The birth of Jesus Christ, the Son of God, the Father, by the Virgin Mary (the incarnation), his ministry, and death on the Cross (the Passion) made a sufficient reparation for that sin. His life and teachings were recorded in the writings of the evangelists Matthew, Mark, Luke and John, and of St Paul, in the New Testament of the Bible. With the help of the Holy Spirit, the third person of the Holy Trinity that made up the Godhead, those who lived in accordance with Christ's teaching could invoke His sacrifice and hope to win salvation.

Over the centuries all sorts of anxieties and controversies had arisen about the means of attaining salvation. The vast majority of Catholics recognised the Church hierarchy (the Pope, cardinals, bishops, abbots and other dignitaries) as the authority which could guide them towards the truth, but by the late Middle Ages it bore little resemblance to the poor and simple apostles of Christ who had founded the Church. The wealth of even relatively minor churches and monasteries and the state in which many prelates lived seemed contrary to the message of the Gospels. Those who expressed their doubts about this apparent contradiction were in danger of being condemned by the Church authorities as heretics, and even totally orthodox members of the clerical elite could not agree on all matters of doctrine.

One unresolved problem was the question of *predestination*: if God was all-powerful and all-knowing, the fate of each Christian to be damned or saved must have always been determined. If this was so there seemed to be no free exercise of the will when individuals made their choice to live a good or evil life. Even supposing the various solutions offered by scholars from the time of St Augustine onwards were convincing, there were other unsatisfactory aspects to the whole question of salvation. Apart from the saints, how could any fallible human deserve to go straight to heaven after death? Surely most people were sinful but not totally evil, only differing in degree in the amount of their merit: how could it be just that one person would be saved whilst another only marginally more wicked neighbour would be damned? These doubts were exacerbated by the crises that assailed the Church at the time of the Papacy's exile in Avignon, the Great Schism and the following controversy over whether popes or general councils of the Church should have supreme authority.

Such doubts increasingly preoccupied both clerics and the more reflective members of the laity. The spread of literacy and the migration of people to towns, where new ideas could more readily be discussed, promoted speculation, and the introduction of printing with moveable type in the mid-fifteenth century stimulated debate even further. This brings us to a major concern of this chapter and, indeed, of most historians who write about religion: to what extent were the Protestant and Catholic reformations of the sixteenth centuries anticipated in the later Middle Ages? Many English-language historians of the past two centuries, often writing from a Protestant standpoint, viewed late medieval beliefs and practices as deeply flawed, inviting the challenges posed by Martin Luther and other reformers. Huizinga saw the preoccupation with death and decay found in the art and literature of the time as symptomatic of a dying culture.[1]

Conversely, in recent decades writers such as Eamon Duffy and R. N. Swanson have demonstrated the vitality of religion and the strong spiritual response that it evoked from many members of the laity and clergy.[2] The work of Francis Oakley and Guillaume Mollat has portrayed a hierarchy that took its duties and the whole question of the validity of ecclesiastical authority far more seriously than earlier commentators allowed.[3] The following sections examine these and other issues; first, the Catholic hierarchy and how it coped with challenges to its power; then the way in which people actually practised their religion, and finally, the fate of heretics and other people who were partly or wholly excluded from the Catholic Church. Throughout the chapter, evidence will be offered that a seismic change in religious belief and practice was under way: this was being brought about not only by religious radicals but by those who wished to reform the Church from within. Some were inspired by a sense of mystical unity with the Divinity, others by a desire to revert to the ways of the early Church, and others by the critical spirit of the first generations of Renaissance humanist scholars.

The written sources for the history of religion in the later Middle Ages differ in quantity and quality from region to region. The greatest archive, in the Vatican in Rome, has never been disturbed by war or revolution. The huge correspondence conducted by the Papacy with all parts of Europe, accounts of receipts and payments and legal documents are monumental. In Germany, Britain, France and the Low Countries a chequered history and the conversion of many areas to the Protestant faith mean that survival is patchy; although good sets of churchwardens' accounts, for example, survive in some English parishes. The same principle applies to the evidence to be found in buildings and artefacts: the interiors of many churches were vandalised during the French Revolution. Monasteries were destroyed or used for other purposes in England during the Reformation. It was a regular practice of the Catholic authorities to destroy any material that was thought to be heretical, pagan or occult.

The relative success of the *Hussites* means that their movement is reasonably well recorded but much *Lollard* material in England was probably destroyed in the late fourteenth and fifteenth centuries. The best evidence of their activities is to be found in court cases, and some *Lollard* tracts and bibles (translated into English) that have survived. The vicious persecution of the Jews in much of northern Europe had a severe impact on the evidence for their activities. Most of the mystics managed to avoid the taint of heresy and many writings, especially by clerics, survive. Even suspect communities, such as the *Béguines* and *Beghards*, have left records. The intrinsic value of many artefacts: church plate, vestments, statues of precious materials, fine manuscripts, has in some cases ensured their survival but in others led to their deliberate destruction or dismemberment for profit or for ideological reasons.

(i) THE PAPACY UNDER PRESSURE

The government of the Church

By the fourteenth century, the Catholic Church had a complex structure that was strictly hierarchical. At the summit was the Pope, who claimed supreme spiritual authority, derived directly from Jesus Christ, over all Christians. He presided over a court or *curia* which was normally based in Rome and which administered the religious, fiscal and political affairs of the Papacy throughout southern, north-western and central Europe. Greece, Russia and surrounding areas were Orthodox – owing obedience to the patriarch of Constantinople and other patriarchs rather than to the Pope – and North Africa and the Ottoman Empire were Islamic. Apart from its moral authority, wealth and far-reaching administrative structure, the Papacy had two formidable weapons with which it could exact obedience. Individuals could be excommunicated, cut off from all the services and graces of the Church, and if they died whilst under this penalty they would certainly be damned. Popes could also place a congregation, an area, or even a whole country under an *interdict*; depriving all those who lived there of the services of the Church and putting their souls in jeopardy. From time to time General Councils of the Church were summoned by the Papacy: composed of prelates and scholars they added weight to administrative or doctrinal changes and initiated reforms.

The cardinals were, after the Pope, the most powerful prelates in the Church. They usually numbered between ten and twenty-five and it was a matter of pride for the major states to produce at least one cardinal. Their most important function was to elect a pope when the incumbent died: they usually chose the successful candidate from amongst themselves. Despite repeated attempts, however, they never managed to exact binding promises about papal conduct after the election. Some, such as Cardinal Henry Beaufort in England or Cardinal Nicholas of Cusa in Germany, played a prominent part in European politics. Others were content with their role as princes of the Church and, like other clergy, they varied in their interpretation of what their position required.

Apart from its embattled frontiers, Christian Europe was divided into dioceses controlled by bishops. They were theoretically appointed by the Papacy but during the late Middle Ages secular princes progressively gained control over this important piece of patronage. In most countries the senior bishops were called 'metropolitans' and had the rank of 'archbishop'. Circumstances varied, but they normally expected to exercise authority over the other bishops in the 'province' (or area) where they had jurisdiction. The bishops, like the cardinals, often played an important part in the secular government of their state: this was inevitable when the majority of well-educated men were clerics and, in contrast to the situation in lay life, the most able and ambitious could rise to the top.

Between the prelates and the ordinary parish priests there were a number of other categories of clerics who enjoyed varying degrees of importance. Bishops were usually based in a city or town which had a cathedral (*cathedra* was the Latin word for their 'seat' or 'throne'): the building and its finances were managed by a college of canons. In England some bishops had their seats in monastic churches. The Pope, cardinals and bishops all needed administrative staffs as well as the chaplains who cared for their spiritual welfare. Secular princes mirrored these arrangements in their bureaucracies and their chapel staff. The government of the Church in each country recognised the authority of the Pope, which he delegated to his bishops, and in turn they controlled the priests (or rectors) who held benefices (i.e., were appointed/presented to parishes). Some priests were appointed directly by the bishops or even by the Pope but in other parishes this right belonged to a local landowner, who might be a layman or the abbot of a monastery. When parishes yielded a high income in tithes and other dues, the person or body who had the right of presentment was often tempted to keep most of it. A vicar (or deputy), a more lowly cleric, was appointed to care for the parishioners. *Appropriation* was another practice that could undermine pastoral care in a parish: tithes intended for its support were transferred to a monastery, convent or priory.

The religious orders

C. H. Lawrence has remarked that inherent in the Christian tradition was a quest for God, involving 'separation from the world and the conquest of sensuality and human ambition'.[4] The earliest and greatest of the monastic orders was founded by St Benedict in Italy in the early sixth century. His rule enshrined the search for a good Christian life through the disciplines of poverty, chastity and obedience and it provided a pattern for later orders, such as the Cistercians and the Carthusians, and the equivalent regimes for nuns. The later orders often adopted even stricter rules in their search for perfection. St Benedict's original plan had balanced prayer in the chapel at the liturgical hours[5] and some contemplation, assisted by the reading of a devotional book, with a substantial amount of physical labour. In later centuries, however, monks and nuns were increasingly drawn from the upper, better-educated orders of society; servants were employed to do the menial tasks. The monks spent most of their time singing and reciting ever more elaborate offices in the chapel and reading and copying devotional works. As early as 1086, Ulrich of Cluny reported that manual work:

> amounts to nothing more than shelling the new beans or rooting out the weeds that choke the good plants in the garden, sometimes making loaves in the bakery. On days when it is done, after holding a shorter chapter than usual [a business meeting attended by all the monks each morning], the abbot says 'Let us proceed to manual labour'. All then process out . . . to the garden. Psalms are sung, and after a spell of weeding, the procession reforms and returns to the cloister.[6]

Monasteries were governed by an abbot or prior, to whom all the monks and servants owed unquestioning obedience. In large establishments he would preside over a number of other senior brothers with specialist responsibilities.[7] The precentor (or cantor) and sacristan, for example, respectively looked after the singing, and the fabric, vessels and vestments of the chapel. The novice master trained new monks; in the early centuries these included young boys but the practice of admitting them was later discouraged. Many monasteries also ran flourishing schools, a recruiting ground for new monks. By the later Middle Ages, many monasteries and convents were situated in or near towns and the presence of a religious house attracted the laity. The poor could get assistance, the chapel services aided piety, some people wished to be buried in the precincts and some even lived there. Patrons and their families enjoyed special privileges if they had founded monasteries or given them substantial gifts. Some of the laity purchased *corrodies*: in return for a sum of money they would be housed and fed in the monastery during their old age.

In many ways the duties and routines of nuns were similar to those of monks. Yet Penelope Johnson in her study of religious women in France suggests that, after a time of near equality, their status declined in the later Middle Ages.[8] Originally they were highly valued for the intercessions they made to heaven for the salvation of souls. Nuns also enjoyed more autonomy than lay women as they were not directly subjected to fathers, brothers or husbands: abbesses were the only women who held power through election rather than by an accident of birth. By the thirteenth century, however, there was an increasing tendency for monks and friars to be ordained as priests. This enhanced their status as they became participants in the sacrifice of the Mass rather than mere spectators like the nuns. It also relieved the monks of the expense of employing priests to celebrate services and hear confession. The lowered status of nuns was compounded by the tendency to enforce strict enclosure on them. Some historians, however, would maintain that the desire of the male hierarchy to confine them within their convents was a characteristic of the Catholic Reformation of the sixteenth century rather than the later Middle Ages. Nuns also contributed to the changing religious climate: some were mystics (see below) and the order of St Bridgit of Sweden, founded in 1346, formed part of a movement for reform, with its emphasis on personal piety.

The Catholic Church in the later Middle Ages has sometimes been described as if it had inherited a pure faith and mode of worship from apostolic times and had gradually allowed this to be overlaid by a complex, inaccessible theology and corrupt, superstitious practices. Over the past century, however, research has highlighted a whole series of reforms, dating from the time of the Emperor Charlemagne in the ninth century, which addressed recurrent anxieties that standards of scholarship, education and clerical conduct were declining. In the thirteenth century one of the last great medieval reforms, the foundation of two orders of friars (*mendicants*), by St Francis (Friars Minor) and St Dominic (Order of Preachers),[9] signalled a commitment to retaining the involvement of the laity in their religion. The Carmelites, the Austin Friars and female orders of the Dominicans and Franciscans (Poor Clares) were founded later. The friars differed from the older monastic orders in that their poverty was manifested by their need to beg for their daily food. They mixed freely with the laity, sometimes alienating parish priests by seeming to usurp their functions: their preaching often exercised a magnetic effect on congregations. In 1370 the Bruges Pact between the four mendicant orders arranged for them to co-operate to challenge the domination and hostility of the secular parish clergy.[10]

The foundation of the orders of friars had recognised a demographic shift to the towns and the need for a style of preaching to appeal to more sophisticated urban congregations. The friars were anxious to enlist new recruits who were well educated, so they targeted university towns such as Montpellier and Oxford. The attraction devout Christians felt for the friars' message and the flexibility they enjoyed in the pursuit of their ministry, often travelling from place to place, enabled them both to encourage backsliders and doubters to renew their faith and to combat heresy. Soon after their foundation, however, the Franciscans had been split by a controversy about how absolute their poverty should be. In the end, those who wished to retain some material possessions, such as the houses in which they lived (*Conventuals*), prevailed and their more extreme opponents were condemned as heretics. From the late fourteenth century, however, Franciscans who wished to follow their rule more strictly (*Observants*) were encouraged and this facilitated improved standards in the order. No such crisis had afflicted the Dominicans, who had been particularly successful in their campaign against the Albigensian heretics (also called *cathars*) in the south of France.

By the mid-fourteenth century there were signs that monasticism was in decline. The population in many monasteries fell by half; in the renowned house of Reichenau, in Germany, there were no more than ten monks by 1339. Pope Benedict XII castigated them for their neglect of divine service, believing that this decline was due to their refusal to admit any but nobles.[11] Many monasteries set limits to the number of postulants they admitted: some clearly wished to exclude social inferiors, others wished to use their endowments to maintain a comfortable lifestyle for the few. In addition, the Black Death hit monks, nuns and friars, and the Hundred Years War led to the devastation of a number of French religious houses. The Avignon Popes used the practice of *commendam* as a means of rewarding their cardinals. The commendatory abbot received his post for life; he would normally be an absentee and was not obliged to concern himself with the welfare of his house. Although some communities did adhere to strict monastic rules until the end of the Middle Ages, the lax and indulgent lifestyle of others shocked observers. Barbara Hardy, for example, has recorded the lavish dining habits of the monks of Westminster Abbey, adjacent to the royal court.[12]

Monks and nuns in the late Middle Ages suffered from two contradictory tendencies. On the one hand, the laity was allowed to associate with them more closely than had been the case in the early centuries of Christianity; on the other, many lay people spent their money seeking more personal, less institutionalised means of salvation. A growing body of literature, serious and profane, criticised the orders for real or imagined faults.

The Papacy in Avignon and the Great Schism

The troubles that assailed the Church in the early fourteenth century did not originate in any inherent weakness in its structure or beliefs. They arose initially, rather, from a long-standing conflict of interest between the Papacy and the great European monarchs. The popes demanded the right to raise money for the support of the Church, to have ultimate jurisdiction over disputes involving ecclesiastical interests and to appoint senior clerics in every Christian country. These claims had been hotly contested by lay princes for centuries since they challenged three of their principal sources of power: taxation, control of the law, and patronage. The German Emperors had originally been the principal protagonists in these disputes but in the early fourteenth century the French king, Philip IV, 'the Fair', had been involved in a vicious conflict with Pope Boniface VIII. French agents in Italy had handled Boniface roughly and he proved unable to mete out any effective punishment for this humiliation. He died soon afterwards leaving the Roman Papacy discredited, and from 1309 his successor, the Frenchman Clement V, moved permanently to Avignon.[13] This represented a break with the tradition that most popes were drawn from one of the states of Italy and that they resided in Rome (at least during the winter; in the summer months they had avoided its heat and disease by staying in one of their smaller towns in the Papal State).[14] Clement V was in poor health and loved his native France. He used the excuse that he was to hold a General Council in Vienne, in 1311–12, to avoid a dangerous journey through the lawless regions of northern Italy and an equally dangerous residence in Rome.

The fact that Avignon was adjacent to the kingdom of France and that all Clement V's successors were Frenchmen suggested to contemporaries that the Papacy had become a pawn of the French king. The situation was condemned as the 'Baylonish Captivity', recalling the time in the Old Testament when the Jews were taken into exile by the king of Babylon. Clement V had never established a permanent residence for himself but his successor, John XXII, altered and extended the episcopal palace at Avignon. In the 1330s a massive and austere papal palace was added to it and a number of palaces and summer residences, churches and monasteries were built in and around the city by the popes and cardinals.

Guillaume Mollat, in *The Popes at Avignon, 1305–1378*, has pointed out that the intense localism of medieval society should be recognised when assessing the political impact of the move to Avignon. Many of the French prelates, who undoubtedly played a predominant role during that period, came from the south and west of France. They did not necessarily respect the wishes of the king in Paris, a city as distant from their needs and interests as Rome, and they seem to have tried to prevent royal interference in papal elections. Avignon, in any case, was technically under the sovereignty of the Emperor, not the French king. The papal court, which included about 600 people, was more stable than the itinerant Roman one and its accessibility to northern Europe brought it more business. It was a brilliant centre of patronage for learning (including a library of 2,000 books), art and literature, attracting renowned writers such as Francesco Petrarch. This is an extract from an account of the entertainment offered to a visiting Italian cardinal in 1343:

> In the interval between the seventh and eighth courses there was a tournament, which took place in the banqueting hall itself. A concert brought the main part of the feast to a close. At dessert, two trees were brought in; one seemed made of silver, and bore apples, pears, figs, peaches and grapes of gold; the other was green as laurel, and was decorated with crystallised fruits of many colours. The wines came from Provence, La Rochelle, Beaune, St Pourcain and the Rhine. After dessert the master cook danced, together with his thirty assistants.[15]

Avignon did contain servile and corrupt people but so did other European courts, secular and ecclesiastical. There is little evidence that the residence of the Papacy at Avignon changed for the worse the quality of faith or practice within the Church. Indeed the more able popes, such as John XXII, took effective measures to enhance their authority and extirpate heresy and lesser forms of dissent. He also concerned himself with his Italian domains, making strenuous but ineffectual attempts to reduce them to obedience. Zutshi, however, does cite examples of pro-French bias shown by the Avignon Popes during the early stages of the Hundred Years War.[16] Many Europeans, especially the enemies of France, perceived that they were partial in their political inclinations and this contributed to an attitude that was growing amongst the laity which can best be described as 'anticlericalism' (see Section (iii) below).

The Romans had seen their city's prestige decline after the departure of the Papacy and they had lost the revenue that had been generated by the presence of so many prelates and by the visits of pilgrims, clerics and foreign envoys. The lawless condition of northern Italy had been improved by Cardinal Gil Albornoz (from 1353 to 1365), who used mercenary soldiers to subdue the Papal State to obedience. Gregory XI was finally prevailed upon to return to Rome in 1377 and he died there in the following year. The College of Cardinals (in which Italians and French predominated) elected an Italian from Naples as his successor, Urban VI. The French cardinals soon regretted their altruism as Urban proceeded, it seemed to them, to give undue weight to Italian interests and generally to behave in an arbitrary and unreasonable manner. Historians often dismissed their claim that the Roman populace intimidated them but Howard Kaminsky's recent account provides plausible evidence that they did so.[17] The cardinals left

Rome, declared that they had voted under duress, and elected a new pope, the cousin of the king of France, as Clement VII. He retired to Avignon, initiating the scandal that is known as 'the Great Schism'.

Disputes between the popes and the emperors in previous centuries had sometimes thrown up 'anti-popes'; they had been used to embarrass and de-stabilise their rivals. It had invariably been clear to the majority of Christians, however, which man was the genuine heir to St Peter (the apostle chosen by Christ as the first head of the Church). The anti-popes had normally been abandoned as soon as the prospect of a solution to the dispute was in sight. The problem with the Great Schism that divided Europe was that the powers were fairly evenly balanced in their support of the two contenders. Urban VI and his successors were recognised by England, the Emperor, Hungary, Bohemia and Poland: these countries generally pursued an anti-French policy. France obeyed Clement VII as did Burgundy, Scotland, Naples, Castile and Aragon. Support in some areas fluctuated between the two popes and Portugal changed sides four times. These alignments were to some extent determined by conflicts such as the Hundred Years War. Yet this factor cannot have been the only reason why the Schism lasted for nearly forty years, since during much of the period there was a lull in hostilities. Avignon had served as an effective base for the Papacy for seventy years and many people there and in other parts of Europe had benefited from the eclipse of Rome. The Popes of the Schism should not be dismissed as ambitious and self-seeking as, over recent decades, work in the papal archives has revealed the plausible *canonical* (according to Church law) claim which each of them could make to be legitimate. Personal ambition seems to have been combined with a conviction that they alone were the rightful leaders of Christendom.

The Avignon Popes in the fourteenth century had improved their fiscal administration to such an extent that they enjoyed unprecedented levels of revenue. The Schismatic Popes who resided there from 1378 had little more than half of the income enjoyed by their predecessors and they were obliged to spend most of it on vain attempts to conquer their Italian possessions. These campaigns were initially led by a brother of Charles V of France, Louis I of Anjou, until his death in 1384. After that, the periodic insanity of Charles VI (when the country was ruled by his pragmatic uncles), and the eventual revival of the Hundred Years War with England, put paid to the Avignon Popes' chances. The financial situation of the Roman Schismatic Popes was even more precarious. They lacked the complex bureaucracy of Avignon and received little revenue from other areas besides Italy. Urban VI's successor was another Neapolitan, Boniface IX, and he imported members of his noble family into Rome. They acquired many papal offices and colluded with him in taking all possible means to raise money. Initially this was to defend Rome against supporters of the Avignon Papacy but it also made it notorious for all kinds of corruption. Boniface's campaigns were reasonably successful but the Papacy had been reduced to the stature of an Italian principality, losing much of its mystique as the moral leader of Christendom.

The memory of the 'Babylonish Captivity' rankled with many members of the Church, and the alacrity with which Clement VII returned to Avignon raised the fear that the Papacy would be further discredited. Eventually European princes and clerics, led by France, showed that their concern for the Christian religion out-weighed more immediate political considerations. Prelates and scholars such as Pierre d'Ailly and Jean Gerson believed that the most effective way in which to end the Schism was by calling a General Council of the Church. These councils had been summoned periodically by the popes, who had invariably dominated them, and had sanctioned doctrinal developments and reforms in practice. In 1409, the cardinals who had defected from both the Roman and Avignon Popes met as a General Council at Pisa. It had been agreed that both popes should resign, thus rescuing the supporters of either from having been in error and at risk of damnation during the previous three decades. Despite the fact that most European powers agreed with the Council's policy both popes refused to resign and, in the meantime, the Council had elected a third.

The Conciliar Movement

The Church and the princes of Europe simply could not tolerate the continuation of a scandalous schism: not only did it promote political and religious discord but it would encourage the Hussite heresy, which was making dangerous progress in Bohemia (see below, Section 5(iii)). Sigismund, king of the Romans, summoned a General Council to meet at Constance, a self-governing imperial city, in 1414. This was unprecedented since councils had previously been convened by popes. Those who attended it believed that it had three main purposes: to end the Schism, to combat heresy and to reform the Church. As the conciliar decree *Haec Sancta* (Holy Things) proclaimed, it:

> has its authority immediately from Christ; and all men, of every rank and condition, including the pope himself, are bound to obey it in matters concerning the Faith, the abolition of the schism, and the reformation of the Church of God in its head and members.[18]

These words seemed to spell the end of papal supremacy, especially as the Council was successful in bringing the Schism to an end.

The Roman Pope resigned, after agreeing to 'summon' the Council (a fiction that was to give the new Papacy a show of continuity), and the other two were deposed. A reunited College of Cardinals and, uniquely, six representatives from the French, German, Italian, English and Spanish (from 1416) nations, elected an Italian, Odo Colonna, as Pope Martin V. These nations were not representative of single countries (the 'Germans', for example, included Poland, Hungary, Bohemia and Denmark) but reflected the divisions in some universities. The system was adopted to prevent the Italian majority from dominating the Council. On the other hand, it was more susceptible to the influence of the lay princes who were the patrons and masters of many of the participants.[19] The Council also seemed to have destroyed the Bohemian heresy with the trial and execution of John Hus, although after his martyrdom his followers actually grew stronger. Sigismund was not really interested in radical reform, and, once the Schism had ended and his great heretic had been destroyed, he was content for the Council to disperse. Before it did so it none the less passed the decree

Frequens, requiring that General Councils should meet at regular intervals and that they should address the issue of reform.

The achievement of the Council of Constance should not be underestimated for it had, after all, been convened without the authority of a generally recognised pope and still managed to bring the Schism to an end. The fact that it did so was due in part to developments in ideas about the relationship between lay and ecclesiastical power that had taken place over the previous century. Much of this thinking originated from Italy, the scene of long-standing conflicts between popes and emperors. It contained a number of small states where highly educated lawyers and clerics waged ideological warfare on behalf of one or other of the protagonists. Marsiglio of Padua, a supporter of the Emperor, had been amongst the influential jurists who cut through papal pretensions to act as secular rulers. In his *Defensor Pacis* (Defender of the Peace) he claimed that the right to govern should belong to the highest civil authority, and the Church should be concerned only with spiritual matters.

The civil authority, although usually exercised by the Emperor, a prince or a group of patricians, was derived from the 'association of the citizens or the people'[20] and was essentially set up by popular sovereignty. This reflected Marsiglio's Italian background where pro-Papal and pro-Imperial city states had long been in conflict. In the process the urban classes, from patricians to minor craftsmen, had achieved a political sophistication that was only matched in the towns of the Low Countries. His thought confined religion within the realm of faith, recognised the complete sovereignty of the temporal power and, according to Ozment, proclaimed a gap between the sacred and secular that was to be irreparable by 1500.[21]

The reasoning that sought a strict limitation of papal power in relation to secular states could also be applied to its interaction with the community of the faithful in the Church. General Councils were composed of the elite: cardinals, bishops, abbots and other prelates as well as scholars and officials, but they could be said to represent all Christians more effectively than one individual, even if he was the Pope. The idea of representation at both municipal and national level was spreading in western Europe in the late Middle Ages. Most towns had some form of conciliar government and assemblies were called to redress grievances and raise taxes in Castile, Aragon, Scotland, Ireland, England, Florence, the Empire and France. They were sometimes manipulated by the most powerful faction or by their prince, and only substantial property owners were involved, but their existence did at least raise new possibilities for politically alert laymen and clerics.

The prelates and scholars who prepared the way for the series of General Councils which met in the first half of the fifteenth century and contributed to the policies they formulated had two major concerns: to end the Schism and to institute a thorough reform of the Church. If they were successful it was to be hoped that such scandals would not recur and that anticlericalism, which was to be found even in highly orthodox areas of Europe, would be quelled. During the Council of Constance, Cardinal Pierre d'Ailly produced a *Treatise on the Reform of the Church*. The reform should be carried out from the Papacy downwards: cardinals should no longer be drawn predominantly from one nation. Only suitable candidates should be selected as bishops and clergy and they should be properly educated. The laity should not be expected to pay fees for spiritual services, and begging by the friars should be discouraged. The multiplication of saints' days, holy images and devotional novelties was bringing Christianity into disrepute and should stop. Whilst some writers have seen these proposals, which were not implemented, as anticipating the programme of Protestant reformers in the sixteenth century, Francis Oakley has suggested that they anticipated the catholic reformation instituted by the Council of Trent (1545–62).[22]

Despite his reform programme, d'Ailly was a moderate and he was careful to be absent from the session at Constance which decreed the supremacy of conciliar authority. His pupil Jean Gerson was also a moderate but he was prepared to engage with the central dilemma for supporters of the Councils: how could they both safeguard the traditional values of the Church and make progress in its reform? He was Chancellor of the University of Paris from 1393 and made its policy of limiting papal power through the exercise of conciliar authority his own. A visit to the papal court of Avignon seems to have shocked him and confirmed his commitment to reform the clergy. Gerson was influenced by the reaction to scholastic learning, especially to the ever more complex commentaries on the Christian scriptures which had been instituted by *nominalists* such as William of Ockham. They argued that the omnipotence and divinity of God made human attempts to explain his law and works by reason futile. This led Gerson conversely to suggest that theology should be conveyed to the laity in very simple terms, firmly based on the teaching of Christ in the Bible. He put his ideas into practice by preaching in Paris, often addressing the royal court. Gerson also believed that, instead of becoming ever more intellectually remote from religious experience, scholars should concentrate on its inherent spirituality. He stressed the individual's chance of achieving a mystical union with God:

> Before the reception of form matter is imperfect, lacks beauty, power and activity. If form is given to it, it immediately attains perfection in accord with the nature of the form. In like manner, the soul . . . when it is united with God, receives a certain divine life.[23]

Gerson saw that the readiness of the French king and the Emperor to support General Councils as a means of ending the Schism was also an opportunity to carry out reforms. The unity of the Church had been undermined by the worldly ambitions of the Papacy and it could only legitimately be restored by the supreme authority of the Church as represented by a council, even one which had not been called by a pope. He played a major role at Constance (until Martin V was elected), securing the deposition of the Pisa Pope and directing the indictment of John Hus. Gerson's reform programme might have contained similarities to that of the heretic but he felt that the challenge Hus presented to orthodox belief justified his punishment. Gerson's involvement in the complex rivalries between the duke of Burgundy and the Armagnac faction (see Chapter 3: ii) forced him to remain outside France for several years. When he returned he lived obscurely, writing devotional works advocating the spiritual piety that he believed was the key to individual salvation.

The decree *Frequens*, passed by the Council of Constance, had provided that Church Councils should meet regularly in the future. One accordingly assembled at Pavia in 1423 but Martin V made his disapproval clear: it was poorly attended and dispersed without achieving any reforms. With the Great Schism so recently resolved the princes and prelates were anxious not to provoke a new rift with the Papacy.

The Council of Basle presented a more formidable challenge to papal power: meeting in 1431 outside Italy it was less amenable to pressure from the Pope. The Emperor and German princes hoped it would support them against the Hussites and a settlement was made with the moderate Utraquists. This enabled the Imperial forces to destroy the radical Taborites, who were threatening to subvert more areas within and adjacent to Bohemia (see below, Section 5(iii)). At the beginning of the Council, Nicholas of Cusa wrote *Of Catholic Concord*, one of the most developed statements of how the authority of Councils and the Papacy could be reconciled. All power came from God, and Christ did not make Peter the head of the Church until he had been chosen by the apostles as their leader. Neither Peter nor the Popes could be greater than the Church since their power was derived from it. Cusa believed that election should be used in choosing all the highest members of the hierarchy: priests should choose their bishops, bishops their archbishops, and archbishops the cardinals. Ideally the Pope and cardinals would work together but, if they came into conflict, the Council's power should be superior to that of the Pope. Indeed, he repeated the view of earlier canonists and of the apologists for Constance, that any pope who was heretical or did any other serious damage to the Church should be deposed. The same principles applied to the Emperor, who ultimately derived his right to rule from the people. Brian Tierney has remarked that in his writings Cusa drew together the ideas on popular sovereignty of the two previous centuries.[24]

Pope Eugenius IV attempted in 1437 to move the Council from Basle to Ferrara on the grounds that it needed to negotiate with the Greek Emperor, John Palaeologus VIII. Constantinople could only hold out against the Turks for a limited time without aid from western Europe. He believed that if the Orthodox Church, which had finally separated from the Western Church in the eleventh century, could be reunited with it aid would be forthcoming: Eugenius was eager to bring this about and to strengthen his position in the process. By 1438 most of the senior prelates, including Nicholas of Cusa, had forsaken Basle for Ferrara, leaving behind the most radical reformers. They passed resolutions that addressed the problems of the Church, especially that of excessive papal power, but without the co-operation of the Pope nothing happened. The reformers finally destroyed any chances of making progress by electing an anti-pope: this alienated most European princes, who were desperate to avoid another schism. In the meantime Eugenius had moved the Council from Ferrara to Florence where, in 1439, an agreement was concluded that the Orthodox and Western churches should be reunited. Compromises had been made on both sides, especially by the Greeks, but it proved impossible for either the Pope or the Greek Emperor to get the reconciliation accepted by their churches. This did not prevent Eugenius from enhancing his prestige by the apparent agreement and thus also improving his position in his conflict with Basle: the Council continued for another decade but support for it progressively diminished. No European prince proved ready to make a serious attempt to rescue Constantinople and it fell to the Turks in 1453.

Whilst no pope could question the validity of Constance, since Martin V and his successors owed their positions to it, they could undermine the claims both that Councils should meet regularly and that they were superior in authority to the Papacy. In *Execrabilis* in 1460, Pius II declared appeals from a pope to a future council anathema (a sin meriting excommunication):

> A horrible abuse, unheard-of in earlier times, has sprung up in our period. Some men, imbued with a spirit of rebellion and moved not by a desire for sound decisions but rather by a desire to escape the punishment for sin, suppose that they can appeal from the pope, vicar of Jesus Christ; – from the pope to whom in the person of Peter it was said, 'Feed my sheep' (John, 21.16) and 'Whatever you bind on earth will be bound in heaven' (Matthew, 16.19) – from this pope to a future council. How harmful this is to the Christian republic, as well as how contrary to canon law, anyone who is not ignorant of the law can understand.[25]

This bull was often seen as ending the late medieval Conciliar Movement but it has more recently been pointed out that, even after 1460, princes found it useful to threaten recalcitrant popes with councils. Some German princes and scholars, in particular, remained faithful to the objectives formulated by the reformers at Basle and these were to re-surface early in the following century. The political ideas generated by the debate are also a matter for controversy: did they lay the foundations of Western constitutional thought of later centuries or did they actually promote the absolute power that many princes claimed to possess during the early modern period? What is clear is that secular rulers had played a crucial part in ending the Great Schism and in diminishing the power of the Papacy and Church hierarchy.

The Church in the later fifteenth century

Princes had profited from the long-drawn-out troubles of the Papacy by increasing control over their national churches. Charles VII negotiated the Pragmatic Sanction of Bourges in 1438 with Eugenius IV: it accepted the moral reforms of Basle and abolished the levy of *annates* (a papal tax) within France and the Pope's right to reserve benefices for his own appointees. These harsh measures were later watered down but the process by which the king assumed unquestioned control over the Church was well under way. This was a logical continuation of the move, fifty years earlier, by the uncles of Charles VI and the bishops to withdraw obedience from the Schismatic Avignon Pope. By doing so they had consciously enhanced the power of the state over the French Church, a policy known as *Gallicanism*.

In 1439 Eugenius had to recognise the Acceptation of Mainz, in which the German princes accepted the reforming decrees of the Council of Basle and severely limited papal powers to raise revenue. These concessions were later modified and the princes remained dissatisfied that they had not achieved the measure of independence enjoyed by England and France. England was ahead in this particular game: in the previous century, during the reign of Edward III, the Statutes Provisors (1351) and Praemunire (1353) had severely limited the papal powers of appointment and the right of appeal from English courts to the Papacy. The perceived evils that these measures addressed were the appointment of uncaring foreigners to benefices financed by English patrons, and the danger that the money gained might be used against England in its war with France. May McKisack, however, has pointed out that the Papacy could use provisions to reward deserving poor clerics and to protect parishes from selfish local interests.[26] By 1487 papal pretensions to influence the affairs of European states had sunk so low that Innocent VIII waited eight months to learn the wishes of James III before making his provisions to Scottish benefices.[27] By exerting so much control over their national churches, rulers in countries such as Scotland, England, some German principalities and France were promoting the emergence of modern nation states.

During the next decades the involvement of the Papal State in the Italian Wars continued the process of reducing the Popes, in the esteem of many Christians, to the status of secular princes. The defence that papalists such as Juan de Torquemada had mounted in the middle of the century, vindicating an absolute and divinely sanctioned use of power, was to be most effectively employed by lay sovereigns. The curtailment of the Papacy's temporal power would not affect its overall authority so gravely, however, if it retained the spiritual dominance it had enjoyed since the days of the early Church. In the late fifteenth century, on the one hand, religion was buoyant, whilst on the other, many Christians were sceptical about aspects of their worship and the suitability of priests and the religious to hold their offices. Scholarship was flourishing: during this period universities produced most of the reformers who were to make such a devastating and learned critique of the Catholic Church early in the next century. Widespread knowledge of classical texts as well as an ability to engage critically with the commentaries of the Fathers, scholastics and later writers was not confined to Renaissance Italy. Huizinga questioned the appearance of the phenomenon of 'Christian Humanism' in France and Burgundy as early as the fifteenth century, where respect for hierarchy and chivalrous aspirations were still predominant.[28] Yet there is plenty of evidence of an active intellectual life well before the orthodox response to the religious crisis provoked by Martin Luther in the 1520s.

A number of devout and orthodox Catholics were critical of aspects of the administration and morals of the Catholic hierarchy and wished to reform them well before the impact of Protestantism. The ideas of some of the writers connected with the Conciliar Movement have been discussed above. Later in the century the work of Wessel Gansfort anticipated Martin Luther's ideas in some respects by questioning the jurisdiction of popes and prelates over ordinary Christians, and their powers in relation to Purgatory. Luther acknowledged in a forward to an edition of Gansfort's works, that 'his spirit is in accord with mine'.[29] Gansfort lived in Groningen in the Netherlands and also had links with adherents of the Modern Devotion, at Windesheim (spiritual Christians who wished to live simply in accord with the teaching of the New Testament, see Section (ii) below). The way in which groups and individuals practised their religion and the effect it was to have on the future of the Catholic Church is the subject of the following section.

(ii) RELIGIOUS EXPERIENCE

Popular religion?

During the second half of the twentieth century the study of the phenomenon of 'popular' religion flourished. It formed part of an endeavour, fuelled by Marxist history, to recover the activities and values of the common people. Cults of the saints and their shrines; pilgrimages; religious plays and processions; rites at birth, marriage and death, are the kinds of subject that lend themselves to this approach. In many ways it is a fruitful one since it directs attention to records and artefacts which have not always been considered by historians of religion in the past. Accounts of the trials of Cathar heretics in the south of France in the early fourteenth century, for example, are very informative about the ideas uneducated people held about the afterlife. Guillaume Fort of Montaillou believed:

> that the souls of good men go to heavenly paradise, but that the souls of bad men, both now and after the last judgement, will go among the cliffs and precipices and that demons will throw them down from the cliffs onto the rocks below. Asked who taught him these errors, he said that he himself had thought up the idea that after death human bodies do not revive and are not resurrected [resurrection of the body was a Church dogma].[30]

It could be objected that the views of a man charged with heresy should not be taken as representative of ordinary peoples' ideas about religion. Indeed, many aspects of so-called 'popular culture' are vitiated by the fact that contemporary records were made by people from the educated elite. Views such as those expressed above were only recorded in exceptional circumstances: the vociferous Cathars had attracted the wrath of the ecclesiastical hierarchy. R. N. Swanson, in his invaluable account of this whole subject, suggests that many Christians were allowed to deviate from religious orthodoxy in peace.[31] It is probable that some ideas that the Church would have considered heretical were discussed along with orthodox ones by lay men and lay women when they met together. In this book we have not devoted a separate section to the 'popular culture' of the peasantry since most of its manifestations were connected, more or less directly, with popular religion. The culture of town dwellers is discussed below in Chapter 6: ii.

Eamon Duffy, besides deploring the excessive attention devoted in recent studies to witches, educated ladies and Lollards, and questioning whether there really was a decline in religious practice in England during the late Middle Ages, has also challenged the whole concept of 'popular' religion. He takes issue with Colin Richmond's suggestion that by the fifteenth century the gentry were distancing themselves from the rest of the parish by their devotional practices. Duffy's scepticism about the division between 'elite' and 'popular' religion is shared by Swanson, who covers the whole of western Europe, not just England, and considers that the distinction that is sometimes made between 'lay' and 'clerical' religion is equally dubious.[32] This section looks at various aspects of worship and of ideas about the soul and the afterlife and will provide some evidence by which the validity of the concept of 'popular' religion can be assessed.

The liturgy

Religion met the spiritual needs of Christians but it was also at the centre of life in the Middle Ages in a physical sense. Activity in every village and town revolved around the churches and monasteries: the status of cities was defined by the presence of a cathedral. One week was divided from another by the holy day/holiday of Sunday, the day when Christ was resurrected, and every Friday, the devout remembered the Crucifixion and fasted. Major saints' days as well as great feasts such as Christmas and Easter were also holidays and were marked by merry-making and by special ceremonies: the lighting of bonfires on the eve of the nativity of St John the Baptist, for example; although some such customs originated in pre-Christian rites.

The most important ceremony of all and the most frequently repeated was the celebration of Mass (or the Eucharist) – the service in which the priest commemorated Christ's institution of the sacrament at the Last Supper. Once the bread and wine had been consecrated (the bread was then called 'the Host') it was thought to become in essence (although not materially) the flesh and blood of Christ: theologians called this process *transubstantiation*. Only the priest drank the wine from the chalice but all those who obeyed the laws of the Church received the Host from his hands. In this way the sacrifice Christ made on the cross was re-enacted: it was both the supreme form of worship and a means of gaining divine grace to assist the progress of the soul to salvation. Many members of the laity only received the sacrament once a year, normally at Easter, but priests, religious (monks, nuns and friars), and those who were gravely ill or especially devout did so much more frequently. Other services were celebrated in monasteries and cathedrals, where the religious and canons would pray at regular intervals during the day and night.

The nature of the rite that celebrated the Eucharist and which culminated in the consecration emphasised the centrality of the priest: the only person who could turn bread and wine into the flesh and blood of God. The authority of the ecclesiastical hierarchy was glorified by this unique power possessed by its representative. There seemed to be little for the laity to do but be mute spectators at a ceremony which, although essential to their chances of salvation, gave them little opportunity for participation. The emphasis laid by historians in recent decades, however, on lay religious experience has revealed that they did increasingly have a role to play. Virginia Reinburg's study of the liturgy in late medieval and Reformation France has considered the use of lay prayer books.[33] Whilst the priests' service books (or *missals*) concentrated on the sacrifice of the Mass, the lay prayer books stressed the reading of the Gospels, prayers and the offertory procession when gifts were given to the Church. The elevation of the consecrated Host was a communal act of worship since the faithful were intended to adore it as Christ raised up on the cross. After Mass, bread that the congregation had brought with them was blessed and given back to them so that a souvenir of the rite could be taken to their own homes.

The kiss of peace, exchanged by members of the congregation, was another means of involving the laity in the Mass. This was increasingly superseded, possibly through fear of infection during bouts of the plague, by kissing the *pax*. This was a tablet, often bearing an image of the crucifix, which was kissed by the priest who was celebrating Mass and then passed among the congregation. Prayer books and books of hours were another means by which the wealthier and better-educated laity could participate in the liturgy. The 'hours' were the periods of the day and night set apart by the Church for devotion; originally intended for those in religious orders; literate members of the laity could recite the appropriate prayers (see Section (i) above). People could adapt these offices to their individual spiritual needs by choosing which parts to follow and adding their own prayers and meditations. Anne Sutton and Livia Visser Fuchs have made a detailed study of the significance of the additions that were made to a book of hours that belonged to Richard III, king of England. Wealthy members of the laity paid large sums of money to acquire beautiful decorated prayer books.

The Church also presided over the administration of the other six sacraments: baptism, confirmation, marriage, penance, ordination and extreme unction. The ministration of a priest was required for baptism, penance and extreme unction although, in the first case, anyone might baptise a dying baby if no priest was available. This was permitted because it was believed that only the baptised had any hope of salvation, although belief in limbo was increasing: this was a place for the souls of un-baptised infants and the just who lived before Christ's incarnation. Bishops normally performed the sacraments of confirmation and ordination, whilst the marriage partners themselves partook of the sacrament of marriage. Yet the Church was not prepared to allow so important a rite to be outside its control and insisted that priests celebrated weddings, which were often followed by nuptial Masses. There were signs by the late Middle Ages that marriage, instead of being regarded as an inferior state required by frail humanity for the avoidance of sin, was beginning to be recognised by some clerics as a vocation and a source of grace. David d'Avray quotes a sermon to this effect that was delivered by Johannes Nider, a Dominican, to his German congregation: another instance of the closer association of the laity in the quest for godliness.[34]

Death

The whole process of serious illness, death, burial and bequests was enormously important in the Middle Ages. Whilst contemporary Western society regards pain and death as unmitigated disasters and dead bodies as unpleasant and unhygienic, devout Christians then took a different view. Few would go as far as the *anchoress* (female hermit) Julian of Norwich, who prayed for a serious illness so that she might benefit spiritually from the experience, but many saw suffering as an aid to salvation. Life was hard and dangerous and, provided that they made a good death, Christians could hope that they would ultimately go to heaven. An essential component of a good death was the sacrament of extreme unction, which enabled the dying persons to confess their sins to a priest, be anointed with oil, and receive absolution. This rite gave enormous power to the Church since failure to experience it at death endangered the soul: one of the reasons why the papal powers of excommunication and interdict were so feared. Those who lost their bodies at death through drowning or burning also risked damnation: the resurrection of the body was required at the Last Judgement, when Christ would come to welcome the just into heaven and condemn the wicked for eternity.

The ways in which people, assisted by Church doctrine and imagery, attempted to ensure their salvation are well documented. Such records mostly concern the more prosperous sections of society, although ornaments and church memorials were seen by all, and Paul Binski has given a recent account of these.[35] Manuals were produced to inform the laity how to die well: one of the most popular in England in the late fifteenth century was William Caxton's printed version of the *Ars Moriendi* (*The Art of Dying*). The manner in which a person's worldly goods were disposed of could make an impact on their prospects of salvation, and donations to the poor and to the Church were especially meritorious. It was also important to concentrate on the passion and death of Christ as an exemplar of how a good Christian should die.

Well before the time of their death the laity were regaled with vivid images and texts that prepared them for what was to come. The horrors of hell awaiting those who died in a state of mortal sin (one that could not subsequently be relieved) were vividly described by preachers. The point was emphasised by church paintings showing the Last Judgement and the fate of the damned in gruesome detail, while the beauty of the Holy Trinity, the Virgin Mary, angels and saints anticipated the joys of heaven. From the early fifteenth century, representations of the Dance of Death were popular, such as the fresco in the cloisters of the churchyard of the Innocents in Paris: the figure of death led a line of skeletal or mummified figures in a macabre dance. Another phenomenon was the portrayal of the wealthy departed in tomb sculpture: shown sometimes in power and splendour but also as naked, rotten corpses. In either case (and sometimes the 'living' and 'dead' images were juxtaposed) spectators could draw the lesson that life was transitory and its grim ending inevitable. One of the most popular ways of contrasting the worldly joys of the wealthy and the noble with what was to come was the vision of the three living and the three dead kings. Three handsome young princes encountered three decomposing corpses, their counterparts, who addressed them in terms such as the following:

> The truth is that death
> Had made us such as we are
> And you will rot as we are now;
> Until now you were so pure and perfect
> However you will rot before the end.[36]

Huizinga took such imagery as a metaphor for a declining culture; later writers have seen it as a reaction to the terrible mortality caused by the Black Death and European wars, or guilt arising from the increasing gulf between rich and poor. (see Illustration 9).

The rich and powerful remained ambivalent about the way in which they provided for their deaths. The very sumptuousness of their tombs, even of those that seemed to portray their humility, was a statement of the elevated position they and their families enjoyed. In the case of royalty this tendency was particularly pronounced. All the great princes of the time had their family mausoleums, such as at St Denis in France and Westminster in England, and Binski shows how they

9 A mass for the dead

The deceased's family stands at either side of the tomb (containing an image rather than the actual corpse which would have been buried in a vault). Behind, the knights of St John conduct the service.

managed to make even more political capital out of their corpses. There was an increasing tendency to have parts of royal corpses, especially hearts and intestines, buried separately from their bodies. The territorial power of the dynasty could thus be stressed by ensuring a kind of princely presence in several parts of the realm. The custom was facilitated by the practice of removing the entrails of princes so that their remains could be preserved: burial was normally a lengthy process entailing slow journeys to the chosen site. An image of the dead prince, dressed in robes of state, was often displayed at the main funeral, emphasising continuity between the authority of the new and the deceased ruler (some of these survive in England and are displayed in Westminster Abbey).

The attitudes taken by poor and ill-educated people towards death and the afterlife are not easy to recover. Whilst the imagery in churches and cathedrals was graphic and available for all, as were sermons by priests and friars, the reaction to them by the common people is hard to estimate. Some, however, did leave wills (especially if they had prospered) and these contain a concern for their salvation in the gifts they made to the Church and for charity equal to that shown by the higher orders. There was also a tendency to be credulous about the existence of demons and ghosts. Preachers used tales about visitations from the dead, hoping to scare their congregations into behaving well, paying their dues to the Church and funding Masses for the departed.

A story that survives from the fifteenth century tells of a man, probably a ploughman or a small farmer, who was returning from a smithy when he encountered the ghost of his late mistress. She told him that her terrible suffering could only be relieved if he paid for many masses for the repose of her soul. He replied: 'I will celebrate Masses for you even if it costs me all my goods, right down to my last penny.'[37] He duly paid for a large number of Masses and the departed returned in a state of bliss to thank and bless him. We must assume that a congregation would accept this and similar stories as likely to be truthful and, if they had the means, would take steps to avoid the penalties that were threatened. Such beliefs were in many cases shared by the higher orders: in the above story the preacher chose a common man and woman as the main protagonists. Like the provision of murals and carvings in the churches this was a deliberate attempt to instruct and involve all orders of society in religious experience and duties. Other beliefs may not have been so effectively controlled by the authorities: the fear, for example, that on All Hallowe'en, the eve of All Souls' Day, the dead briefly returned to earth. Ghosts, when they were reported by the laity, were viewed with suspicion: in 1397 an inhabitant of a Herefordshire parish was charged with causing scandal by claiming that the spirit of his father haunted the area at night.[38]

The dilemma of how a Christian could enjoy the pleasures of the world and still achieve salvation was a constant preoccupation. During the later Middle Ages it seemed that a solution to the problem might be offered by the growing belief in purgatory and in the efficacy of indulgences in relieving those who acquired them from the consequences of their sins.

Purgatory, Masses for the dead and indulgences

Belief in purgatory was not a late medieval phenomenon: its existence had been assumed by many priests and lay people for centuries. Until the Council of Florence in 1437 affirmed it as an official doctrine it was for believers to decide whether or not they accepted the idea of a kind of waiting room in which departed souls who had committed venial sins stayed until the Last Judgement. It was not a pleasant place and those sent there had a great agony to bear: they were denied the supreme bliss of God's presence. The idea of purgatory solved one of the problems raised in the Introduction to this chapter: apart from the saints, all Christians were sinful in some degree, burdened by the heritage of the disobedience of Adam and Eve. Provided they had avoided the taint of mortal sin at death, it seemed to accord with God's intention in sending Christ as a redeemer to allow them eventually to purge themselves of sin. The difficulty for theologians was that, once dead, a Christian had no further opportunity to make reparation for the sins that had been committed in life. This could, however, be overcome by tapping into the great resource of grace that the sacrifice of Christ and the lives of the Virgin Mary and the saints had accumulated. The advantage of this belief from the point of view of the Church was that it could control the release of this grace, thus enhancing its authority and also raising large amounts of revenue. Masses for the dead were perceived as an effective means by which the sacrament of the Eucharist could be used to invoke Christ's help for a soul suffering in purgatory: in England sums paid to priests to say Masses varied between 1d and 4d.

Rich people often left substantial sums of money in their wills to pay for Masses and some even founded *chantries* where a priest was paid to pray and say them, full-time or part-time, for their souls. These could be located at an existing altar in a church or monastery or in a specially built chapel. The childless Sir John

Fastolf, for example, had a grandiose plan to found a *chantry* college at his castle at Caister in Norfolk but nothing came of it: only a proportion of those established in wills were ever set up. In Germany a variation on this practice was the *Seelhaus* (Soul-house): a group of women would be endowed by a family to pray for their souls. Less wealthy people could leave money for a *chantry* priest to say Masses for a limited period or at particular times of the year: the anniversary of the death was popular. Ordinary parish priests and ordained monks and friars were also paid to carry out these duties, which often made an important contribution to their income. Barrie Dobson has addressed the question of whether the popularity of *chantries* and similar bequests in the late Middle Ages marked a preference for a more personal, private kind of religious practice.[39] In a study of York, however, he found that, while many individuals and associations set up *chantries*, the latter were anxious that the work of the priests should be properly integrated into the religious life of the community for the benefit of all.

In a bull of 1343, Pope Clement VI encouraged the issue of indulgences by referring to the 'treasury of merits'. Christians could either buy remission of the years to be spent in purgatory by departed members of their family, or buy relief for their own sins. Indulgences could be acquired in a variety of ways: by visiting a local shrine, making a pilgrimage to a holy city such as Rome or Jerusalem, giving alms, paying for church building works and decorations, or by going on Crusade. Indulgences could also be purchased in lieu of carrying out any of the religious duties listed above. A plenary indulgence, which absolved a person from all punishment due for sins committed up to the time of purchase, was the most desirable. Originally indulgences were sold directly by the Church but increasingly the right to issue them was passed to lay men known as 'pardoners'. They would only be effective for the living if they confessed their sins and received absolution from a priest. Another way of avoiding the penalties of sin was to pay someone else to undertake a pilgrimage; friars often made themselves available to do this.

Despite the bad press that the practice of granting indulgences has received from generations of Protestant historians, the original conception had several advantages. Many people in the late Middle Ages seem to have been oppressed by terrible doubts about their chances of salvation, leading them to what Huizinga has characterised as 'lax practice, chequered by spasmodic effusions of ardent piety',[40] and a fevered, desperate attitude to life which could result in violent, illogical behaviour. Indugences catered for 'the anxieties of whole masses of repentant sinners'.[41] Swanson cited purgatory as one of the beliefs that the Church accepted rather than instituted, bowing to pressure from the laity to recognise their need for reassurance.[42] Belief in purgatory had a positive side: people were encouraged to live well, give to the poor and use their resources at death, at least in part, to improve the lives and surroundings of their fellows. Difficulties arose as much from the increasingly urgent demands of the laity for more indulgences, which remitted longer periods in purgatory, as from the greed and cynicism of the Church.

An obvious problem with the issue of indulgences was that the laity might be tempted into complacency about their sins if, by the expenditure of a few coins, they could buy remission. It was also a very unequal system since the rich could afford to buy more immunity than the poor. A wealthy man or woman could found a *chantry* chapel or at least pay for regular Masses for their souls and buy indulgences to relieve them of punishment for all sins. The best a poor man could afford was one or two Masses after death and to participate in any special graces that the Church or local benefactors might offer (one form of almsgiving was to pay for Masses for all departed souls in a particular place). Another flaw in the practice was that there was always a temptation to exploit an easy source of revenue and thus devalue its spiritual appeal. The papal sojourn at Avignon, followed by the Great Schism and the Conciliar Movement, led popes to placate European princes by colluding in the withdrawal of taxes formerly paid to the Holy See (see Section (i) above). The sale of indulgences both at local level and throughout Christendom helped with rising costs and declining revenue. Those who supplied them were sometimes decent, devout people but it only took a few rogues, such as the Pardoner described by Geoffrey Chaucer in *The Canterbury Tales*, to bring the whole process into disrepute:

> But of his craft, from Berwick to Ware
> Never was there such another pardoner
> For in his trunk he had a pillow-case
> Which that he said, was our Lady's veil:
> He said, he had a gobbet of the sail
> That saint Peter had, when that he went
> Upon the sea, until Jesus Christ him held.
> He had a cross of metal, full of stones,
> And in a glass he had pigs' bones.
> But with these relics when he found
> A poor parson dwelling upon land,
> Upon a day he got him more money
> Than that parson got in months two.[43]

Corpus Christi, saints and shrines

The veneration of the saints played a very important part in late medieval religious practice; yet even more central to the Christian rite was the worship of Jesus Christ and his mother the Virgin Mary. The desire to utilise their great treasury of merits and, in the case of the Virgin and the saints, to ask for their intercession for the forgiveness of sins and the relief of punishment, was a major factor in the success of these cults.

Many of the most renowned saints originated from the New Testament and early Christian periods. The twelve apostles and St Paul figure in the scriptures; they travelled widely and were in some cases martyred, so tremendous prestige was attached to any places associated with them. The most daring pilgrims travelled to the Holy Land to worship at the many shrines linked to Christ's ministry, passion and resurrection, and some, like Nompar, seigneur of Caumont, brought back souvenirs. He purchased fine coloured silk, four pieces of rope the length of the Holy Sepulchre, four purses, thirty-three silver rings, and twelve silver crucifixes (which had touched the Sepulchre), a bag of soil, two pairs of golden spurs, four roses and a phial of Jordan water. He distributed these to his family and tenants, on his return to France.[44] The great basilica of St Peter's in Rome reminded the faithful of the authority Christ had given to that apostle to govern the Church, and the city contained many other holy sites. Pilgrims could gain spiritual refreshment by visiting Rome, and indulgences were attached to particular shrines.

St James the Great (Zebedee), another apostle, had been adopted as the patron saint of Spain and become an icon as a supernatural leader (*Santiago matamoros*) in their fight against the Moors. His martyred body had reputedly been transported miraculously to Galicia, where a rich shrine was erected in the basilica of St James in Compostela. It became enormously popular with pilgrims, especially those from France and Britain. Great merit was earned by making the journey on foot across the Pyrenees, but it was tempting for British pilgrims to take one of the many ships from southern English ports to Corunna, not far from the shrine. William Wey, a priest and fellow of Eton College, visited Compostela in 1456 and left a detailed account of his experiences. Such reports could either act as guide books or give the reader a vicarious experience of what it was like to be a pilgrim – without undertaking the danger and expense of travel. Here is an extract from his long list of the spiritual benefits pilgrims derived from the shrine:

> A third part of all their sins are remitted for anyone who makes a pilgrimage to the church of the blessed James Zebedee at whatever time. If they die on the way there, or at the shrine or returning, if they have repented of their sins, these are all remitted. Item, those who go every Sunday to the procession of the church of St James are given for the procession and consecration forty days of indulgence and are given the same throughout the week. If it is a feast day they are given three hundred more days in addition to the indulgence for a third part of all their sins. Item, on the vigil of St James and on the feast for the dedication of his church they are given six hundred days in addition to the indulgence for a third part of all their sins.[45]

Many saints flourished during the early Christian era: there were the great Fathers of the Church, Augustine, Ambrose, Jerome and Gregory, and martyrs such as Catherine and George. The Fathers were revered for their sanctity and learning but perhaps seemed too remote and intellectual for many worshippers. Women could relate more easily to St Catherine, a beautiful and well-educated princess who repelled the lustful advances of a pagan emperor and, after many trials, was martyred. She was the most popular of a whole clutch of virgin saints: some modern writers have wondered if the reaction to accounts of tortures, including scourging and the removal of teeth, eyes and breasts, may have contained an element of sadistic sexual gratification. St George manfully bore many agonies before he was killed: portrayed as a young, handsome knight, he served as a male role model. In recent times the Papacy has subjected the histories of the early saints to close scrutiny with the result that Catholics are not now encouraged to venerate those whose careers and very existence are extremely dubious.

The location and creation of saints had doubtless always had a political dimension but during the later Middle Ages this became increasingly overt. Sanctity was conferred by God but the process of canonisation, which recognised an individual as a saint, was the responsibility of the Papacy. All the major European dynasties wanted the prestige conferred by possessing a saintly member of the family. England led the way when Edward the Confessor was canonised in 1161; France rejoiced that the pious Louis IX became a saint in 1297, as did the Angevin dynasty which produced St Louis of Toulouse, who was canonised in 1317 during the papal sojourn in Avignon. A preponderance of late medieval saints came from Italy: the further away from Rome or Avignon that holy individuals lived, the smaller were their chances of canonisation. Some attempts to get princes and nobles who had led pious lives canonised failed: the cause of Henry VI was promoted by the early Tudors but the break with Rome in the early 1530s ended his chances of sainthood.

Whilst some believed that: 'to a registrar [clerical official] the miracle of a single nobleman was worth a dozen dead and revived peasant children',[46] the common people made a substantial contribution to the formation of saintly cults. Although only a proportion of the laity and priests whose shrines were associated with miracles after their decease were canonised, prayers were offered and pilgrimages were made despite the absence of any official authorisation. The life of Dorothy of Montau, a married woman of peasant stock (who was eventually canonised in 1976), illustrates the kind of holiness that appealed to her contemporaries. Apart from dragging her unwilling husband off on pilgrimages, she spent most of her life in Danzig, bearing nine children, eight of whom died young. She regularly denied herself sleep, scourged and burnt her body and aggravated the wounds with nettles or nutshells. She had mystical experiences, feeling her love for the divine so intensely that her body grew hot. When she was widowed she was enclosed in a cell in the cathedral of Marienwerder as an *anchoress*. Her cult was fostered by her confessor, who wrote several accounts of her life: miracles occurred at her tomb, and devotion to her remained strong in Germany. Richard Kieckhefer shows that her hagiographer portrayed her as carrying out political as well as religious tasks. God had placed her in Prussia in order that lawless contemporaries on the borders of Christendom could be weaned away from violence by her prayers and example.[47] Her career also exemplifies the anguished pursuit of holiness that some believe characterises late medieval north-western Europe. Veneration by ordinary people could eventually push the Church into recognising a person as holy.

When the English conquerors of Wales tried to marginalise local saints the process worked in reverse: Glanmor Williams suggests that the Welsh largely ignored Anglo-Norman imports and remained attached to saints David (Dewi), Teilo, Dyfrig and Euddogwy.[48] Throughout Europe saints and holy people received special devotion in the localities where they had lived or, as in the case of St James at Compostela, where there was a special reason to venerate them.

A new cult, which originated amongst the *Béguines* (communities of women living a religious life but without a monastic rule) of Liège in the mid-thirteenth century, swiftly grew in popularity. Devotion to the 'Corpus Christi' (or body of Christ) received strong papal approval from John XXII at Avignon in 1317. The feast of Corpus Christi soon became popular throughout France, Germany and Britain. The cult should not be confused with the veneration for Christ, the son of God and the second person in the Trinity, which had always been an integral part of the Christian religion. Corpus Christi concentrated specifically on his passion and crucifixion, using his suffering as a means by which the devout could face their own sinful nature and draw on his merits to pray for redemption. Attendance at Mass was the climax of a programme of prayer and meditation that brought Christians closer to God. Devotion was concentrated on the Host, whether held on high by the priest during the Eucharist or displayed in a monstrance during special rites or in processions (see Illustration 10).

10 A religious procession at Strasbourg

The celebrations at Strasburg after the defeat of Burgundy at Nancy in 1477. In the procession a priest bears the Host in a monstrance under a canopy. Images of the Virgin and Child and the Crucified Christ are also carried out of the cathedral. (*Heinrich Knoblochzer, woodcut, Strasburg, 1477*)

Miri Rubin, in her study *Corpus Christi: The Eucharist in Late Medieval Culture*, has shown that a large number of handbooks were produced for the clergy and laity, to instruct them how to administer and receive the Sacrament. Moral tales or *exempla* that demonstrated the power of the consecrated Host were a staple ingredient of these books. Some dwelt on visions granted to the pious while they received the Sacrament, which demonstrated the true presence of the body of Christ. Nuns, *Béguines* and lay women sometimes reported seeing a young child or baby in the Host. Another sort of tale involved unusual behaviour by animals or humans in awe of the Eucharist: kneeling oxen were involved on at least one occasion. Finally, Eucharistic properties: flesh, blood, or Christ as the Man of Sorrows (bound, bleeding and wearing the crown of thorns) might appear, to confound negligent priests, thieves, Jews and witches.

An advantage of the cult of Corpus Christi was that no official sanction was required to establish a rite or a shrine in its honour. Any church or cathedral could set up an altar, usually surmounted with a crucifix, where special devotions could be held. A liturgy, which may have been composed by St Thomas Aquinas, circulated throughout Europe. It included a Mass, and an office for the feast and its octave (eight days including the festival) which expounded the eucharistic doctrine:

> Though his flesh as food abideth,
> And his blood as drink – he hideth
> Undivided under each.[49]

The Ascension of Christ and his nature as God posed a problem as far as the veneration of physical remains was concerned. For centuries, however, relics purporting to be derived from his passion had been treasured, including many pieces of the cross, nails from the crucifixion, the crown of thorns, St Veronica's veil (with which she wiped Christ's face on the way to Calvary) and the shroud at Turin. With the cult of Corpus Christi these now became the objects of ever more intense devotion.

An extreme manifestation of popular enthusiasm for the new cult was the case of Wilsnack, near Wittenberg in Saxony. In 1383 its church was destroyed by fire but the parish priest claimed to have found three consecrated hosts, marked with drops of blood, in the rubble. The church was quickly rebuilt and granted an indulgence by Urban VI: large numbers of 'plebeian persons who cannot be trusted', including many children (often without their parents), made the pilgrimage to the new shrine.[50] The ecclesiastical authorities became alarmed by the hysterical atmosphere that the shrine seemed to engender and by fraudulent claims about miracles. They unsuccessfully attempted on several occasions to ban worship there but it continued to flourish until the mid-sixteenth century when Wilsnack fell under Protestant control. This is one of the best known of a number of instances, stressed by historians in recent decades, of the lower clergy and laity taking devotional initiatives in the later Middle Ages and getting away with it.

The problem for the Church and for theologians like Jean Gerson was that while Corpus Christi confirmed and intensified religious belief and increased revenue from Masses and visits to shrines and images it also tended to drag devotion down to a very physical level. It encouraged the laity and some ordinary priests to claim direct access to religious experience unmediated by the authority of the hierarchy. Cheap images of the Man of Sorrows, which the laity could purchase and set up in their own houses or carry about with them, multiplied after the spread of printed material. This detracted from the mystery and awe that many felt should attend worship, and undermined the centrality of the Church in providing images of God: Gerson criticised the irreverence of many celebrations. During the fifteenth century there was a growing tendency to limit the public showing of the Host and to divide the altar from the nave by the erection of *rood* screens. The name *rood* referred to the crucifix that often surmounted the screen: this was presumably intended to comfort the laity in the nave, who were cut off visually from the rite of consecration.

The cult of the Virgin Mary shared the advantage enjoyed by Corpus Christi, that no special ecclesiastical approval had to be obtained for a church to promote worship. The mother of God had always been venerated by the Church but it was not until the late Middle Ages that special devotion to her became so widespread. One theory links it to the dissemination of chivalric values amongst the nobility, with their emphasis on the respect that should be paid to worthy women. Feminist studies have seen the Virgin, together with other female saints, as a valued role model and intercessor for all kinds of women. Increased literacy and the growing availability of books fostered enthusiasm for the cult, and the many lives of the Virgin, such as that contained in *The Golden Legend*, were read by priests, the religious and the laity.

The problem of surviving relics presented itself, since the Virgin did not suffer a passion and was thought to have been taken up bodily into heaven (the Assumption). Intense devotion to her cult, however, was able to overcome these difficulties: phials containing her milk (Walsingham and Ipswich) and pieces of her clothing (Durham) were revered. Her house, which was thought to have been miraculously transported by angels away from the infidels in Palestine, was a growing attraction for pilgrims to Loreto in Italy. Any location where her image was considered to possess special powers or where she had appeared to a believer was a popular focus of adoration (*Mariolatry*). The people of Ypres were devoted to a statue of the Virgin that had protected them during an attack by the English in 1383. In the diocese of Strasburg, eighteen new Marian shrines were established after 1350, and similar examples of the growth of her cult could be cited throughout Europe.

Yet there were potential challenges to the authority of the Church hierarchy in the popular desire for direct revelations from the Virgin, as well as from the Corpus Christi, and these are exemplified in Richard Wunderli's *Peasant Fires: The Drummer of Niklashausen*.[51] In 1476, after a very cold, hard winter, Hans Behem, an illiterate shepherd in Franconia, south-central Germany, claimed that the Virgin had appeared to him. She had warned that God was angry with mankind, punishing them with bad weather because they were failing to worship him devoutly. Nobles, prelates and priests were lax and self-indulgent; they should renounce their comfortable lives and allow the ordinary people to own land in common. Hans was to go to the nearby church of the Virgin at Niklashausen, burn his drum and shepherd's pipe and encourage others to destroy their

11 Hans Behem preaching to the common people at Niklashausen, Germany

A friar, who was supposed by Behem's critics to be his evil genius, lurks behind him. (*Hartmann Schedel, woodcut, 'The Nuremberg Chronicle', 1493*)

vain possessions. He should preach as the Virgin dictated and make the church a place of pilgrimage. During the next few months thousands of ordinary people flocked there to hear 'the Drummer' and destroy their vanities: those with nothing else even burnt their clothes. By early July, alarmed by reports that 'the Drummer' was urging the peasantry to arm themselves, the bishop of Wurzburg seized him and rapidly had him tried and burnt as a heretic. Two accomplices, a particularly insurgent peasant and a *Beghard* (a man who lived a holy life without a monastic rule, the equivalent of the female *Béguines*) hermit, were beheaded (see Illustration 11). In this case the ecclesiastical authorities were able to nip the cult in the bud because its leader was naive and made statements which could be condemned as heretical. Such ideas, when aired in the early sixteenth century by educated reformers enjoying powerful political support, could not so easily be suppressed.

The advantages of Mariolatry for the Church were, nevertheless, plentiful. It provided a satisfying emotional outlet for celibate nuns and priests and presented a gentler aspect to a religion that necessarily concentrated on the suffering and sacrifice of Christ and the awful fate of unrepentant sinners. Yet the temptation to capitalise on a beautiful statue or on the unsupported claims of a visionary was manifest: if Hans Behem had not preached a revolutionary political programme he might have been tolerated or even encouraged by the hierarchy. Churches such as Walsingham (dismissed as 'Falsingham' by the Lollards) derived great financial gain from their relics. It was difficult for the credulous and uneducated to distinguish between the Mother of God as a virtuous person to be emulated and petitioned as an intercessor and as a powerful deity in her own right. Worship at some of her shrines seemed to have crossed this delicate line, to the scandal of the growing band of reformers who wished to purge Christianity of superstitious and idolatrous practices. Yet the appeal that the Virgin had for so many members of the laity was symptomatic of the way in which they were appropriating, changing and strengthening the Christian faith for their individual needs.

Another exemplar of this kind of lay intervention in religious practice is the guilds and fraternities, which John Bossy has described as 'the most characteristic expressions of late medieval Christianity'.[52] These associations were essentially urban, and varied considerably throughout Europe in their composition and purpose. They will be described below (see Chapter 6: (ii)).

Mystics

Discussion in this section has dwelt on the way in which the laity and ordinary clerics interacted with the ecclesiatical hierarchy in the development of religious practice. Whilst there were marked regional variations, throughout northern Europe the general trend was for the laity to become more deeply involved and in some cases even to take the initiative. A similar process can be discerned in mysticism as a dimension in the religious experience of groups and of individuals in the late Middle Ages. Mysticism had constituted an element in Christian worship since the earliest times: passages in the New Testament could be so interpreted, and the writings of St Augustine in the fifth century were a model for later devotional meditations.

Generalisations about the phenomenon of mysticism are not particularly helpful since each individual or group had their own characteristics. What set them apart from other Christians, however, was an intense longing for union with God, to be achieved by meditation, emptying the mind of all extraneous matters and, in some cases, mortification of the body. The following extract from *The Scale of Perfection* by the English mystic and writer Walter Hilton incorporates some of these characteristics:

> And when thou feelest this desire to God, to Jesus (all is one), helped and comforted by ghostly might so great that it is turned into love and affection, ghostly savour and sweetness, into light and knowing of truth – so great that for the time the point of thy thought is set upon nothing that is made, nor feelest no stirring of vainglory, nor none other evil affection, for they must not impair that time, but only is enclosed, rested, softened, anointed in Jesus – then has thou found somewhat of Jesus. Not yet him as he is, but a shadow of him. For the better that thou findest him, the more shall thou desire him. Then by what manner of prayer, or meditation, or occupation that thou may have greatest desire to him, and have most feeling of him: by that occupation, thou seekest him best, and best findest him.[53]

Those who attempted to achieve this kind of direct, personal relationship with God were by implication undermining the role of the Church as interpreter of doctrine and custodian of the sacrament of the Eucharist: the rite through which the individual could partake of the divine. At no stage in the Middle Ages was mysticism subject to official condemnation, indeed some mystics were praised and supported by the authorities. Most were, in any case, either priests or in religious orders but the danger remained that immersion in contemplation and contempt for worldly matters could lead to heretical statements.

A new intensity of mystical experience was introduced into northern Europe in the twelfth century by the visions and writings of the German nun Hildegard of Bingen. During the three centuries that followed her death a number of men and women, clerics, religious and lay folk, took a similar path to achieve insight into the divinity of God and union with his person. This could involve the capacity to see visions and/or hear the voices of God and the saints, or might be a purely internal enlightenment, usually granted after prolonged prayer and meditation. Mystics often shunned the formulaic prayers to be found in missals and books of hours, preferring to use their own words informed by their spontaneous feelings. It was not necessary, however, to be exclusively devoted to such exercises: a strong feeling was expressed by mystical theologians such as Meister Eckhart and Jan van Ruysbroek that holy lives should mix contemplation; with work. St Bridgit of Sweden and St Catherine of Siena were two powerful personalities who combined a mystical engagement in their faith with political activism. They deplored clerical abuses and the papal sojourn in Avignon, inspiring such respect that they were both canonised rather than condemned for their strictures.

The ideal of living a holy life in the lay world was exemplified by those who belonged to the *Béguine* and *Beghard* movement, although only a small number were mystics. They were communities of men and women who lived in a new way: without a monastic rule but devoted to prayer and good works. Unlike the religious orders they did not rely on patrons or on begging for their upkeep but were expected to work. There was a constant danger that the looseness of their organisation and the mysticism of individual members would expose them to the charge of *antinomianism* (a claim not to be bound by the moral law): in 1310 the *Béguine* Margaret Porete was burnt for heresy.

Over a century later, political rather than theological considerations led to the condemnation of Joan of Arc in Normandy. She is not normally classed with the mystics but her claim to have heard the voices of St Margaret and St Michael drew on the tradition of pious individuals communing with the divine without the intervention of the Church hierarchy. The reports of Joan's trial show that her interrogators did make some attempt to establish whether or not she had received genuine communications from the saints. The fact that she was illiterate deprived them of the written evidence that was often used to test orthodoxy. The Church authorities were generally concerned not so much to quell mystical experiences but to ensure that they remained within the orthodox canon of Christian beliefs: when they did so faith could be strengthened by accounts of devout lives. The Dominican nuns of south-western Germany and Switzerland compiled a collection of spiritual, mystical biographies, *The Lives of the Sisters*, which was influential on later generations.

England was another country where mystical devotion flourished at this time and a number of treatises and memoirs survive which attest to this. The anonymous author of *The Cloud of Unknowing* was probably a priest from the north-east Midlands, writing in the late fourteenth century. It was intended to provide spiritual direction to nuns or monks who were living as contemplatives and it shows signs that it was influenced by the near contemporary treatise, Hilton's *The Scale of Perfection*. The 'cloud of unknowing' is not a physical entity but it hides God from human beings. To penetrate it they must put a 'cloud of forgetting' between themselves and all created things so that by intense meditation on the incarnation of Christ they can release a gift of grace that will enable them to contemplate the divinity of God. *The Cloud* was an orthodox account of how the individual soul might approach the divine: it avoided the dangers of *antinomianism* inherent in the thought of some European mystics such as Meister Eckhart. At his death he had been under investigation for heresy at Avignon for his claim that exterior acts add nothing to the goodness of interior devotion.

Julian of Norwich the *anchoress* was enclosed in a cell in the church of St Julian, Norwich. When she was a young woman during a serious illness she had had sixteen visions or 'showings' of Jesus. Most dwelt on his sufferings during the Passion or discussed theological points, mainly reassuring her of his love and forgiveness for mankind. The final one reaffirmed the truth of all Julian had experienced:

> I am a woman, ignorant, weak and frail. But I know very well that what I am saying I have received from the revelation of him who is sovereign teacher.[54]

Her conviction earned Julian a high reputation as a pious hermit and spiritual director. Margery Kempe, a married woman from Kings Lynn, visited her as part of her quest to achieve union with God. Maureen Fries suggests that much of the criticism aimed at Margery both in her own time and in the strictures of later commentators arises from her refusal to accept a conventional role.[55] She bore her husband fourteen children but was constantly leaving home to make pilgrimages and badgering him to allow her to live in chastity. She did eventually persuade him to embrace celibacy, after which she received the ring, staff and cloak of a *vowess*, but she continued her travels. Margery was thus neither a good wife nor a nun: sufficient shortcomings to damn her in the eyes of her neighbours and fellow pilgrims (who also found her incessant weeping very trying). Modern writers have tended to subject her life, a kind of autobiography which was recorded for her in a book by priests, to a Freudian interpretation where most of her characteristics are considered to be due to sexual problems, hysteria, post-natal depression or a combination of factors. Margery seems to have been emulating St Bridgit, who was also married (there were also similarities between her life and the career of Dorothy of Montau). Despite her extravagances, she provides valuable evidence about how an illiterate lay woman attempted to live a holy life.

The fourteenth century marked a high spot in mystical devotion to God but it remained an important influence within the Catholic Church for centuries to come. The first section of this chapter recorded Jean Gerson's concern with spiritual development, especially for the laity. In 1453 the statesman and reformer Nicholas of Cusa sent a small book, *The Vision of God, or the Icon*, to aid the contemplative exercises of a community of Benedictine monks at Tegernsee in Austria. The book was accompanied by a painting of God, whose eyes seemed to gaze on the observer. Cusa used this as a starting point to teach that, while God could not be perfectly known by any human being, if he was approached with a kind of 'learned ignorance' in which reason was put in abeyance, some intimation of his divinity might be received. Just at the time when humanists in northern Europe and Italy were using ancient learning to refine their understanding of philosophy, literature and the natural world, one of the most vital movements within the Church was leading its members away from the use of reason.

R. R. Post, in *The Modern Devotion* (or *Devotio Moderna*, communities of sisters and brethren of the Common Life, which started in Holland in the late fourteenth century), rejects the idea that it fostered humanism or concedes that it only did so when the Renaissance was well under way.[56] Many were initially lay men and women, although there was a later tendency for them to accept a monastic rule. They were associated with the community at Windesheim (see Section (i) above). Whilst the Modern Devotion stressed the importance of education and founded a number of schools, its religious aims were entirely orthodox. There was a strong mystical element exemplified in *The Imitation of Christ*, which was probably written by Thomas à Kempis, a Regular Canon who was a member of the movement in Holland. Readers were exhorted to practise the traditional monastic virtues of humility, obedience, purity and poverty but also to maintain a perpetual communion with God and the saints and constantly to reflect on the Passion and on making a good death. The strong spiritual element in the Modern Devotion and the stress laid upon good education was influential on several reformers and humanists at the end of the fifteenth century: Martin Luther had studied with the brethren. Post may be correct in seeing their engagement with the new learning as a late development but the thinking they represented was to be an element in the Protestant programme during the following century. Like the *Béguines*, *Beghards* and mystics such as Meister Eckhart and Julian of Norwich, those who embraced the Modern Devotion wanted a direct relationship with God, which left little space for the authority of Church tradition.

In this section, evidence has been reviewed for the degree to which the laity and ordinary priests, nuns and religious could control the practice of their religion. There does not seem to have been a great gulf between the laity and their priests. Only when there was a threat that a person or belief could be considered heretical might local churchmen be obliged to retreat from popularly supported practices (in the case of the Drummer of Niklashausen, for example). Late medieval north-western Europe contained huge tracts of sparsely populated and often inaccessible land: there was little to prevent local communities worshipping in the way that was best suited to their needs. Nobles, clergy and the people established shrines, made pilgrimages, venerated holy men and women and celebrated their local saints in processions and plays without causing social or theological conflict. The religious culture of ordinary people was vital and flourishing and it was shared to a large extent by the higher orders of society: that would only change if the nature of religion itself changed.

(iii) HERESY AND OTHER FORMS OF EXCLUSION

Exclusion and the 'universal' Church

'Catholic' means 'universal' or 'all-embracing' and in the Middle Ages the Church was thought by its members to be truly catholic. There were categories of people residing in Europe, however, who were excluded wholly or partly from the Christian community. Despite the persecution that many of them suffered, their very existence carried some intimations of the changes that were to come about in the Catholic Church during the following centuries. Moslems and Jews were seen as presenting a serious threat to the integrity of Christendom. The Ottoman Turks dominated much of the eastern Mediterranean by the fifteenth century. Islam was the main religion in North Africa, and Moors lived in the enclave of Granada in southern Spain (their presence recalled a time when Spain had been invaded from North Africa). Much rhetoric was expended on the subject of a Crusade, but after the West's defeat at Nicopolis in 1396, little was done to stop the Ottoman advance through Hungary. In Spain, King Ferdinand and Queen Isabella had conquered Granada by the end of the fifteenth century and instituted a harsh policy of conversion to Christianity. Moslem diplomats and traders visited almost all European states but they were usually tolerated because they were small in number, represented rich and powerful interests and were often only temporarily resident. The fate of Jews in north-western Europe will be discussed below.

A number of people who had been baptised as Christians were wholly or partially excluded from the Church during their lifetimes or even after death. 'Leper' is still a word that is used for someone who is socially unacceptable and separated from the rest of the community. This was literally true in the Middle Ages both because of the fear that lepers would infect healthy people and because of the feeling that victims of the disease must have sinned greatly to be so severely punished by God. In his later years, Henry IV of England suffered from a disease which some believed to be leprosy; it was assumed that his condition was a consequence of the deposition and murder of Richard II or of the execution of Archbishop Scrope.[57] Ordinary lepers were required to submit to a religious ceremony similar to the rites for the dead, to forfeit their possessions, to wear distinctive clothes and to carry a clapper and begging bowl. They frequently lived in hospitals, subject to a strict, quasi-monastic regime: those who cared for them earned great spiritual merit.

People who committed suicide were thought to have incurred damnation by their self-murder and were posthumously denied all religious rites. The body was dragged (sometimes it did not cross the threshold if it was found in a house but was thrown out of a window or pulled underneath the threshold) to the local scaffold and hung there. Eventually it was put, without a burial service, in an unmarked grave on unconsecrated land. The suicide's goods were confiscated, so his or her family suffered both shame and hardship. Evidence of court cases involving suicide shows that the authorities could show compassion to surviving relatives: doubtful incidents such as drowning without witnesses could be classified as accidents. Alexander Murray records a number of merciful court decisions when there could have been no doubt that death had been self-inflicted.[58] In 1423, for example, the Court of Requests in Paris allowed the widow of an embroiderer to keep his goods and to bury him in consecrated ground 'provided that no solemnity attends the burial'. The reason for this leniency seems to have been that the man had been honest and hardworking, that he was ill when he threw himself out of a window and that he left six children, with another on the way. When our contemporaries speak of 'medieval' cruelty such instances of compassion and common sense are invariably overlooked.

Lepers, suicides and those born into different faiths were not deliberately withdrawing from the religious life of Christendom, even if this was to be the outcome of their situation. Most heretics, witches and magicians understood the risks that they ran but continued their practices from conviction, a desire for knowledge, self-delusion or hope of gain. In another very amorphous category of people were those who expressed anticlerical or sceptical sentiments. In extreme cases they might be branded as heretics and incur total exclusion from the Church, but many more either criticised the clergy and got away with it or were subjected to relatively mild penalties.

Anticlericalism and scepticism

A conference on anticlericalism in late medieval and early modern Europe, held in 1990, agreed that it could be defined as engendering 'literary, political or physical action against what were perceived as unjust privileges constituting the legal, political, economic, sexual, sacred or social power of the clergy'.[59] This ponderous definition does not perhaps encompass drunken conversations in taverns concluding that friars were lecherous, priests lazy and monks rapacious, but it is useful to distinguish between casual anticlericalism and ideas that arose out of a specific agenda. In some cases resentment at the economic power of the clergy might arise from nothing more than a disinclination to pay rent or tithes; complaints about violations of celibacy vows could come from husbands jealous of the attractions of charismatic preachers. The Burgundian Jean Molinet's New Year rhyme probably did not emanate from deep-seated doubts about clerical privileges:

> Let us pray God that the Jacobins
> May eat the Augustinians,
> And that the Carmelites may be hanged
> With the cords of the Minorites.[60]

The above instances identify an anticlericalism that did not question the doctrines of the Church or call for a general reform: all that was required was that clerks should live up to the high standards of pastoral care set by Christ. Jane Dempsey Douglas sees anticlericalism in the works of Christine de Pizan:[61] she was very orthodox and pious in her beliefs, ending her days in a nunnery, but she crossed swords with clerical writers on several occasions. She was involved in 'the quarrel about women', caused by the second part of a poem, *The Romance of the Rose*, in which the author attributed all sorts of faults and frailties to them.

Later, in her *Book of the City of Ladies*, Christine used gentle satire to poke fun at the way in which writers, nearly all of them clerks, indulged in unjust invective against women. She accused them of misunderstanding and undervaluing the nature of women and criticised popes and clergy for allowing such a wrongful tradition to grow up, especially as their own morals were often suspect. Christine was no reformer but the fact that a woman, even an exceptional one, dared to take the whole hierarchy to task was evidence of a new spirit of criticism that was spreading amongst the laity. This exemplifies the scholarly achievements that are sometimes attributed to 'the early French Renaissance'.

Anticlericalism of a different kind is identified by Michael Burleigh in an article on Prussia in the fifteenth century. He takes issue with the suggestion by Robin Du Boulay that Prussian society was inherently violent and that it therefore rejected the clergy's claim to immunity from normal legal penalties ('benefit of clergy', as it was called in England, was recognised throughout medieval Europe). Burleigh takes the case of a long confrontation between the Order of Teutonic Knights and the bishop, knights and townspeople of Ermland over jurisdiction. He argues that it arose out of the aggressive assertion of clerical privilege rather than from violence in a society that no longer accorded automatic deference to the knights.[62]

In the long run it was anticlericalism arising out of a feeling that the clergy were failing in their role as priests and religious which presented most dangers to the Church. There was a widespread expectation in the fourteenth and fifteenth centuries that the clergy were likely to be persecuted or even killed. This only actually happened in Bohemia during the Hussite wars but many of the laity felt that standards were so low that it was inevitable. In the first half of the fifteenth century the followers of Hus attacked both the spiritual and material power of the clergy: questioning the doctrine of *transubstantiation*, demanding that the laity should have the consecrated wine as well as the bread at the Eucharist and confiscating much Church property. Their success sent shock waves throughout the Catholic Church.

John van Engen identifies a strong anticlerical element in the lives and teachings of adherents of the Modern Devotion.[63] Their founder, Gert Grote, felt that advancement within the Church and the acquisition of too much learning endangered clerics' chances of salvation. He refused ordination although he became a deacon so that he could preach. The Church authorities in Deventer saw his stance as a threat, and during his last years he was prohibited even from preaching. This was the only time, however, when the movement was seriously censured; many Brothers and Sisters of the Common Life eventually took monastic vows and this may have saved the Modern Devotion from the charge of heresy. By the sixteenth century, however, many people felt that the clergy and the religious had betrayed the ideals of Christianity and were looking for radical means of reforming them.

Susan Reynolds, in her article 'Social Mentalities and the Case of Medieval Scepticism' concedes that scepticism in that period is hard to identify. There are good reasons for this: most writers were clerics who wished either to suppress the evidence or to present it as something else. Deviance could be described as ignorance, madness, heresy or the inspiration of the Devil. It is unlikely that the

Londoner Elena Dalok had a conventional belief in God when she declared in 1493 that she enjoyed a heaven on this earth, so did not care about the world to come.[64] The experience of the sceptics who were hauled before the authorities for blasphemy, heresy or witchcraft would encourage others who were harbouring doubts to remain silent.

Reynolds suggests that the difficulties modern writers have with the possibility of scepticism (and atheism) in the Middle Ages is that they regard medieval society as far more homogeneous than it really was, and set it in an 'Age of Faith'. She accepts that the great majority did have a conventional belief in Christianity but cites some evidence of scepticism. Many miracle stories, for example, show how those who scoffed at the powers of a saint, a relic or the Host were confounded: if such people did not exist in reality they would not have featured in these tales. Thomas Walsingham in his *History* blamed the outbreak of the Peasants' Revolt in 1381 on the sins of the lords, for some of them even doubted the existence of God. She concludes that: 'the evidence suggests that some people found Christianity, or parts of it, hard to believe in, and that some may not have tried very hard'.[65]

When scepticism was expressed too publicly it was firmly discouraged by the authorities: they assigned it to one of the accepted categories of deviance and punished it accordingly. If the doubters were influential lords, however, it was less likely that action would be taken and in the long run such sentiments were held by so few people that they hardly presented a threat to the Church. Anticlericalism was more dangerous, and could range from the gentle satires of Geoffrey Chaucer and Christine de Pizan to the excesses of the Hussite movement. In some cases material considerations were involved, and little long-term damage was done to the Church. Yet even the piety of the Modern Devotion could alarm the authorities by raising the spectre of heresy: a fear that seemed all too justified with the rise of the Lollards in England and the Hussites in Bohemia.

Heresy

Gordon Leff, in his study *Heresy in the Later Middle Ages, c.1250–c.1450*, distinguishes the common characteristics of the major heretical sects of that period.[66] They had a sense of election, of being Christ's chosen people; they were prepared to reject the laws of the Church; the major means of religious reform was for the prelates to adopt poverty. There was also a tendency for the intellectual origins of a heresy to be developed by clerics and to be taken up by nobles and gentry: the later more militant stages were headed by the lower orders. A further belief common to most heretics was that there had been a pure, Apostolic age of Christianity but that the prelates in subsequent centuries had betrayed the teachings of Christ. Leff suggests that the decision of the Lateran Council of 1215 to block the foundation of any new monastic orders created a vacuum for devout reformers that could readily be filled by heretical beliefs.

Heresy was not a new phenomenon in the late Middle Ages; deviant doctrines had shaken the Church since its early days. Most heresies had started as attempts by sincere churchmen to reform morals and standards but some, such as *Catharism*, were strongly influenced by ideas that had penetrated France from the south-eastern Mediterranean. The Cathar outlook was dominated by dualism: the dichotomy between the spiritual and the material, between the good Cathar church and the evil Catholic Church. Cathars (or *Albigensians*) denied so many of the basic tenets of Christianity that they effectively constituted a separate faith. The kings, prelates and nobles of northern France had subdued the heresy, after a long struggle, by the early fourteenth century. They were assisted by the orders of friars, especially the Dominicans (see Section (i) above), who travelled throughout Languedoc preaching the orthodox faith and rooting out Cathars. The defeat of this heresy was not just a triumph for the Church hierarchy: it was part of the process in the late Middle Ages by which the monarchy brought the outlying regions of France steadily under its political control.

The Inquisition had been set up by the Papacy in the thirteenth century: judges acting directly on the authority of the Popes could go into any area and work independently of the local bishop. Inquisitors (who were often Dominicans) had a fearsome array of powers over those suspected of heresy: trials could be secret, torture was used and witnesses were often anonymous (as far as those accused were concerned). Some escaped with penances such as making gifts to the Church or going on pilgrimage; other punishments were the sequestration of goods, the demolition of houses, or long terms of imprisonment. Those who violently resisted their persecutors, refused to recant and repent or who lapsed after recantation were excommunicated. They were degraded from their orders if they were clerks, handed over to the secular authorities and executed, frequently by being burnt alive. Right to the end, however, priests would try to persuade the condemned men and women to repent so that their souls might be saved.

The *Waldensians* shared some of the heretical beliefs of the Cathars and had some common ground with them such as their use of *perfecti* in preference to priests. These were men and women, usually from the laity, who had achieved true holiness. They did not work, but lived chastely without possessions, begging for their food and shelter, preaching and administering the sacraments to believers. The cult, which was particularly popular with the poorer members of the laity, spread widely throughout northern Europe (with the exception of the British Isles) and northern Italy. Waldensians were regularly persecuted but their beliefs continued in some areas into the early modern period: in Bohemia they shared some beliefs with the Hussites. Other small heretical movements, such as the *Flagellants* and the *Free Spirit*, survived into the fifteenth century but they presented no substantial threat to the Church.

When a serious challenge was made to the authority of the ecclesiastical hierarchy it came from an unlikely source: John Wyclif was a priest and doctor of divinity at Oxford University. Most of his ideas had been debated by scholars for centuries but he pushed his conclusions to extremes. For a time, he got away with it because his friends at court included John of Gaunt and the Queen Mother. They probably found his call for the king to assert his supremacy over the Church to reform clerical abuses congenial. It was one often made by loyal churchmen and such demands were to culminate in the Conciliar Movement's push for reform early in the following century. Wyclif embraced the doctrine of *predestination*, an issue that had been debated without a dogma emerging since the early days of the Church:

> Holy church is of those that God has ordained to dwell with him in bliss, of what state so they be, priests or seculars, lords or commoners, ladies or poor women, that endlessly love God.[67]

It was the conclusion that Wyclif drew from his belief in predestination that was to cause some of the troubles experienced by Hus and his followers. No one could be sure who was to be saved and who damned but, on the basis of an individual's obedience to the precepts of the Bible, 'we may guess and that is enough'.[68] Priests who seemed by their laxity or other sins to be predestined to damnation had no authority and could be disregarded. In 1377 the Pope condemned nineteen articles in Wyclif's *Of Civil Rule* and prohibited him and some of his followers from preaching in Oxford. In the meantime he lost his powerful protectors by publishing *On the Eucharist*, in which he undermined the central doctrine of *transubstantiation*. He did not question that the bread and wine were spiritually the body and blood of Christ but maintained that their essence remained after consecration (*remanence*). He took this approach because it was the only way in which he could reconcile his *realist* philosophy with church dogma.

Plato had been the first to argue that everything that exists is a reflection of an archtype: somewhere there exists the ultimate reality of tables, trees, apples etc. and what we experience are dim copies of them. It followed that the archtypes of the bread and wine used at the Eucharist could not cease to exist once they had been consecrated and must continue to co-exist with the spiritually present flesh and blood of Christ. This may seem to be a very abstruse way of arriving at a slightly different doctrine from the official one but people suffered and died for it during the following decades and centuries. Jeremy Catto explains the loyalty of the hierarchy and of many lay people to the belief in transubstantiation in terms of the strong social and emotional bonds that had been forged by the cult of the Host expressed in the festival of Corpus Christi (see Section (ii) above).[69] Intellectuals, orthodox as well as heretical, might be questioning the value of *sacramentals* (practices such as kissing the *pax*), but the hierarchy probably felt that they were necessary to engage the interest of the uneducated.

In 1382, the archbishop of Canterbury banned twenty-four propositions from Wyclif's writings. John of Gaunt and his former supporters amongst the friars had been alienated by his ideas about the Eucharist and he retired from Oxford to his parish of Lutterworth, where he died two years later. On the Continent, heretics had been persecuted with fire and imprisonment for over a century, so Wyclif seems to have had a fortunate escape. The slowness of communications, the fact that he had a number of well-placed sympathisers in Westminster and supporters in the University of Oxford, and that his ideas were buried in abstruse academic treatises, assisted his survival. It was to be his followers and those who later adopted his ideas, the Lollards, who would suffer for their heresies.

'Lollard' was a term of abuse when it was coined: it meant 'mumbler' and referred to the habit of incessantly reading from the Bible. Wyclif's first followers were university dons and students, who concentrated on attempting to get the authorities to accept their interpretation of Church doctrines and practices. There was still a hope that well-placed sympathisers might achieve this: pinning Twelve Conclusions to the door of Westminster Abbey during a parliamentary session in 1395 seems to have been such an attempt. The Conclusions did not cover the whole Lollard programme for reform but gave an idea of their priorities. They condemned endowments; the powers of the priesthood; vows of chastity; the doctrine of the Eucharist; priests holding secular offices; pilgrimages; the worship of images; oral confession; exorcisms; blessings of objects like oil and water; some capital punishment; the chastity of women in holy orders; and the production of luxury goods. The programme attracted no influential support and Lollards were increasingly persecuted. The fact that they were thought to have encouraged the Peasants' Revolt of 1381 harmed their case despite the fact that Wyclif had condemned it. Yet the movement continued to attract supporters; mostly drawn from the lower orders of society, they were concentrated in the Midlands and Western counties of England.

The danger that Lollardy was thought to present to the Church was underlined in 1401 when the newly established King Henry IV passed the *Act of the Burning of Heretics*. This adopted the continental practice of burning relapsed and obdurate heretics, although only two were actually executed by fire during his reign. The measure may have had more to do with a new dynasty establishing its orthodoxy and godliness than with a fear that the country was swamped with Lollards. The reign of Henry V initiated the first serious wave of persecution. The rebellion of Sir John Oldcastle in 1414 seemed dangerous: he mustered very few supporters, was hunted down and burnt, but his alleged intention had been to kill the royal family, confiscate clerical property and destroy their buildings.[70] Whatever the truth may have been, this, and another even less successful rising sixteen years later, justified the authorities in rooting out Lollardy amongst the lower orders whenever they found it. Nicholson suggests that Lollardy penetrated Scotland largely as a result of English influence. The recently founded University of St Andrews thought the threat grave enough in 1416 to include a promise in the oath for graduands: 'to defend the kirk against the attack of Lollards'.[71]

In the trial of John Burrell, servant of Thomas Mone, in Norwich in 1429, the defendant blamed his employer, sister and brother-in-law for involving him in their heresies. These included the beliefs that: confession was only to be made to God; 'it would be better for many priests to take wives and to use them carnally, as many priests do in diverse remote parts'; no priest had the power to make the body of Christ; the church was the soul of every good Christian; prayers said in church had no special efficacy; there was no obligation to observe feast days; tithes should not be paid to priests; prayers and Masses did not help the dead; and the friars were destroying the world.[72] This report is interesting since it shows the way in which some of the ideas of Wyclif and his immediate followers had been retained and how others, in the perception of ordinary people like John Burrell, had been developed.

Lollardy continued as a minority and underground movement up to the time of the Reformation. Occasionally someone was indicted for heresy but the strongest evidence for its survival was the number of devotional works and bibles in the vernacular that were circulated. Margaret Aston and Colin Richmond suggest that there was a difference between the ways the common people and the gentry were treated.[73] The latter, from the number of manuscripts that survive, seem to have been able to read prohibited works in privacy and safety whilst the former, who were often illiterate, expressed their heretical beliefs openly and were more likely to be persecuted.

The extent of the influence that the ideas of Wyclif exerted on the contemporary Hussite movement in Bohemia and Moravia has been much debated. They were certainly well known to John Hus and other academic reformers and were quoted by their opponents as proof of their heresy; but other factors have also been given greater or lesser weight. Howard Kaminsky, writing during the last years of communist hegemony in Eastern Europe, typified *Hussitism* as a 'revolution', the reaction of the people against narrow-minded and conservative ecclesiastical and political domination.[74] Frantisek Smahel, who suffered under the communist regime, paints a more complex picture in which racial and economic pressures played a part.[75] British historians such as Gordon Leff and Malcolm Lambert have concentrated on the importance of Wyclif to the scholars who called for reform.[76] They also emphasise that Hus and his contemporaries were working within a Bohemian reforming tradition which was not essentially heretical, and which had been fostered in its early days by the Emperor Charles IV. Recently John Klassen, while agreeing with the extent of Wyclif's influence on Hus, has emphasised the importance of the nobility.[77] They managed to preserve their power during the attempted radicalisation of the movement by the Taborites and some reformers in Prague, and by the end of the century were unassailable.

During the earlier part of his career there was little to distinguish Hus from his orthodox reformist precursors except that he preached in Czech rather than German at the Jerusalem Chapel in Prague. His eloquence and dedication to the moral renewal of the laity and clergy gave him a following that included many from the lower orders. The writings of Wyclif were discussed at the University of Prague, where Hus was a master, but he lacked the Englishman's intense intellectual engagement with the theological issues: he supported Wyclif primarily for his defiance of the authority of the ecclesiastical hierarchy. Wenceslas, the king of Bohemia and deposed king of the Romans, had mixed feelings about the reformers, alternately tolerating and discouraging them. In 1403 the Germans, who had a majority vote at the university, secured the condemnation of forty-five articles from Wyclif's works. They especially objected to his *realism* since most were *nominalists* (they did not believe that there were universal archetypes that were reflected in all created things). Hus supported Wyclif's condemnation of clerical abuses and his view of predestination but did not accept some of his other propositions, including his modification of the doctrine of transubstantiation. As he was to write:

> Christ by his own power and words [that is, not through a priest's consecration] transubstantiates the bread into his body and the wine into his blood. ... Wherefore I have sung the song approved by the church from the time that I learned to sing and I have sung it in the schools and the churches.[78]

In the following years it was as much the manner as the content of Hus's preaching that alienated some of his former supporters: he remained a thorn in the side of Wenceslas but was little known beyond Bohemia. In 1409, as part of the intricate politics of the Empire and its relationship with the Schismatic Popes, it suited Wenceslas to support the Czechs in the university against the Germans and to give them a voting majority. A number of Germans quit Prague for Leipzig and other universities in the Empire and their hostility was to prejudice opinion against Hus at the Council of Constance. He started to preach against the granting of indulgences by the Papacy and local prelates and this made him more enemies. In 1411 he was excommunicated and forced to leave Prague so that its citizens did not suffer the consequences of an interdict. He continued to preach in the countryside, probably contributing to the ground swell of radical religion that was to break out a few years later.

Hus welcomed the chance to go to Constance in 1414, with a safe-conduct from the Emperor-elect Sigismund, to explain and defend his beliefs. Malcolm Lambert suspects that Sigismund and his brother and rival Wenceslas may have come to an arrangement: Sigismund would be left free to seek coronation as Emperor in return for quelling Hus.[79] Initially Hus was allowed to speak at the Council but most of the prelates regarded him as a heretic and he was soon imprisoned. In June 1415 he was put on trial, charged with a number of heresies including *remanence*, which he did not believe in: Pierre d'Ailly was his prosecutor, supported by Jean Gerson. There was a paradox here: one of the heresies of which Hus stood accused was the wish to limit papal power, at a time when the majority at the Council, including d'Ailly and Gerson, had made a determined attempt to achieve the same thing. Hus demonstrated that he did not hold a number of the beliefs that had been credited to him but he was unable to recant on a few of them. 'I cannot lie before God',[80] he declared, and was burnt the following day, 6 July 1415. Had he not been credited with Wyclif's heresies, some of which he did not share, he might have escaped with a lighter punishment.

Contrary to the expectation of the Emperor and divines at Constance, the death of Hus did not end the split between reformers and the orthodox in Bohemia and Moravia: it affronted national pride and actually encouraged his followers: 452 nobles signed a protest at his execution, and a widespread demand arose for the laity to receive the Sacrament in both kinds (Utraquism). Many clergy who refused these requests were driven from their parishes, and the University of Prague (rather than Councils or the Papacy) was declared to be the final authority in ecclesiastical disputes. Radical brotherhoods, including women and children, sprang up in the countryside: the most extreme were the Taborites, who occupied a deserted fortress, naming it 'Tabor' after the mountain occupied by the Israelites in the Old Testament. In 1420 they issued the Four Articles that formed the basis of Hussitism for the next twenty-five years: the word of God should be preached freely throughout Bohemia; the Eucharist should be administered in both kinds; the clergy should give away their excess goods and live a simple life in emulation of the apostles; and all mortal sins of the laity and clergy should be extirpated.

Wenceslas died in 1419 and was succeeded as king of Bohemia by the Emperor Sigismund, who was determined to crush his heretical subjects. He launched a series of Crusades against them during the following years but his soldiers were always soundly beaten by the Hussites. They had a succession of able military leaders, first John Zizka and then Prokop the Bald. Nationalist fervour against the Germans who dominated the Empire, and fear of being subjugated and treated as heretics by Sigismund, kept the moderate and radical Hussite factions together. As one popular song went:

> Children let us praise the Lord,
> Honour Him in loud accord!
> For he frightened and confounded,
> All those thousands of Barbarians,
> Suabians, Misnians, Hungarians
> Who have overrun our land
> With his strong protecting hand
> To the winds He has them waved,
> And we children now are saved.
> Faithful Czechs, let's sing our love
> To our father high above.[81]

They dealt with their own extremists harshly: a populist preacher was executed in Prague, and the Taborites burnt some of the Adamites, whose practices (including free love and going naked in public), both real and imagined, scandalised the majority.

As the brotherhoods achieved security, trade and industry flourished and their beliefs and way of life became more stable. The extremists were eradicated in a series of internal confrontations and by the alliance of Prokop the Bald with some of the moderates in Prague. Most of the Hussite nobles and the merchants had always wished for compromise with their king and with the Bohemians, who had remained orthodox Catholics. The prelates at the Council of Basle, meeting in Germany under the guidance of the pragmatic Cardinal Caesarini, were prepared to broker a compromise. In 1436, Sigismund and the moderate Hussites, who had won a victory over their rivals at Lipany two years earlier, came to an agreement (which was never accepted by the Papacy). By its terms, communion in Bohemia could be available in one or both kinds; the punishment of mortal sins was to be confined to those whose concern it was (the clergy); the right to preach was limited to deacons and clergy. Priests were to have no hereditary possessions although the Church would retain its property (much had already been taken into lay hands).

A moderate form of Hussitism survived in Bohemia and Moravia until it was amalgamated with the more extreme Protestant creed at the Reformation. The only body to hold some of the original doctrines and practices are the Moravian Brethren, who survive to this day. Hussitism never spread beyond Bohemia and Moravia although other heresies such as Waldensianism had enjoyed a wide and long-lasting appeal in Europe. Germans felt excluded by the strongly nationalist character of the movement and it may have confirmed many within the Empire in their orthodox beliefs. The Lollards probably regarded it as an offshoot of their own agitation for reform and there is some evidence of co-operation between the two creeds in the early fifteenth century. France, ravaged by the wars with England, showed little interest in heretical doctrines: the awful fate of the Cathars may have acted as a deterrent in the South. In the following century, however, Calvinism was to attract many educated and prosperous people. As in the case of Catharism, regional identities played an important part in predisposing individuals and groups to heretical beliefs.

The Jews

Judaism was the one faith, besides Christianity, which could be practised in some parts of Europe in the Middle Ages (the situation of Moslems has been referred to above). Yet it was only barely tolerated and the lives and culture of Jewish communities were always subject to sudden and violent persecution. The hostility which most felt towards the Jews originated from the accounts given in the New Testament Gospels of how Christ was treated by his own people during his ministry, culminating in his condemnation and crucifixion. The choice made by the crowd before Pontius Pilate, that the robber Barabbas rather than Christ should be spared, and the cries, 'Let him be crucified', and 'His blood be on us and on our children' (New Testament, Matthew, 27), condemned them down the generations. Jews were subject to draconian taxes, and to limitations on where they might live and the clothes they might wear, which were intended to distinguish them from the Christian community. They frequently engaged in money lending, one of the few professions open to them as it was forbidden to Christians if it involved usury (charging interest on loans). The presence of wealthy and submissive communities in many European towns and cities was very useful to Christian princes and merchants. Despite periodic persecution, the Jews in many parts of Europe in the high Middle Ages were reasonably secure (they were protected by special laws in Germany), but there was a marked deterioration in their situation during the late Middle Ages.

By the mid-fourteenth century some princes had expelled Jewish communities from their lands: Edward I of England had done so, in 1288 from Gascony, and in 1290 from England (there were scarcely any Jews elsewhere in the British Isles). In 1321 in France, lepers, Jews and 'the King of Granada' were accused of a great plot to kill Christians by poisoning wells and cisterns. As a result of this fantasy many were burnt and their goods were confiscated: the lepers who survived were kept in strict confinement but the Jews were expelled. Later, under the financial constraints of the wars with the English, a few were allowed to return but they were suspected of spreading the Black Death, more were murdered and they were finally banished from the kingdom in 1394. The absence of Jews, however, did not stop myths about their wickedness from circulating long after they had gone: Chaucer's Prioress told a heartrending tale about a virtuous little Christian boy who was supposedly murdered by them. This closely resembled the case of little St Hugh of Lincoln, a child reputed to have been killed by the Jews a few decades before they were expelled from England. These and similar stories constituted the 'blood libel' which was widely believed by Christians throughout Europe.

Miri Rubin has shown how such stories and another later one about the abuse of consecrated Hosts were used to justify the imprisonment, fining, torture, murder or expulsion of thousands of Jews during the later Middle Ages.[82] The Host story originated in Paris in the late thirteenth century: according to the *Chronicle of St Denis*, a Christian woman in debt to a Jew was suborned by him to steal a Host. He tortured it in various ways to test if it was really God: it bled and later, while it was being boiled, a crucifix hovered over the cauldron. The Jew was apprehended and executed but his wife and family converted to Christianity and a chapel was built on the site of his house. Versions of this story were circulated throughout northern Europe until the Reformations.

Jews certainly felt a religious distaste for some aspects of Christianity: the Virgin Birth, the Incarnation and the Trinity, for example, but they seem to have regarded the possibility of a divine presence in bread and wine as 'a perplexing joke'.[83] One explanation for the persecution their communities suffered is that there was always a temptation to evade debts by whipping up righteous indignation against imagined sacrilege. The story about the testing of hosts may also have reflected Christian anxieties about the dogma of transubstantiation, which had only recently been promulgated and which was quite hard to understand. Persecution, fuelled by murder or sacrilege narratives, often took place when a society was under stress: Jews were suspected of spreading the plague and of colluding with the Hussites in Bohemia, so they became scapegoats and credence was given to the most unlikely libels against them.

J. M. Minty has also suggested a demographic reason for the persecutions: Jewish quarters had often been built on the outskirts of towns, in poor districts. With greater prosperity, towns expanded and wealthy citizens and nobles found that they and their churches were adjacent to Jewish homes and synagogues, although such communities were relatively small. In many German towns persecution and expulsion were followed by the appropriation of Jewish property by the civic authorities or the Church. In 1426 in Cologne, the provost and archdeacon granted the magistrate permission to convert the synagogue of the Jews into a church, since they:

> refused to recognise our dear lord Jesus Christ as God and man, had a synagogue next to the town hall of the said city of Cologne and behaved therein in ways which good Christians would never tolerate in such a holy town. And so that, in place of the damned Jewish customs and practices, fitting praise and honour might be given to Almighty God, Jesus Christ his only son and the blessed Virgin Mary on that same site.[84]

The Papacy derived a large income from its Jews and protected them both in Rome and in Avignon. Clement VI remonstrated with persecutors of Jews in France during the Black Death, pointing out (to no avail) that it occurred in areas not inhabited by them and also that they too succumbed to the disease. The Emperors were also reasonably sympathetic, finding Jews to be a useful source of loans and taxes. Towns, on occasions, were prepared to give them the benefit of the doubt: in 1409 in Schlettstadt, Alsace, a Christian thief maliciously placed a Host in a Jewish house but the owner was exonerated and the thief was punished. Isolated incidents like these, however, did not reverse the tendency in north-western Europe to expel Jews from Christian communities. By the end of the fourteenth century they had been forced to leave Brabant and by 1520 about ninety German cities had expelled their Jews. Some went to Italy or the Ottoman Empire and others travelled eastward into Poland and Russia.

Evidence of Jewish attitudes to their Christian neighbours is scanty, mostly confined to theological works and a few songs and poems. There was a danger in expressing any kind of criticism, but a lament by Rabbi Avigdor Kara deploring the 1389 massacre of Prague survives:

> Now my soul is eaten up for these great men, experts in book and in discourse, for leaders and cantors [leaders of synagogue services, often fine singers] and community benefactors,
> for scholars and men of manners [ethics]
> Take them from me, they are my congregation
>
> Old synagogue was the meeting place of their families
> their house of prayer.
> There the sword of fire will devour them.
> They were sacrificed whole to their God![85]

Cecil Roth has made the point that the Christians who accepted the 'blood libel' or Host narratives attributed extraordinary mentalities to the Jewish murderers and blasphemers.[86] Their persecutors acted as if Jews believed that the little boys were holy and that the Hosts were the flesh of God, or why torment them in the first place? Having been given irrefutable and visible proof by children who were resurrected and Hosts which bled and over which crucifixes or Christ figures appeared, they still remained obdurate unbelievers. Their own scriptures forecast the advent of a messiah and they lived in the middle of pious Christian communities observing the work of God and seeing the faithful attending church, so how could they not be converted? Roth accounts for this anomaly by suggesting that most Christians believed that Jews were in thrall to the Devil and thus incapable of redemption. This made them less than human and explains how normally reasonable communities could subject Jews to atrocious treatment.

The association of Jews with the Devil in the popular mind led to the suspicion that they practised witchcraft. Some of the blasphemous and murderous rites of which they were accused could be described as sorcery. The use of Christian children's blood and the tortures to which Hosts were said to be subjected were similar to occult means of gaining strength and special knowledge. Anna Fra, in 'The Witch and the Jew: Two Alikes Were Not the Same', questions whether, in practice, Jews were condemned as witches. The Papacy was generally protective of Jews, so they usually suffered when a particular local problem such as the plague or excessive debt got out of control. She points out that the large number of people burnt at the stake as witches in Europe 'simply did not include Jews'.[87]

One of the reasons why some civic authorities allowed Jews to remain as residents was the belief that eventually the superiority of the Christian religion would convince them and they would accept conversion. Yet Jonathan Elukin points to another anomalous attitude: those who were converted to Christianity were often regarded with deep suspicion by their new co-religionists.[88] Conversions often took place under duress as alternatives to the loss of home and goods, or even death. There was a suspicion that Rabbinic thought allowed such converts to have the effects of baptism annulled. Any sign of backsliding from their adopted faith put them in danger of condemnation by the Church as lapsed heretics and of being burnt. Rejected and despised by their own race and community, many converted Jews faced a harsh fate. Furthermore, John Edwards believes that not all Jews who retained their faith had a constantly wretched life: the rich and well connected could exercise some influence on their societies.[89]

Magic and witchcraft

The Church had an ambivalent attitude towards the belief in witches and demons: whilst it generally discouraged superstitious practices it recognised the danger that deviant behaviour could, in fact, be inspired by the Devil. Keith Thomas, in *Religion and the Decline of Magic*, pointed to the problem that whilst many kinds of magic and its practitioners were officially condemned, the Church itself by its use of prayer, the sacraments and surrounding beliefs was indulging in a form of magic. Officially only natural magic, where no supernatural powers other than God and the saints were invoked, was acceptable. Some believed that demons, who had been regarded as benign powers in late classical, neo-Platonic philosophy, could be summoned by necromancers (people skilled in the magic arts) to do their will. By the Christian era these demons were progressively identified with Satan and his attendant devils, who appeared only to delude magicians and bring about their damnation.

Practitioners of natural magic were generally able to work without interference from the authorities. In England they were often known as 'wise women' or 'cunning men' and they acted as healers and advisers. Their knowledge of the properties of herbs, the behaviour of animals and the vagaries of the weather could yield spectacular results in ill-educated and impoverished communities. Yet their services were not entirely confined to the common people: priests, monks and nuns could also exercise these skills. There was always a danger of crossing the line between the use of innocent magic and the practice of rituals that were condemned as consorting with demons. Alice Hancock, for example, was accused in 1438 before the bishop of Bath and Wells for sending out health remedies: she blessed a girdle or garment of the diseased person.[90] Her blessing was presumably thought to have a diabolic origin. About fifty years later, Elizabeth of York, the queen of Henry VII, paid 6s 8d for a girdle of Our Lady for use in childbirth: its origins were clearly unexceptionable.[91]

Members of royalty, the nobility and gentry availed themselves of the services of natural magicians, while Louis XI of France in later life festooned himself with holy amulets and relics in an attempt to ward off mortality. They also employed physicians, astrologers and alchemists, whose activities often strayed from what we might describe as science, into the occult. The aim could simply be to improve personal health and avoid death but there could be a desire to seek propitious times for marriage or going into battle. Magic might also be used to discover one's enemies, learn their intentions and frustrate them. This process is known as *divination*, and astrology was favoured in European courts as the means of achieving it (this should be distinguished from astronomy, which later developed as the scientific study of the heavenly bodies).

Knowledge of astrology increased in the later Middle Ages after a number of Arabic works on the subject had been translated by the scholastics. The future health and prosperity of an individual could be discovered by casting their horoscope from the conjunction of the planets and the stars at the time of their birth (a version of this process is still available in the pages of newspapers and magazines). Horoscopes could be cast for other times depending on the requirements of the patron. Christine de Pizan's father was astrologer to Charles V of France and the art was practised in other contemporary courts, sometimes by men who were primarily employed as physicians. Edward III of England was warned of the dangers of astrology by Bishop Thomas Bradwardine and he seems to have taken the advice seriously. His grandson Richard II, however, possessed several astrological instruments and a book of divination. Pious French writers such as Philippe de Mézières and Jean Gerson condemned the practice. During the reign of Charles VI various people had attempted to cure him of his madness: for example, a court physician, master Jean de Bar, was burnt with his books as a sorcerer in 1398.

The political dangers to astrologers were considerable for whereas some monarchs allowed the practice of divination, an insecure king like Henry VI of England regarded the unofficial casting of his horoscope as treasonable. The case of Eleanor Cobham, duchess of Gloucester, in 1441 hinged on the charge that she had suborned a witch and two clerks, one of whom was an astrologer, to plot the king's death. They had cast his horoscope and predicted that he would die young: it was the conspirators who died and the duchess spent the rest of her life in confinement. This was not a simple case, as the charges had been brought forward by political enemies of Humphrey, duke of Gloucester, but Henry VI took it seriously enough to commission a new horoscope which offered him a better life expectancy. Some thirty-five years later, friends of the disgraced duke of Clarence were charged (and some were executed) for casting the horoscopes of Edward IV and the Prince of Wales: the duke was murdered in the Tower soon afterwards.

Alchemy, like astrology, owed its popularity to the work of Arab scholars whose treatises had been translated into Latin. It derived from Aristotle's theory that all matter could be reduced to four elements: earth, air, fire and water. Metals were composed of these elements in various proportions, so with the aid of an 'elixir' or 'Philosopher's stone' they could be re-combined to obtain higher forms of matter such as silver and gold. Alchemy was not condemned by the Church: the pious Henry VI of England actually appointed a commission to look into the possibility of transmuting base metals into gold and silver to relieve his financial problems. The popular handbook for rulers, mostly a translation of an Arabic original, *The Secret of Secrets*, had a section on the occult sciences including the 'Philosopher's Stone'. There was, however, widespread scepticism about the basic premise of alchemy and practitioners tended to be regarded as fools or rogues. Some members of the upper orders of society practised magic without any attempt to present it as a science or pseudo-science. The *Munich Handbook*, probably written by a priest, was clearly intended for an educated reader. It explained how to conjure demons to achieve three kinds of magic: illusions (a fine banquet or a castle), psychological benefits (arousing love or gaining favour at court), and divinitory techniques for past, present and future. Many of the magical rites started with *scrying*: an assistant gazed at a reflecting surface until he saw figures; these were taken to be spirits who could achieve the desired result.[92]

Our main knowledge of occult practices comes from the trials of those who were caught and indicted. Gilles de Rais was a Breton noble; he may have been a paedophile, and resorted to alchemy to boost his failing fortunes. He was involved in disputes over land in the course of which he unwisely had a priest beaten. In 1440 his enemies accused him, amongst other things, of heresy, apostacy, conjuring demons, sodomy, sacrilege, the murder of children and violation of the immunities of the Church. One of the charges gives a picture of what was thought to occur during a demonic conjuration:

> In a certain low room of the castle or fortress of Tiffauges, in the diocese of Nantes ... about 5 years ago Monsieur Francesco Prelati, self-styled expert in the art of geomancy [divination], and Jean de la Rivière, made many magic signs, circles, and characters. Also, in a certain wood near the said fortress, Antoine de la Palerme, of Lombardy, and one named Louis, with other magicians and conjurers of demons, practiced divinations and summons to evil spirits, named Orion, Beelzebub, Satan and Belial, with fire, incense, myrrh, aloes, and other fragrant substances.[93]

Because he confessed after torture and had shown penitence, de Rais was conceded the mercy of being strangled rather than being burnt alive. Several of his accomplices were also executed although those who gave evidence against him were pardoned. As in the cases of important offenders discussed above, the charge of practising magic was linked to other complex social and political issues.

The distinction between witchcraft and sorcery (or necromancy) is a fine one. Hugh Trevor-Roper argued that witchcraft had sprung from Aristotelian thought whilst high magic or sorcery was a product of neo-Platonism. Others have seen witchcraft as a kind of folk religion which had co-existed, largely undetected, with Christianity in Europe. Margaret Murray in her publications in the mid-twentieth century believed that it represented the survival of a pre-Christian fertility cult, although Norman Cohn, in *Europe's Inner Demons*, has accused her of manipulating her evidence.[94] The distinguishing feature of witchcraft in the Middle Ages was *maleficium*, the desire to do evil by supernatural means. Others, particularly sorcerers, might seek the same result as part of their occult practices but witches were generally believed to be dedicated to harming their neighbours. They were usually drawn from the lower orders of society and were predominantly but not exclusively female.

People had been sporadically accused of witchcraft throughout the Middle Ages. In Ireland in 1324–5, for example, the wealthy Lady Alice Kyteler and her associates were charged with having bewitched her four husbands. Her stepchildren and an unpopular English bishop were instrumental in bringing her to trial: she escaped to England but some of her associates were burnt.[95] The family's desire for Lady Alice's property and a power struggle between indigenous and English clergy seem to have been the main features in this case and there were no more recorded witch trials in Ireland for over two centuries. Similarly in Scotland, persecution did not commence until after the Protestant Reformation.

Most writers on the subject originally believed that the persecution of witches started on a large scale in southern France in the early fourteenth century but Cohn has shown this to be based on erroneous later accounts. The Order of Knights Templar had been suppressed with the use of torture, forced confessions and burnings in early fourteenth-century France by Philip IV but they had been charged with vile sexual misconduct and diabolic rites, not witchcraft.

The large-scale persecution of witches was a north-west European phenomenon of the fifteenth, sixteenth and early seventeenth centuries. It was carried out sporadically in England and with more enthusiasm in parts of France, Burgundy and the Empire during the fifteenth century. The nature of the offence was refined and acquired particular details during this period: details that Carlo Ginsburg suggests largely existed in the minds of the accusers.[96] In 1435–7 Johannes Nider wrote the *Formicarius* or *Anthill*, in which he compared the virtues and vices of men and the customs of ants. In the fifth book he described the practices of witches: they were people who stole and killed children, using parts of their bodies to make ointment to change themselves into other creatures, and liquid to drink in diabolical ceremonies. Initiates renounced the Christian faith, trampling on crosses at every opportunity. In Switzerland in 1428, over a hundred men and women had been burnt after confessing, under torture, that they had flown to gatherings on sticks or brooms. They had magically entered cellars, drinking the best wine and defecating in the barrels. They could change themselves into wolves to devour cattle and could cause the illness and death of children and adults. Theory and alleged practice combined to produce accounts of witches' sabbaths: the name for meetings was a reference to the Jewish holy day and the horrible rites that were thought to take place.

In 1484 Pope Innocent VIII issued his bull *Summis desiderantes* (*Much desiring*), reiterating the Church's condemnation of witchcraft and encouraging the vigorous prosecution of culprits. He did so at the instance of two Dominican inquisitors, Heinrich Institoris and Jacob Sprenger, who were carrying out a witch-hunt in the Alps. Two years later they published their *Malleus Maleficarum* (*The Hammer of Witches*), which described the defining characteristics of witchcraft: evil intention, the help of the Devil, and the permission of God. No orthodox thinker could allow the Devil to work any evil without such permission – to do so would deprive humankind of the freedom to choose salvation or damnation. Many saw the witch-hunt as an extension of the drive against heresy: in France the word for witchcraft and *Waldensian* was the same – *vauderie*.

Keith Thomas in the early 1970s raised some pertinent questions about why society colluded with the Church in the persecution of witches. On some occasions there were obvious material gains to be made, as in the case of Lady Kyteler. But he suggested that the way in which most people practised their religion, through a series of rituals, could easily be transferred in popular imagination to a subversion of Christian rites: the so-called sabbath. Witchcraft (especially after the suppression of other scapegoats: Templars, Jews and heretics) accounted for the otherwise inexplicable misfortunes of life. The loss of goods, the failure of crops or the sudden death of members of the family were made more bearable if a local person could be blamed: if they were unattractive, poor and socially isolated so much the better. The fact that the ecclesiastical authorities encouraged the persecution of witches must have reassured many doubters. The uneducated would not usually have been aware of the distinction made by theorists between what actually happened and the delusions sent by the Devil. Witches were not condemned by the authorities for flying through the air or turning themselves into wolves but for heresy in rejecting Christianity and making pacts with the Devil under the delusion that he would give them such powers.

Even stranger to modern eyes is the fact that so many people actually confessed to participating in the extravagant rites of witchcraft. Torture was regularly used as part of the trial process, so many of the accounts may be explained for that reason. The judges were working to an agenda set by previous cases, the theological view of witchcraft, and treatises such as the *Anthill*. As Richard Kieckhefer has pointed out, these expectations vitiated the evidence in many trials.[97] Those presided over by lay judges, who were not so knowledgeable, and the depositions of witnesses, and trials for defamation by the wrongly accused, are most likely to reflect contemporary popular ideas. Yet in addition to these more plausible accounts, confessions do exist from a number of 'witches' who had not been tortured or who volunteered information about their supernatural activities. Some may have been mentally deranged: but the work of Ginzburg, in particular, *The Night Battles*, shows that people either in dreams, or in a drugged state induced by a particular diet, or through group hysteria, genuinely believed themselves to be capable of magical acts.[98]

CONCLUSION

The question raised at the beginning of this chapter can now be addressed: how far did the changes in practice and belief both within the Church and by heretical sects anticipate the sixteenth-century Catholic and Protestant Reformations? Ozment maintains that the laity had failed to find consolation from a piety based on the penitential practices of monks.[99] But the section on religious experience has suggested that the faith of many priests and lay people was strong during the later Middle Ages. Ample evidence survives of belief in the doctrines of the Church, such as the redeeming sacrifice of Christ and the alternative paths to salvation or damnation. There were also means by which these doctrines could be refined, and practices developed as a result of pressure from ordinary people: the doctrine of purgatory, and the *sacramentals* are examples. Lay people were not hostile to the Church but wished to be more closely associated with it (see below, Chapter 6). Clerical and lay mystics showed the need many felt for a closer relationship with the divine. Lay bodies such as the *Béguines*, *Beghards* and Brethren of the Common Life had a semi-monastic existence, deliberately shunning the conventional orders as they feared the corruption of worldly values. A sort of reformation was taking place within these associations and, by their example, they influenced others.

There was always a danger that new religious bodies would be accused of lapsing into heresy. Their concerns, however: superstitious practices, excessive clerical wealth, and poor standards of education and pastoral care, were shared by many prelates and the reformers who participated in the Conciliar Movement.

The manner in which English-language historians have tended to concentrate on the Protestant Reformation has, until recently, tended to obscure the reform of the Catholic Church that took place in the sixteenth century, culminating in the provisions of the Council of Trent. The nature of reform might have been different had the Protestants not supplied an impetus, but the need for it had been urged by loyal churchmen during the later Middle Ages, and changes would have taken place.

Only the Hussites succeeded in bringing about permanent changes within their church but their example seems to have had an impact on other reformers. Malcolm Lambert sees the Lollardy that survived in England into the sixteenth century as contributing to English Protestantism by its anticlericalism, scripture reading and denial of transubstantiation. The Brethren of the Common Life were not considered heretical but their lifestyle and values anticipated the Reformations in many ways and were influential on reformers such as Luther. Political factors that predisposed some rulers to support changes, the impact of the Renaissance on the authority of traditional learning, the wider availability of books through printing, and the strength of popular piety, combined with orthodox and heretical demands for religious reform, created an irresistible force by the early sixteenth century.

Attempts, such as those made in this chapter, to penetrate the ideas and values of past peoples, whose belief systems are largely alien to present commentators, may yield more fruitful results than the quest to establish differences between popular and elite cultures. As Huizinga remarked:

> When we see side by side the most striking contrasts of passionate piety and mocking indifference, it is so easy to explain them by opposing, as if they made up distinct groups, the worldly to the devout, the intellectuals to the ignorant, the reformers to the conservatives. But, in so doing, we fail to take sufficient account of the marvellous complexity of the human soul and of the forms of culture.[100]

6

Culture and Society

INTRODUCTION: THEMES AND SOURCES

This chapter builds on the rest of the book to suggest ways in which social, economic, political and ideological developments involved cultural change. There were limitations to these trends: we observed in the Introduction that life for the poor and uneducated in remote parts of north-western Europe probably changed little during the period. The subjects chosen for discussion, therefore, involve locations where literate, politically active people were concentrated: princely courts, universities and other educational institutions, towns and cities.

By 1350, princely courts flourished in all the realms of north-western Europe. They had developed out of the households that had surrounded lords and rulers throughout the Middle Ages. Their size, organisation and magnificence will be shown to have borne a direct relationship to the prestige a prince enjoyed and, to some extent, his power. Whilst today we tend to denigrate those who ostentatiously display their wealth, a poverty-stricken prince cut a poor figure with his subjects and foreign observers in the late Middle Ages. It was important for rulers to receive sufficient revenues to finance suitably splendid courts, but their discriminating use of patronage, both to reward followers and to commission stylish art, literature and architecture, was also a sign of success.

The growth in court studies has revealed the rich records and material that have survived from the late Middle Ages. Inventories, accounts, correspondence, the reports of envoys and ambassadors, can be valuable sources of evidence. Many buildings and works of art, treasured in the past for their intrinsic historical and aesthetic interest, can now be assembled to reconstruct a court environment. The work of museums (such as the Victoria and Albert, and the National Maritime Museum at Greenwich, in England) in mounting special exhibitions devoted to particular late medieval and Renaissance courts has done much to increase the enthusiasm of both historians and non-specialists for the subject.

With regard to schools and universities, these generated their own records, which survive in large quantities subject to the usual caveat concerning the effects of war and civil unrest in some parts of our study area. Manuscripts and early printed books (*incunabula*) have a high value for collectors and this has also served to help in their preservation. The increasing numbers of personal family documents, including wills, can help assess the spread of book ownership and interest in those produced by the new technology of printing. Our main concerns in examining these subjects here are to look at the motives for the evident

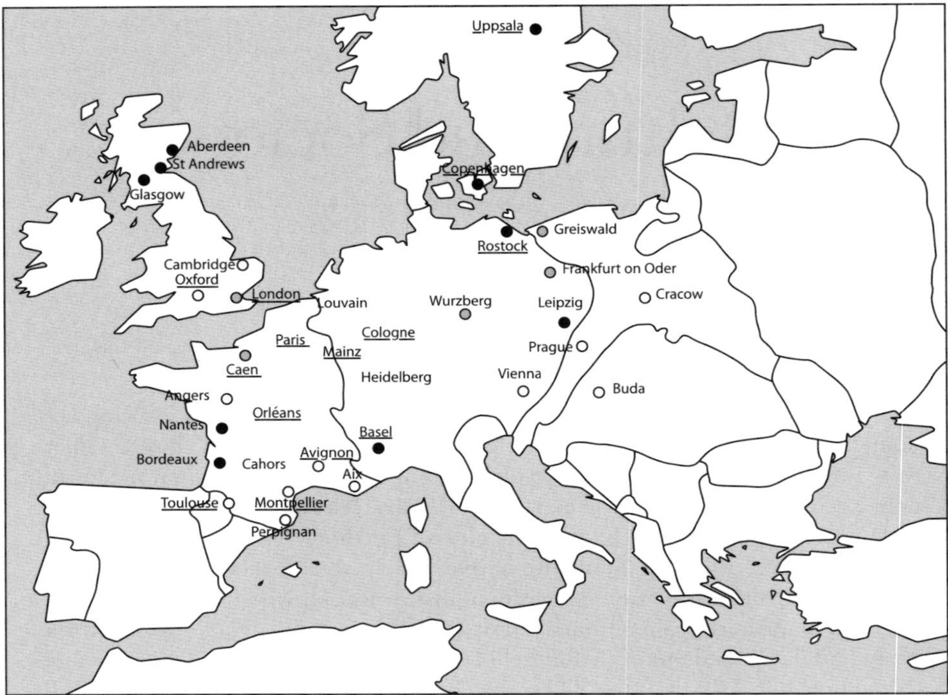

Map 5 Universities and printing centres

expansion in universities in our period (see Map 5), and to try to assess whether any noticeable change was under way in the curriculum or the methods of teachers. This also applies to schools, and the increasing importance of formal education for boys from the upper levels of society. Another important question is whether the intellectual attitudes associated with the Renaissance are evident in northern Europe in the fifteenth century. We have already tentatively associated the work of Christine de Pizan with the idea of the early Renaissance in France; here we will look more closely at this concept in relation to a wider range of scholars and institutions.

The last section of the chapter examines the special culture of towns. There seems little doubt that life in one of the successful urban centres of our period was very attractive to many mostly young people from the countryside or smaller centres. This is clear from the way in which the population of these cities was maintained not by 'natural increase' but by a constant flow of immigrants. Our aim here is to analyse the nature of late medieval urban culture and to see how it is related to the ideas of both continuity and change which have been advanced in relation to our period. Was the communal element in town life still prominent or had the more individualistic attitudes, often associated with the Renaissance, made a noticeable impact?

(i) COURT SOCIETY

What exactly was a princely court in the later Middle Ages? Until recent decades the answer to this question would have seemed to be fairly obvious: the court existed in whatever place the prince happened to be, and consisted of the members of his family, the nobility, officials and servants who accompanied him. This definition will do as a starting point, but recent scholarly interest in the phenomenon of the court has generated debate about its nature and significance and extended knowledge of its culture. A question to ask about our period is whether the political and cultural character of courts was changing. Every medieval prince had a household. When he married, his wife usually established a separate but smaller one and their children too might have households. These were regulated bodies of men, women and older children, often numbering between 200 and 500 people, who were assembled for the purpose of serving their prince. They ranged from great officials, often of noble rank, to kitchen boys and chambermaids. Some of these followed the princes as they toured their domains, others stayed in the principal residences to maintain and protect them. Princes invariably ruled with the aid of councils composed of members of the ruling dynasty, nobles, knights, clerics, lawyers and non-noble officials. Courts included the upper ranks of the household, members of the councils who regularly attended the prince, and other nobles, ladies and men who were accepted as courtiers. Early descriptions of courts tended to treat them as synonymous with princely households but the recent emphasis on court studies has shown the need for a more precise definition.

Norbert Elias made a decisive contribution to the growth of court studies.[1] He was primarily concerned with the *ancien régime*, the period of absolute European monarchies, which historians define as extending from the Renaissance to the French Revolution. He concentrated on the French court under Louis XIV, but distorted his arguments by paying undue regard to the criticisms contained in the *Memoirs* of the duke of Saint Simon (a man who never achieved the offices he felt he deserved at court). Elias, however, recognised that a great deal of continuity existed between the institutions and culture of courts in the later Middle Ages and the early modern period. He emphasised characteristics which they shared, such as the connection between influence at court and the acquisition of political power, and the importance of princely patronage. One of the most recent critics of the Elias view of the court is Jeroen Duindam. He thinks that all the instruments for achieving power that Elias said were used by rulers were also available to the nobility, and that their pedigrees defined their status independently of princely favours. He also accuses Elias of being uncritical in accepting the myth of omnipotence that monarchs created.[2]

The agenda was set for English court studies in a book edited by David Starkey, *The English Court: From the Wars of the Roses to the Civil War.*[3] The central argument is proclaimed in the title: the political supremacy of the court as an instrument of royal policy survived until the power of the Monarchy itself was temporarily destroyed in the mid-seventeenth century. This argument defied a whole school of historians that from the nineteenth century onwards had stressed the importance of the institutions of government through which monarchs had governed: the law, the royal council and Parliament, both in the later Middle Ages and in the early modern period. Their views culminated in the middle decades of the twentieth century in the work of G. R. Elton, who claimed that Henry VIII's Secretary of State, Thomas Cromwell: 'reformed administration by replacing medieval household methods by modern national and bureaucratic methods'.[4] The issues this argument raises about the power and importance of the English court as an institution in the late Middle Ages will be considered below in the wider context of north-western Europe.

Location

One of the problems in describing and analysing the nature of court society in the late Middle Ages was its impermanent location, which arose out of the peripatetic habits of princes. The idea that a prince should have a fixed principal residence, typically in his or her capital city, is essentially a development of the Renaissance period. A medieval prince would normally set up court in a large number of locations throughout the year; only warfare, sickness or extreme youth or age would vary this pattern. The dukes of Burgundy, for example, had principal residences in Paris (the Hôtel d'Artois); Brussels in Brabant; Bruges, Ghent and Lille in Flanders; Valenciennes in Hainault; and Dijon and Hesdin in Burgundy (that is, their original French duchy). They were influenced by the expansion of their domains. The first two, Philip the Bold and John the Fearless, regarded themselves as French princes and frequented their residences in Paris and the old duchy of Burgundy. The steady acquisition of territory in the Low Countries meant that Philip the Good and Charles the Bold were more frequently to be found in Brussels, Bruges and Lille. Much of their administration, especially the financial offices, was eventually situated at Malines/Mechlin, near Brussels. The itineraries that were followed by princes were, as Fiona Kisby has shown, to some extent determined by the feasts of the liturgical calendar.[5] It was important, for example, to spend Christmas in a comfortable residence where plentiful supplies of food and drink would be available.

In addition to their main residences princes stayed at their smaller castles, houses and hunting lodges and also enjoyed the hospitality of great nobles, cities, towns and monasteries. When the court was transferred to smaller residences and when it was on the road its less important members often had to face the same discomforts and dangers that were the lot of private travellers. Officials and servants were responsible for organising and protecting the huge baggage trains which accompanied princes on their travels. Many household goods were designed to be dismantled and then re-erected frequently: for example, folding altars, chests of clothes, tapestries and even glass windows, which were extremely expensive. The costs of endless and frequent changes of location were considerable and provided many opportunities for profit to court officials and local merchants. Princes and their councils did their best to minimize these by formulating strict regulations to control expenditure, and visiting places where they could receive partially or totally free entertainment.

The nobles, ecclesiastics and townspeople who were expected to extend hospitality to visiting princes could find their obligations burdensome. Paul-Joachim Heinig has recorded the impact of a visit by the Emperor Frederick III, just after his coronation in 1442, to the Imperial free city of Frankfurt.[6] Besides demanding very low prices for hay, straw, beds and stallage (the Imperial retinue normally included about 600 horses), the court officials expected to receive free food and drink for the Emperor's lodging and wood and coal for his kitchen. The Jews of Frankfurt traditionally provided parchment for the Chancellery, beds for the Imperial lodging, pots and pans for the kitchen and special favours for certain officials. The city had to present gifts to the Emperor and his entourage: those who supported Frankfurt's interests at court, such as the notary of the court tribunal, were treated especially generously. Louis de Male, count of Flanders, seems to have feared that his practice of leaving his horses and dogs to be kept at the expense of Flemish abbeys might imperil his soul. In his will in 1384 he conceded:

> We recognise that we have sometimes imposed our great horses and dogs on the abbeys of our land, and that they have been kept and fed there, and still are, and this has been by requisition and grace, not by right. And we do not wish that the Church should in any way be harmed in possession of its rights and liberties.[7]

The architectural layout of princely residences varied considerably. The fortress of the Louvre in Paris, for example, was not modified for the needs of a large and splendid Renaissance court until the sixteenth century, remaining until then essentially a medieval castle. The palace of Linlithgow in Scotland, on the other hand, was reconstructed by James I in the 1420s. It incorporated recent developments in French design, such as a large central courtyard flanked by fine façades, external stair turrets in the corners of the courtyard and a triple fireplace in the Great Hall (see Illustration 12). James could also have been influenced by what he saw during his captivity in England: the palaces of Cardinal Beaufort and the palace of Sheen (see Figure 2).[8] The location of the principal royal English palace at Westminster was largely due to the development of the cult of St Edward the Confessor, whose shrine was located in the adjacent abbey. From the time of Henry III and during the reigns of the next three kings (who bore the name of Edward) and of Richard II, work was constantly in progress embellishing and extending both the abbey and the palace. Yet no overall plan was ever formulated for the latter and existing structures, such as the Great Hall and the Parliament building, prevented any radical changes to what remained a rambling and old-fashioned conglomeration of buildings[9]

The Emperor Frederick III achieved a compromise in one of his favourite residences, Wiener Neustadt in Lower Austria. His principal seat was a castle but all sorts of other buildings sprang up in the town to cater for the needs of his court: royal stables, mews for hawks, gardens and lodgings for court officers. Frederick was so short of money that he was confined for the middle decades of his reign to his patrimonial lands, and his movements were therefore more limited than was usual for princes. In Burgundy, residences such as the Princenhof in Bruges were

12 Linlithgow Palace, Scotland

This was always planned as a palace rather than a castle, and demonstrates the confidence of James I who started the work in the 1420s. French influence may be seen in features such as the external staircase and elaborate fountain. (*The east and south courtyard fronts drawn by R. W. Billings, c. 1850, engraved by J. H. L. Keux*)

to prove influential on later palace buildings in northern Europe. The *donjon* (castle keep), which contained the ducal quarters, was set with the chapel, kitchens and Great Hall in a series of courtyards, which also housed lodgings for the heir and courtiers, gardens, a tiltyard and tennis courts. Most of the buildings were made of brick. These arrangements had several advantages for the dukes: their quarters in the *donjon* gave them privacy and security without the need for a full-scale, old-fashioned castle structure; they were also surrounded by facilities for recreation without having to leave their residence.

Henry VII had visited modern palaces on the Continent during his long exile and was almost certainly influenced by their design when he started to rebuild the palace of Sheen in 1497. He renamed it 'Richmond' after the title he had borne before he seized the throne. Its arrangement was very similar to the residence at Bruges and it impressed observers by its convenience and luxury; one described the orchard at the time of the reception of Catherine of Aragon in 1501:

> many marvellous beasts, as lions, dragons, and such other divers [many] kind, properly fashioned and carved in the ground, right well sondid [based] and compassed with lead, with many vines, seeds, and strange fruit right goodly beset. ... In the lower end of this garden be pleasant galleries and houses of pleasure to disport in.[10]

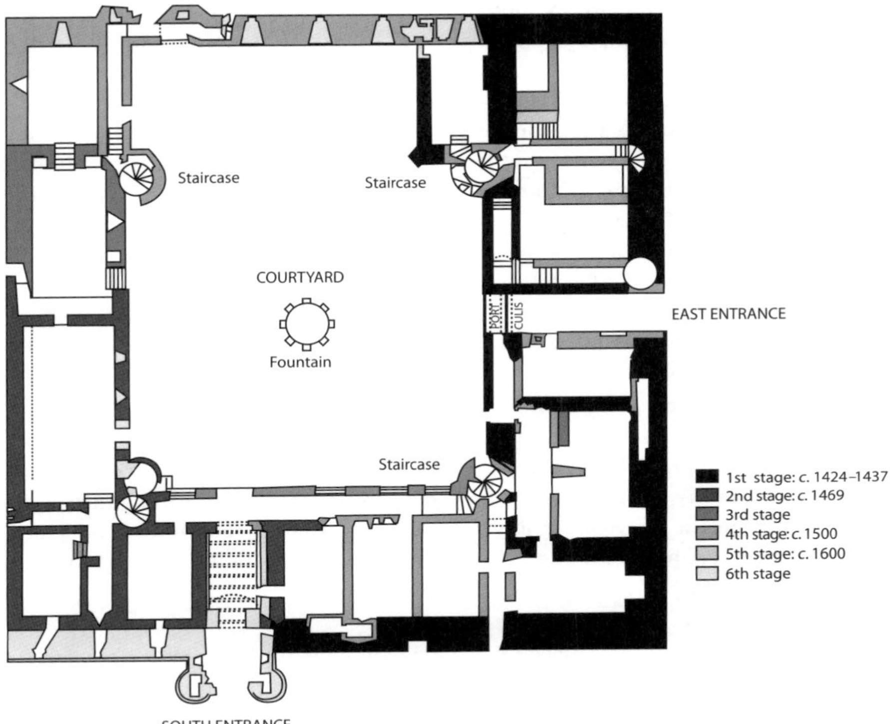

Figure 2 Plan of Linlithgow Palace, Scotland: the groundfloor

A courtyard layout was probably planned from the beginning. This can be compared to Angers where the dukes had to work with an existing structure.

Henry was not, however, the first English king to introduce such standards of luxury to his court, for Edward IV had visited the duchy of Burgundy as an exile and seems to have emulated much of the splendour he experienced there and some of its building styles. While he was duke of Gloucester and during his short reign, Richard III also carried out ambitious new building works, especially in his northern castles.

Organisation

The need to get value for money and the recognition that a well-ordered court reflected the power and prestige of the prince, led to the formulation of regulations for the conduct of the household, and descriptions of court ceremonies. English kings had issued ordinances about how their households should be organised and financed from at least the eleventh century. It was not until the middle of the fifteenth century, however, that sufficiently detailed instructions survive to give us a vivid picture of the life of the royal household and the court that it sustained. David Starkey believes that *The Ryalle* [Royal] *Book*, which is usually assigned to the early Tudor period, was actually written by a former gentleman usher of Henry VI for the instruction of the new Yorkist officials in the early 1460s.[11] It describes a richly furnished and ceremonious court such as is portrayed in the testimony of foreign visitors to England in the years before the outbreak of the Civil Wars. Previously it was thought that the penury and dowdiness, that were associated with the later days of Henry VI, were also characteristic of his early adulthood. If Starkey is correct about the dating, it pushes back the consciousness about the importance of keeping a magnificent establishment by several decades. Edward IV, the first Yorkist king, has been credited with this policy mainly because an elaborate description of his court, its officials and their duties survives, which was probably written in 1471/2.

The Black Book of the Household of Edward IV provides a detailed account, supported by ancient and Christian authorities, of the duties and rewards of officials. It is divided into two parts, 'the magnificent house' and 'the provident house', which combine the aims of arranging an impressive, ceremonious court and enjoining strict economy and accounting in the way in which it was to function. The esquires of the body, for example, should be:

> noble of condition; of them always ii be attendant upon the king's person to array and undress him, to watch day and night, to dress him in his clothes. And they be callers to the chamberlain if anything lack for his person or pleasure; their business is many secrets, some sitting in the king's chamber, some in the hall, with persons of like service, which is called knight's service. Taking every of them for his livery [allowance] at night a wheaten loaf, a quart wine, a gallon ale; and for winter livery, from All Halloween-tide until Easter, a tall wax candle, a wax candle, ii Paris candles, chopped wood. And wages in the counting house if he be present in court, daily viid, and clothing with the household winter and summer, or xls besides his other fee of jewel house, or of treasurer of England; and besides his watching [night-time] clothing of chamber, of the king's wardrobe, he hath abiding in this court but ii servants, livery sufficient for his horses in the country by the king's purveyor. And if any squire of the body be let blood or else wearied with waking or watching, he shall have sick livery with knights; litter and rushes all the year of the sergeant usher of the hall and chamber. Often times these stand instead of carvers and cupbearers.[12]

The advice contained in this treatise seems to have been only partially successful. Edward certainly impressed observers with his magnificence but he still felt that it was all costing too much. Ordinances were issued in 1478 that attempted to enforce a tighter control on the numbers of household servants, their pay and allowances. Henry VII, whilst maintaining an opulent and stately court, found it necessary through the treasurer of his chamber to keep expenses under constant surveillance.[13]

The distribution of power within princely households varied from country to country, although the functions they were expected to carry out were broadly the same. In England the Chamberlain presided over the magnificent, public side and the Steward over the provident, practical side. In the Empire the household was divided into five parts: the house, yard, stable, kitchen and wardrobe. Maximilian I chose Innsbruck as his principal residence and when he visited his second wife, Bianca Maria Sforza, there, her household of between 150 and 200 people merged with his travelling household. The Empress does not seem to have been greatly valued by her husband once he had spent her large dowry: in 1497 he abandoned her in Worms for several months, a prisoner of her creditors. She was given a meagre allowance for her own needs and those of her household although she was expected to employ all the servants required for the maintenance of her state. These included four washerwomen, two chaplains with two servants, a furrier and his assistant, three senior and two junior door-keepers, three lutanists, three drummers and pipers, and the master of the stable with one assistant. There were also seven noble pages, two silversmiths, an assistant to clean the silverware, a candlemaker, eight wagoners, one dancing master, four guards, a gardener, two fools and various cleaners and porters.[14]

Maximilian had huge debts throughout his long reign and selections of the royal plate and linen were periodically pawned. The wages and clothes due to officials and servants were frequently in arrears but at least they had the right to two meals a day (except in Lent, when only one was served). Breakfast was eaten at 9.00 am and consisted of soup, fried meat or game, cabbage, porridge, bread and wine. Dinner followed at 16.00 and the menu was similar to breakfast: cabbage or beets, stew, salted calf's head or similar dishes according to the season, bread and wine. The royal family and senior officials were served with white bread, everyone else had black, rye bread. The menus compare poorly with those served in the courts of England and Burgundy, reflecting as they do, regional tastes and the poverty of the Emperor. On feast days, however, richer and more varied food would have been available. The dilatory payment of salaries was typical of all late medieval courts: the provision of board and, sometimes, lodging dated from a much earlier period; money had only assumed a major role in employment in recent centuries. Princes could normally give it a low priority, for their subjects were equally dilatory in paying their taxes and Customs dues.

The identification of the household structure within the court with the prince's military role varied from state to state. In England, apart from the royal guards, the emphasis was on ceremony and good housekeeping. Ralph Griffiths, however, has pointed out that a change occurred during the crisis of Lancastrian authority in the later 1450s. Not only did Henry VI withdraw to his strong castles in the Midlands but he also looked to the court that accompanied him for his army commanders, and to their retinues for loyal soldiers.[15] Not since the days of the Black Prince and Henry V's campaigns in France had the court been put on such a martial basis. This was a more permanent element in the Burgundian court, where chivalric ideals were associated with the duchy's ability constantly to expand its territories. The first Chamberlain was not only the director of all the household services, in time of war he was expected to serve as the duke's Lieutenant and Standard-bearer.[16]

Power and prestige

Are Norbert Elias, David Starkey and other historians of courts correct in making such a close connection between their functioning and the exercise of political power? Princes were not always surrounded by splendid courts, so were they necessarily less effective on those occasions? What about other members of princely families, nobles and able officials, could they only exert influence by means of the court? Did the situation change between the mid-fourteenth and the end of the fifteenth century, and did the same developments occur in all the states we are discussing?

The French court provides a useful case study to enable us to answer some of these questions and it can then be compared with the other states. It is an obvious choice for close attention: throughout the late Middle Ages, even when France was weak politically, the French language and the culture of the upper orders of society were strongly influential throughout north-western Europe. Marie Thérèse Caron suggests that by the late thirteenth century the court had assumed the character that it would keep until the fifteenth century, while J. F. Solnon has claimed that the king did not have a court in the Middle Ages.[17] The royal council was detached from the court, indeed some of the royal princes who were members had regional courts of their own. Lawyers were also useful councillors and they had a professional existence apart from the royal court in the various law courts, including the *parlements* that were described above in Chapter 3. Yet throughout our period the power and prestige of the monarchy was reflected in the nature of the court that it was able to maintain.

In the mid-fourteenth century the parts of France ruled directly by its kings were limited and mainly confined to the north. They visited their castles in the Loire valley from time to time, but by the reign of John the Good, they spent much of the year in or near Paris. The Palais de la Cité on the island in the river Seine, the Louvre and the Hôtel de Nesle were favourite residences in the capital as were Saint-Ouen, Saint-Germain-en-Laye, and Bicêtre in the outskirts. John's son, the Dauphin (later Charles V), had more direct impact on the development of French court life than did his father. He and his brothers, the dukes of Anjou, Berry and Burgundy, cultivated the values of chivalry. This confirmed a hierarchical power structure based on the bearing of coats of arms, which was important for proof of noble lineage, in battle and in tournaments (see above, Chapter 1 and Chapter 4).[18] As a relatively new dynasty the Valois needed to enhance the prestige of their family and affirm its legitimacy by every possible means: not easy to do while Edward III of England and the Black Prince were occupying large areas of France. The brothers established mausolea for themselves: John of Berry in the cathedral at Bourges; Philip of Burgundy at the Carthusian monastery, the Chartreuse de Champmol, outside Dijon; Louis of Anjou at Angers; and Charles V in the abbey of St Denis in the outskirts of Paris. The king rewarded some of his most prominent servants, such as the general Bertrand du Guesclin, by allowing them to be buried in the abbey: the princes were to keep their retinues even in death. The dukes of Burgundy were to challenge French royal authority during the following century but, under Charles V, their power and splendour enhanced his prestige.

The court of Charles V attained great sophistication in literature and the arts, which also contributed to the good reputation of the French monarchy. Writers such as Christine de Pizan and Philippe de Mézières ensured that the king's good reputation would survive him. His piety, demonstrated in his elaborate coronation rites, meant that he avoided the condemnations that were sometimes made of lavish courts such as that of his cousin, Richard II of England. After years of defeat at the hands of the English, the court provided Charles with a magnificent environment in which he could both negotiate foreign alliances and restore the morale of his subjects. His son, Charles VI, in his early years kept an equally splendid court: indeed it was at a fête that he suffered the accident which contributed to his decline into insanity. The power vacuum during his later reign was filled both by the conflicting ambitions of the great French princes and by the resurgent power of England under Henry V.

Whilst the courts of the dukes of Burgundy and the other French princes were important centres during the early fifteenth century, Charles VI and his household, situated in and around Paris, were little more than puppets of the English. After the death of his brother, Henry V, in 1422, the English Regent, John, duke of Bedford, held his own peripatetic court in northern France. The wealth acquired by the booty of war and his revenues as a great magnate enabled him to amass fine manuscripts, jewels, precious relics and furnishings, which have been traced and described by Jenny Stratford.[19] The rival court held by Charles VII at Bourges was initially a poor affair in comparison, but it was essential to provide a 'tangible alternative' to English rule.[20] A factor in the success of the English and their Burgundian ally, and the dismal showing of the French kings, seems to have been the power of their courts to impress their subjects and foreign ambassadors.

The death of Bedford and the alliance of Charles VII with Philip the Good of Burgundy in 1435 underlined the gradual reversal of the fortunes of England and France. Henry VI may have kept a splendid court until the 1450s but he then went virtually bankrupt. The German knight Jorg von Ehingen found nothing to remark on when he visited Henry's court beyond the fact that he gave him 'his order'. This was probably the Lancastrian SS collar, which was usually given to important supporters or members of the king's affinity, rather than the Garter, which was reserved for the nobles closest to the king.[21] The splendid celebrations for the marriage of the Dauphin to Margaret of Scotland in 1436 proclaimed to Europe that France was not only recovering its lands from the English but could achieve the grandeur of style appropriate to a great kingdom. Even after Paris was restored to him, however, Charles preferred to reside in his *châteaux* in the Loire valley. Despite their differences his son, later Louis XI, also spent most of his time in that region, especially at Tours and Amboise. This might seem to have been a risky policy so soon after the reconquest of much of France but Louis was effective in exacting respect and obedience from his subjects. He was also congenitally suspicious and had good reason to fear the machinations of the Yorkist kings of England and the expansionist ambitions of Charles the Bold of Burgundy. He probably felt more secure in the heart of his kingdom, far from marauders on the northern coasts or the border with Burgundy.

The marriage of Charles VIII to the duchess Anne of Brittany introduced the influence of one of the great fifteenth-century regional courts. Like her forebears, she patronised the arts and literature from her capital at Nantes and founded an order for great ladies, which had the girdle of St Francis as its insignia. As queen she continued to keep great state, financing her household out of the income from her duchy. After the premature death of Charles she married his cousin and successor, Louis XII, the former duke of Orleans. He had kept a cosmopolitan court like his cultivated father, centred on the family's great château of Blois in the Loire valley. After he ascended the throne the royal couple preferred that residence above all others and carried out extensive building works to modernise and beautify it. Although the kingdom was drained of resources by the wars fought by Charles VIII, Louis XII and Francis I, the courts they held became ever more brilliant and ceremonious. This reflected the growing power that they wielded even over the greatest of their subjects, and was linked to the impact of Italian Renaissance culture. This encouraged princes to achieve fame and glory both by their political acumen and by commissioning great works of art and literature such as their building projects in the Loire valley, and employing renowned artists like Leonardo da Vinci. As the court of the French kings became more brilliant, so the courts of the princes withered away. Most of the duchies, Brittany, Orleans, Anjou and part of Burgundy, had in any case been incorporated into the lands ruled directly by the kings by the end of the fifteenth century.

In France the political fortunes of the kings seem to have been reflected very clearly in the renown of their courts. The reign of Charles V and the second half of the reign of Charles VII marked recoveries from English occupation and revivals in the splendour of their courts. The increasing strength and authority of the Monarchy in the late fifteenth and early sixteenth century was also mirrored in the magnificence of its setting. A similar phenomenon is to be found in England, although the most lavish and cultivated court of the fourteenth century, kept by Richard II, did not save him from destruction. Indeed his reputation for extravagance and self-indulgence was fostered by the kind of state he kept and probably contributed to his downfall. Charles the Bold of Burgundy also held a fine court, where military virtues were pursued through the cult of chivalry. He kept a firm hold on his subjects, who obeyed him despite his unwise expansionist policies. His court did not save him from defeat and death at Nancy in 1477: prudent princes did not expose themselves to the chances of battle. Had Charles survived and continued to live within his magnificent court, it is unlikely that the humiliation of defeat would have left his reputation as a great prince unimpaired.

In the case of the Empire, wealth and a renowned court went hand in hand. The Emperor Charles IV avoided unnecessary wars and drew sufficient income from his ancestral lands to undertake great building works and patronise the arts in Bohemia. His was one of the most cosmopolitan and brilliant courts in Europe. Paul Crossley has described the work of his architect Peter Parler as 'flamboyant and inventive'.[22] Yet his successors, less able and mired in the Hussite wars, sank into indigence and wielded little authority beyond their ancestral lands. Maximilian I's marriage to Mary of Burgundy gave the Empire a new direction and greater resources that were, in the following century, to enhance its authority. The court was certainly a factor in demonstrating their power and prestige but, after the days of Charles IV, it could not match the magnificence of England and France at their best and of Burgundy under the Valois dukes.

The German lay and ecclesiastical princes all had their courts, but in the fourteenth and fifteenth centuries they were not especially distinguished by their patronage of the arts or by their political significance. Jorg von Ehingen had already served both Duke Sigismund of the Tyrol and Duke Albert of Austria when he toured the western European courts in the 1450s. It could have been the family alliance with the former that elicited such praise for Scotland from him:

> The king was my gracious lady's [the wife of Duke Sigismund] brother and he received me graciously and well. The Queen was a Duchess of Guelders and a Low German.
>
> Item. The King presented me with two tents and a cloth of black satin, and to each of my pages gave ten ducats, there being four pages.
>
> Item. The Queen gave me a fine jewel worth 30 ducats and a stallion worth quite 100 gulden, and much honour was shown me in hunting, dancing and feasting.[23]

The lavish hospitality offered to a relatively unimportant visitor is notable, especially as the Scots kings had fewer resources to draw on than neighbouring monarchs. This extract also provides testimony to the cosmopolitan nature of European courts, a characteristic which was clearly valued by James II, who was desperately trying to cut a fine figure and show his independence of his English rival.

A magnificent court did not necessarily guarantee that a prince would achieve renown and influence and it was not the automatic key to greatness for subjects. John, duke of Berry, and René, duke of Anjou and titular king of Naples and Jerusalem, were not famous warriors but in their own smaller circles, independently of the French court, they achieved a reputation for their sophistication and love of the arts. Despite his failure to conquer his kingdom of Naples, René established a great reputation for his patronage of art and literature. He completed the building of a graceful and comfortable small palace within the old curtain walls of the château of Angers; this was one of many such projects that he undertook (see Illustrations 13 and 14). A great English magnate such as Richard, earl of Warwick, rose to prominence during the later reign of Henry VI through his enormous wealth and his alliance with the duke of York. Both nobles were hostile to the court and they finally achieved power by force of arms rather than by royal favour. Lesser men, administrators and household servants, were much more likely to gain influence through the court, where they might catch the eye of their prince or one of his nobles. Sometimes a pleasing manner or handsome person was the key to success, as with the favours enjoyed by the mistress of Charles VII, Agnes Sorel. She first entered court circles through her service to the wife of René of Anjou. Others, such as the Chancellor Nicolas Rolin, were employed by Philip the Good of Burgundy for their talents as administrators. He was to be disgraced, however, after court intrigues: a common fate for those who only enjoyed influence through their prince, a benefit that could easily be withdrawn.

In earlier centuries great churchmen had served their princes alongside the nobility. The careers of Nicolas Rolin in Burgundy and Adam Moleyns, Keeper

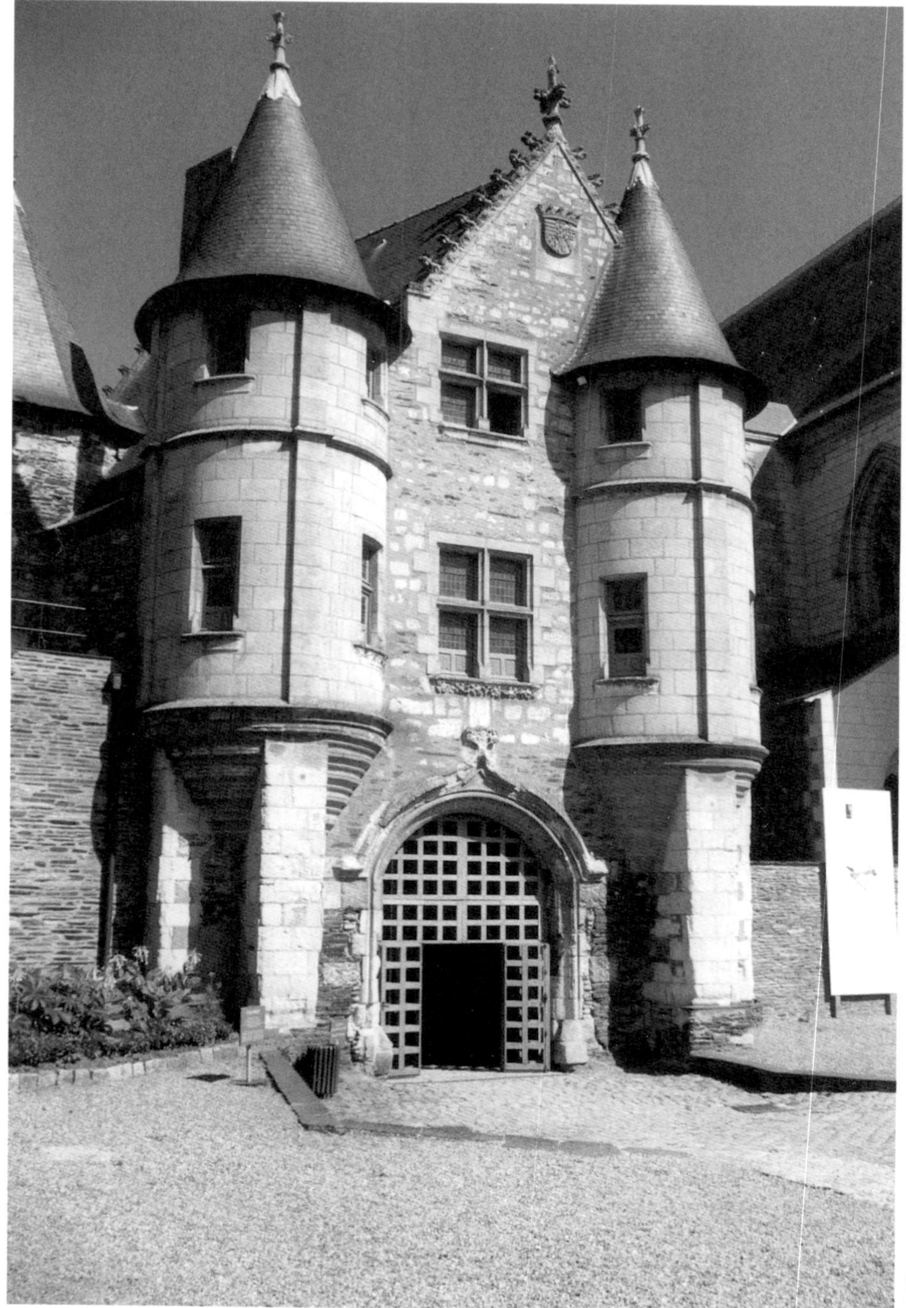

13 King René's gatehouse, 1450, Angers Castle, France

One of a series of elegant buildings with which the dukes of Anjou, titular kings of Sicily, modernised the old castle in the fourteenth and fifteenth centuries.

14 The curtain wall, Angers Castle, built in the thirteenth century

King René put the moat to good use two hundred years later keeping some of his menagerie there.

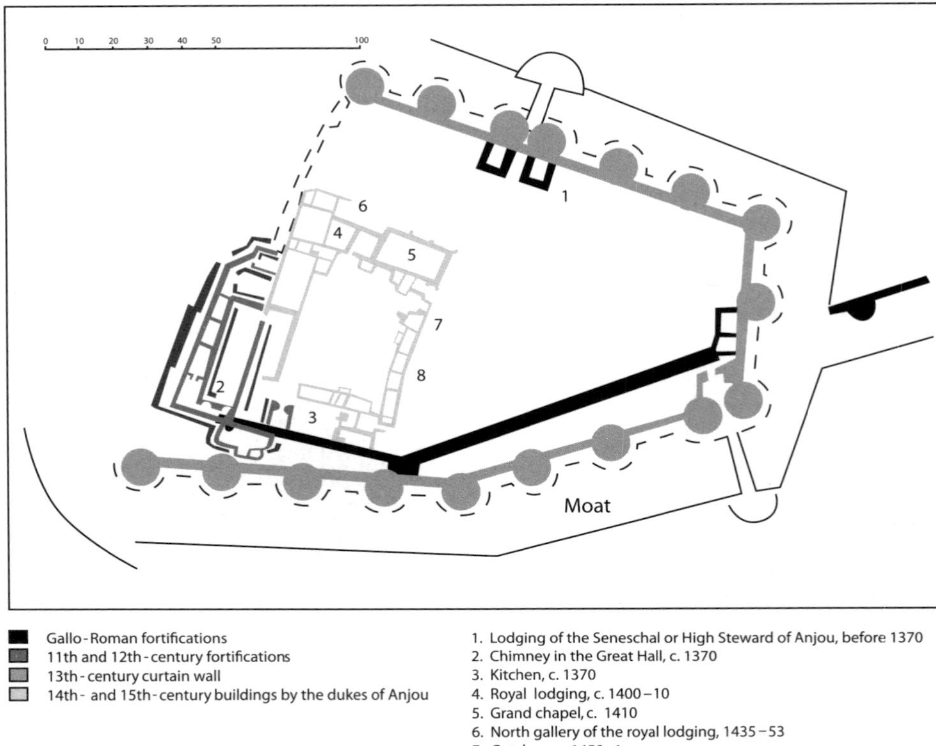

Figure 3 Plan of Angers castle in the fourteenth and fifteenth centuries

The dukes of Anjou, titular kings of Sicily, inserted a modern palace into the huge space enclosed by the earlier medieval walls.

of the Privy Seal and bishop of Chichester in England (who was murdered during the popular unrest in 1450), demonstrate that relatively humble men were being employed by princes in the later Middle Ages if they were sufficiently able. Great wealth and high office could be their reward: even if some suffered bad ends, a professional official class capable of servicing the European states was in the process of formation.

Court culture

It should not be too readily assumed that a distinctive court culture invariably existed. In the fourteenth century a good case can be made that the individual taste and patronage of rulers such as the Emperor Charles IV, Charles V of France and Richard II of England imparted a characteristic style to their courts. The dukes of Burgundy, disposing of ever increasing wealth, employed writers and artists in the fifteenth century who set new standards of luxury and refinement. For much of the century, however, a series of political crises and a besetting lack of sufficient revenue atrophied the development of most northern European courts. This changed as the style that had been developed in the courts of Italy during the early Renaissance penetrated Scotland, England, France and Germany. It should also be recognised that court culture was not necessarily the preserve of the elite: Malcolm Vale's recent study has stressed that codes of behaviour and recreations encompassed a much wider section of those who lived in princely households than simply the courtiers.[24] The quotation from Edward IV's *Black Book* demonstrates that a whole structure of rights and customs had been built up amongst the household servants of all degrees.

In the fourteenth century, religion informed the style of those courts that could claim a distinctive culture. The Emperor Charles IV was very devout and his patronage was almost exclusively extended to the building of churches and the production of religious art. Even his castle/palace of Karlstein was arranged to reflect 'the convergence of spiritual and secular power'.[25] The building was erected on a steep hill with the palace quarters at the lowest level, there was then a tower containing the chapels of the Virgin and St Catherine, and at the top of the structure was a large tower which housed the chapel of the Holy Cross. The chapels contained the Emperor's collection of relics and were richly decorated with gold, semi-precious stones and fresco cycles. In the chapel of the Holy Cross, monumental pictures were executed by the Bohemian Master Theodoricus and formed the climax of a scheme which associated Charles with the Church, presenting him as 'the vicar of Christ on earth'.[26] There was a direct connection between the pious but opulent image he created for himself and his court and the authority he enjoyed as Emperor.

Charles V of France was equally successful in impressing his subjects and other states that he was a good Christian and an effective monarch. His court was not held in the magnificent surroundings of Prague or Karlstein but artists and writers flourished there. The praises he received from writers such as Christine de Pizan, and the illuminated manuscripts and other works of art which recorded his regal acts, contributed to the renown that he enjoyed amongst his contemporaries and with posterity. Richard II of England was influenced both by the court culture of his French cousin and, through his wife Anne of Bohemia, by that of Prague. The location of his court at Westminster encouraged him to continue to exploit the cult of Edward the Confessor, which had been developed over the previous century. Richard's portraits that survive in Westminster Abbey and in the Wilton Diptych set the agenda: he was presented with all the attributes of an anointed king who enjoyed the approval of the Virgin and the saints. Some contemporary writers, such as Roger Dymmok, defended his court by recounting how the Queen of Sheba had been impressed by the magnificence of King Solomon and saw it as an attribute of his wisdom.[27] Yet more people condemned him for extravagance and exalting himself over his subjects, to whom he became 'Richard the Redeless'.

Court culture in the fifteenth century retained its religious character but, according to historians such as Huizinga, it had become simply a veneer that disguised declining ideals. The forms of chivalry expressed most notably through the knightly orders and through tournaments and other court displays were a defining feature of this culture. Edward III of England had founded the Order of the Garter in 1348 and many princes emulated him, seizing the opportunity to achieve prestige throughout Europe. The most famous and admired of the fifteenth-century foundations was the Order of the Golden Fleece, which was instituted by Philip the Good of Burgundy in 1430. The heyday of the Order, under the duke and his son Charles the Bold, coincided with their court's most brilliant period: its wealth, and the refinement of style and the art which it generated, indicate that it was strongly influential on other contemporary courts. Werner Paravicini has subjected this assumption to careful investigation. He suggests that Burgundy may seem to have developed a more sophisticated court, because it is usually contrasted with states such as France and England that were impoverished by decades of internal and external warfare.[28] Much is made of the detailed accounts of the regulation of the court that survive, encouraging historians to dwell on the uniqueness of Burgundian culture, but, apart from the strong emphasis laid upon the practice of chivalry, there was not so much to distinguish it from other courts. Those who had close contacts with the dukes, such as Edward IV of England and some German princes, probably did respond to their example but this should not be over-emphasised. The question of how far Burgundy developed a characteristic court culture relates to the wider claim, made by Henri Pirenne in his *Histoire de Belgique* in 1902, that under the Valois dukes it began to develop some of the characteristics of a nation state. This was refuted by Huizinga in a series of articles, and his objections have recently been supported by the studies made by Graeme Small of the work of the Burgundian historian George Chastelain. He believes that French culture was still supremely important in the court circle even towards the end of the fifteenth century.

Knightly participation in tournaments, with all their chivalric trappings, emphasised the hierarchical, exclusive nature of courtly society. This was also true of other favourite pursuits at court such as hunting and games of chance. The peasantry suffered when huntsmen's horses trampled their crops and the hunting dogs killed their animals. Little heed was paid to these hardships although compensation was sometimes paid: in 1302, in two months, the count of Flanders had to pay for the destruction of eighteen sheep, two lambs, two calves and three geese by a wolf that he kept.[29] Board games, especially chess, were immensely popular with the elite and the pieces were often made of precious or semi-precious materials such as ivory. The order of the chess pieces: the kings and queens, bishops, knights, castles and pawns reflected the structure of society, as appropriately high or low values were assigned to each. Heavy betting was often made on the outcome of these games: itself a form of the conspicuous consumption that was a characteristic of court life.

Patronage was an essential element in activities and relationships in late medieval courts. A straightforward transaction occurred when a member of a household or an artist was paid in money or in kind for performing a service or executing a commission. A more indirect form of patronage is illustrated by this letter, sent in 1447/50 to Jane Carew, a rich widow, by Queen Margaret of Anjou, wife of Henry VI:

> Right dear and well-beloved we greet you well and, for as much as our trusty and well-beloved squire Thomas Burneby, sewer [server at table] of our mouth, as well as for the great zeal, love, and affection that he hath unto your person, as for the womanly and virtuous governance that ye be renowned of, desireth with all his heart to do you worship by way of marriage, before all creatures living, as he saith. We desiring the increase, furtherance and preferring of our said squire, for his manifold merits and deserts, as for the good service that he hath done unto my lord [the king] and us, and yet therin daily continueth, pray you right affectuously [earnestly] that, at reverence of us, ye will have our said squire towards his said marriage especially recommended.[30]

In this case the Queen's pressure was ineffective, the lady eventually married a noble, a brother of the earl of Oxford.

The princely patrons of artists and writers wished to enhance their reputations by ornamenting their courts with rare and beautiful objects and by their taste for literature. Prestige was attached to employing the finest artists: the Rhine and Meuse areas, for example, produced musicians who specialised in playing loud instruments such as trumpets and shawms. Their music often took the form of *virelais-ballades* (three stanzas and a refrain), which were suitable for accompanying songs and dances (see Illustration 15). Such minstrels were employed at the court of Albert of Bavaria and by Philip the Bold of Burgundy.[31] Princes also expected praise; while artists could present images of pious and powerful rulers, writers were even more direct:

> I praise highly the magnificence and grandeur of the king's household, for within it is the supreme academy for the nobles of the realm, and a school of vigour, probity and manners by which the realm is honoured and will flourish.[32]

Not all writers took Fortescue's sanguine view of courts: in Chapter 3 the strictures of John Skelton in the *Bowge of Court* were quoted. He based his poem on an early fifteenth-century work by the French writer and courtier Alain Chartier, who was drawing on a long European tradition of literature critical of courts. Rosemary Horrox has discussed this in 'Caterpillars of the Commonwealth', concluding that the charges of ambition and decadence often levelled against individual courtiers did not mean that the institution of the court itself was widely unpopular.[33] Extravagant condemnations were the preserve of literature rather than everyday life.

Malcolm Vale's recent study concludes by tackling the question of how far late medieval courts were instrumental in the emergence of nation states. Despite changes such as the increased use of local vernacular languages (Dutch was replacing French in the Low Countries as early as 1300), he sees continuity in the conduct of courts. Whilst princes were surrounded with greater ceremonial than had been usual in earlier times, courts remained the product of the economic demands and customs of the households on which they were founded.[34] On the other hand, under effective rulers such as the Emperor Charles IV, Charles V of France, Philip the Good of Burgundy and Henry VII of England, the court was a good instrument for projecting a powerful princely image. Until

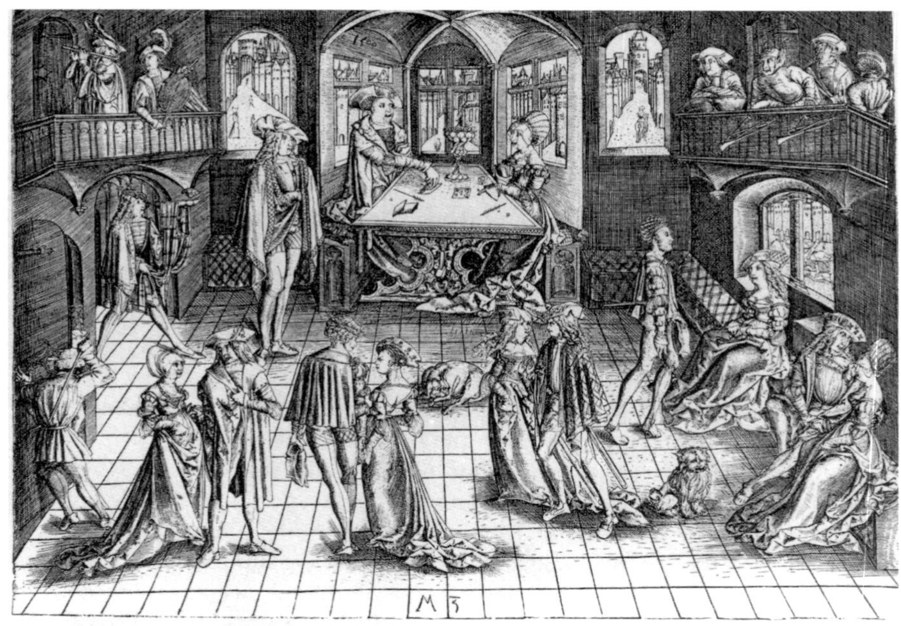

15 A ball at the court of duke Albert the Wise of Bavaria, 1500

The duke sits at a table playing cards with a lady (*an engraving by the anonymous master MZ*)

later centuries when subjects became progressively involved in political decision-making, courts, as David Starkey and others have demonstrated, played a central role in the governance of European states.

(ii) UNIVERSITIES AND LEARNING: THE CULTURE OF THE ELITE

Universities

Universities had been a feature of medieval life since the thirteenth century but they were originally closely associated principally with the study of theology and Roman law. The sophisticated appreciation of art and beauty associated, for example, with John Duke of Berry (the original owner of the *Très Riches Heures* among other things) or with the designer of Jacques Coeur's house in Bourges, did not come from any system of education but originated in an individual's private enthusiasms. There was no formal education in the visual arts. Artists themselves were considered as craftsmen who learnt their skills in the workshops of their elders, usually combined with an apprenticeship and formal membership of a guild. In Bruges, sculptors were members of the carpenters' guild until 1431. In Ghent, only native-born artists could join the guild. Foreigners' work had to be sold at two special markets, one on Shrove Tuesday when, for the day, the butchers' stalls in the market were taken over by artists. Patrons acquired their taste by experience of a culturally rich environment: the court itself sometimes provided the education needed.

Formal education was not, however, despised. Our period sees not only the foundation of schools intended for a much wider section of society than just future clerics but also the increasing acceptance of a university education as desirable for many young men who had no intention of going into the Church or the law. In the Paston family much greater emphasis was laid on formal education by the end of the fifteenth century. John I's older sons do not seem to have had any education in a school or college. John II was at court by the time he was nineteen. His next brother, John III, was closely associated with his patron the duke of Norfolk and then made a career in local affairs as an MP and Sheriff of Norfolk. The next boy, Edmund II, was in London training as a lawyer at Staple Inn in 1470. The two youngest went to school and university. Walter was at Oxford taking the BA degree in June 1479, when he was probably about twenty-four. He died that summer but there is no record that he had his eye set on a clerical career. William Paston III, the youngest of the family, was at Eton College in the same year. Like many schoolboys since, he wrote home asking for money and for extra food (in his case no less than 12 lb of figs and 8 lb of raisins) and about a girl he had some interest in.[35] For boys, by the 1470s, the informal education obtained by living in a noble household was no longer sufficient for gentlemen.

The mid fourteenth-century, the period just before and just after the Black Death, marks something of a watershed for universities in our study area. At the outset of the century the old foundations of Bologna, Paris and Oxford still towered over the others, of which there was only a small number. The new institutions recognised as true universities (certified as such by the Papacy by being granted the status of a *studium generale*, which allowed its graduates to teach 'world wide') increased rapidly during the course of the century, with a particular concentration in the later years. Why was this? What forces were at work in Europe to produce this result? One motivation was that which drives a great deal of the expansion of education, particularly university education, in the modern world. Attendance at a university seemed to be the passport to a lucrative career and improved social standing, something not to be decried in the hierarchical society of the day.

Guenée has drawn attention to the increasing number of royal servants, councillors and other functionaries who were lawyers. This meant, in most of southern Europe, that they had been trained at Bologna; in France, from 1248, lawyers at court might be graduates of the university at Orleans. This trend became even more noticeable in the later fourteenth century, particularly in the courts of German rulers. In France these men were often of noble birth; this applies to all those admitted to the Council by Philip the Fair and even to large numbers in the lower administrative ranks, *baillis* and *sénéchaux*.[36] Lewis sees the rising numbers of lawyers of both noble and *bourgeois* backgrounds as constituting almost a separate group in society. They could be found working not only for the king and in the sovereign courts but also for town authorities and private landowners. The Jouvenel family in the fifteenth century, for example, were all lawyers and of noble rank and renowned for their loyalty to the Crown. The father, Jean I, was a member (in fact second president) of the *parlement* of Poitiers; the son, Jean II, was an advocate of the king; and his son Guillaume was a knight and *conseiller lai* (lay counsel) in the court.[37]

There is also the issue of prestige; this related not to what we would call nationalism but to the standing of a ruling family or dynasty or the self-confidence of a city of importance. R. C. Schwinges expressed this very clearly; a university was 'as clear an expression of princely and ruling authority as the building of castles and towns, and the founding of churches and monasteries'.[38] It seems to have become accepted that the presence of a university in a ruler's territory or within a city was a sign of the honour due to that place and its ruler. This applied, for example, to the university in Prague, established in 1347–8 by the Emperor Charles IV. Neighbouring rulers then seem to have wished to emulate him by similarly setting up rival institutions in Vienna (1364), Cracow (1364) and Pest (1367).

An even clearer instance of this kind of motivation is the establishment of the University of Louvain in Brabant in 1425. The lands of the duke of Burgundy contained no university; in the past, students had gone to Paris. At this date Paris was within the English sphere of influence in France so that the founding of this new institution had some political significance; the foundation also had some attraction for the citizens of Louvain, who felt that their city was overshadowed by Brussels at this period. Even more pointedly political was the setting up of the University of Caen by the English in 1436. The need for lawyers in government service has already been mentioned. Although the theology faculty at Paris was without equal at this period, civil (Roman) law could not be studied there. Orleans and Angers were the leading law schools in France. Allmand has linked the move in favour of the foundation of the university of Caen with the English failure to take Orleans in 1429. Now Normandy looked like the real base of the English in France and a local institution was needed to train lawyers and other graduates, even if this infuriated the scholars of Paris.

At the point when Parisian indignation reached a peak the city fell to the Dauphin's forces, making the case for the new body even stronger. By August 1436, three masters had been appointed and in the following May the Pope granted the coveted status of *studium generale*. The institution did not really get off the ground until 1439 but then enjoyed a degree of success despite financial problems. In the first eleven years there were about 250 students at any one time, mostly from nearby in the dioceses of Bayeux and Coutances, but also including a small group of Italians from Milan, attracted by the Italian chancellor Zeno da Castiglione. This may seem like a very small student body but the older university at Cahors, for example, never had more than a few dozen students.[39] The university happily survived the fall of Normandy to the French king, to become a genuinely successful institution.

Another factor of perhaps equal importance was religious differences. The most important of these was the divisions caused by the Great Schism in the Church (see Chapter 5). Once a ruler had declared for the Roman pontiff as opposed to the Pope in Avignon, the universities in his realm were expected to follow suit. It became difficult, if not impossible, to recruit clergy or lay graduates from a university with the opposite allegiance. There was also the fact that some university teachers or masters disagreed violently with the choice made by, or forced on, their institution and were looking for opportunities elsewhere. Thus we find that a whole group of universities in Germany were founded after the rulers of this region had declared their support for the Pope in Rome. Students from this area who wished to study theology and the arts had formerly gone to Paris; France was now the centre of support for the Avignon Pope and going to university in Paris was no longer politically possible. The exodus from Paris re-invigorated both Prague and Vienna and helped found new universities at Erfurt (1379–89), Heidelberg (1385) and Cologne (1388), among other places. Cracow, which had initially not been a success, was also re-opened with the active support of the king, Ladislas Jagiellon. Other religious problems also had an impact on the fortunes of various universities. Prague was closely associated with support for the Hussites (John Hus was rector of the university in 1402), while Vienna, in Habsburg territory, was the centre for those who opposed them. The fact that Wyclif was an Oxford master and taught in the schools there for more than thirty years helped to cast a pall over the university throughout much of the fifteenth century, associating it with heresy, something which redounded to the benefit of Cambridge.

Cologne and Rostock (1419) in Brandenburg (both members of the Hanseatic League) are examples of universities that largely owed their foundation to the enthusiastic support of the leading citizens of these towns. Cologne had long had schools run by Dominicans and the other orders of friars but it was support from the city that was crucial to its success in becoming a fully-fledged university. This is a pleasant contrast to the situation in many other places, where the townsmen bitterly resented the students' privileges. It was only too easy for a brawl in an alehouse to spill over into rioting between the two groups. In Scotland, the initiative came not from townspeople but from the bishops, with St Andrews being founded by Bishop William Elphinstone, in 1411–12, Glasgow in 1451 and Aberdeen in 1494–5 although it did not begin to function until 1500.

Because of the fact that only the Papacy could issue the bull that gave an institution the status of a university, there was a degree of uniformity in the privileges of students and in the syllabus and the teaching methods throughout Europe. Technically all students had clerical status, usually being in minor orders (the lowest rank of the clergy). This did very little to restrain student behaviour and was largely forgotten by the fifteenth century but it was the justification for allowing students to escape the jurisdiction of town courts. The Clerk of Oxenford (Chaucer's model student from *The Canterbury Tales*) was a cleric, not a clerk in the modern sense of the word. He is described as studying logic, a subject from the Arts curriculum, and living in poverty on handouts from his friends.[40] The Arts was the lowest of the faculties, often being seen merely as a preparation for study in the higher faculties of Law, Theology and Medicine. Following the whole course from matriculation (registration) to acquiring the status of a regent or master took many years. It was not considered unusual or shameful to leave the university before graduating even as a bachelor (one step on the way to being a master). Once the status of master had been achieved there was an obligation to teach for a number of years. Spending a whole career as a teacher in the schools as Wyclif did was unusual.

Living from hand to mouth on the generosity of friends, like Chaucer's Clerk, was the lot of many students. During the fourteenth century, however, help perhaps became more easily available to students in difficulties. In Germany, poor students were often excused the fees or did not have to comply with regulations on dress or residence. At Oxford, some benefactors founded chests; these were literally large, secure wooden storage boxes. A student in need would deposit in the chest an item of value, often a book, as a pledge against the repayment of a loan provided from the charity funds of the donor. Other wealthier donors founded colleges, endowed residential institutions which made provision for fellows (teaching masters) and scholars. These offered greater security to the masters, most of whom in the older universities had had to rely on student fees for their income, and to the few, mostly advanced (post-bachelor), students who were included in the foundation. Colleges did not exist only in Oxford and Cambridge. In Prague in 1366, the Collegium Caroli (Charles College) was founded for twelve Masters of Arts: one was to teach the Bible using the usual set book of the *Sentences* of Peter Lombard. They would all be supported by benefices belonging to the Royal Collegiate Chapel of All Saints. In Vienna, a Ducal College was established in 1384 by Duke Albert of Habsburg, with rather similar conditions. In Cologne, in contrast, a college established in 1430 was financed by the bequests of two merchants, one from Westphalia and one from Alkmaar. This had a rector and twelve fellows, including a theologian, and canon and civil lawyers.

In France, the earliest college consisted simply of one room in the Hospital of the Blessed Mary of Paris, tucked alongside the West front of the cathedral of Notre Dame. In 1180 a certain Jocius of London bought the room from the hospital and endowed it for the support of eighteen scholars, with 'sufficient' beds (not necessarily one each) and a small monthly stipend. Much more splendid was the College of Navarre, founded in 1304 by Queen Joanna of Navarre for a total of 70 scholars, some studying Arts, but at least twenty being advanced students of Theology. There were separate kitchens, halls and dormitories for the various groups of students. The master or 'principal of the artists' (students studying the Arts) was expected to 'diligently hear the lessons of the Scholars studying in the Faculty of Arts and faithfully instruct them alike in life and in doctrine'.[41] Fifty colleges were founded in Paris in the fourteenth and fifteenth centuries.

It is hard to be precise about the age of those attending universities; in some places the Arts faculty was treated almost like a preparatory course, so that students might be only thirteen or fourteen. In other places students went straight to the advanced faculties of Law or Medicine since they had received tuition in grammar and logic elsewhere. There are some surprising references to students who were apparently in trouble with their courses because they could not read. This is the case at Vienna in 1455 and Heidelberg in 1466: it is fairly clear that a basic lack of literacy is implied, not an inability to understand advanced texts, since the Heidelberg students are instructed to listen in silence to a lecture (based on a text) and not distract their fellow students by chatting.[42]

We have much better information regarding the schools, deliberately designed to feed boys into university life, which were founded in this period in England. The most important of these are Winchester College (1379) and Eton College, each of which was linked to a sister foundation at a university;

Winchester to New College, Oxford, (1380s) and Eton to King's College, Cambridge. The 1440 foundation charter of Eton, a project very dear to the heart of Henry VI, lays down that the school will provide for:

> 70 scholars whose duty it is to learn the science of grammar and 16 choristers whose duty it shall likewise be when they have been sufficiently instructed in singing to learn grammar.

For this purpose there will be a master teacher and an 'usher'; the king's final hope for his school was that it should be 'called the lady mother and mistress of all other grammar schools'.[43] The statutes of King's College from 1443 lay down the kind of student to be admitted; they are to be:

> poor, indigent scholar clerks who have received the first tonsure [are in minor orders, see above] adorned with good manners and birth, sufficiently grounded in grammar, honest in conversation [well behaved], able and apt for study, desiring to proceed further in study not already graduates and not bound to any other college except our royal college of Eton.

A later statute sets out how Etonians wishing to go to King's are to be examined at the school in 'reading, plainsong, and Donatus'.[44] (Donatus was the standard Latin grammar textbook of medieval schools.) New humanist (see below) views on education are associated with Magdalen College School, Oxford, in the 1480s. John Anwykyll, the first headmaster of the school, prepared a new Latin grammar book for his boys. This may not sound very revolutionary, but Donatus had been written in the fourth century CE so the new book replaced one that was about a thousand years old. Its full Latin title, which refers to the fact that examples have been carefully collected from authors like the Italian grammarian Perotti, excluding what it calls 'barbarisms', makes clear that it was based on the work of Italian humanist scholars of the early Renaissance.[45] This book was also printed at the press of Theodoric Rood, the first printer in Oxford, whose workshop was set up in a building owned by Magdalen College.[46]

All this seems to link these schools with the new attitudes to learning which are associated with Italy and the new technology of printing. It has also been suggested that the Brethren of the Common Life (see Chapter 5) were largely responsible for opening schools in the Netherlands which taught in a more *humanist* way than either Louvain or Cologne, the nearest universities, both institutions associated with the old approach of *scholasticism*. The school at Deventer, which was attended by Erasmus, one of the most famous humanist scholars in Europe in the early sixteenth century, was run not by the Brethren but by the canons of the local cathedral. The headmaster, Alexander Hegius, introduced a humanist approach to the teaching of classics, something that greatly influenced his famous pupil. The school may have been the first north of the Alps to teach Greek. Other schools at pre-university level, particularly in the Netherlands and Germany, followed this example.

In general, the achievements of scholars in the fourteenth century have been acclaimed. Jacques Verger, who has written very widely on medieval universities, associates the early fourteenth century with 'dazzling' teaching of theology and law at Oxford, Paris and Bologna. He mentions Thomas Bradwardine, who eventually became archbishop of Canterbury, Bartolus Sassoferrato, who became a councillor to the Emperor Charles IV, and Nicolas d'Oresme, who was close to Charles V of France.[47] It might be thought that the disaster of the Black Death and the crisis of the Great Schism would undermine universities and make it difficult for them to maintain these high standards. It seems, however, that universities in Europe in general, including those in our study area, did not suffer as much as one might imagine from losses caused by plague. Numbers held up well (Cambridge, for example, doubled in size from 700 to 1,500 students in the fifteenth century) and may well have increased as a proportion of the population as a whole. As we have seen, many new foundations date from the last quarter of the fourteenth century or the first years of the fifteenth. Plague was seen by the end of the fourteenth century not as a disaster but as an unwelcome intruder breaking the continuity of learning. By this time the students of most universities dispersed into the countryside if plague broke out. The Great Schism had more potent effects. In Swanson's opinion,

> the years of the schism were the focal years for the transformation of medieval universities as they became increasingly fragmented, politicised, laicised, and diverted to other more local issues.[48]

It has also often been felt that in the fifteenth century, university curricula as a whole ossified. Many were still based on a set of texts that had to be studied at the various stages of the journey from newly enrolled student to regent master. Teaching is often said to have consisted largely of formal disputations concerning dry logical points which took little account of the new spirit of humanist study (the study of classical authors in their original language, with full attention to their style and meaning). It is certainly true that the works of Aristotle translated into Latin, and other set texts, dominated much learning. At the University of Pavia, Lorenzo Valla was so rude about his colleagues' lack of Greek and the inelegance of their Latin style that he was expelled. There were, however, some signs of change. Some courses at the College of the Sorbonne in Paris were updated. In Cambridge, John Doket, the provost of King's College, began to teach the ideas of some of the Italian *neo-Platonists* as an antidote to the excessive rationalism of scholasticism. Neo-Platonists fused the ideas of Plato with Christianity to produce a more mystical view of humanity and the world, including the important idea that 'Man is a microcosm of all creation, free to determine his destiny',[49] as an antidote to the excessive rationalism of scholasticism. ('Scholasticism' is the term used to describe the medieval philosophy based on the study of logic, especially using the works of Aristotle.) James Overfield has argued that in Germany humanists dedicated themselves to the improvement of university teaching and opening the curriculum up to humanist attitudes to scholarship. Peter Luder, at the University of Heidelberg in 1456, used his inaugural oration to promote the study of history, oratory and poetry, the basic elements of *studia humanitatis* (the term used for study in this new way). He finished in the words of Cicero: study of this kind can 'inspire youth, give pleasure in old age, embellish prosperity, offer escape and solace in adversity and give enjoyment at home'.[50]

The success of the campaign led by Luder is shown by the fact that every university in Germany, even that in Rostock, had courses in *studia humanitatis* by the 1490s.[51] We can also frequently trace connections between scholars from the northern universities and their colleagues south of the Alps.

Finally, it must be said that even if on occasion university statutes were abused, so that young nobles graduated without fulfilling all the requirements, or students seemed excessively rowdy, or the curriculum was dry as dust, there was still enough enthusiasm for the idea of the university for donors to endow colleges or other benefactions, and for many young men to exert themselves to attend them.

Humanists and lawyers

In England the spread of humanist ideas, outside universities, has been associated with Duke Humphrey of Gloucester, Henry V's youngest brother, and John Tiptoft, earl of Worcester. Duke Humphrey was in close contact with a number of Italian scholars, one of whom, Tito Livio Frulovisi, was commissioned to write a life of Henry V. Another was Zeno da Castiglione, whom we have already met as chancellor of the University of Caen. Duke Humphrey is also remembered for his munificent donations of books to Oxford; these amounted to nearly three hundred separate titles during his lifetime, which the University hoped to house in a specially built room over the new Divinity School.[52] Tiptoft was a student at University College Oxford in the 1440s but also studied in Italy at the University of Padua. He was an avid book collector, owning copies of newly discovered texts as well as two printed bibles, and certainly intended to be a generous benefactor to Oxford. But his execution in 1470 during the turmoil following Henry VI's restoration to the throne made it difficult for his executors to carry out his wishes. Weiss, however, cautions against making too much of these examples. In England, as in much of our study area, learning at the end of our period was a blend of the 'old' (scholasticism) and the 'new' (humanism), and often valued in a pragmatic way for its usefulness in diplomacy and in the study of philosophy and theology.[53]

Law stood apart from these studies in some respects. In France, Burgundy and the Empire the study of canon (Church) law led to prominent positions in Church courts. The study of Roman civil law led to an increasingly secure and lucrative career in royal service, whether in the courts or as a bureaucrat. In England, however, while careers could be made in the Church courts in much the same way as in the rest of Europe the system of law in the royal courts was different and required a different form of professional training. The practices of the Courts of King's Bench and of Common Pleas were grounded on English common law, a system based largely on precedent and not on the writings of Justinian, which were studied in law schools like that of Bologna or Orleans. This had led by the mid-fourteenth century to the establishment of the Inns of Court in London, where young lawyers could be educated. These were not formal law schools but vocational training colleges, to use modern phraseology. The emphasis was on learning the techniques of pleading in the courts and the drafting of documents, by a mixture of apprenticeship and mock trials or moots, not on the study of abstract principles of law.[54] The training was seen as useful for any gentleman who had property or might wish to be involved in public affairs, since many students of the Inns never practised as lawyers. However, those who did gain acceptance as 'utter barristers' (those who finished their training and were qualified to plead in the King's Bench and other royal courts), found this in many cases a path to social advancement and even wealth.

Printing

As we have seen, the universities were no longer the only places were contacts might be made with scholars. Moreover, from the middle of the century the development and spread of printing greatly increased the possible number of accurate copies of a book and the choice of reading. It also notably reduced the price of written material. The idea of using inked carved blocks to produce multiple copies of a picture or even of a small amount of text had been put into practice in the late fourteenth century. The woodcut of the torture of St Erasmus is a good example of this kind of production (see Illustration 16).

The technical development which made printing so powerful a tool in the dissemination of learning and information was the use of moveable type, individual letters cast in metal, which could be put together in a frame to make up a text and then re-used many times. The first person to do this was not, according to a tradition in the sixteenth century, Johann Gutenberg of Mainz, but Janszoon Coster of Haarlem.[55] Gutenberg was, however, certainly responsible for the success of the new technology; his first surviving work is a proclamation of an indulgence from 1454, while his great printed bible dates from about the same time. This new, commercially successful technology rapidly spread to other towns in Germany, including Nuremberg and Strasbourg, and to Italy where two German printers set up a press in Subiaco, moving to Rome in 1467. Paris had a press before 1470, while by 1500 there were nine important presses in the Netherlands, including Deventer, Louvain and Antwerp. William Caxton first set up a press in Bruges to produce books and other items for the English market in 1474, and moved to Westminster in 1476.

The influence of printing in universities, however, seems at first to have been muted. Most had a well developed system of scribes copying books in sections, which were then hired out quite cheaply to the students as needed. Libraries (in which the most heavily used books were sometimes chained to the reading desks) had become more common and better endowed. Erfurt, for example, had a library of over 1,400 books by 1433. Printers tended to set up business in commercial centres like London or Venice rather than in university towns. Where they did print textbooks these were aimed more at schoolboys than scholars: Donatus's Latin grammar was an early 'bestseller'. The great explosion in the printing of classical texts in handsome editions in the original Greek or Latin, associated with, for example, the Aldine Press in Venice, did not occur until the early years of the sixteenth century.

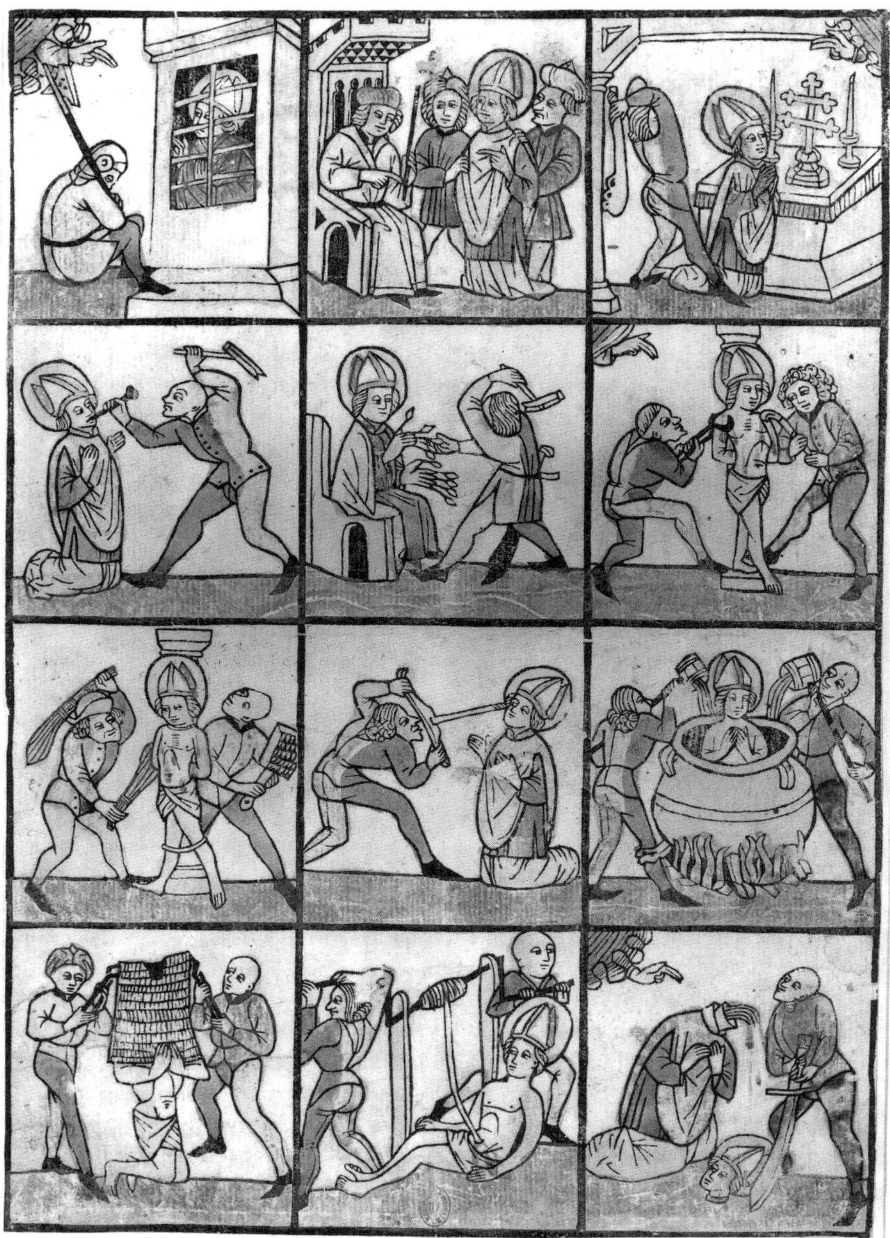

16 The martyrdom of St Erasmus

This woodcut of the truly horrible death of St Erasmus was made and printed in the early fifteenth century before the printing of books and other texts with moveable type had begun. It shows how printing led to the wide dissemination of all kinds of information, here a popular 'horror story' with a religious slant. The woodcut also gives an idea of how the cult of saints was seen by ordinary laypeople.

Printers' work did mean, however, that lay men and women had easier access to a much wider range of written material than ever before. By 1500, some 36,000 separate titles had been issued from the presses of Europe, the average size of an edition being around 1,000 copies.[56] Larissa Taylor has shown that there was a great demand for printed collections of sermons and related preaching aids: over 5,000 were produced in France between 1460 and 1500.[57] Readers could also have much greater confidence in the accuracy of the text of any printed book, especially a copy of a classical text. The reading and enjoyment of books of all kinds was thus more widely spread in society by the end of the fifteenth century. Romances, histories, instructional manuals and religious texts were supplied to an eager market. Two of the first books printed by Caxton in Bruges were an edition of stories about the siege of Troy and a book on how to play chess; in Westminster the early output of his press included a book about manners for boys, *The Canterbury Tales*, and two editions of the most popular English prayer book of the day, the Sarum Hours.

In our period the world of learning expanded rapidly. New universities were founded in large numbers; schools with clear aims and clearly drawn up statutes also appeared. Education was moving away from the exclusive control of the Church and was no longer seen as really only of importance for intending clergy. This did not mean, however, that universities in particular were able to act freely and without any interference from the authorities. Rather, it seems that as the influence of ecclesiastics declined, the influence of the ruler increased. We have already seen the important role that reasons of dynastic or civic pride played in the foundation of some new institutions. Rulers did not relinquish control of their university once it was established. In the same way the older universities found the state more and more prepared to take an interest in their affairs. The reform of the University of Paris in 1452 was largely motivated, according to Verger, by the desire, 'to restore order to an institution whose repeated strikes, critical spirit and corporate arrogance were particularly irritating to the king'.[58] At Oxford, Edward IV insisted on the replacement of George Neville as chancellor after the involvement of the head of the Neville family, the earl of Warwick, in the temporary return of Henry VI. The university's attempt to placate Edward and retain his goodwill by then appointing Lionel Woodville (a relation of the queen) to this position came unstuck when Richard III insisted on Woodville's removal in 1483, after Richard's seizure of the throne.[59]

The greater openness of learning in the later fifteenth century, coupled with the growing spread of printed books, made both schools and universities attractive to young men both of gentle birth and with ambitions to rise in society. At the same time it brought these institutions to the attention of rulers and reinforced their desire to have some say in their organisation and control.

(iii) URBAN CULTURE

Town life

Did some of the current of innovation in cultural life filter down to the ordinary townspeople, prefiguring the changes associated with the Renaissance? Were towns in general characterised by a more vibrant and exciting way of life, one with more varied cultural opportunities, than could be found in villages? We are, of course, dealing with a period of some one hundred and fifty years and a wide range of different societies spread over much of northern Europe. Any generalisations attempted must be viewed with some suspicion. We should also not forget the disadvantages of urban life as well as discussing the possible benefits.

Towns in our period suffered from high death rates; infectious diseases naturally flourished in the crowded and unhygienic conditions found in most of them. The frequent recurrence of the plague in the years after 1348 only served to emphasise this aspect of urban life and it became usual, for those who could, to leave a town when plague broke out, in the hope of escaping the infection. Yet despite this, towns continued to attract immigrants from the countryside. Although there are no freemen's registers for London we know that over 46 per cent of the apprentices of London skinners and tailors came not just from outside London but specifically from the north of England. The records of the little town of Romney in Kent reveal that half of the freemen were born within five miles of the town but others came from all over East Kent and about a quarter came from over fifty miles away. A town was attractive not only for the economic opportunities which it represented but also because of other features like religious sites or shrines, or the seat of government and the attendant courts. It is hard to estimate the 'pull' of urban culture compared with these more practical matters but to contemporaries town life was clearly worth the risks. This ensured that the proportion of the population living in towns did not fall and may even have increased during the late Middle Ages.

Once he had arrived in a town, the sheer variety of trades and skills pursued by the inhabitants would probably have amazed a country boy. In the 1260s a *Livre des Métiers* (Book of Trades) was drawn up in Paris which listed 101 different crafts, mostly in the textile, leather, building and metal trades and in the supply of food and drink. London had no similar list but 51 crafts were involved in the elections to the Common Council in 1377. The town of Beverley addressed the members of 37 different trades including occupations like coverlet weavers and *latteners* (makers of items in a kind of brass), when establishing the obligation on the craftsmen of the town to participate in the celebration of Corpus Christi.

By the fourteenth century, in many but not all towns, the ability to pursue a craft would depend on the membership of the appropriate guild. Although there were local variations the main features of this system could be found throughout our study area. An apprenticeship was necessary in order to learn a trade, a process that could take anything between one and twelve years. An apprentice would hope to become a journeyman (from the French *journée*, meaning 'day'), working by the day for a master. The master ran the workshop and would normally be eligible for full rights as a burgess, burgher or freeman of the town concerned. It must be remembered, however, that not all crafts were rigidly separated from others using similar tools or materials. In London, potters made spurs and candlesticks as well as brass pots, while in the fifteenth century the leather-based crafts of glovers, pursers, *whittawyers* (tanners of white leather) and pouchmakers amalgamated with the leather sellers' guild. The term 'guild', however, was used not only for trade organisations but also for those whose original purpose was social or religious, helping members who were sick or who needed a decent burial or who shared a devotion to a particular saint. All these functions could be combined in the trade guild, along with a desire not only to control the quality of work in a trade but also to regulate entry to it and the terms on which it operated. In Flanders, for example, in the fifteenth century, only those who owned a shop and employed journeymen to do the actual work could have mastership in a guild.

Guilds also had a place in civic life, being involved in the ceremonial at public events like, for example, the wedding of Charles the Bold and Margaret of York in Flanders in 1468. The wedding party came in procession from Damme, where the bride had landed, to Bruges. At the city gates the welcoming party included the guilds as well as foreign merchants and clerics. Such events also contributed to the excitement of living in a town for even the humblest of the people. We have already described (see Chapter 2) the elaborate welcoming pageant put on in London for Henry V on his return from Agincourt. Another example of the importance of ceremonial and spectacle in town life would be the Joyous Entries made by the rulers of the Netherlands into the chief cities usually on acceding to power. The funeral procession of Philip the Good of Burgundy in Bruges in June 1467 was also watched by some 20,000 townspeople. They were clothed in black at their own expense and were expected to keep absolutely still and silent as the cortege passed; in this way they were in effect part of the event, not just spectators.[60]

Though towns might suffer very severely from dearth in times of food shortages it is also the case that the authorities in many cases took great care to regulate the sale of food and drink in their town. This could take the form of trying to ensure supplies in bad times, something that was most unlikely to happen in the countryside in similar circumstances. Both Ghent and Bruges used public stocks of grain to alleviate the distress in the cities in 1436–8 and in the 1480s. In Aberdeen the corporation sometimes bought whole cargoes of grain or salt to sell on at a reasonable price. More usually the town council and its officers tried to control quality and to prevent prices rising beyond what was considered fair. Both what were known as *forestalling* (buying up goods before they reached the market in order to force up the price) and *regrating* (buying goods in a market to sell later at a higher price) were regarded with great disfavour and could be punished by fines imposed by the town court. In 1372 in London, a man admitted forestalling three thousand eggs; the eggs were confiscated and resold at a lower price. Also in London in 1422, a group of people were brought to the court accused of buying up fish, cheese, chickens and other foodstuffs directly from boatmen on the quay at Queenshythe in the evening in order to sell them later. Their plot came to nothing when the stench from the fish led to its discovery.[61] Earlier, in 1382, the city authorities forced a fishmonger to reduce the price of his herrings. The original price agreed was 6 for a penny to the hucksters (street sellers), so that they could charge 5 for a penny to their customers. He was, however, discovered to have made an agreement with a man from outside London to sell him herrings at 10 for a penny. The record states that 'he and all other freemen were bound of right to sell to their neighbours at as low a rate as to strangers or even cheaper'.

Thus the Mayor and Aldermen insisted that he must sell his herrings at 9 to the penny within the city and no more.[62]

In France there was a similar concern to control prices and prevent fraud; in the market at Montpazier in Gascony, stone vessels, which are standard grain measures, still exist in the market hall.[63] Townsmen in France also seem to have had a considerable degree of access to lands and gardens near the town where they could produce their own food and wine, which somewhat lessened their dependence on supplies brought from some distance. Around Toulouse and Arles, for example, there were large areas under vines which belonged to the townspeople and which were used to supply their needs. At Tours no less than 170 litres of wine per head was produced from vineyards owned by the citizens.

In both English and French towns there were regulations to control the quality of bread and wine or ale on sale in the town as well as the prices charged. There is some evidence from archaeological investigations that the diet, at least for some people, in a medieval town was relatively healthy (and should have ensured a reasonable life expectancy provided they survived the many infectious diseases). Investigation of bones from a cemetery in London largely dating from the eleventh and twelfth centuries revealed that only 17 per cent suffered from a deficiency disease. Further study of a larger group of remains from the tenth to the fifteenth centuries showed that the average heights of both men and women did not differ radically from those of a late nineteenth-century population.[64] The height of adults has been considered as a reliable indicator of the overall health and nutrition of a population.

Taverns, alehouses and inns were a common and welcome feature of town life. Inns had rooms for travellers, and by the end of our period the best equipped provided a fair degree of comfort. There was even an inn at St Paul's Wharf in London in 1390, which could offer a 'suite' of rooms. Taxing the sale of alcoholic drink was common: in 1405 the city of Toulouse raised over a quarter of its revenue from a tax on the sale of wine. Prostitution, traditionally defined as the 'oldest profession', also flourished in late medieval towns. Many German towns in the fifteenth century, including Nuremberg, Munich and Strasbourg, had set up brothels controlled by the town council; in Lübeck, prostitutes had their own guild.[65] It was also common for prostitution to be confined to a particular area of the town. This was the case in London, where the 'stews' were to be found south of the river in Southwark, and it was also the case in Perpignan. In Paris, prostitutes were divided into two groups: those working in brothels, and those who plied their trade in dark alleys, cemeteries or by the city walls. This latter group had no official recognition and were liable to be brought before the courts.[66]

In old age or sickness, some form of charitable care was much more likely to be available in an urban than in a rural setting. It was not uncommon for guilds to provide for members who had fallen on hard times. This happened in both Bruges and Ghent, and also in London where the Grocers' Company built a range of almshouses, financed by a gift from Robert Knolles in the 1430s.[67] More general charities also existed for the care of the sick and aged; in Nuremberg the Mendel Foundation provided[68] for poor and honest artisans who had fallen on hard times, offering asylum to craftsmen who ranged from chain-mail makers, to wooden shoemakers and city scribes.[69] The full extent of the poor relief available in Ghent in the fourteenth century has been shown by Nicholas: it included two orphanages, a leper hospital, and special institutions for the blind, poor foreigners, old ladies and the insane.[70]

The physical appearance of a town would always have differentiated it sharply from the rural world of the village. In the first place the great majority of towns in north-western Europe were walled; this clearly marked the boundary between urban and rural space. Within the walls, even after the depopulation caused by the Black Death, buildings were much more closely packed together than in a village and we have already mentioned in Chapter 2 the very high densities which have been calculated for some towns. The typical *burgage tenement* (standard urban landholding) in an English town had a relatively short frontage to the main street but was fairly deep, allowing for quite a long garden and warehouses or workshops to exist behind the main building. This plan can still be seen in many towns today, although frequently, in later periods, side roads were run across the original burgage plots. In the centre of the town, round the market square, most towns erected public buildings, many of which were enlarged or renewed in our period. Norwich rebuilt its old Toll House as a Gild Hall when its new charter allowed for the election of a mayor in 1404. In 1429, the town also undertook the repair of the town mills on the river Wensum. This was clearly necessary but the new works caused upstream flooding and claims against the corporation.

Our period also saw the erection of public buildings on a grander scale. This is particularly noticeable in the towns of the Hanseatic League in northern Germany. In Bremen the town hall or *Rathaus* was rebuilt in 1405–10 and occupied one side of the large market place. Although the present appearance of the exterior dates from 1595, the *Untere Rathaus* or lower trading hall, inside the building, by its sheer size gives us an impression of the vigour of the trading which took place there. Outside the hall stands a very large statue of Roland, one of Charlemagne's knights and a hero of many romances, which was placed there in 1404. This well expressed the way in which Bremen saw itself as part of the wider European community. To contemporaries the statue also symbolised the rights granted to the town traditionally by Charlemagne himself.[71] In Lübeck, the leading town in the Hanseatic League, the public buildings were mostly built or renewed in the late fourteenth and fifteenth centuries when the city became the largest town in Germany apart from Cologne. One of the most impressive of the surviving buildings from that period is the Holstein Gate or *Holstentor*, the entrance to the city from the south. This was modelled on the gates of Bruges by the designer Heinrich Helmstede and built between 1469 and 1478. The two towers capped with conical roofs loom over those approaching, while the central gate itself is decorated with friezes and arcades. No visitor could fail to understand that he was entering a powerful and wealthy town (see Illustration 17).

In Brabant, the element of competition between the leading towns was a powerful spur to the erection of splendid public buildings. Both Louvain and Brussels erected new town halls in the fifteenth century. That in Brussels was specifically designed to express its position as the leading city in the county, and its close connection with the court of the dukes of Burgundy. As well as a façade with

17 Holstentor gate of Lübeck, the leading town of the Hanseatic League

The buildings to the right are storehouses used for salt by merchants.

over 200 statues, the new town hall had a balcony, on which it was intended that the duke would appear with the city council on the occasion of his Joyous Entry. Blockmans and Prevenier point out that the tower of the town hall triumphed 'over all the other towers in the city' including those of the churches.[72]

Inside the town itself, the houses of the people would vary, from those built quickly by speculators to let, like those round the market place in Coventry put up by the Prior of St Mary's Abbey, to the palaces of the great. We can cite here the examples of John of Gaunt's Palace of the Savoy, just outside the gates of London on the Strand, or the magnificent house built in Bourges, for the merchant and financier Jacques Coeur. By the end of the fifteenth century, chimneys and glazed windows could be found in even quite modest town houses, greatly improving the living conditions of those who had suffered from the smoky dark rooms of earlier times.

Perhaps the best way of appreciating the lifestyle that by our period was within the reach of successful town dwellers is to read the description of the guildsmen from the *General Prologue* to Chaucer's *Canterbury Tales*. Chaucer, as the son of a London vintner, came from this level of society and knew it well. His group of townsmen includes a haberdasher, a carpenter, a weaver, a dyer and a tapestry maker. They are, therefore, all artisans, the 'middling sort' in town society, not from the elite merchant guilds. They are, however, well dressed, with knives with silver mounts, clearly wealthy and expecting the respect of fellow citizens. Their wives, explains Chaucer, particularly enjoy their status:

> It is very fine to be called, 'my lady'
> And go to feasts on holiday eves leading the procession,
> And have a gown with a train royally carried.

These men no longer dined on the potage of peasants but on dishes like 'poudre-marchant tart', roasts and pies, all washed down with good draughts of London ale.[73]

Even if many could not hope for such a standard of living we can still understand from this and the other amenities and excitements of urban life, why the lure of towns remained potent throughout our period.

Guilds, processions and plays

The feasts these guildsmen so enjoyed were, of course, a different aspect of a guild's functions from the concern with crafts and trades already mentioned. John Bossy has described guilds and fraternities as 'the most characteristic expressions of late medieval Christianity.'[74] Fraternities were virtually indistinguishable from guilds, although they were sometimes founded with the express intention of promoting a particular objective: hunting, music-making or a religious practice such as devotion to Christ, the Virgin or a particular saint. Membership of fraternities might include university students, nobles, priests and other orders of society who would not usually have participated in craft or merchant guilds. Whilst women sometimes joined the latter they were regularly recognised as full members of fraternities, although they never held official positions within them. Fraternities were immensely popular with the laity in the late Middle Ages: in Great Yarmouth about eighteen flourished, from 1430 to 1530, and in Geneva there were thirty-eight in 1487. Some were short-lived: Caroline Barron shows, for example, that the fraternity founded in honour of the Conception of the Virgin in the parish of St Sepulchre at Newgate, London, by 'poor people of the parish' before 1349, only lasted for a few decades.[75] In this case the low status of the members may have contributed to its brief existence: some fraternities that are known to have been founded in about the same period were still flourishing in the reign of Henry VIII.

There were national variations in the degree of popularity of the patrons of fraternities. Whilst Christ and the Virgin were adopted universally there was, for example, a particularly strong devotion to the Holy Spirit in France. In many cases these fraternities included the whole population of a parish; their chief purpose was to hold a dinner at Pentecost (the commemoration of the time when the Holy Spirit descended upon the apostles), distribute food to their members at the same time, and say Masses for the dead. There seems to have been little which distinguished associations of this kind from the activities of congregations in ordinary, well-functioning parishes: it could be that they provided a congenial and religious means by which wealthier members could help the poor. In the case of both guilds and fraternities, their religious and social activities made up a very important element in urban culture. Since their functions in these areas overlapped to a great extent we will use the word 'guild' to refer to them both.

Churches, chapels and altars would often have a link with a particular guild: this might be because there was an obvious reason for the association, for example, St Christopher was the patron of water carriers, or because members had a special devotion to a saint, to the Virgin or to Christ. They would attend Masses together on occasions that had significance for the guild, such as the feast of their patron saint, or when one of them was to be buried. Although the services were conducted by priests, the timing and, to some extent, the content were decided by the lay guildsmen. Their patronage could bring considerable amounts of revenue to a church and its priests and this gave them influence in an ecclesiastical preserve.

A 1389 description of the rules of the guild of the Tilers of Lincoln typifies the mixture of religious and secular values that were characteristic of these associations:

> The gild of the Tilers of Lincoln, commonly called 'Pointers', was founded AD 1346.
>
> Every incomer shall make himself known to the Graceman, but must be admitted by the common consent of the guild, and be sworn to keep the ordinances. And each shall give a quarter of barley, and pay iid to the ale, and id to the Dean.
>
> Four 'soulcandles' shall be found [provided], and used in the burial services.
>
> A feast shall be held on the festival of Corpus Christi; and, on each day of the feast, they shall have three flagons, and four or six tankards; ale shall be given to the poor; and prayers shall be said over the flagons.
>
> Pilgrims shall be helped.
>
> Burials shall be provided for, by the Graceman, the two Wardens and the Dean [guild officials].
>
> If any brother does anything underhanded and with ill-will, by which another will be wronged in working his craft, he shall pay to the guild a pound of wax, without any room for grace.
>
> No tiler nor 'pointer' shall stay in the city, unless he enters the guild.[76]

Religious processions, especially those to mark the great feasts of the year (often also popular holidays), were an important part of the culture of most towns. Whilst some villages were too remote to participate in them, in densely populated areas such as the Netherlands and southern England, many country people would travel to watch them: they could be very elaborate and contain dramatic elements. In Leuven in the Netherlands, for example, a procession for the Virgin contained tableaux of scenes from her life, drawn on carts. They were followed by walking episodes concerning holy women of the Old Testament (each sponsored by a different guild), including Sarah, Rebecca, Ruth and Jael; the last carried a hammer and was followed by the lecherous Sisera with a nail in his head. These parts would almost certainly have been played by men and boys, for Lynette Muir suggests that it was rare for women to take parts in public shows or performances before the sixteenth century.[77]

Peter Arnade's study of Ghent exemplifies the social and political influence that prosperous guilds could enjoy in a community. He argues that it is impossible to distinguish clearly between the sacred and the secular in discussing the religious ceremonies and processions that took place.[78] The city's four large parish churches housed chapels of several guilds as well as of numerous religious fraternities: the most important was the weavers' guild and there were fifty-three lesser guilds for crafts dealing with other aspects of the textile trade, transport and the sale of local goods.

The greatest civic event of the year was a procession in late July which carried the relics of the local martyr, St Lieven, from an abbey in Ghent to the village of Houtem (where a fair was held) and back again. It was accompanied by many guildsmen in their liveries with flags, musicians, theatrical troupes and persons of all ages and backgrounds, and was symbolic of the wealth, power and solidarity of the citizens. Such harmony was not always easy to achieve, however: in 1430 the parish church of St Nicholas and guild officials had to resolve a potentially damaging dispute about which guild would have the coveted place next to the Holy Sacrament in the annual Corpus Christi procession. On this occasion the prestigious mercers had to yield to the fruitmongers and be content with a place between the cheese merchants and fishmongers. The enthusiasm with which the guilds and fraternities organised and participated in the great religious festivals seems to have been closely linked to their commitment to help their city remain semi-independent.

In the later Middle Ages the religious processions connected with the great feasts of the Church or with popular local saints were sometimes enhanced or even replaced by plays: the Leuven procession marked a typically transitional event. Dramatic representations were not a new phenomenon within the Church: for centuries priests and monks had arranged for tableaux and animated portrayals of some episodes from the Bible as a means of instructing and inspiring the laity and this liturgical drama continued in some places until the sixteenth century. Philippe de Mézières, for example, wrote a play of the Presentation of Mary for her feast day (2 February, called 'Candlemas' in England), which was performed for over a decade in Avignon in the late fourteenth century. There were also bands of professional entertainers who roamed Europe performing interludes and dramas as well as working as acrobats, jugglers and fire-eaters. The Church generally disapproved of these groups and the secular authorities regarded them as little better than beggars.

The Mystery Plays, which were regularly performed from the fourteenth to the sixteenth centuries, were altogether more elaborate and expensive to stage than liturgical or entertainers' dramas. 'Mystery', like the French 'mystères' and German 'mysterienspeil', refers to the service or occupation of those who performed the plays. The plays were cycles portraying episodes from the Bible, from the Creation to the Last Judgement, usually performed to coincide with a great feast, often Corpus Christi. The presence of the Host in some of the processions or the plays was calculated to increase the piety of onlookers. In Innsbruck, for example, in the play of the Three Kings, it was placed on an altar and the kings made their offerings to it rather than to the Virgin. Conversely, when the Sacrament was not present the behaviour of both the players and the crowd could be less than reverential. Joseph, for example, expressed his doubts about the paternity of her child robustly to Mary:

> Ah, such words make me full sorry,
> With great mourning to make my moan.
> Therefore be not so bold,
> That no such tales be told,
> But hold thee still as stone.
> Thou art young and I am old –
> Such works if I do would
> Those games from me are gone!
> Therefore tell me privately,
> Whose is the child thou is with now?[79]

By the late Middle Ages responsibility for financing and performing plays had been largely taken over by merchants and tradesmen in the towns. The characteristically close involvement of the guilds is demonstrated by this extract from the Burgh Records of Aberdeen in 1442; it relates to a play which was performed at Candlemas:

> the tailors shall find [provide]
> our Lady, saint Bridget, saint Helen, Joseph
> and as many squires as they may
>
> the skinners shall find
> two bishops, four angels and as many honest
> squires as they may
>
> the websters [weavers] and walkers [fullers of cloth] shall find
> Simeon and his disciples and as many honest
> Squires, etc.[80]

The Spurriers and Lorimers (makers of spurs and horse bits) in York in 1494 ordered that:

> Every master of the said craft upon Corpus Christi day every year shall be present with the pageant wagon [on which the play was performed] from the time the play begins at the first place until such time as the play is played and finished at the last place in the town and whosoever is absent at any place unless he is sick or has another reasonable excuse shall forfeit 2s in the manner aforesaid.[81]

The honour of the guild, no small matter to its members, required that all should be seen to take part in events like this.

Saint (or Miracle) Plays were very popular in Europe: copies of over a hundred survive in France alone and these do not include the guilds' performances that enacted the lives of their patron saints. The Virgin was the most regular subject; a number concentrated on her childhood as well as on her place in the life of Christ. In comparison with France, very few Saint Plays were performed in England or Germany. The choice of saints could have political connotations: national and local heroes and heroines were popular. St George had originally been venerated in France, but perhaps because Edward III of England chose him as the national saint during the early stages of the Hundred Years War, the only time a play of his life was performed there was during the English occupation of the north of the country in the 1420s. St George figured prominently in English Mummers' Plays, which were performed by ordinary people in towns and villages. In most cases little evidence survives about the authorship of Mystery or Saint Plays: many were performed for a considerable number of years and were probably adapted by different people as time passed. They were likely to have been originally composed by clerics: in the texts that survive there are some bawdy, secular episodes but the religious content is treated in an orthodox fashion.

The Morality Plays were another type of religious drama that was developed, probably in England, in the course of the fifteenth century. They were more abstract and conceptual than the strongly narrative Mystery and Saint Plays and more likely to have been composed by a single author to appeal to the increasingly well-educated urban bourgeoisie. *The Castle of Perseverance*, the most elaborate of the English Morality plays that are known to survive, traces the temptations of a symbolic figure, 'Mankind'. He is assailed by people representing the World, the Flesh and the Devil and by all kinds of particular vices, like Backbiter and Gluttony. For a time he is rescued by his Good Angel and by various virtues, who protect him in their castle, but he relapses. Returning to the sins of the world he eventually dies and is mocked by them as he is taken off to Hell: yet the mercy of God still prevails and he is rescued and admitted to Heaven. The genre of Morality Plays was widely adopted in northern Europe: *Everyman*, the best known of all, originated in the Netherlands. These plays marked the growing sophistication of a laity for whom thieving shepherds and farting devils no longer possessed such fascination.

The performance of Mystery, Saint and Morality Plays could take place in various locations and be presented in a number of styles. Since many of the guild plays were associated with processions and religious festivals they were seen in the street. They might be performed in a series of fixed booths or stages, the number depending on how many plays were to be presented, or they could be enacted on wagons that were drawn to various parts of the town in the course of a day or of several days. Alternatively plays could be enacted in a large open space, a square or an area on the edge of town. Some of these latter were staged in the round: in Jean Fouquet's miniature of the martyrdom of St Apollonia, in a play in France (see Illustration 18), the area was enclosed within a fence and a hedge, part of the action taking place in the arena, part in fixed booths on the periphery.[82] Onlookers were not normally expected to pay to see religious plays and the most the actors could expect would be small gifts of wine or contributions towards their expenses. The existence of the enclosure in the Fouquet picture, however, implies that there might have been some circumstances in which charges were made. Religious drama could also be enacted in great halls: the English bishops at the Council of Constance arranged a feast for their continental fellows in 1417 and

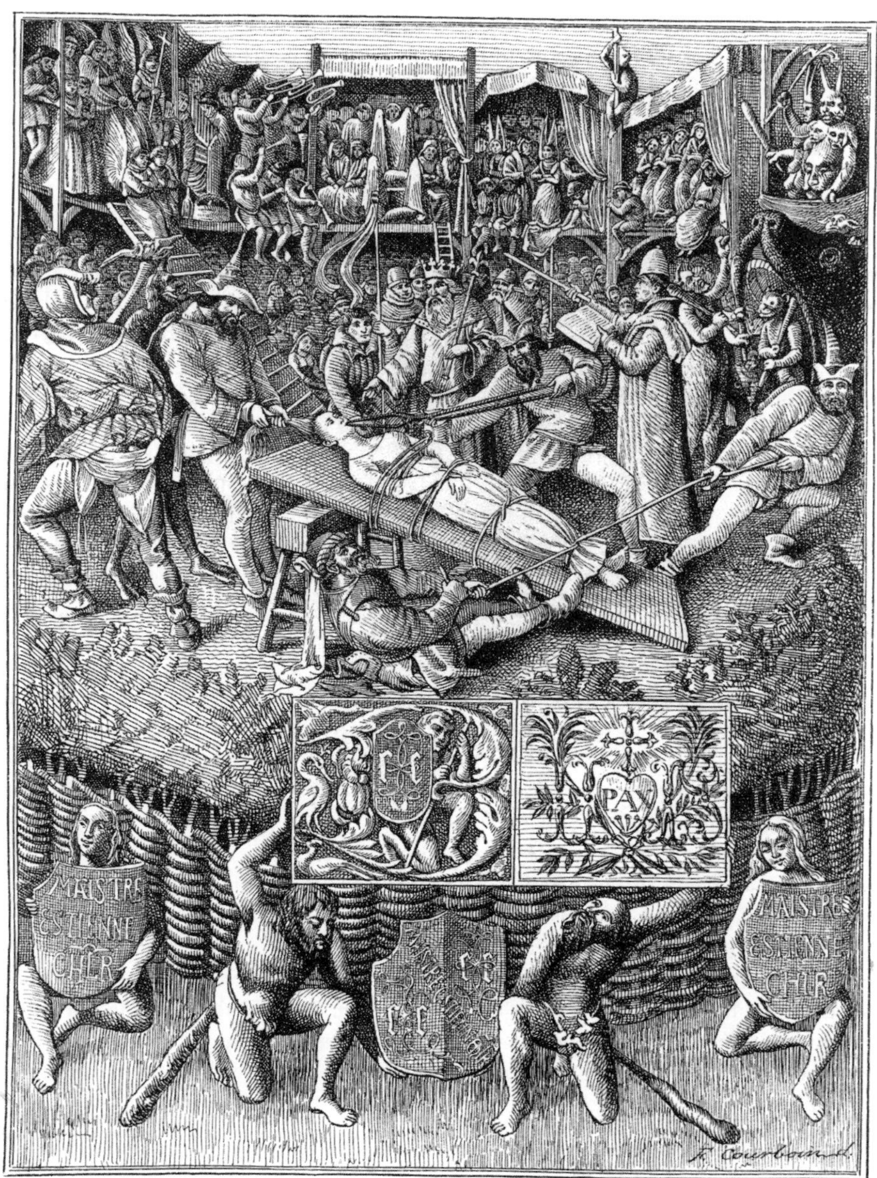

18 The martyrdom of St Apollonia

This image of the martyrdom of St Apollonia from Jean Fouquet's miniature *c.* 1455 was engraved for Bapst's *Essai sur l'histoire du théatre* (Paris, 1893). The saint's teeth are being brutally pulled out. The action takes place in a theatre in the round enclosed within a fence and containing five scaffolds as well as the central area occupied by players in the foreground and the audience at the back.

between the first and second courses a play of the Nativity was performed. This type of performance was, in a sense, restoring religious drama to the Church where it had started: by the fifteenth century the laity had made substantial inroads into its monopoly as interacting spectators, producers and players.

CONCLUSION

In this chapter we have looked at the issue of cultural change in both the upper levels of medieval society and also the more mundane world of townsmen and women. Perhaps the first conclusion to draw is to emphasise the degree to which these apparently different aspects of late medieval society interacted. The Joyous Entry of the duke of Burgundy into one of the leading towns of his possessions in the Netherlands was at once an opportunity for the court to show itself at its most splendid and a means to make plain its authority. The town could demonstrate its wealth and the townspeople could contribute their presence to what was almost a form of theatre. In the same fashion, if we consider the world of the universities and of learning we can see that many aspects of university life had changed little since their first beginnings. Overwhelmingly the method of teaching was the same, as was the structure of faculties and degrees. However, the student body was no longer mainly made up of intending clerics or the dedicated wandering scholars of the early medieval period but of the gentry or nobility of the area, leavened by a much smaller proportion of those intending ordination. Swanson described the secularisation of universities in somewhat disparaging terms but this trend brought them much more into the main stream of contemporary life. Similarly, reading, once the recreation of a small minority of the elite, was becoming a leisure activity for many, and a necessity for those in an increasing number of occupations.

Conversely, we can also discern developments which tended to mark clearer boundaries between different levels of society and between the learning of the elite and those of lower status. If courts did have the political influence which has been claimed for them, it was easier for a ruler to be aloof from the mass of his people and increasingly to draw more and more power into his own hands and those of his immediate advisers. It could be argued that this would be a step on the way to the more powerful centralised monarchies of sixteenth- and seventeenth-century Europe. Similarly, as enthusiasm for humanist learning grew among learned men both inside and outside universities this would set them further apart from the culture of everyday people with its mixture of custom, tradition, and religion, based much more on experience and celebrations than on the study of texts.

Perhaps it may be better to see society in our chosen study area as becoming more diverse and more open. The old threefold division into those who fought, those who prayed and those who worked was beginning to lose its force. Particularly in large prosperous towns, greater opportunities were opened up. Printing had made books available in unheard of variety and quantity. Even if little had changed on the surface, new currents of thought were increasing in strength. Many of these have been associated by historians with the advent of the Renaissance. Little in the world of townsmen, however, seems to hint at the wholesale rejection of many of the most popular features of urban cultural life, so intimately bound up with religious celebrations, which was to characterise the Reformation in northern Europe. Features like the Corpus Christi plays performed by guildsmen and the use of both private and public funds for the erection of buildings with communal purposes seem to be at a peak in the fifteenth century.

Drawing conclusions about the significance of princely courts seems more problematic though it is not clear that this is due to an increasing appreciation of national differences and a new sense of national identity among either princes or their people. Clearly courts were sophisticated and cultured places but conclusions about their political importance perhaps depend more on the personality and fortunes of the ruler concerned than on any inherent feature of the institution itself. It is certainly possible to see northern Europe in the fifteenth century as culturally and intellectually backward compared with the Italian city states. Colin Richmond's view of the 'badness of English art in the fifteenth century',[83] and the more general view that later medieval universities 'manifested the symptoms of organisational and intellectual decline',[84] have perhaps obscured the fact that, in northern Europe, much of the most admired so-called medieval art and architecture dates from our period rather than from the thirteenth or fourteenth centuries.

Conclusion

The Preface to this book quoted Guenée's view that the fourteenth and fifteenth centuries were 'part of a transitional period when the medieval state gradually gave way to the modern'.[1] The extent to which this was true of the political, social, economic, religious and cultural history of north-western Europe has been a major concern of this book. The arguments of historians about this issue have polarised around two kinds of question. Were culture, beliefs, political and economic institutions so decayed that they would be swept away by the Renaissance, Reformations and technological advances of the early modern period? Conversely, were many of these developments already under way by the late Middle Ages so that continuity rather than change predominated? The views expressed in this book have tended to favour the second version of history.

In social and economic terms the impact of the Black Death, with the consequent fall in population and labour shortages, initiated a period of stagnation and conflict over rights between landlords and their peasants. The latter proved unwilling to accept any longer unreasonable feudal obligations or excessive taxation and popular revolts taught their masters the practical limits of their powers. Land was relatively plentiful in Britain, France and western Germany, agricultural prosperity was gradually restored and the peasants managed to discard many of their feudal burdens. In the eastern parts of the Empire, where frontier conditions still prevailed, some lay and ecclesiastical landowners began to enforce a new and harsher form of serfdom on most of their peasants. Subsistence farming was still the norm in many parts of Europe but where surpluses could be produced and sold, wool in England, for example, and wine in Bordeaux, improved agricultural practices were fostered. Great merchant associations like the Hanseatic League and the Merchant Adventurers established international trade of a sophistication and volume that signified the beginning of a new economic era. This was facilitated by the increasing use of bills of exchange and by the foundation of banking houses on the model of those earlier developed in Italy.

In the Low Countries, southern England and western Germany towns and cities had an importance comparable to that of the large country estates of princes, prelates and the nobility. Yet despite the fact that town dwellers were still in a minority, from nobles with urban residences, via merchants, lawyers, artisans and servants to the dangerous people who existed on the margins of society, they were a force for change. A city like Ghent simply refused to accept ancient views of the deference owed to the counts of Flanders. Other cities, such as London, were less successful in achieving political independence of their prince but economically they exerted a powerful influence. If revenue in the form of taxes or loans was withheld from the Emperor or the king of England their ability to operate effectively was fatally impaired. The poverty of Frederick III confined him to his patrimonial lands for much of his reign. The loss of the French lands and the breakdown in royal authority in England in the 1450s were partly due to the virtual bankruptcy of the Crown.

The most successful sovereigns appreciated the need to change the way in which they exercised their power whilst appearing to conform to the Christian stereotype of the 'good prince'. The Emperor Charles IV overcame the difficulties of ruling a huge, racially diverse area by avoiding large-scale wars and cultivating the traditional, medieval image of a just, magnificent and pious king. Charles V of France replicated these features, keeping the war with England on a low key, and successfully avoiding pitched battles, in which the French had had little success in the 1350s and 1360s. The reign of Henry V was perhaps too short for his kingly qualities to be properly assessed and he left his son an ambivalent legacy: enormous loyalty and respect on the one hand, French conquests that were almost impossible to defend, on the other. James II of Scotland was a forward-looking king but he was prematurely killed by one of his own modern weapons.

Perhaps the best exemplars of the characteristics of this new approach to monarchy were Charles VII and Louis XI of France, Henry VII of England and the Emperor Maximilian. Louis, Charles and Henry combined a ruthless determination to crush all internal opposition to their government with an understanding that they could not afford to alienate their subjects by appearing to violate the traditional standards of good rule as they were formulated in mirrors for princes. Louis was well placed between his father's expulsion of the English and his heirs' expensive Italian wars to profit from France's growing prosperity, and he exacted high taxes from his subjects. Henry was largely successful in avoiding external wars and taxed all orders of society to put his new dynasty on a sound financial basis: he well understood how to balance magnificence and prudence at his court. When possible, Maximilian used guile rather than great and expensive armed force to achieve his ends. His brilliant marriage to Mary of Burgundy virtually bought the Imperial crown for the Habsburg dynasty in perpetuity; his second marriage, to Bianca Maria Sforza, rescued him, at least temporarily, from dire financial straits.

'The military revolution', which many historians believe transformed warfare in the early modern period, grew out of developments in the Middle Ages. The expansion of towns and the increasing sophistication of crafts like metal work was a phenomenon of our period. Cannons were used with increasing frequency, especially in siege warfare, and in response the art of fortification was developed to repulse their fire. Better knowledge of the physical terrain of Europe and its surrounding seas promoted improved communications, which were utilised by military commanders. Most important of all was the growing capacity of rulers to tax their subjects heavily and regularly so that they could pay for professional armies. This released them from any reliance on the feudal levies, who only expected to serve for fixed periods and whose loyalties were often primarily to their own lords. As the ability of princes to raise and equip armies outstripped that of even their most powerful subjects, so their authority was enhanced. The reigns of Charles VIII, Louis XII and Francis I of France and of Henry VIII of England were to show that such princes could suffer defeats abroad without experiencing serious threats to their sovereignty at home. Princes continued to pay lip service to the crusading ideal but in practice none of them were prepared to commit substantial resources to it after the disaster of Nicopolis in the late fourteenth century. The wars against the Turks were called 'crusades' but they were essentially fought to defend the eastern borders of Europe.

By 1500 the European conflicts of the previous two centuries had promoted the emergence of several nation states. Adrian Hastings believes that despite the fact that Lowland Scots shared a language and some institutions with the English, the long wars with their neighbour had forged them into a nation state. The Irish and the Welsh, on the other hand, whilst having a strong national identity defined by their cultural heritage, were prevented by England from forming separate states. England was the prototype nation state in north-western Europe: it had been developing central institutions of government and law since Anglo-Saxon times and the Hundred Years War confirmed its ethnic and national character. The Empire had a predominantly German language, law and literature, so that, with the exception of countries such as Bohemia, it had a national identity of a kind. The emergence of a nation state, however, had to await the dissolution of the Empire and the unification of Germany in the late nineteenth century.[2] Most commentators recognise a strongly religious element in the developing French view of their nationhood. Françoise Autrand also believes that the way in which the monarchy survived the crises of 1356 to 1361, and the English occupation of France, from 1418 to 1436, strengthened it and laid the foundations of the state.[3]

The religious conflicts of the late Middle Ages also tended to enhance princely authority. The temporal power of the Papacy was permanently weakened by the Great Schism and the Conciliar Movement, even if the reforms of the following century were needed to restore its spiritual credibility. By 1500 most princes had achieved a large measure of exemption from papal taxation and had established some control over appointments to high ecclesiastical offices. During the Protestant Reformation it was the will of the prince that invariably decided whether or not his or her country should remain in communion with the Catholic Church. The laity and ordinary clerics also gained greater control over the way in which their religion was practised and, in some cases, promoted developments in doctrine. The work of Eamon Duffy, Robert Swanson and others has shown the strength of popular piety in this period. The will of the prince had largely determined the amount of dissent that should be allowed within a realm. The Lancastrians chose to persecute Lollardy, whose early manifestations, along with Wyclif's writings, had been tolerated by their predecessors. The Papacy normally managed to encourage protection of the Jews for financial reasons, but in times of crisis when scapegoats were required its effectiveness was limited.

Robert Bartlett has suggested that by 1300 Europe existed as a cultural entity defined by its personal names, saintly cults, coinage, charters of rights, schools and universities.[4] Cultural elites had done much to develop the nature of Europe in the late Middle Ages to the benefit of posterity. Court society in France, Valois Burgundy, the England of Richard II and Henry VII and late fifteenth-century Scotland reflected princely power and sophistication. Able monarchs used the court to enhance their prestige and further their diplomatic aims. Towards the end of our period it was also a means by which the new humanist scholarship that was emerging in Italy, entered northern Europe. The universities were not exactly flourishing; although exceptional individuals such as

John Wyclif or Jean Gerson could achieve notoriety or renown, they were certainly not the only means by which intellectual advances could be made. Political theorists like Philippe de Mézières and Sir John Fortescue were just as likely to be courtiers or lawyers as academics. The art of printing was developed largely independently of the universities. The larger towns, not only capital cities like Paris and London but trading centres like Cologne or Bruges, were vibrant and exciting places in our period. In London many of the more important guilds or livery companies built halls for their communal festivities. In Flanders, painters like Hans Memling and the Van Eyck brothers produced work of outstanding merit commissioned by their fellow citizens. The renown of merchants like Richard Whittington of London or Jacques Coeur of Bourges reflects the power and wealth now to be found in towns.

Terms like 'the later Middle Ages', 'Renaissance' and 'Reformations', the creation of later historians and commentators, are essentially arbitrary – one of the reasons why we have gone back to the thirteenth century and forward to the early modern period in some of our discussions has been because of the elasticity of these terms. Yet the century and a half from 1350 to 1500 did have defining characteristics such as those that have been suggested above. Without those developments the political, cultural, economic and ideological changes of the following centuries in north-western Europe would not have happened or would have taken a very different form.

Notes

Introduction

1. J. R. Hale, *The Civilization of Europe in the Renaissance* (London: Harper Collins, 1993), p. 3. The origin of the name, according to Ovid in the *Metamorphoses*, was a nymph 'Europa' who was seduced by Jupiter in the form of a bull. The children she had by him were known as 'Europeans'.
2. J. Huizinga, *The Waning of the Middle Ages* (Harmondsworth: Penguin, 1955); D. Hay, *Europe in the Fourteenth and Fifteenth Centuries* (Harlow: London, 1989); B. Guenée, *States and Rulers in Later Medieval Europe*, trans. J. Vale (Oxford: Basil Blackwell, 1988), p. 18.
3. J. Burckhardt, *The Civilization of the Renaissance in Italy*, was first published in 1860; T. A. Brady, H. A. Oberman and J. D. Tracy (eds), *Handbook of European History, 1400–1600* (Leiden, 1994–5), pp. xiv, xvii.
4. J. Kelly-Gadol, 'Did Women Have a Renaissance?', *Becoming Visible: Women in European History*, ed. R. Bridenthal and C. Koonz (Boston, MA: Houghton Mifflin, 1977), p. 137.
5. *The Brenner Debate: Agrarian Class Structure and Economic Development in Pre-industrial Europe*, ed. T. H. Aston, C. H. E. Philpin (Cambridge: Cambridge University Press, 1985).
6. Q. Skinner, *The Foundations of Modern Political Thought*, 2 vols (Cambridge: Cambridge University Press, 1978).
7. A. Ayton and J. L. Price, *The Medieval Military Revolution: State, Society and Military Change in Medieval and Early Modern Europe* (London: Tauris Academic Studies, 1995).
8. E. Duffy, *The Stripping of the Altars: Traditional Religion in England, c.1400–c.1580* (New Haven, CT: Yale University Press, 1992).
9. S. Ozment, *The Age of Reform, 1250–1550: An Intellectual and Religious History of Late Medieval and Reformation Europe* (New Haven, CT, and London: Yale University Press, 1980) p.181.

1 The Countryside and its People

1. T. H. Aston and C. H. E. Philpin (eds), *The Brenner Debates: Agrarian Class Struggle and Economic Development in Pre-industrial Europe* (Cambridge: Cambridge University Press, 1985).
2. J. Hatcher and M. Bailey, *Modelling the Middle Ages: The History and Theory of England's Economic Development* (Oxford: Oxford University Press, 2001), p. 79.
3. G. Bois, *The Crisis of Feudalism: Economy and Society in Eastern Normandy, c.1300–1550* (Cambridge: Cambridge University Press; Paris: Editions de la Maison des Sciences de l'Homme, 1984).

4. Hatcher and Bailey, *Modelling the Middle Ages*, p. 57.
5. The most important writer from this point of view is R. H. Britnell, particularly in *The Commercialisation of English Society, 1000–1500* (Manchester: Manchester University Press, 1996).
6. Hatcher and Bailey, *Modelling the Middle Ages*, p. 120.
7. B. Hanawalt, *The Ties that Bound: Peasant Families in Medieval England* (Oxford: Oxford University Press, 1986).
8. N. J. Mayhew, 'Scotland: Economy and Society', in S. H. Rigby (ed.), *A Companion to Britain in the Middle Ages* (Oxford: Blackwell Publishing, 2003), p. 107.
9. B. Graham, 'Ireland: Economy and Society', in ibid., p. 143.
10. G. Duby, 'The Manor and the Peasant Economy: the Southern Alps in 1338', *The Chivalrous Society* (London: Edward Arnold, 1977), pp. 188–215.
11. C. Friedrichs, 'German Social Structure, 1300–1600', in B. Scribner (ed.), *Germany: A New Social and Economic History, 1450–1630* (London: Edward Arnold, 1996), p. 234.
12. D. Herlihy, *The Black Death and the Transformation of the West* (Cambridge, MA and London: Harvard University Press, 1997), pp. 26–31. See also S. K. Cohn Jr, *The Black Death Transformed: Disease and Culture in Early Renaissance Europe* (London: Edward Arnold, 2002); he denies the disease was bubonic plague but does not commit himself to another identification.
13. Henry Kinghton, *Chronicle*, quoted in D. Baker (ed.), *England in the Later Middle Ages* (Dallas, TX: Academia, 1993), p. 160.
14. J. L. Bolton, *The Medieval English Economy, 1150–1500* (London: Dent, 1985), p. 49.
15. Hatcher and Bailey, *Modelling the Middle Ages*, p. 32.
16. Bolton, *The Medieval English Economy*, p. 51.
17. B. Campbell, 'England: Land and People', in S. H. Rigby (ed.), *A Companion to Britain in the Middle Ages* (Oxford: Blackwell Publishing, 2003) p. 9.
18. Mayhew, 'Scotland: Economy and Society', p. 111.
19. Graham, 'Ireland: Economy and Society', p. 151.
20. H. A. Miskimin, *The Economy of Early Renaissance Europe, 1300–1460* (Cambridge: Cambridge University Press, 1975), pp. 25–32.
21. R. Froissier, *Peasant Life in the Medieval West* (Oxford: Basil Blackwell, 1988), p. 12; W. Rösener, *Peasants in the Middle Ages* (Cambridge: Polity Press, 1992), p. 34.
22. E. Le Roy Ladurie and M. Morineau, *Histoire économique et sociale de la France*, vol. II (Paris: Presses Universitaires de France, 1977) p. 485. He gives high, medium and low estimates for the population in 1328.
23. G. Bois, *The Crisis of Feudalism*, pp. 24–57.
24. E. Le Roy Ladurie, *The Peasants of Languedoc*, trans. J. Day (Urbana and London: University of Illinois Press, 1994), pp. 11–14.
25. Le Roy Ladurie and Morineau, *Histoire économique et sociale de la France*, vol. II, pp. 483–4.
26. D. Nicholas, 'Economic Reorientation and Social Change in Fourteenth Century Flanders', *Past and Present*, 70 (1976), p. 24, n. 75.
27. D. Nicholas, *Medieval Flanders* (London: Longman, 1992), pp. 260–1.

28. Ibid., p. 266.
29. B. J. P. van Bavel, 'Land Lease and Agriculture: the Transition of the Rural Economy in the Dutch River Area from the Fourteenth to the Sixteenth Century', *Past and Present*, 172 (2001), p. 10.
30. Rösener, *Peasants in the Middle Ages*, pp. 255–6.
31. W. F. Hagen, 'Village Life in East-Elbian Germany and Poland, 1400–1800', in T. Scott (ed.), *The Peasantries of Europe from the Fourteenth to the Eighteenth Centuries* (London: Longman, 1998), p. 163.
32. W. Abel, *Agricultural Fluctuations in Europe from the Thirteenth to the Twentieth Centuries*, trans. O. Ordish (London: Methuen, 1986), p. 44.
33. T. Scott, *Society and Economy in Germany, 1300–1600* (Basingstoke: Palgrave Macmillan, 2002), pp. 56–7.
34. M. Bailey, 'Demographic Decline in Late Medieval England: some Thoughts on Recent Research', *Economic History Review*, 49 (1996), p. 1.
35. J. Langton, 'The Historical Geography of European Peasantries', in T. Scott (ed.), *The Peasantries of Europe*, p. 375.
36. P. J. P. Goldberg, *Women, Work and Life Cycle in a Medieval Economy: Women in York and Yorkshire, c.1300–1520* (Oxford: Clarendon Press, 1992), p. 337.
37. Bailey, 'Demographic Decline in Late Medieval England, pp. 1–19.
38. G. Bois, *The Crisis of Feudalism*, pp. 316, 327, 346.
39. Ibid., pp. 335–45.
40. Scott, *Society and Economy in Germany*, pp. 68–71.
41. P. Contamine, *La Vie quotidienne pendant la Guerre de Cent Ans: France et Angleterre* (Paris: Hachette, 1976), p. 138.
42. G. Duby, *Rural Economy and Country Life in the Medieval West*, trans. C. Postan (Columbia: University of South Carolina Press, 1968), p. 269.
43. Bois, *The Crisis of Feudalism*, p. 176, quoting M. de Bouard, *Histoire de Normandie* (Toulouse: n.p., 1970), p. 166.
44. The estate of one particular husbandman in 1401 comprised 2 horses, 2 cattle, 2 small pigs and 40 sheep. His house was well furnished with ample beds, bedlinen, and kitchen equipment. A smallholder in 1413 living not far from Rouen owned 1 cow, 8 sheep and a bare minimum of furniture (Bois, *The Crisis of Feudalism*, pp. 181–2).
45. E. Le Roy Ladurie and M. Morineau, *Histoire économique et sociale de la France*, vol. I, p. 522.
46. Bois, *The Crisis of Feudalism*, p. 364.
47. E. Le Roy Ladurie, *The French Peasantry, 1450–1660* (Aldershot: Scolar Press, 1987), p. 56.
48. Le Roy Ladurie and Morineau, *Histoire économique et sociale de la France*, p. 518.
49. Ibid., p. 539.
50. Le Roy Ladurie, *The Peasants of Languedoc*, pp. 11–50.
51. D. C. Munro (ed.), *Custumals of Battle Abbey* (1934), pp. 94–8, in D. Baker (ed.), *England in the Later Middle Ages: Portraits and Documents* (Dallas: Academia, 1993), p. 156.
52. S. H. Rigby, *English Society in the Later Middle Ages: Class Status and Gender* (London: Macmillan, 1995), p. 33.

53. R. B. Dobson (ed.), *The Peasants' Revolt of 1381* (London: Macmillan, 1970), pp. 80–3.
54. Ibid., extract from the Anonimalle Chronicle, p. 165.
55. C. Dyer, 'A Redistribution of Incomes in Fifteenth-Century England?' *Past and Present*, 39–41 (1968), p. 33.
56. E. B. Fryde, *Peasants and Landlords in Later Medieval England* (Stroud: Alan Sutton, 1996), p. 227.
57. Bolton, *The Medieval English Economy*, p. 185.
58. Dobson, *The Peasants' Revolt*, p. 64.
59. Fryde, *Peasants and Landlords*, p. 172.
60. Details of Hopton's properties come from C. Richmond, *John Hopton, a Fifteenth Century Suffolk Gentleman* (Cambridge: Cambridge University Press, 1981). Information on Blythburgh is to be found on pp. 34–55, and on Easton Bavents on pp. 78–94.
61. D. Nicholas, 'Economic Reorientation and Social Change in Fourteenth Century Flanders', *Past and Present*, 70 (1976), p. 27.
62. Bas J. P. Bavel, 'Land, Lease and Agriculture: the Transition of the Rural Economy in the Dutch River Area from the Fourteenth to the Sixteenth Century', *Past and Present*, 172 (2001), pp. 3–43.
63. Rösener, *Peasants in the Middle Ages*, p. 40.
64. Hans Rosenberg, quoted in T. Scott, *Society and Economy in Germany, 1300–1600*, p. 182.
65. Scott, *Society and Economy in Germany*, p. 153.
66. Ibid., p. 194.
67. Ibid., pp. 18, 196.
68. Ibid., p. 157, quoting Werner Rolevinck.
69. C. Friederichs, 'German Social Structure, 1300–1600', in B. Scribner (ed.), *Germany: A New Social and Economic History, 1450–1630* (London: Edward Arnold, 1996) p. 249.
70. Scott, *Society and Economy in Germany*, pp.196–7.
71. W. L. Urban, *Dithmarschen: A Medieval Peasant Republic* (Lewiston and Lampeter: Edward Mellen Press, 1991) tells the story of this state.
72. Hatcher and Bailey, *Modelling the Middle Ages*, pp. 238–40.
73. Rösener, *Peasants in the Middle Ages*, pp. 62, 80–1.
74. G. G. Astill, 'Economic Change in Later Medieval England: an Archaeological Review', in T. H. Aston and others (eds), *Social Relations and Ideas: Essays in Honour of R. H. Hilton* (Cambridge: Cambridge University Press, 1983), pp. 232–3.
75. Ibid., pp. 223–5.
76. Hanawalt, *The Ties that Bound*, p. 158.
77. P. Fleming, *Family and Household in Medieval England* (Basingstoke: Palgrave Macmillan, 2001), p. 68.
78. Rösener, *Peasants in the Middle Ages*, pp. 187–90.
79. Le Roy Ladurie and Morineau, *Histoire économique et sociale de la France*, p. 546.
80. Fleming, *Family and Household*, p. 66; for inheritance pp. 110–22, and for retirement pp. 122–4.

81. C. Dyer, *Standards of Living in the Later Middle Ages: Social Change in England c.1200–1520* (Cambridge: Cambridge University Press, 1989), pp. 170–1.
82. Rösener, *Peasants in the Middle Ages*, pp. 103–4.
83. B. Scribner (ed.), *Germany, a New Social and Economic History, 1450–1630* (London: Edward Arnold, 1996), p. 90.
84. Sir J. Fortescue, *On the Laws and Governance of England*, ed. S. Lockwood (Cambridge: Cambridge University Press, 1997), p. 89.
85. Rösener, *Peasants in the Middle Ages*, p. 183.
86. S. Shahar, *The Fourth Estate: A History of Women in the Middle Ages* (London: Routledge, 1993), p. 224.
87. Anon., *Piers Ploughman's Crede*, quoted in E. Power, *Medieval Women* (Cambridge: Cambridge University Press, 1975), p. 74.
88. Hanawalt, *The Ties that Bound*.
89. P. Ariès, in P. Ariès, *Centuries of Childhood*, trs. R. Baldick (London: Pimlico, 1996), put forward the idea that parents at this time showed little affection for their children.
90. Fleming, *Family and Household*, p. 65.
91. P. Freedman, *Images of the Medieval Peasant* (Stanford, CA: Stanford University Press, 1999), p. 44.
92. R. Hilton, *Class Conflict and the Crisis of Feudalism* (London: Hambledon Press, 1985), p. 249.
93. Quoted in the *Viking Portable Medieval Reader*, p. 196.
94. Freedman, *Images of the Medieval Peasant*, p. 201.
95. Scott, *Society and Economy in Germany*, p. 231.
96. D. Potter, *A History of France, 1460–1560* (Basingstoke: Macmillan, 1995), p. 168.
97. Le Roy Ladurie, *The French Peasantry, 1450–1660*, pp. 63–4.
98. Potter, *A History of France*, pp. 180–1.
99. Scribner, *Germany*, pp. 236–7.
100. Nicholas, 'Economic Reorientation and Social Change', pp. 366–7.
101. H. S. Bennett, *The Pastons and Their England* (Cambridge: Cambridge University Press, Canto edition, 1990), p. 1, quoting J. Gairdner (ed.), *The Paston Letters*, Introduction, p. xxxv.
102. For more information on the Stonor family, see C. Carpenter (ed.), *Kingsford's Stonor Letters and Papers* (Cambridge: Cambridge University Press, 1996).
103. K. Dockray, *Edward IV: A Source Book* (Stroud: Sutton, 1999), pp. 40–3; M. Hicks, *Warwick the Kingmaker* (Oxford: Blackwell Publishers, 2002), 258–9, puts forward a different view.
104. Shahar, *The Fourth Estate*, p. 135.
105. E. Amt, *Women's Lives in Medieval Europe: A Source Book* (London: Routledge, 1993), pp. 164–5.
106. Fleming, *Family and Household*, p. 63.
107. Bennett, *The Pastons and Their England*, p. 63.
108. The story of the Knyvet dispute comes from J. R. Lander, *English Justices of the Peace, 1461–1509* (Stroud: Sutton, 1989), pp. 99–100.

109. Details of Alice de Bryene's household can be found in F. F. Swabey, *Medieval Gentlewoman: Life in a Widow's Household in the Later Middle Ages* (Stroud: Sutton, 1999). Details of the food served are on pp. 84–8.
110. R. Vaughan, *Charles the Bold* (Woodbridge: Boydell, 2002), p. 194.
111. C. M. Woolgar, *The Great Household in Late Medieval England* (New Haven and London: Yale University Press, 1999), p. 160.
112. W. C. Dickenson, G. Donaldson and I. A. Milne (eds), *A Source Book of Scottish History* (London and Edinburgh: Nelson, 1952), vol. 1, pp. 206–7.
113. F. Baumgartner, *France in the Sixteenth Century* (New York: St Martin's Press, 1995), p. 50.
114. P. S. Lewis, *Later Medieval France: The Polity* (London: St Martin's Press, 1968), p. 174.
115. Literally, 'full world'; this is the phrase used in Le Roy Ladurie and Morineau, *Histoire économique et sociale de la France.*
116. Scott, *Society and Economy in Germany*, p. 19.

2 Townsmen, Traders and Unrest

1. John Munro's major work is *Wool, Cloth and Gold: The Struggle for Bullion in Anglo-Burgundian Trade* (Brussels: Editions de l'Université de Bruxelles; Toronto: University of Toronto Press, 1973), but he has also written many articles on the topic, some collected in *Bullion Flows and Monetary Policies in England and the Low Countries* (Aldershot: Variorum, 1994). Peter Spufford's major works are *Power and Profit: The Merchant in Medieval Europe* (London: Thames & Hudson, 2002) and *Money and its Use in Medieval Europe* (Cambridge: Cambridge University Press, 1988).
2. B. Guenée, *States and Rulers in Later Medieval Europe* (Oxford: Basil Blackwell, 1985) p. 194.
3. C. R. Friedrichs, 'German Social Structure, 1300–1600', in R. B. Scribner (ed.), *Germany: A New Social and Economic History, 1450–1630*, vol. I (London: Edward Arnold, 1996), p. 238.
4. B. Dobson, 'Urban Europe', in *The New Cambridge Medieval History*, vol. VII, p. 121.
5. C. Dyer, 'Small Places with Large Consequences: the Importance of Small Towns in England, 1000–1540', *Historical Research*, 75 (2002), p. 2.
6. This figure, from D. Nicholas, *The Later Medieval City, 1300–1500* (London: Longman, 1997), is disputed by H. A. Miskimin (*The Economy of Early Renaissance Europe, 1300–1460* (Cambridge: Cambridge University Press, 1975), p. 73), who puts the population of Paris before the Black Death at 80,000.
7. C. Dyer, *Standards of Living in the Later Middle Ages: Social Change in England, c.1200–1520* (Cambridge: Cambridge University Press, 1989), p. 189.
8. T. Scott and R. B. Scribner, 'Urban Networks', in R. B. Scribner (ed.), *Germany*, vol. I, p. 115.
9. D. Nicholas, *The Later Medieval City*, p. 107.

10. A. Curry, 'Towns at War: Relations between the Towns of Normandy and their English Rulers, 1417–1450', in J. A. F. Thomson (ed.), *Towns and Townspeople* (Stroud: Alan Sutton, 1988), pp. 149–50.
11. L. A. Burgess (ed.), *The Southampton Terrier of 1454* (London: Her Majesty's Stationery Office, 1976).
12. R. H. Hilton, *English and French Towns in Feudal Society: A Comparative Study* (Cambridge: Cambridge University Press, 1992), p. 128.
13. T. Scott, *Society and Economy in Germany, 1300–1600* (Basingstoke: Palgrave Macmillan, 2002), p. 38.
14. S. Rigby, 'Urban Oligarchy in Late Medieval England', in J. A. F. Thomson (ed.), *Towns and Townspeople* (Stroud: Alan Sutton, 1988), p. 66.
15. M. Lynch, 'Towns and Townspeople in Fifteenth Century Scotland', in Thomson, *Towns and Townspeople*, p. 185. More general information can be found in M. Lynch, M. Spearmen and G. Stell (eds), *The Medieval Scottish Town* (Edinburgh: John Donald, 1988).
16. F. J. Baumgartner, *France in the Sixteenth Century* (New York: St Martin's Press, 1995), p. 74.
17. Hilton, *English and French Towns in Feudal Society*, p. 103.
18. P. S. Lewis, *Later Medieval France: The Polity* (London: St Martin's Press, 1968), p. 270.
19. T. Scott, *Society and Economy in Germany, 1300–1600*, p. 22.
20. W. Blockmans and W. Prevenier, *The Promised Lands: The Low Countries under Burgundian Rule, 1369–1530* (Philadelphia: University of Pennsylvania Press, 1999), p. 127.
21. D. Nicholas, *Medieval Flanders* (London: Longman, 1992), p. 285.
22. G. Williams, *Renewal and Reformation: Wales, 1415–1642* (Oxford: Oxford University Press, 1993), p. 20.
23. H. Swanson, *Medieval British Towns* (Basingstoke: Palgrave Macmillan, 1999), p. 20.
24. A. R. Myers (ed.), *English Historical Documents 1327–1485*, vol. IV (London: Eyre & Spottiswoode, 1969), p. 445.
25. Ibid., p. 475.
26. Ibid., pp. 580–5.
27. C. Phythian-Evans, *Desolation of a City: Coventry and the Urban Crisis of the Late Middle Ages* (Cambridge: Cambridge University Press, 1979).
28. R. Britnell, *Growth and Decline in Colchester, 1300–1525* (Cambridge: Cambridge University Press, 1986), p. 267.
29. A. Dyer, *Decline and Growth in English Towns, 1400–1640* (Basingstoke: Palgrave Macmillan, 1991), pp. 58–9.
30. This saint had supposedly travelled to the city with her many companions only for them all to be martyred.
31. M. C. Howell, *Women, Production and Patriarchy in Medieval Cities* (Chicago and London: University of Chicago Press, 1986), pp. 95–161, has much information on women's involvement in the economy of Cologne. The portraits of the Rinke family can be found in A. d'Haenens, *Europe of the North Sea and the Baltic: The World of the Hanse* (Antwerp: Fonds Mercator, 1984), pp. 219, 221.

32. Nicholas, *Medieval Flanders*, p. 222.
33. Blockmans and Prevenier, *The Promised Lands*, pp. 138–40.
34. Nicholas, *Medieval Flanders*, p. 399.
35. *The Relation of England*, in D. Baker (ed.), *England in the Later Middle Ages* (Dallas, TX: Academia, 1993), pp. 147–9.
36. Myers, *English Historical Documents*, vol. IV, pp. 215–18.
37. K. Dockray, *Henry VI, Margaret of Anjou and the Wars of the Roses: A Source Book* (Stroud, Alan Sutton, 2000), pp. 135–6.
38. Myers, *English Historical Documents*, vol. IV, pp. 1101–2.
39. Ibid., p. 1104.
40. H. Swanson, *Medieval British Towns*, pp. 24–6.
41. Scott, *Society and Economy in Germany, 1300–1600*, pp. 132–7, 150.
42. Details of Southampton's trade can be found in O. Coleman (ed.), *The Brokage Book of Southampton, 1443–44* (Southampton: Southampton Record Series, 1960) and H. S. Cobb (ed.), *The Local Port Book of Southampton for 1439–40* (Southampton: Southampton Record Series, 1961).
43. A. A. Ruddock, *Italian Merchants in Southampton, 1270–1600*, pp. 206–1.
44. M. E. Mallett, *The Florentine Galleys in the Fifteenth Century* (Oxford: Clarendon Press, 1967), pp. 132–43.
45. R. S. Lopez and I. W. Raymond, *Medieval Trade in the Mediterranean World* (New York and London: Columbia University Press, 1955), pp. 109–14.
46. Ibid., p. 179.
47. Ibid., p. 232.
48. E. S. Hunt and J. M. Murray, *A History of Business in Medieval Europe, 1200–1550* (Cambridge: Cambridge University Press, 1999), p. 72.
49. P. Spufford, *Power and Profit: The Merchant in Medieval Europe* (London: Thames & Hudson, 2002), p. 44.
50. Hunt and Murray, *A History of Business in Medieval Europe, 1200–1550*, p. 141.
51. Spufford, *Power and Profit*, p. 15.
52. Spufford, in ibid., pp. 359–72, discusses the new mines and the towns founded on the back of this industry in detail.
53. J. H. Munro, 'Patterns of Trade, Money and Credit', in T. A. Brady, H. A. Oberman, and J. D. Tracy, *Handbook of European History, 1400–1600* (Leiden, 1994–5), pp. 147–57; P. Spufford, 'Trade in Fourteenth Century Europe', in M. Jones (ed.), *The New Cambridge Medieval History*, vol. VI: *c.1300–1415* (Cambridge: Cambridge University Press, 2000), p. 199, provides details of the decline in the availability of bullion at this date.
54. W. Childs, 'Commerce and Trade', in C. T. Allmand (ed.), *The New Cambridge Medieval History*, vol. VII: *c.1415–c.1500* (Cambridge: Cambridge University Press, 1998), p. 153.
55. P. Dollinger, *The German Hansa* (London: Macmillan, 1970), pp. 530–1.
56. Ibid., pp. 474–5.
57. Ibid., p. 85.
58. T. H. Lloyd, *The English Wool Trade in the Middle Ages* (Cambridge: Cambridge University Press, 1977), p. 119.
59. Ibid., p. 211.

60. E. Power and M. M. Postan, *Studies in English Trade in the Fifteenth Century* (London: George Routledge & Sons, 1933), p. 75.
61. E. E. Rich (ed.), *The Ordinance Book of the Merchants of the Staple* (Cambridge: Cambridge University Press, 1937).
62. Myers, *English Historical Documents*, vol. IV, p. 1026.
63. A. Hanham, *The Celys and their World* (Cambridge: Cambridge University Press, 1985), p. 120.
64. Hanham, *The Celys and their World*, p. 210.
65. R. Hilton, 'Was there a General Crisis of Feudalism?', *Class Conflict and the Crisis of Feudalism* (London: Hambledon Press, 1985).
66. M. Mollat and P. Wolff, *The Popular Revolutions of the Late Middle Ages*, trans. A. L. Lytton-Sells (London: Allen & Unwin, 1973), p.178. B. Guenée has identified this chronicler as the cantor Michel Pintoin.
67. Hilton, see note 12; R. Brenner, various writings, including 'The Rises and Declines of Serfdom in Medieval and Early Modern Europe', in M. L. Bush (ed.), *Europe, Serfdom and Slavery: Studies in Legal Bondage* (London and New York: Longman, 1996).
68. B. Guenée, *L'Opinion publique à la fin du Moyen Age* (Perrin, 2002), p. 99.
69. R. Cazelles, 'The Jacquerie', in ed. R. H. Hilton and T. H. Aston (eds) (Cambridge: Cambridge University Press, 1984), *The English Rising of 1381*, pp. 74–82.
70. Nicholas, *Medieval Flanders*, p. 252.
71. Ibid., p. 312.
72. B. Harvey, 'Introduction', *Before the Black Death: Studies in the 'Crisis' of the Early Fourteenth Century*, ed. Bruce M. S. Campbell (Manchester and New York: Manchester University Press, 1991), p. 23.
73. R. B. Dobson (ed.), *The Peasants' Revolt of 1381* (Basingstoke: Macmillan, 1983) from the *Anonimalle Chronicle*, pp. 164–5.
74. S. Justice, *Writing and Rebellion: England in 1381* (Berkeley, CA: University of California Press, 1994), chapter 4.
75. H. A. Miskimin, 'The Last Act of Charles V: the Background to the Revolts of 1382', *Cash, Credit and Crisis in Europe, 1300–1600*, ed. H. A. Miskimin and H. Alvin (London: Variorum Reprints, 1989), pp. 433–42.
76. C. Barron, 'The Reign of Richard II', in Jones (ed.), *New Cambridge Medieval History*, vol. VI: *c.1300–c.1415*, p. 306.
77. M. Aston, *Lollards and Reformers: Images and Literacy in Late Medieval Religion* (London: Hambledon Press, 1984); A. Hudson, *The Premature Reformation: Wycliffite Texts and Lollard History* (Oxford: Clarendon Press, 1988).
78. Quoted in Mollat and Wolff, *The Popular Revolutions of the Late Middle Ages*, p. 258.
79. Guenée, *L'Opinion publique*, p. 196.
80. B. Geremek, *The Margins of Society in Late Medieval Paris*, trans. J. Burrell (Cambridge: Cambridge University Press, 1987).
81. S. Walker, 'Rumour, Sedition and Popular Protest in the Reign of Henry IV', *Past and Present*, 166 (2000), p. 34.
82. I. M. W. Harvey, *Jack Cade's Rebellion of 1450* (Oxford: Clarendon Press, 1991), pp. 78–9.

83. Ibid., p. 187.
84. M. L. Kekewich et al. (eds), *The Politics of Fifteenth Century England: John Vale's Book* (Stroud: Alan Sutton, 1995), pp. 205–6.
85. Harvey, *Jack Cade's Rebellion*, p. 185.
86. E. S. Hunt and J. M. Murray, *A History of Business in Medieval Europe, 1200–1550* (Cambridge: Cambridge University Press, 1999) p. 141.
87. Spufford, *Power and Profit*, pp. 99–103.
88. P. C. Maddern, *Violence and Social Order: East Anglia, 1422–1442* (Oxford: Oxford University Press, 1992).
89. Guenée, *L'Opinion publique*, p. 200.

3 Princes: Ideal and Reality

1. B. Guenée, *States and Rulers in Later Medieval Europe*, trans. J. Vale (Oxford: Basil Blackwell, 1985), pp. 169–70.
2. J. P. Genet, 'Politics: Theory and Practice', C. T. Allmand (ed.), *The New Cambridge Medieval History*, vol. VII: *c.1415–c.1500* (Cambridge: Cambridge University Press, 1998), pp. 3–28.
3. R. A. Jackson, *Vive le roi! A History of the French Coronation Ceremonies from Charles V to Charles X* (Chapel Hill, NC: University of North Carolina Press, 1984), pp. 57–8.
4. P. S. Lewis, 'Pouvoir, "speculative" et "pratique": quelles voix entendre?', *Penser le Pouvoir au Moyen Age (VIIIe–XVe siècle)*, Etudes d'histoire et de littérature offertes à Françoise Autrand, ed. D. Boutet and J. Verger (Paris: Ed. Rue d'Ulm, 2000), pp. 157–70.
5. Q. Skinner, *The Foundations of Political Thought*, vol. I (Cambridge: Cambridge University Press, 1978), Introduction.
6. See, for example, M. L. des Garets, *Le Roi René, 1409–80: Un Artisan de la Renaissance Française au XVe siècle* (Paris: La Table Ronde, 1980).
7. Christine de Pizan, *Le Livre du Corps de Policie*, ed. R. H. Lucas (Geneva: Ambilly-Annemasse, 1967), pp. 31–2.
8. M. Bateson (ed.), *George Ashby's Poems* (London: EETS, Extra Series, 76, 1899), stanza 24, 18.
9. K. de Lettenhove, *Chastellain, Oeuvres diverses* (8 vols), vol. 7 (Brussels: F. Heussner, 1865), p. 297; trans. M. Kekewich.
10. M. Nejedly, 'L'idéal du roi en Bohème à la fin du XIVe siècle', *Penser le Pouvoir*, pp. 247–60.
11. R. Mitchinson, *A History of Scotland* (London: Methuen, 1970), p. 71.
12. J. M. Brown, 'The Exercise of Power', *Scottish Society in the Fifteenth Century*, ed. J. M. Brown (London: Edward Arnold, 1977), p. 54.
13. Ibid., p. 44.
14. Andrew of Wyntoun, *Andrew of Wyntoun's Orygynale Cronykil of Scotland*, vol. III, ed. D. Laing, Historians of Scotland, 9 (Edinburgh: William Patterson, 1879), pp. 104–5.
15. R. Nicholson, *Scotland: The Later Middle Ages* (Edinburgh: Oliver & Boyd, 1974), pp. 164–83.
16. Wyntoun, Orygynale Cronykil of Scotland, vol. III, p. 55.

17. A. Grant, *Independence and Nationhood: Scotland 1306–1469* (Edinburgh: Edinburgh University Press, 1991), p. 179.
18. Brown, 'The Exercise of Power', p. 46, quoting *Moray Registrum.*
19. Ibid., p. 186.
20. Grant, *Independence and Nationhood*, p. 48.
21. W. Goodall (ed.), *The Scotichronicon of John Fordun and Walter Bower*, 2 vols (Edinburgh: Robert Flaminius, 1759), vol. II, p. 511.
22. Nicholson, *Scotland: The Later Middle Ages*, p. 423.
23. N. MacDougall, *James III: A Political Study* (Edinburgh: Donald, 1982), chapter 12.
24. N. MacDougall, 'Richard III and James III, Contemporary Monarchs, Parallel Mythologies', in P. W. Hammond (ed.), *Richard III: Loyalty, Lordship and Law* (London: Richard II and Yorkist History Trust, 1986), p. 151.
25. Guenée, *States and Rulers*, p. 114.
26. J. Kail (ed.), *Twenty-Six Political Poems from the Oxford MSS Digby 102 and Douce 322*, part I (London: Early English Texts Society, 124, 1904), p. 55, 'Dede is worchyng'.
27. W. M. Ormrod, 'England in the Middle Ages', in R. Bonney (ed.), *The Rise of the Fiscal State in Europe, c.1200–1815* (Oxford: Oxford University Press, 1999), pp. 19–52.
28. *Calendar of Close Rolls*, Edward III, vol. I (1327–1330), p. 100.
29. C. Given-Wilson, *The English Nobility in the Late Middle Ages* (London: Routledge, 1996), pp. 36–7.
30. C. Plummer, in his edition of Sir John Fortescue, *The Governance of England* (Oxford: Clarendon, 1885), pp. 15–16.
31. M. Hicks, *Bastard Feudalism* (London: Longman, 1995); C. Carpenter, *The Wars of the Roses* (Cambridge: Cambridge University Press, 1997).
32. N. Saul, *Richard II* (London and New Haven, CT: Yale University Press, 1997), p. 109.
33. D. Gordon, L. Monnas and C. Elam (eds), *The Regal Image of Richard II and the Wilton Diptych* (London: Harvey Miller Publishers, 1997).
34. Saul, *Richard II*, p. 394.
35. T. Wright (ed.), *Political Poems and Songs Relating to English History*, vol. I (London: Rolls Series, 1859), p. 370.
36. Saul, *Richard II*, p. 467.
37. A. R. Myers (ed.), *English Historical Documents, 1327–1485*, vol. IV (London: Eyre & Spottiswoode, 1969), p. 413; *RP* (Parliament Rolls), vol. 3, p. 416.
38. H. G. Richardson, 'The Commons and Medieval Politics', in H. G. Richardson and G. O. Sayles (eds), *The English Parliament in the Middle Ages* (London: Hambledon, 1981), p. 21–48.
39. E. Wright, 'Henry IV, the Commons and the Recovery of Royal Finance in 1407', in *Rulers and Ruled in Late Medieval England: Essays Presented to Gerald Harriss*, ed. R. Archer and S. Walker (London: Hambledon Press, 1995).
40. G. Hodges, *Owain Glyn Dwr: The War of Independence in the Welsh Borders* (Almeley: Logaston, 1995), p. 37.
41. E. M. Thompson (ed. and trans.), *Chronicon Adae de Usk, 1377–1404* (London, 1876), p. 194.

42. R. R. Davies, *The Revolt of Owain Glyn Dwr* (Oxford: Oxford University Press, 1995), pp. 102, 321.
43. G. L. Harriss (ed.), *Henry V: The Practice of Kingship* (Stroud: Alan Sutton, 1993), p. 31. For a recent biography, see C. T. Allmand, *Henry V* (London and New Haven, CT: Yale University Press, 1997).
44. *Forty-first Report of the Deputy Keeper of the Public Records* (London, 1881), pp. 313–15, put into chronological order.
45. Harriss, *Henry V*, p. 210.
46. See especially, John Watts, *Henry VI and the Politics of Kingship* (Cambridge: Cambridge University Press, 1996).
47. R. A. Griffiths, *The Reign of Henry VI* (London: Ernest Benn, 1981), especially pp. 248–54.
48. M. L. Kekewich, C. Richmond, A. F. Sutton, L. Visser-Fuchs and J. Watts (eds), *The Politics of Fifteenth Century England* (Stroud: Allan Sutton, 1995), p. 136.
49. M. Hicks, *Warwick the Kingmaker* (Oxford: Blackwell Publishers, 1998), pp. 258–59.
50. C. D. Ross, *Edward IV* (London and New Haven, CT: Yale University Press, 1997), especially pp. 421–3.
51. *The Great Chronicle of London*, ed. A. H. Thomas and I. D. Thornley (Gloucester: Alan Sutton, 1983), pp. 231–2 raises the possibility that Edward IV was illegitimate.
52. A. F. Sutton, '"A curious searcher for our Weal Public": Richard III, Piety, Chivalry and the Concept of the "Good Prince"', in P. W. Hammond (ed.), *Richard III: Loyalty, Lordship and Law* (Stroud: Alan Sutton, 1986), pp. 58–90.
53. N. Pronay (ed.), *The Crowland Chronicle Continuations: 1459–1486* (London: J. Cox, 1986), pp. 157–85.
54. C. Richmond, '1485 and All That, or What Was Going On at the Battle of Bosworth?', in Hammond, *Richard III: Loyalty, Lordship and Law*, pp. 172–206.
55. A. Fox, *Politics and Literature in the Reigns of Henry VII and Henry VIII* (Oxford: Basil Blackwell, 1989), p. 32, from 'The Bowge of Court' (court rations).
56. After Arthur's death in 1502, his younger brother Henry became heir to the throne.
57. Jackson, *Vive le Roi!* p. 29.
58. R. Cazelles, *Société Politique, Noblesse et Couronne sous Jean le Bon et Charles V* (Geneva: Mémoires et Documents publiés par la Société de l'Ecole des Chartes, 1982), pp. 42–4, 46–7.
59. P. S. Lewis, *Later Medieval France: The Polity* (London: St Martin's Press, 1968), p. 374.
60. Ibid., pp. 197–8. See above, Chapter 2 for Simon Caboche, a Parisian butcher who led a rising in that year: the ordinance was for the reform of the tax collection and accounting system.
61. R. Vaughan, *Valois Burgundy* (London: Allen Lane, 1975), p. 95.
62. Lewis, *Later Medieval France: The Polity*, p. 110.
63. M. S. Blayney (ed.), *Fifteenth Century Translations of Alain Chartier's 'Le Traité de l'Espérance' and 'Le Quadrilogue Invectif'* (London: Early English Texts Society, 1974), pp. 270, 281, 1, 245–7.

64. F. Autrand, *Naissance d'un corps de l'Etat: les gens du Parlement de Paris, 1345–1454* (Paris: Publications de la Sorbonne, 1981); R. G. Little, *The Parlement of Poitiers: War, Government and Politics in France, 1418–1436* (London: Royal Historical Society, 1984).
65. Mathieu d'Escouchy, *Chronique*, 3 vols, ed. G. du Fresne de Beaucourt (Paris: Société de l'Histoire de France, 1863–4), vol. 3, p. 18, quoted in M. Vale, *Charles VII* (London: Eyre Methuen, 1974), p. 80.
66. Vale, *Charles VII*, p. 80.
67. E. Bourassin, *Louis XI: homme d'état, homme privé* (Paris: Tallandier, 1995).
68. Kekewich et al., *The Politics of Fifteenth Century England*, p. 217.
69. Bourassin, *Louis XI*, p. 13.
70. J. Huizinga, *The Waning of the Middle Ages* (Harmondsworth: Penguin, 1955), p. 94.
71. J. Michelet, *Histoire de France* (1855), quoted by I. Cloulas, *Charles VIII et le Mirage Italien* (Paris: A. Michel, 1986), front page.
72. Lewis, *Later Medieval France: The Polity*, pp. 276–7.
73. D. Hay, *Europe in the Fourteenth and Fifteenth Centuries* (Harlow: Longman, 1989), pp. 129–31.
74. R. Sablonier, 'The Swiss Confederation', in Allmand (ed.), *New Cambridge Medieval History*, vol. VIII: *c.1415–c.1500*, p. 645.
75. Guenée, *States and Rulers*, p. 211.
76. H. J. Cohn, *The Government of the Rhine Palatinate in the Fifteenth Century* (Oxford: Oxford University Press, 1965), pp. 152–74.
77. T. Scott, 'Germany and the Empire', in Allmand (ed.), *New Cambridge Medieval History*, vol. VII: *c.1415–c.1500*, pp. 337–66.
78. P. Dollinger (trans.), D. S. Ault and S. H. Steinberg, *The German Hansa* (London: Macmillan, 1970), p. 113.
79. S. Harrison Thomson, 'Learning at the Court of Charles IV', *Speculum* (1950), pp. 25, 8.
80. R. du Boulay, *Germany in the Later Middle Ages* (London: Athlone, 1983), p. 38.
81. E. Isenmann, 'The Holy Roman Empire in the Middle Ages', in Bonney, *The Rise of the Fiscal State in Europe*, p. 260.
82. Kekewich et al., *The Politics of Fifteenth Century England*, p. 242.

4 Waging War

1. Sir J. Fortescue, *In Praise of the Laws of England*, ed. S. Lockwood (Cambridge: Cambridge University Press, 1997), p. 53.
2. P. Contamine, *War in the Middle Ages* (Oxford: Basil Blackwell, 1986), p. 210.
3. Ibid.
4. C. J. Rogers, *War Cruel and Sharp* (Woodbridge: Boydell, 2000); M. J. Prestwich, *Armies and Warfare in the Middle Ages: The English Experience* (New Haven, CT: Yale University Press, 1996); A. Ayton and J. L. Price (eds), *The Medieval Military Revolution: State, Society and Military Change in Medieval and Early Modern Europe* (London: I. B. Tauris, 1998).
5. Contamine, *War in the Middle Ages*, pp. 282–3.
6. See below, p. 140.

7. K. de Vries, 'The Effect of Killing the Christian Prisoners at the Battle of Nicopolis', in L. J. A. Villalon and D. J. Kagan (eds), *Crusaders, Condottieri and Cannon: Medieval Warfare in Societies around the Mediterranean* (Leiden and Boston: Brill, 2003), p. 167.
8. J. Barnie, *War in Medieval Society: Social Values and the Hundred Years War, 1337–99* (London: Weidenfeld and Nicolson, 1974), p. 77.
9. A. Curry, *The Battle of Agincourt: Sources and Interpretations* (Woodbridge: Boydell, 2000), p. 438.
10. Prestwich, *Armies and Warfare in the Middle Ages*, p. 106.
11. C. J. Rogers, 'The Vegetian "Science of Warfare" in the Middle Ages', *Journal of Medieval Military History*, I (2002), pp. 1–5.
12. C. J. Rogers fully discusses Gillingham's views in ibid., pp. 1–19.
13. S. Morillo, 'Battle Seeking: the Contexts and Limits of Vegetian Strategy', in *Journal of Medieval Military History*, I (2002), pp. 21–41.
14. M. Keen, *Chivalry* (New Haven, CT, and London: Yale University Press, 1984), p. 2.
15. T. Jones, *Chaucer's Knight: The Portrait of a Medieval Mercenary* (London: Methuen, 1982).
16. Keen, *Chivalry*, p. 191.
17. Prestwich, *Armies and Warfare in the Middle Ages*, p. 232. The incident comes from Froissart's *Chronicle*.
18. *Viking Portable Medieval Reader*, ed. James Bruce Ross and Mary Martin. McLaughlin (Harmondsworth: Penguin, 1977), p. 112.
19. Keen, *Chivalry*, p. 173. The motto translates as 'Honour conquers all'.
20. J. Barnie, *War in Medieval Society*, p. 94.
21. Ibid., p. 96.
22. D. A. Cohen, 'Secular Pragmatism and Thinking about War in some Court Writings of Pere III el Cerimonios', in Villalon and Kagan (eds), *Crusaders, Condottieri and Cannon*, p. 46.
23. J. C. Fuller, quoted in Rogers, *War Cruel and Sharp*, p. 219.
24. This view is put forward by Allmand, Michael Prestwich, Fowler and Keen among others; there is a full discussion of the historiography of the campaign in Rogers, *War Cruel and Sharp*, chapter 10, pp. 217–37.
25. Ibid., pp. 277–1.
26. Ibid., pp. 273–85.
27. Ibid., p. 421.
28. J. Palmer, 'The War Aims of the Protagonists and the Negotiations for Peace', in K. Fowler (ed.), *The Hundred Years War* (London: Macmillan, 1971), p. 68.
29. Extracts from chronicle accounts of Agincourt, details of the French battle plan and many other sources relating to the battle can be found in A. Curry, *The Battle of Agincourt: Sources and Interpretations* (Woodbridge: Boydell, 2000).
30. Froissart, *Chronicles*, ed. and trans. G. Brereton (Harmondsworth: Penguin, 1968), pp. 49–50.
31. J. Barnie, *War in Medieval Society*, p. 50, quoting Knighton's chronicle.
32. R. Vaughan, *John the Fearless* (London: Longman, 1979), p. 138.
33. Ibid., pp. 143, 149–50.

34. Quoted in R. Vaughan, *Valois Burgundy* (London: Allen Lane, 1975), p. 81.
35. A full account of the battle can be found in R. Vaughan, *Charles the Bold*, new edn (Woodbridge: Boydell, 2002), pp. 418–32.
36. Ibid., p. 428.
37. Contamine, *War in the Middle Ages*, pp. 132–7.
38. M. Bennett, 'The Development of Battle Tactics in the Hundred Years War', in A. Curry and M. Hughes (eds), *Arms, Armies and Fortifications in the Hundred Years War* (Woodbridge: Boydell, 1994), p. 19.
39. Duke Philip of Cleves, quoted in D. Eltis, 'Towns and Defence in Later Medieval Europe', *Nottingham Medieval Studies*, V (1989).
40. H. J. Hewitt, *The Organisation of War under Edward III* (Manchester: Manchester University Press, 1966), pp. 50–63.
41. Prestwich, *Armies and Warfare in the Middle Ages*, pp. 259–61.
42. R. W. Kaeuper, *War, Justice and Public Order: England and France in the Later Middle Ages* (Oxford: Oxford University Press, 1988), p. 26.
43. M. Hicks, *Bastard Feudalism* (London: Longman, 1995).
44. C. Allmand, *Society at War: The Experiences of England and France during the Hundred Years War* (Edinburgh: Oliver and Boyd, 1973), pp. 58–60.
45. A. R. Myers (ed.), *English Historical Documents*, vol. IV (London: Eyre & Spottiswoode, 1969), pp.498–500.
46. C. Allmand, *Lancastrian Normandy, 1415–1450: The History of a Medieval Occupation* (Oxford: Clarendon Press, 1983), p. 53.
47. M. Hughes, 'The Fourteenth Century French Raids on Hampshire and the Isle of Wight', in Curry and Hughes, *Arms, Armies and Fortifications*, p. 142.
48. Hewitt, *The Organisation of War under Edward III*, p. 39.
49. Ibid., p. 87.
50. Prestwich, *Armies and Warfare in the Middle Ages*, p. 246.
51. Myers, *English Historical Documents*, vol. IV, p. 62.
52. Prestwich, *Armies and Warfare in the Middle Ages*, p. 262.
53. *Letter and Papers Illustrative of the Wars of the English in France*, vol. II ed. Joseph Stevenson, pt 2 (London: Longman, Green, 1861) pp. 575–85.
54. Allmand, *Society at War*, pp. 55–7.
55. P. Contamine, *Guerre et Société en France, en Angleterre et en Bourgogne, XIV–XV siècles* (Villeneuve d'Asq: Lille, 1991), p. 333.
56. Contamine, ibid., p. 171.
57. See Chapter 3.
58. H. J. Cohn, *The Government of the Rhine Palatinate in the Fifteenth Century* (Oxford: Oxford University Press, 1965), pp. 152–74.
59. F. R. H. du Boulay, *Germany in the Later Middle Ages* (London: Athlone, 1983), p. 27
60. N. Houseley, *The Later Crusades: 1274–1580 from Lyons to Alcazor* (Oxford: Oxford University Press, 1992), pp. 252–3.
61. J. Riley-Smith, *The Crusades* (London: Athlone, 1990), pp. 233–4.
62. D. S. Bachrach, 'A Military Revolution Reconsidered: the Case of the Burgundian State under the Valois Dukes', in *Essays in Medieval Studies*, 15 (1998), pp. 9–14.

63. J. de Venette, *The Chronicle of Jean de Venette*, trans. J. Birdsall, ed. R. A. Newhall (New York: Columbia University Press, 1952), p. 94.
64. Allmand, *Society at War*, p. 88.
65. Ibid., p. 91.
66. N. Wright, *Knights and Peasants: The Hundred Years War in the French Countryside* (Woodbridge: Boydell, 1998).
67. Myers, *English Historical Documents*, vol. IV, pp. 516–22.
68. D. Potter, *A History of France, 1460–1560* (Basingstoke: Macmillan, 1995), p. 144.
69. P. Chaunu and R. Gascon, *Histoire économique et Sociale de la France*, ed. F. Braudel and E. Labrousse, vol. I (Paris: Presses Universitaires de la France, 1970–82).
70. Vaughan, *Charles the Bold*, p. 415.
71. Barnie, *War in Medieval Society*, p. 97.
72. P. S. Lewis, *Later Medieval France: The Polity* (London: St Martin's Press, 1968), p. 77.
73. Ibid., pp. 60, 64.
74. Barnie, *War in Medieval Society*, p. 48.
75. W. M. Ormrod, 'The Domestic Response to the Hundred Years War', in Curry and Hughes, *Arms, Armies and Fortifications in the Hundred Years War*, p. 87.
76. Allmand, *Society at War*, pp. 141–50.
77. A. D. M. Barrell, *Medieval Scotland* (Cambridge: Cambridge University Press, 2000), p. 121.

5 The Church, Religion and Dissent

1. J. Huizinga, *The Waning of the Middle Ages* (Harmondsworth: Penguin, 1955).
2. E. Duffy, *The Stripping of the Altars: Traditinal Religion in England, c.1400–1580* (New Haven, CT, and London: Yale University Press, 1992); R. N. Swanson, *Religion and Devotion in Europe, c.1215–c.1515* (Cambridge: Cambridge University Press, 1995).
3. F. Oakley, *Natural Law, Conciliarism and Consent in the Late Middle Ages* (London: Variorum Reprints, 1984); G. Mollat, *The Popes at Avignon, 1305–1378*, trans. Janet Love (London: Thomas Nelson & Sons, 1963).
4. C. H. Lawrence, *Medieval Monasticism: Forms of the Religious Life in Western Europe in the Middle Ages* (London: Longman, 2001), p. 2.
5. The hours were matins (late night or early morning), lauds (sunrise), prime (6 a.m.), terce (9 a.m.), sext (noon), none (3 p.m.) and vespers (sunset).
6. Lawrence, *Medieval Monasticism*, p. 111, quoting J. P. Migne (ed.), *Patrologiae Cursus Completus* (Paris, 1853), p. 149, and pp. 675–7.
7. The film *The Name of the Rose* (based on the book *The Name of the Rose*, by Umberto Eco), starring Sean Connery, gives a good idea of the working of a medieval monastery even if the mortality rate was not normally so high!
8. P. D. Johnson, *Equal in Monastic Profession: Religious Women in Medieval France* (Chicago, IL: University of Chicago Press, 1991).

9. From the beginning the Dominicans were associated with combating heresy as St Dominic preached against the Cathars in Languedoc, see section 5(iii).
10. A. Jotischky, *The Carmelites and Antiquity: Mendicants and their Pasts in the Middle Ages* (Oxford: Oxford University Press, 2002), pp. 22–3.
11. Lawrence, *Medieval Monasticism*, p. 280.
12. B. Harvey, *Living and Dying in England, 1100–1540: The Monastic Experience* (Oxford: Clarendon Press, 1993).
13. P. N. R. Zutshi, 'The Avignon Papacy', in M. Jones (ed.), *The New Cambridge Medieval History*, vol. VII: *c.1300–c.1415* (Cambridge: Cambridge University Press, 2000), pp. 653–73. Avignon belonged to the count of Provence, a papal vassal, and was adjacent to the Comtat-Venaissin, a papal possession since 1274. In 1348 Clement VI bought Avignon for 80,000 crowns. There have not been many general works published on the Avignon Papacy and Great Schism in English over recent decades. The *New Cambridge Medieval History* has recently provided a welcome summary of what is available.
14. The Papacy exerted only a moral control over parts of northern Italy, much of it was under the sovereignty of the Emperor. The Papacy ruled some parts of central and northern Italy, such as Rimini and Bologna, directly (at least in theory); they were known as the Papal State or States.
15. Oakley *Natural Law, Conciliarism and Consent*, p. 314.
16. Zutshi, 'The Avignon Papacy', p. 659.
17. H. Kaminsky, 'The Great Schism', in Jones (ed.), *New Cambridge Medieval History, c.1300–c.1415*, p. 675.
18. S. Ozment, *The Age of Reform, 1250–1550: An Intellectual and Religious History of Late Medieval and Reformation Europe* (New Haven, CT, and London: Yale University Press, 1980), p. 156.
19. 'A. Black, 'Popes and Councils', in C. T. Allmand (ed.), *The New Cambridge Medieval History*, vol. VII: *c.1415–c.1500* (Cambridge: Cambridge University Press, 1998), pp. 65–86.
20. A. Black, *Political Thought in Europe, 1250–1450* (Cambridge: Cambridge University Press, 1992), p. 60.
21. Ozment, *The Age of Reform*, pp. 152–5.
22. Oakley, *Natural Law, Conciliarism and Consent*, pp. 40–57.
23. D. Catherine Brown, *Pastor and Laity in the Theology of Jean Gerson* (Cambridge: Cambridge University Press, 1987), p. 201.
24. B. Tierney, *Religion, Law and the Growth of Constitutional Thought, 1150–1650* (Cambridge: Cambridge University Press, 1982) p. 70.
25. C. M. D. Crowder, *Unity, Heresy and Reform: The Conciliar Response to the Great Schism* (London: Edward Arnold, 1977), p. 180.
26. M. McKisack, *The Fourteenth Century* (Oxford: Clarendon, 1959), pp. 272–5.
27. J. Wormald, *Court, Kirk and Community: Scotland, 1470–1625* (Edinburgh: Edinburgh University Press, 1981/1991), p. 76.
28. Huizinga, *The Waning of the Middle Ages*, pp. 333–4.
29. C. Augustijn, 'Wessel Gansfort's Rise to Celebrity', in F. Akkerman, G. Chuisman and A. J. Vanderjagt (eds), *Wessel Gansfort (1419–1487) and Northern Humanism* (Leiden, New York, and Cologne: Brill, 1993), pp. 3–21.

30. D. Englander et al. (eds), *Culture and Belief in Europe, 1450–1600: An Anthology of Sources* (Oxford: Basil Blackwell/Open University, 1990), p. 103.
31. R. N. Swanson, *Religion and Devotion in Europe, c.1215–c.1515* (Cambridge: Cambridge University Press, 1995), p. 40.
32. Duffy, *The Stripping of the Attars*, pp. 2–4; C. Richmond, 'Religion and the Fifteenth Century Gentleman', in B. Dobson (ed.), *The Church, Politics and Patronage in the Fifteenth Century* (Gloucester and New York: Alan Sutton, 1984), p. 199; Swanson, *Religion and Devotion in Europe*, p. 187.
33. V. Reinburg, 'Liturgy and Laity in Late Medieval and Reformation France', *Sixteenth Century Journal*, 23 (1992), pp. 526–47.
34. D. d'Avray, 'The Gospel of the Marriage Feast of Cana and Marriage Preaching in France', in *The Bible in the Medieval World: Essays in memory of Beryl Smalley*, ed. K. Walsh and D. Wood (Oxford: Basil Blackwell, 1985), pp. 220–1.
35. P. Binski, *Medieval Death: Ritual and Representation* (London: British Museum Press, 1997).
36. Ibid., from the psalter of Robert de Lisle, *c.*1310, p. 136.
37. Englander, *Culture and Belief in Europe*, p. 17.
38. K. Thomas, *Religion and the Decline of Magic: Studies in Popular Beliefs in Sixteenth and Seventeenth Century England* (London: Weidenfeld & Nicolson, 1971), p. 588.
39. B. Dobson, 'Citizens and Chantries in Late Medieval York', in *Church and City, 1000–1500: Essays in Honour of Christopher Brooke*, ed. D. Abulafia, M. Franklin and M. Rubin (Cambridge: Cambridge University Press, 1992), p. 312.
40. Huizinga, *The Waning of the Middle Ages*, p. 179.
41. N. Vincent, 'Some Pardoners' Tales: the Earliest English Indulgences', *Transactions of the Royal Historical Society*, 6th series, 12 (2002), pp. 23–58.
42. Swanson, *Religion and Devotion in Europe*, p. 39.
43. W. W. Skeat, *The Students' Chaucer: A Complete Edition of his Works* (Oxford: Clarendon, 1895), *The Canterbury Tales*, pp. 427–8.
44. J. Sumption, *Pilgrimage: An Image of Medieval Religion* (London: Faber & Faber, 1975), pp. 259–60.
45. Englander, *Culture and Belief in Europe*, p. 22.
46. R. C. Finucane, *Miracles and Pilgrims: Popular Beliefs in Medieval England* (Basingstoke: Macmillan, 1995), p. 155.
47. R. Kieckhefer, *Unquiet Souls: Fourteenth Century Saints and their Religious Milieu* (Chicago: University of Chicago Press, 1984), p. 8.
48. G. Williams, *Wales and the Reformation* (Cardiff: University of Wales Press, 1997), p. 10.
49. M. Rubin, *Corpus Christi: The Eucharist in Late Medieval Culture* (Cambridge: Cambridge University Press, 1991), p. 192.
50. Sumption, *Pilgrimage*, pp. 282–4.
51. R. Wunderli, *Peasant Fires: The Drummer of Niklashausen* (Bloomington and Indianapolis: University of Indiana Press, 1992).
52. J. Bossy, *Christianity in the West, 1400–1700* (Oxford: Oxford University Press, 1985), p. 58.
53. B. Windeatt (ed.), *English Mystics of the Middle Ages* (Cambridge: Cambridge University Press, 1994), pp. 154–5.

54. R. Bradler, 'Julian of Norwich: Writer and Mystic', in P. E. Szarmach (ed.), *An Introduction to the Medieval Mystics of Europe* (Albany: State University of New York Press, 1984), p. 197.
55. M. Fries, 'Margery Kempe', in Szarmach, *An Introduction to the Medieval Mystics of Europe*, pp. 217–35.
56. R. R. Post, *The Modern Devotion: Confrontation with Reform and Humanism*, Studies in Medieval and Reformation Thought, 3 (Leiden: E. J. Brill, 1968).
57. Scrope participated in a nobles' rebellion against Henry IV in 1405. It was highly unusual for prelates to be executed.
58. A. Murray, *Suicide in the Middle Ages*, 2 vols (Oxford: Oxford University Press, 2000), vol. 1, p. 221.
59. P. A. Dykema and H. A. Oberman (eds), *Anticlericalism in Late Medieval and Early Modern Europe* (Leiden, Cologne and New York: E.J. Brill, 1993), p. x.
60. Huizinga, *The Waning of the Middle Ages*, p. 180.
61. J. Dempsey Douglas, 'A Report on Anticlericalism in three French Women Writers, 1404–1549', in Dykema and Oberman, *Anticlericalism in Late Medieval and Early Modern Europe*, pp. 243–56.
62. M. Burleigh, 'Anticlericalism in Fifteenth Century Prussia: the Clerical Contribution Reconsidered', in C. M. Barron and C. Harper Bill (eds), *The Church in Pre-Reformation Society Essays in Honour of F. R. H. Du Boulay* (Woodbridge: Boydell Press, 1985), pp. 38–47.
63. J. van Engen, 'Late Medieval Anticlericalism: the Case of the New Devout', in Dykema and Oberman, *Anticlericalism in Late Medieval and Early Modern Europe*, pp. 19–52.
64. Thomas, *Religion and the Decline of Magic*, p. 168.
65. S. Reynolds, 'Social Mentalities and the Case of Medieval Scepticism', *Transactions of the Royal Historical Society*, 5th series, 1 (1991), p. 39.
66. G. Leff, *Heresy in the Later Middle Ages: The Relation of Heterodoxy to Dissent, c.1250–c.1450*, 2 vols (New York: Manchester University Press/Barnes & Noble, 1967).
67. A. Hudson, *The Premature Reformation: Wycliffite Texts and Lollard History* (Oxford: Clarendon Press, 1988), p. 314.
68. Ibid., p. 315.
69. J. I. Catto, 'John Wyclif and the Cult of the Eucharist', in K. Walsh and D. Wood (eds), *The Bible in the Medieval World* (Oxford: Basil Blackwell, 1985), pp. 269–86.
70. C. Allmand, *Henry V* (New Haven, CT, and London: Yale University Press, 1997).
71. R. Nicholson, *Scotland: The Later Middle Ages* (Edinburgh: Oliver & Boyd, 1974), p. 241.
72. S. Justice, 'Inquistion, Speech and Writing: a Case from Late Medieval Norwich', in R. Copeland (ed.), *Criticism and Dissent in the Middle Ages* (Cambridge: Cambridge University Press, 1996), p. 290.
73. M. Aston and C. Richmond (eds), *Lollardy and the Gentry in the Later Middle Ages* (Stroud: Sutton, 1997).
74. H. Kaminsky, *A History of the Hussite Revolution* (Berkeley and Los Angeles: University of California Press, 1967).

75. F. Smahel, *La Révolution Hussite: une anomalie historique* (Paris: Presses Universitaires de France, 1985).
76. Leff, *Heresy in the Later Middle Ages*; M. Lambert, *Medieval Heresy: Popular Movements from Bogomil to Hus* (New York: Holmes & Meier, 1976).
77. J. Klassen, 'Hus, the Hussites and Bohemia', in Allmand (ed.), *New Cambridge Medieval History*, vol. VII: *c.1415–c.1500*, pp. 367–91.
78. Leff, *Heresy in the Later Middle Ages*, vol. 2, pp. 657–8.
79. Lambert, *Medieval Heresy*, p. 310.
80. Leff, *Heresy in the Later Middle Ages*, vol. 2, p. 654.
81. T. A. Fudge, 'The "Crown" and the "Red Gown": Hussite Popular Religion', in B. Scribner and T. Johnson (eds), *Popular Religion in Germany and Central Europe, 1400–1800* (Basingstoke: Macmillan, 1996), p. 52.
82. M. Rubin, *Gentile Tales: The Narrative Assault on Late Medieval Jews* (New Haven, CT, and London: Yale University Press, 1999).
83. Ibid., p. 99.
84. J. M. Minty, 'Judengasse to Christian Quarter: the Phenomenon of the Converted Synagogue in the Late Medieval and Early Modern Holy Roman Empire', in Scribner and Johnson, *Popular Religion in Germany and Central Europe*, pp. 58–86.
85. Rubin, *Gentile Tales*, p. 197.
86. C. Roth, 'The Medieval Conception of the Jew: a New Interpretation', *Essential Papers on Judaism and Christianity in Conflict from Late Antiquity to the Reformation*, ed. J. Cohen (New York and London: New York University Press, 1991), pp. 298–309.
87. A. Fra, 'The Witch and the Jew: Two Alikes Were Not the Same', in J. Cohen (ed.), *From Witness to Witchcraft: Jews and Judaism in Medieval Christian Thought* (Wiesbaden: Harrassowitz Verlag, 1996), p. 368.
88. J. M. Elukin, 'From Jew to Christian? Conversion and Immutability in Medieval Europe', in J. Muldoon (ed.), *Varieties of Religious Conversion in the Middle Ages* (Gainesville, FA: University Press of Florida, 1997), pp. 171–89.
89. J. Edwards (ed. and trans.), *The Jews in Western Europe, 1400–1600* (Manchester: Manchester University Press, 1994), p. 23.
90. S. Wilson, *The Magical Universe: Everyday Ritual and Magic in Pre-Modern Europe* (London and New York: Hambledon, 2000), p. 347.
91. Thomas, *Religion and the Decline of Majic*, p. 28.
92. R. Kieckhefer, *Forbidden Rites: A Necromancer's Manual of the Fifteenth Century* (Stroud: Sutton Publishing, 1997).
93. R. Hope Robbins, *The Encyclopaedia of Witchcraft and Demonology* (London: Peter Neville, 1960), p. 405.
94. N. Cohn, *Europe's Inner Demons: The Demonization of Christians in Medieval Christendom* (London: Pimlico, 1993), p. 160.
95. R. Kieckhefer, *European Witch Trials. Their Foundations in Popular and Learned Culture, 1300–1500* (London: Routledge and Kegan Paul, 1976), pp. 13–14.
96. C. Ginzburg, *Ecstacies: Deciphering the Witches' Sabbath* (London: Penguin Books, 1992).
97. Kieckhefer, *European Witch Trials.*

98. C. Ginzburg, *The Night Battles: Witchcraft and Agrarian Cults in the Sixteenth and Seventeenth Centuries*, trans. J. and A. Tedeschi (London: Routledge & Kegan Paul, 1983).
99. Ozment, *The Age of Reform*, p. 222.
100. Huizinga, *The Waning of the Middle Ages*, p. 179.

6 Culture and Society

1. N. Elias, *The Court Society*, trans. E. Jephcott (Oxford: Blackwell, 1983).
2. J. Duindam, *Myths of Power: Norbert Elias and the Early Modern European Court* (Amsterdam: Amsterdam University Press, 1995).
3. D. Starkey (ed.), *The English Court: From the Wars of the Roses to the Civil War* (Harlow: Longman, 1987).
4. G. R. Elton, *The Tudor Revolution in Government* (Cambridge: Cambridge University Press, 1953), p. 184.
5. F. Kisby, 'Kingship and the Royal Itinerary: a Study of the Peripatetic Household of the Early Tudor Kings, 1485–1547', *The Court Historian*, 4 (1999), pp. 29–39.
6. P. J. Heinig, 'How Large was the Court of Emperor Frederick III?', in R. G. Asch and A. M. Birke (eds), *Princes, Patronage and the Nobility: The Court at the Beginning of the Modern Age*, German Institute of Historical Research (London: Oxford University Press, 1991), p. 142.
7. M. Vale, *The Princely Court: Medieval Courts and Culture in North West Europe, 1270–1380* (Oxford: Clarendon Press, 2001), p. 158.
8. J. G. Dunbar, *Scottish Royal Palaces: The Architecture of Royal Residences during the Late Medieval and Early Renaissance Periods* (East Lothian: Tuckwell Press, 1999).
9. S. Thurley, *Whitehall Palace: An Architectural History of the Royal Apartments, 1240–1698* (New Haven, CT, and London: Yale University Press, 1999). Westminster remained the royal residence until 1529 when Henry VIII received York Place from the disgraced Cardinal Wolsey. It was transferred from the archdiocese of York to the Crown and re-named Whitehall.
10. S. Thurley, *The Royal Palaces of Tudor England* (New Haven, CT, and London: Yale University Press, 1993).
11. D. Starkey, 'Henry VI's Old Blue Gown: the English Court under the Lancastrians and Yorkists', *The Court Historian*, 4 (1999), pp. 1–28.
12. A. R. Myers (ed.), *The Household of Edward IV: The Black Book and the Ordinance of 1478* (Manchester: Manchester University Press, 1959), pp. 111–112.
13. Starkey, *The English Court*, pp. 71–118.
14. G. Beneke, *Maximilian I (1459–1519): An Analytical Biography* (London: Routledge & Kegan Paul, 1982), p. 105.
15. R. Griffiths, '"Ffor the myght off the lande, aftir the myght off the grete lordes theroff, stondith most in the kynges officers", the English Crown, Provinces and Dominions in the Fifteenth Century', in A. Curry and E. Mathew (eds), *Concepts and Patterns of Service in the Later Middle Ages* (Woodbridge: Boydell Press, 2000), pp. 80–98.

16. G. Small, *George Chastelain and the Shaping of Valois Burgundy* (Woodbridge: Boydell Press, 1997), p. 77.
17. M. T. Caron, *Noblesse et Pouvoir Royale en France, XIIIe–XVIe siècle* (Paris: Armand Colin, 1994), pp. 55–6; J. F. Solnon, *La Cour de France* (Paris: Fayard, 1987), p. 15.
18. Caron, *Noblesse et Pouvoir Royale en France*, pp. 128–9.
19. J. Stratford, *The Bedford Inventories: The Worldly Goods of John, Duke of Bedford, Regent of France* (London: Society of Anriquaries of London, 1993).
20. M. Vale, *Charles VII* (London: Eyre Methuen, 1974), pp. 25–6.
21. M. Letts (ed. and trans.), *The Diary of Jorg von Ehingen* (London: Oxford University Press, 1929), p. 28.
22. P. Crossley, 'The Politics of Presentation: the Architecture of Charles IV of Bohemia', in S. Rees Jones, R. Marks and A. J. Minnis (eds), *Courts and Regions in Medieval Europe* (York: York Medieval Press, 2000), p. 99.
23. Letts, *The Diary of Jorg von Ehingen*, p. 40.
24. M. Vale, *The Princely Court.*
25. J. Fajt and J. Royt, *Magister Theodoricus, Court Painter of Charles IV* (Prague: National Gallery, 1997), p. 11.
26. Crossley, 'The Politics of Presentation', p. 112.
27. P. Eberle, 'The Politics of Courtly Style at the Court of Richard II', in G. S. Burgess and R. A. Taylor (eds), *The Spirit of the Court* (Cambridge: D. S. Brewer, 1985), pp. 168–78.
28. W. Paravicini, 'The Court of the Dukes of Burgundy: a Model for Europe?' in Asch and Birke, *Princes, Patronage and the Nobility*, pp. 69–102.
29. M. Vale, *The Princely Court*, p. 181.
30. C. Munro (ed.), *The Letters of Queen Margaret of Anjou and Bishop Beckington and Others* (London: Camden Society, 1863), pp. 97–8.
31. F. Willaert, '"Hovedans": Fourteenth-century Songs in the Rhine and Meuse area', in E. Kooper (ed.), *Medieval Dutch Literature in its European Context* (Cambridge: Cambridge University Press, 1994), pp. 168–87.
32. S. Lockwood (ed.), *Sir John Fortescue, On the Laws and Governance of England* (Cambridge: Cambridge University Press, 1997), p. 64.
33. R. Horrox, 'Caterpillars of the Commonwealth? Courtiers in Late Medieval England', in *Rulers and Ruled in Late Medieval England: Essays presented to Gerald Harriss*, ed. R. Archer and S. Walker (London: Hambledon Press, 1995), pp. 1–15.
34. Vale, *The Princely Court*, pp. 299–300; see also W. Prevenier, 'Court and City Culture in the Low Countries from 1100–1530', in Kooper, *Medieval Dutch Literature*, pp. 11–29, who makes the point that the culture of the bourgeoisie and the court was converging in some instances.
35. N. Davis (ed.), *The Paston Letters* (Oxford: World's Classics edition, Oxford University Press, 1963), letters 130 and 131.
36. B. Guenée, *States and Rulers in Later Medieval Europe*, trans. J. Vale (Oxford: Basil Blackwell, 1985), pp. 200–1.
37. P. S. Lewis, *Later Medieval France* (London: Macmillan, 1968), p. 186.
38. R. C. Schwinges, 'On Recruitment in German Universties from the Fourteenth to the Sixteenth Centuries', in W. J. Courtney and J. Miethke (eds),

Universities and Schooling in Medieval Society (Leiden, Boston and Cologne: Brill, 2000), p. 32.

39. C. Allmand, *Lancastrian Normandy, 1415–1450: The History of a Medieval Occupation* (Oxford: Clarendon Press, 1983), pp. 105–20.
40. G. Chaucer, *The General Prologue to the Canterbury Tales*, ed. J. E. Cunningham (Harmondsworth: Penguin, 1989), lines 284–309.
41. F. M. Powicke and A. B. Emden, *Rashdall's Universities*, vol. I (Oxford: Oxford University Press, 1936), p. 516.
42. A. Cobban, *English University Life in the Middle Ages* (London: UCL Press, 1999), p. 22.
43. A. R. Myers (ed.), *English Historical Documents, 1327–1485*, vol. IV (London: Eyre & Spottiswode, 1969), p. 918.
44. Ibid., p. 895.
45. *Compendium totius grammaticae ex variis autoribus Laurentio, Servio, Perotto diligenter collectum et versibus cum eorum interpretatione conscriptum totius barbarei destructorum et latine lingue ornamentorum non minus quam pueris nece necesarium.*
46. V. Davies, *William Wayneflete, Bishop and Educationalist* (Woodbridge: Boydell Press, 1993), pp. 85–9.
47. J. Verger, 'The Universities', in M. Jones (ed.), *The New Cambridge Medieval History*, vol. VI: *1300–1415* (Cambridge: Cambridge University Press, 2000), pp. 76–7.
48. R. N. Swanson, *Universities, Academics and the Great Schism* (Cambridge: Cambridge University Press, 1979), p. 206.
49. J. Gregory (ed.), *The Neoplatonists* (London: Kyle Cathie, 1991), p. 247.
50. J. Oldfield, 'Germany', in R. Porter and M. Teich (eds), *The Renaissance in National Context* (Cambridge: Cambridge University Press, 1992), pp. 105–6.
51. Ibid., p. 107.
52. R. Weiss, *Humanism in England during the Fifteenth Century* (Oxford: Basil Blackwell, 1967), pp. 62–7.
53. Ibid., p. 182.
54. R. O'Day, *The Professions in Early Modern England, 1450–1800* (London: Longman, 2000), pp. 113–17.
55. A. G. Dickens, *The Age of Humanism and Reformation* (London: Prentice Hall, 1972), p. 45.
56. Ibid., p. 46.
57. L. Taylor, *Soldiers of Christ: Preaching in Late Medieval and Reformation France, 1460–1560* (Oxford: Oxford University Press, 1992), p. 5.
58. J. Verger, 'Schools and Universities', in C. T. Allmand (ed.), *The New Cambridge Medieval History*, vol. VII: *1415–1500* (Cambridge: Cambridge University Press, 1998), p. 236.
59. R. L. Storey, 'Universities in the Wars of the Roses', *England in the Fifteenth Century: Proceedings of the 1986 Harlaxton Symposium* (Woodbridge: Boydell, 1987), p. 320.
60. R. Vaughan, *Charles the Bold* (Woodbridge: Boydell, 2002), pp. 1–2.
61. R. H. Hilton, *English and French Towns in Feudal Society: A Comparative Study* (Cambridge: Cambridge University Press, 1992), p. 80.
62. Myers, *English Historical Documents*, vol. IV, p. 1067.

63. K. D. Lilley, *Urban Life in the Middle Ages, 1000–1450* (Basingstoke: Palgrave, 2002), p. 230.
64. Ibid., p. 221.
65. T. Scott, *Society and Economy in Germany, 1300–1600* (Basingstoke: Palgrave, 2002), p. 46.
66. Lilley, *Urban Life in the Middle Ages, 1000–1450*, p. 245.
67. P. Nightingale, *A Medieval Mercantile Community* (New Haven, CT, and London: Yale University Press, 1995), p. 406.
68. D. Nicholas, *The Metamorphosis of a Medieval City: Ghent in the Age of the Arteveldes, 1302–1390* (London: University of Nebraska Press, 1987), p. 42.
69. F. R. H. du Boulay, *Germany in the Later Middle Ages* (London: Athlone, 1983), pp. 165–6.
70. D. Nicholas, *The Metamorphosis of a Medieval City*, pp. 41–66.
71. Illustrations of buildings in Bremen and other Hanse cities can be found in A. d'Haenens, *Europe of the North Sea and the Baltic: The World of the Hanse* (Antwerp: Fonds Mercator, 1984).
72. W. Blockmans and W. Prevenier, *The Promised Lands: The Low Countries under Burgundian Rule, 1369–1530* (Philadelphia: University of Pennsylvania Press, 1999), p. 221.
73. Chaucer, *The General Prologue to the Canterbury Tales*, lines 361–87. The translation into modern English is from http://www.courses.fas.harvard.edu/~chaucer/contales.html.
74. J. Bossy, *Christianity in the West, 1400–1700* (Oxford: Oxford University Press, 1985), p. 58.
75. C. Barron, 'The Parish Fraternities of Medieval London', in C. M. Barron and C. Harper Bill (eds), *The Church in Pre-Reformation Society: Essays in Honour of F. R. H. Du Boulay* (Woodbridge: Boydell Press, 1985), p. 35.
76. *English Gilds: The Original Ordinances of more than One Hundred Early English Gilds*, ed. Toulmin Smith and L.Toulmin Smith, translated from Latin (London: Early English Texts Society, 1870), pp. 184–5.
77. L. R. Muir, *The Biblical Drama of Medieval Europe* (Cambridge: Cambridge University Press, 1995), p. 55.
78. P. Arnade, *Realms of Ritual: Burgundian Ceremony and Civic Life in Late Medieval Ghent* (Ithaca and London: Cornell University Press, 1996).
79. Extract from the Pewterers' and Founders' play, 'Joseph's Trouble about Mary', in D. Englander et al. (ed.), *Culture and Belief in Europe, 1490–1600: An Anthology of Sources* (Oxford: Basil Blackwell, 1990), p. 13.
80. A. J. Mill, *Medieval Plays in Scotland*, Ph.D. thesis 1924, University of St Andrews (Edinburgh and London: William Blackwood and Sons, 1927), p. 61.
81. Extract from the records of the York guild of Spurriers and Lorimers in Alexandra F. Johnston and Margaret Rogerson (eds), *Records of Early English Drama: York*, vol. 1 (Manchester: Manchester University Press, 1979), p. 176.
82. W. Tydeman, *English Medieval Theatre, 1400–1500* (London: Routledge & Kegan Paul, 1986), p. 80.
83. C. Richmond, 'The Visual Culture of Fifteenth Century England', in A. J. Pollard (ed.), *The Wars of the Roses* (Basingstoke: Macmillan, 1995), p. 87.

84. A. B. Cobban, *The Medieval Universities: Their Development and Organisation* (London: Methuen, 1975), p. 116.

Conclusion

1. B. Guenée, *States and Rulers in Later Medieval Europe*, trans. J. Vale (Oxford: Basil Blackwell, 1988), p. 18.
2. A. Hastings, *The Construction of Nationhood: Ethnicity, Religion and Nationalism* (Cambridge: Cambridge University Press, 1997), pp. 5, 46, 69, 71, 99, 107.
3. F. Autrand, *Naissance d'un corps de l'Etat: les gens du Parlement de Paris, 1345–1454* (Paris: Publications de la Sorbonne, 1981), p. 267.
4. R. Bartlett, *The Making of Europe: Conquest, Colonization and Cultural Change, 950–1350* (London: Allen Lane, Penguin Press, 1993), chapter 11, pp. 269–91. In fourteenth-century Dresden, for example, approximately 30% of the town councillors bore the name John, 24% Nicholas, and 15% Peter, rather than bearing Germanic names.

Bibliography

GENERAL TITLES

Allmand, C. T. (ed.), *The New Cambridge Medieval History, c.1415–c.1500*, New Cambridge Medieval History, vol. VII (Cambridge: Cambridge University Press, 1998).

Aston, M., *The Fifteenth Century: The Prospect of Europe* (London: Thames & Hudson, 1968).

Burns, J. H. and Goldie, M., *The Cambridge History of Political Thought, 1450–1700* (Cambridge: Cambridge University Press, 1991).

Guenée, B., *States and Rulers in Later Medieval Europe*, trans. J. Vale (Oxford: Basil Blackwell, 1985).

Hay, D., *Europe in the Fourteenth and Fifteenth Centuries* (London: Longman, 1989).

Huizinga, J., *The Waning of the Middle Ages* (Harmondsworth: Penguin Books, 1955).

Jones, M. (ed.), *The New Cambridge Medieval History, c.1300–1415*, New Cambridge Medieval History, vol. VI (Cambridge: Cambridge University Press, 2000).

Mackay, A. and Ditchburn, D. (eds), *Atlas of Medieval Europe* (London and New York: Routledge, 1997).

Miskimin, H. A., *The Economy of Early Renaissance Europe, 1300–1460* (Cambridge: Cambridge University Press, 1975).

Myers, A. R. (ed.), *English Historical Documents, 1327–1485*, English Historical Documents, vol. IV (London: Eyre & Spottiswoode, 1969).

CHAPTER 1: THE COUNTRYSIDE AND ITS PEOPLE

Bois, G., *The Crisis of Feudalism: Economy and Society in Eastern Normandy, c.1300–1550* (Cambridge, Cambridge University Press, 1984).

Bolton, J. L., *The Medieval English Economy, 1150–1500* (London: Dent, 1985).

Campbell, B., *English Seigniorial Agriculture, 1250–1450* (Cambridge: Cambridge University Press, 2000).

Dyer, C., *Standards of Living in the Later Middle Ages: Social Change in England, c.1200–1520* (Cambridge: Cambridge University Press, 1989).

Fleming, P., *Family and Household in Medieval England* (Basingstoke: Palgrave Macmillan, 2001).

Froissier, R., *Peasant Life in the Medieval West* (Oxford: Basil Blackwell, 1988).

Fryde, E. B., *Peasants and Landlords in Later Medieval England* (Stroud: Alan Sutton, 1996).

Hatcher, J. and Bailey, M., *Modelling the Middle Ages: The History and Theory of England's Economic Development* (Oxford: Oxford University Press, 2001).

Ladurie, E. le Roy, *The Peasants of Languedoc*, trans. J. Day (Urbana and London: University of Illinois Press, 1994).
Nicholas, D., *Medieval Flanders* (London: Longman, 1992).
Rösener, W., *Peasants in the Middle Ages* (Cambridge: Polity Press, 1992).
Rigby, S. H., *English Society in the Later Middle Ages: Class Status and Gender* (London: Macmillan, 1995).
Scott, T. (ed.), *The Peasantries of Europe from the Fourteenth to the Eighteenth Centuries* (London: Longman, 1998).
Scott, T., *Society and Economy in Germany, 1300–1600* (Basingstoke: Palgrave Macmillan, 2002).

CHAPTER 2: TOWNSMEN, TRADERS AND UNREST

Blockmans, W. and Prevenier, W., *The Promised Lands: The Low Countries under Burgundian Rule, 1369–1530* (Philadelphia: University of Pennsylvania Press, 1999).
d'Haenens, A., *Europe of the North Sea and the Baltic: The World of the Hanse* (Antwerp: Fonds Mercator, 1984).
Dollinger, P., *The German Hansa* (London: Macmillan, 1970).
Dyer, C., *Standards of Living in the Later Middle Ages: Social Change in England, c.1200–1520* (Cambridge: Cambridge University Press, 1989).
Hanham A., *The Celys and their World* (Cambridge: Cambridge University Press, 1985).
Hilton, R. H., *English and French Towns in Feudal Society: A Comparative Study* (Cambridge: Cambridge University Press, 1992).
Howell, M. C., *Women, Production and Patriarchy in Medieval Cities* (Chicago and London: University of Chicago Press, 1986).
Lilley, K. D., *Urban Life in the Middle Ages, 1000–1450* (Basingstoke: Palgrave Macmillan, 2002).
Lloyd, T. H., *The English Wool Trade in the Middle Ages* (Cambridge: Cambridge University Press, 1977).
Lloyd, T. H., *England and the German Hanse, 1157–1611: A Study of their Trade and Diplomacy* (Cambridge: Cambridge University Press, 1991).
Nicholas, D., *Medieval Flanders* (London: Longman, 1992).
Nicholas, D., *The Later Medieval City* (London: Longman, 1997).
Power, E. and Postan, M. M., *Studies in English Trade in the Fifteenth Century* (London: George Routledge and Sons, 1933).
Scott, T., *Society and Economy in Germany, 1300–1600* (Basingstoke: Palgrave Macmillan, 2002).
Swanson, H., *Medieval British Towns* (Basingstoke: Macmillan, 1999).
Thomson, J. A. F. (ed.), *Towns and Townspeople* (Stroud: Alan Sutton, 1988).

CHAPTER 3: PRINCES: IDEAL AND REALITY

Beneke, G., *Maximilian I (1459–1519): An Analytical Biography* (London: Routledge and Kegan Paul, 1982).

Bonney, R. (ed.), *The Rise of the Fiscal State in Europe, c.1200–1815* (Oxford: Oxford University Press, 1999).

Davies, R. R., *The Revolt of Owain Glyn Dwr* (Oxford: Oxford University Press, 1995).

Du Boulay, F. R. H., *Germany in the Later Middle Ages* (London: Athlone, 1983).

Given-Wilson, C., *The English Nobility in the Late Middle Ages* (London: Routledge, 1996).

Grant, A., *Independence and Nationhood: Scotland, 1306–1469* (Edinburgh: Edinburgh University Press, 1991).

Griffiths, R. A., *The Reign of Henry VI* (London: Ernest Benn, 1981).

Harriss, G. L. (ed.), *Henry V: The Practice of Kingship* (Stroud: Alan Sutton, 1993).

Hicks, M., *Warwick the Kingmaker* (Oxford: Blackwell, 1998).

Hodges, G., *Owain Glyn Dwr: The War of Independence in the Welsh Borders* (Almeley: Logaston, 1995).

Lewis, P. S., *Later Medieval France: The Polity* (London: St Martin's Press, 1968).

MacDougall, N., *James III: A Political Study* (Edinburgh: Donald, 1982).

Nicholson, R., *Scotland: The Later Middle Ages* (Edinburgh: Oliver and Boyd, 1974).

Potter, D., *A History of France, 1460–1560* (Basingstoke: Macmillan, 1995).

Ross, C. D., *Edward IV* (London and New Haven: Yale University Press, 1997).

Saul, N., *Richard II* (London and New Haven: Yale University Press, 1997).

Skinner, Q., *The Foundations of Modern Political Thought*, vol. I (Cambridge: Cambridge University Press, 1978).

Vale, M. G. A., *Charles VII* (London: Eyre Methuen, 1974).

Vaughan, R., *Valois Burgundy* (London: Allen Lane, 1975).

Watts, J. L., *Henry VI and the Politics of Kingship* (Cambridge: Cambridge University Press, 1996).

CHAPTER 4: WAGING WAR

Allmand, C., *Society at War: The Experiences of England and France during the Hundred Years War* (Edinburgh: Oliver and Boyd, 1973).

Allmand, C., *The Hundred Years War: England and France at War, c.1300–c.1450* (Cambridge: Cambridge University Press, 1989).

Aston, T. H. and Hilton, R. H., *The English Rising of 1381* (Cambridge: Cambridge University Press, 1984).

Barnie, J., *War in Medieval Society: Social Values and the Hundred Years War, 1337–99* (London: Weidenfeld and Nicolson, 1974).

Curry, A., *The Hundred Years War* (Basingstoke: Macmillan, 1993).

Curry, A. and Hughes, M. (eds), *Arms, Armies and Fortifications in the Hundred Years War* (Woodbridge: Boydell Press, 1994).

Dobson, R. B. (ed.), *The Peasants' Revolt of 1381* (London: Macmillan, 1970).

Fortescue, Sir J. (ed.), *In Praise of the Laws of England* (Cambridge: Cambridge University Press, 1997).

Fowler, K. (ed.), *The Hundred Years War* (London: Macmillan, 1971).

Froissart, *Chronicles*, ed. and trans. G. Brereton (Harmondsworth: Penguin, 1968).

Geremek, Bronislaw, *The Margins of Society in Late Medieval Paris*, trans. J. Birrell (Cambridge: Cambridge University Press, 1987).

Harvey, I. M. W., *Jack Cade's Rebellion of 1450* (Oxford: Clarendon Press, 1991).

Hilton, R., *Class Conflict and the Crisis of Feudalism: Essays in Medieval Social History* (London and New York: Verso, 1990).

Justice, S., *Writing and Rebellion: England in 1381* (Berkeley, CA: University of California Press, 1994).

Kaeuper, R. W., *War, Justice and Public Order: England and France in the Later Middle Ages* (Oxford: Oxford University Press, 1988).

Mollat, M. and Wolff, P., *The Popular Revolutions of the Late Middle Ages*, trans. A. L. Lytton-Sells (London: George Allen and Unwin, 1973).

Miskimin, H. A., *Cash, Credit and Crisis in Europe, 1300–1600* (London: Variorum Reprints, 1989).

Nicholas, D., *Medieval Flanders* (London: Longman, 1992).

Perroy, E., *The Hundred Years War* (London: Eyre & Spottiswoode, 1962).

Pollard, A. J., *Late Medieval England, 1399–1509* (Harlow: Longman, 2000).

Prestwich, M., *Armies and Warfare in the Middle Ages: The English Experience* (New Haven and London, Yale University Press, 1996).

Rodger, N. A. M., *The Safeguard of the Sea: A Naval History of Britain*, vol. I (London: HarperCollins, 1997), pp. 660–1649.

Vaughan, R., *Valois Burgundy* (London: Allen Lane, 1975).

Vaughan, R., *John the Fearless* (London: Longman, 1979).

Walker, S., 'Rumour, Sedition and Popular Protest in the Reign of Henry IV', *Past and Present*, 166 (2000), pp. 31–65.

Wright, N., *Knights and Peasants: The Hundred Years War in the French Countryside* (Woodbridge: Boydell, 1998).

CHAPTER 5: THE CHURCH, RELIGION AND DISSENT

Arnade, P., *Realms of Ritual: Burgundian Ceremony and Civic Life in Late Medieval Ghent* (Ithaca and London: Cornell University Press, 1996).

Barron, C. M. and Harper Bill, C. (eds), *The Church in Pre-Reformation Society: Essays in Honour of F. R. H. Du Boulay* (Woodbridge: Boydell Press, 1985).

Binski, P., *Medieval Death: Ritual and Representation* (London: British Museum Press, 1997).

Black, A., *Monarchy and Community: Political Ideas in the Late Conciliar Controversy* (Cambridge: Cambridge University Press, 1970).

Bossy, J., *Christianity in the West, 1400–1700* (Oxford: Oxford University Press, 1985).

Brown, D. Catherine, *Pastor and Laity in the Theology of Jean Gerson* (Cambridge: Cambridge University Press, 1987).

Cohen, J. (ed.), *From Witness to Witchcraft: Jews and Judaism in Medival Christian Thought* (Wiesbaden: Harrassowitz Verlag, 1996).

Cohn, N., *Europe's Inner Demons: The Demonization of Christians in Medieval Christendom* (London: Pimlico, 1993).
Davidson, C. (ed.), *The Saint Play in Medieval Europe* (Kalamazoo: West Michigan University, 1986).
Duffy, E., *The Stripping of the Altars: Traditional Religion in England, c.1400–c.1580* (New Haven, CT, and London: Yale University Press, 1992).
Dykema, P. A. and Oberman, H. A. (eds), *Anticlericalism in Late Medieval and Early Modern Europe* (Leiden, Cologne and New York: E. J. Brill, 1993).
Finucane, R. C., *Miracles and Pilgrims: Popular Beliefs in Medieval England* (Basingstoke: Macmillan, 1995).
Hudson, A., *The Premature Reformation: Wycliffite Texts and Lollard History* (Oxford: Clarendon Press, 1988).
Ginsburg, C., *Ecstacies: Deciphering the Witches' Sabbath*, trans. R. Rosenthal (London: Penguin Books, 1992).
Huizinga, J., *The Waning of the Middle Ages* (Harmondsworth: Penguin Books, 1955).
Kieckhefer, R., *Unquiet Souls: Fourteenth Century Saints and their Religious Milieu* (Chicago: University of Chicago Press, 1984).
Kieckhefer, R., *Magic in the Middle Ages* (Cambridge: Cambridge University Press, 1990).
Lambert, M., *Medieval Heresy: Popular Movements from Bogomil to Hus* (New York: H. M. Holmes and Meier, 1976).
Leff, G., *Heresy in the Later Middle Ages: The Relation of Heterodoxy to Dissent*, 2 vols (New York: Manchester University Press/Barnes and Noble, 1967).
Mollat, G., *The Popes at Avignon, 1305–1378*, trans. Janet Love (London: Thomas Nelson and Sons, 1963).
Muir, L. R., *The Biblical Drama of Medieval Europe* (Cambridge: Cambridge University Press, 1995).
Murray, A., *Suicide in the Middle Ages*, 2 vols (Oxford: Oxford University Press, 2000).
Oakley, F., *Natural Law, Conciliarism and Consent in the Late Middle Ages* (London: Variorum Reprints, 1984).
Ozment, S., *The Age of Reform, 1250–1550: An Intellectual and Religious History of Late Medieval and Reformation Europe* (New Haven, CT: Yale University Press, 1980).
Post, R. R., *The Modern Devotion: Confrontation with Reform and Humanism*, Studies in Medieval and Reformation Thought, 3 (Leiden: E. J. Brill, 1968).
Reinburg, V., 'Liturgy and the Laity in Late Medieval and Reformation France', *Sixteenth Century Journal*, 23 (1992), pp. 526–47.
Richmond, C., 'Religion and the Fifteenth-Century English Gentleman', *The Church, Politics and Patronage in the Fifteenth Century*, ed. B. Dobson (Gloucester: Alan Sutton, 1984).
Rubin, M., *Corpus Christi: The Eucharist in Late Medieval Culture* (Cambridge: Cambridge University Press, 1991).
Rubin, M., *Gentile Tales: The Narrative Assault on Late Medieval Jews* (New Haven, CT: Yale University Press, 1999).
Scribner, B. and Johnson T. (eds), *Popular Religion in Germany and Central Europe, 1400–1800* (Basingstoke: Macmillan, 1996).

Sumption, J., *Pilgrimage: An Image of Medieval Religion* (London: Faber & Faber, 1975).

Swanson, R. N., *Religion and Devotion in Europe, c.1215–c.1515* (Cambridge: Cambridge University Press, 1995).

Szarmach, P. E. (ed.), *An Introduction to the Medieval Mystics of Europe* (Albany, NY: State University of New York Press, 1984).

Taylor, L., *Soldiers of Christ: Preaching in Late Medieval and Reformation France, 1460–1560* (Oxford: Oxford University Press, 1992).

Tierney, B., *Religion, Law and the Growth of Constitutional Thought, 1150–1650* (Cambridge: Cambridge University Press, 1982).

Thomas, K., *Religion and the Decline of Magic: Studies in Popular Beliefs in Sixteenth and Seventeenth Century England* (London: Weidenfeld & Nicolson, 1971).

Tydeman, W., *English Medieval Theatre, 1400–1500* (London: Routledge & Kegan Paul, 1986).

Weiss, R., *Humanism in England during the Fifteenth Century* (Oxford: Basil Blackwell, 1967).

Windeatt, B. (ed.), *English Mystics of the Middle Ages* (Cambridge: Cambridge University Press, 1994).

Wunderli, R., *Peasant Fires: The Drummer of Niklashausen* (Bloomington and Indianapolis: University of Indiana Press, 1992).

CHAPTER 6: CULTURE AND SOCIETY

Asch, R. G. and Birke, A. M. (eds), *Princes, Patronage and Nobility: The Court at the Beginning of the Modern Age*, German Institute of Historical Research (London: Oxford University Press, 1991).

Barron, C. and Saul, N. (eds), *England and the Low Countries in the Late Middle Ages* (Stroud: Alan Sutton, 1995).

Chaucer, G., *The General Prologue to the Canterbury Tales*, ed. J. E. Cunningham (Harmondsworth: Penguin, 1989).

Cobban, A., *English University Life in the Middle Ages* (London: UCL Press, 1999).

Courtney, W. J. and Miethke, J. (eds), *Universities and Schooling in Medieval Society* (Leiden, Boston and Cologne: Brill, 2000).

Crossley, P., 'The Politics of Presentation: The Architecture of Charles IV of Bohemia', in *Courts and Regions in Medieval Europe*, ed. Sarah Rees Jones, Richard Marks and A. J. Minnis (Woodbridge: Boydell Press, 2000).

Davis, N. (ed.), *The Paston Letters*, World's Classics edition (Oxford: Oxford University Press, 1963).

Dunbar, J. G., *Scottish Royal Palaces: The Architecture of Royal Residences during the Late Medieval and Early Renaissance Periods* (East Lothian: Tuckwell Press, 1999).

Elias, N., *The Court Society*, trans. E. Jephcott (Oxford: Basil Blackwell, 1983).

Goodman, A. and Mackay, A., *The Impact of Humanism on Western Europe* (London: Longman, 1990).

Horrox, R., 'Caterpillars of the Commonwealth? Courtiers in Late Medieval England', *Rulers and Ruled in Late Medieval England: Essays Presented to Gerald Harriss*, ed. R. Archer and S. Walker (London: Hambledon Press, 1995).

Nauert, C. G., *Humanism and the Culture of Renaissance Europe* (Cambridge: Cambridge University Press, 1995).

Powicke, F. M. and Emden, A. B., *Rashdall's Medieval Universities* (Oxford: Oxford University Press, 1936).

Starkey, D. (ed.), *The English Court: From the Wars of the Roses to the Civil War* (Harlow: Longman, 1987).

Starkey, D., 'Henry VI's Old Blue Gown: the English Court under the Lancastrians and Yorkists', *The Court Historian*, 4 (1999).

Stratford, J., *The Bedford Inventories: The Wordly Goods of John, Duke of Bedford, Regent of France* (London: Society of Antiquaries of London, 1993).

Swanson, R. W., *Universities, Academics and the Great Schism* (Cambridge: Cambridge University Press, 1979).

Thurley, S., *The Royal Palaces of Tudor England* (New Haven, CT: Yale University Press, 1993).

Weiss, R., *Humanism in England during the Fifteenth Century* (Oxford: Basil Blackwell, 1967).

Index